"Oi, Mate, Gimme Some More!"

A Yoof-Speak Guide to the Complete Novels of Charles Dickens, Innit

BY MARTIN BAUM

Visit us online at www.authorsonline.co.uk

An Authors OnLine Book

Text Copyright © Martin Baum 2010

Cover design by Martin Baum and Jamie Day ©

British Library Cataloguing Publication Data.
A catalogue record for this book is available from the British Library

ISBN 978-07552-0603-2

Authors OnLine Ltd
19 The Cinques
Gamlingay, Sandy
Bedfordshire SG19 3NU
England

www.yoofspeak.net
www.baumskifilks.com

This book is also available in e-book format, details of which are available at www.authorsonline.co.uk

In Memory of Greg Smith

CONTENTS

INTRODUCTION

When *To be or Not To Be, Innit, a Yoof-Speak Guide to Shakespeare* was first published there were sceptics who baulked at the very idea of the Bard being so unceremoniously 'dissed'. But such was the demand for a book that made Britain's greatest playwright more accessible to the masses that I felt a strong compulsion to spread the yoof-speak net a little wider to include the novels of Charles John Huffam Dickens - storyteller, journalist and philanthropist.

This was a man who knew what deprivation was and empathised with the people who suffered it, and if Dickens' quill was still seeing action then I am certain, as a writer living in the Gads Hill frontline in the Higham turf, with a keen eye for contemporary detail and a street name of Boz, he would have no alternative but to reflect life as it is on the streets today by writing classics like 'Dombey and Sprog', 'Well Small Dorrit', 'Da Tale of Two Turfs', 'Minging Times' and 'Well Good Expectations'.

For the purists, however, I have remained faithful to the

original text; Oliver still asks for more grub, Wackford Squeers is still a sadist and the ghost massive still messes with Scrooge's mojo.

It is what it is.

Respect.

DA TALE OF TWO TURFS

It was da best of times, and not being funny or nuffing, but it was da worst of times, to be honest. Da year was 1775 and fings were looking well suss in da French turf coz da peasants were minging, or rather they was revolting, and not just coz they was Frogs, innit. Da common geezas were largeing it with da nobs all over da Froggy yard, which meant da rank smell of revolution was going down, big time.

But despite da risks, people like da geeza Jarvis Lorry was still boating it across da Channel what separated da English from da French. He worked for da Tellson's Bank and was on his way to da Froggyland hood with da well fit seventeen year old Lucie Manette. Da reason why dis older geeza was hanging with da much younger girl wasn't coz Jarvis was pervy or nuffing, but coz unknown to Lucie, Jarvis Lorry had been looking after all of her farva's stuff after he had been busted by da filth and slung into da Bastille turf for da last eighteen years. Dis geeza was Doctor Alexandre Manette and now he'd been released from da French slammer they was gonna finally be all friends reunited again, which was well good.

And so after they got to da Paris ghetto, Jarvis and Lucie went straight over to da home turf of Ernest Defarge. Now dis geeza was da doctor's servant from before everyfing went belly up, and ever since he'd been sprung from da Bastille, Ernest and his bitch – Theresa - had been looking after and helping da doctor to so get over it. Not only that, coz unknown to any of them, da Defarges was also secret French revolutionaries, which was well off da hook, innit.

Anyhoo - and despite all da care in da community stuff what was being given by Ernest – Doctor Manette was losing it big time after all da years locked up in da Bastille. He was da geeza on da edge who didn't even know his own daughta when they met up.

"Yo, nursie, is it time for da bed bath yet?"
"Oh my God, I cannot believe you said that though! I ain't no nurse, coz we is family and not being funny or nuffing but coz you is my farva and I is your daughta means that I ain't going nowhere near your bits! Now then, you is in safe hands coz me and me main man Jarvis Lorry is gonna get you back to da English turf, you get me."
"Sweet."

So they loaded up da horse and cart and got demselves back to da London ghetto where Lucie's farva began to chillax by resting and eating proper English grub like Kebabs and Pot Noodles instead of all that Froggy slop, innit. Well, it wasn't long before he really began to get himself togevva and eventually back into da medical groove of being da official turf doctor. Sometimes, though, he still went just da bit strange in da head by doing da 'I'm da little teapot' rap but even so, all fings considered, fings seemed to be finally working out.

So everyfing stayed cool until five years later when they was unexpectedly called to give evidence at da courts of da Old Bailey for da trial of some French geeza called Charles Darnay, who had been living in da London turf and was being fingered for da heavy crime of treason. Although he looked well banged to rights, Darnay wasn't really no treacherous Froggy scumbag, coz he had actually been stitched-up like da kipper fish by some spy geezas.

They had accused him of grassing up da British troops to da Frogs, which was so not true and they might have got away with it too if it hadn't been for Lucie and her farva, who was able to tell da court that da Paris One was, in fact, da victim of da huge miscarriage of justice. Da whole fing was well gay after Darnay had been seen yakking and going through some suss documents with some dodgy looking geezas what made him look so guilty in da eyes of da filth. However, and despite him being French, Lucie remembered that he had been well good to her farva when they was on da boat what brought them back from da French turf all those years ago and knew that he was so not guilty.

Maybe it was coz she was fit and da jury was too busy looking at her boobies, but somehow Charles Darnay walked away da free man, which was well jammy. Mind you, what also might have swung da verdict was when Darnay's brief, Sydney Carton, removed his wig and everyone fought that he looked *exactly* like Charles Darnay which meant that dere was now da strong element of doubt. Simples. In other words, coz nobody in da courtroom could be sure it was him what did it, da possibility of da mistaken identity meant it couldn't be proved for certain that Darnay did what da filth said he did. Get in dere Sydney Carton - job done.

Well now da pressure was off, everyone was hanging in Doctor Manette's home turf acting like they was well tight homies. Dere was Charles Darnay, da bank geeza Jarvis Lorry and Sydney Carton, but as chilled as everyone was, not all da posse fought too much of Sydney Carton though. Da geeza drank like da fish animal and kept coming on to da well fit Lucie and violating her space, which was so embarrassing. However, no matter how much he tried to get her to chizzle da nizzle, da fact was Sydney Carton was no match for da silver-tongued Charles Darnay and when he proposed, dere was no contest. After all, who could blame Lucie for choosing him over da drunken, potty-mouthed Sydney Carton?

One day, Jarvis Lorry had been yakking to Charles Darnay about da mysterious letter what he had received for some geeza called da Marquis St Evrémonde. Although Jarvis didn't know who dis Frog geeza was, luckily Charles Darnay did and said that he would return to da French turf, do da Postman Pat fing and deliver it himself. However, as it turned out, dis was nuffing less than da real cunning ruse, coz Charles Darnay and da Marquis St Evrémonde - who was da actual descendant of da corrupt rulers of France - was really one and da same!

Da letter was all about some geeza what had been busted to da Bastille ghetto and needed help before he was going to be guillotined all dead, as you do. Despite realising how revolting da peasants were (and coz he was part of da nob family himself Darnay knew they was *really* revolting), he also knew he had to help out da bruvva from da gutter despite da danger. Well, as soon as he arrived, Darnay realised that perhaps, after all, it wasn't da brightest idea to be hanging on da Paris frontline. Da revolution had so kicked off and da peasants was taking down anyone they fought was nobs and of course as soon as they saw him, Charles Darnay was busted straight into da Bastille.

However, soon news got back to Lucie and her farva and without da single fought for dere own safety, togevva with Jarvis Lorry and Sydney Carton, they got dere booties straight over to da French turf to try to get Darnay away from da peasants who, by da way, were still revolting. Well, they were French, innit. Although they was expecting da worst, they was actually welcomed like they was returning heroes and all coz of da way Doctor Manette had been banged up all those years.

But now da rebels was in charge, and coz they had given da nobs da right royal kicking, they was happy to do anyfing for da doctor.

7

"Hey Doc, respect. Dere is nuffing what we wouldn't do for you."

"Really?"

"For sure coz you is da man, innit."

"Well, in that case, citizen dude, do you happen to know anyfing about some geeza by da name of Charles Darnay who is in da Bastille waiting to be sliced and diced?"

As soon as da rebels had Googled all da info for da doctor, he legged it over to where Darnay was and before he could say "Don't you know who I am, dawg?", Doctor Manette had managed to talk da peasants out of separating Charles Darnay's head from da shoulders like it was da piece of nob salami. Phew.

Well, although he'd just got off, da peasant massive couldn't let it go. Even though they was bang out of order coz Darnay was innocent, he was put on trial again and all coz Ernest Defarge and his bitch Theresa (remember, they was da crew who looked after Doctor Manette all those years ago when he got out of da prison) got gobby. Without doubt, Ernest Defarge proved himself to be nuffing more than da two-faced douchebag after he gave da peasants somefing da doctor had written years after he'd been in da Bastille turf and it was well incriminating.

It all concerned da well dodgy going ons of da dead Marquis St. Evrémonde who was Charles Darnay's farva, and his twin bruvva. They was real badass geezas what murdered and raped loads of peasants in da ghetto and were able to get away with it just coz they was nobs. Anyhoo, all dis had been carefully written in his journal by da doctor who fought that da bruvvas was worse than chavs and hoodies, innit, and had written to da government telling them what he knew. So when da Evrémonde bruvvas found out about what he had done they got Doctor Manette busted into da Bastille turf without nobody - not even his family - knowing where he was. Dis was why he wrote it all down, slagging off all da Evrémondes including da current Marquis St. Evrémonde who, and unknown to da doctor, was none other than Charles Darnay.

Well, after da letter was read out in da court, everyone went well nuts coz dis time Darnay really was banged to rights, end of, which meant he was as good as toast, and he knew it. But all was not lost, fanks to some real clever finking by da ill-mannered but well good brief Sydney Carton who still fancied Lucie, even though she had dissed him big time by becoming Mrs Darnay. He discovered that one of da spy geezas what tried to frame Darnay at da Old Bailey all those years ago was now working in da prison. And so, with da little bit of charm and blackmail, da spy geeza agreed to help which allowed Carton to apply all his powers of cunning to spring Darnay from da slammer.

Da plan was well good. Remembering da time in court when he whipped off his wig showing that they so looked like each other, Sydney Carton's idea was to get to Darnay, trip him out with da heavy sleeping pill, take his place and hope that nobody would notice. So, quickly swopping his freads with da spaced out Darnay, Carton got da spy to smuggle da wasted geeza out of da Bastille and into da waiting carriage what had Jarvis Lorry, Lucy and her farva in it. And not one of them even noticed da smooth switcharoony, which was wicked.

In no time at all they was well away from da French turf, which was just as well coz da evil little minx Madame Theresa Defarge wanted them all turned over to the revolutionary filth. Once upon da time, her peasant bruvva had been whacked by da Evrémonde bruvvas, so she wanted her minging revenge and that was da true reason for shafting him in da first place.

But while it all worked out for everyone else, da same could not be said for da soon to be guillotined Sydney Carton who, top geeza that he was, had da unselfish but well cool fought as he waited for his neck to feel da draught:

"It is da far, far cooler fing that I do, than I have ever done; it is da far, far cooler kip that I go to, than I have ever known. Stuff happens."

Sydney Carton. Respect.

OLIVA TWIST

Hundreds of years ago da England turf was full of badass hoodies, living on da frontline and giving it loads. Dese geezas were well tasty and was always largeing it big time by saying fings like "Talk to da blade", "What is you looking at douchebag?" and "Is you talking to me or is you chewing da brick?" Although they was always well tooled up and so hardass, it really wasn't dere fault or nuffing that they was full of bad attitude to everyone they was mugging in da turf. Alright, so it wasn't no excuse to say that they was so gangsta coz they didn't have no bling, cool freads or nuffing what could be pimped up but even so, they was just da victims of da times, end of. Neverdaless, though they was poor, they was still scum and they was all busted into da ghetto workhouses when they was just sprogs, just like da nippa called Oliva Twist in dis story.

Oliva's life was so screwed after his muvva popped him out of da womb and then came over all dead. Even his own farva had legged it, da swine, which meant that not only was da poor kid up da creek without da paddle, but dere was no other choice but to dump him in da workhouse for unwanted nippas and it sucked. Da workhouse turf sucked. Da freads what all da nippas had to wear sucked. Da grub sucked. In other words, everyfing sucked and all coz of da chief bullyboy what bossed da workhouse who was called Mr Bumble. Dis geeza was always getting in da faces of all da nippas what was starving with da hunger, coz Bumble would never give them nuffing but gruel to eat. Not only was dere never enough, but it looked and tasted minging. However, as if fings weren't bad enough in da workhouse turf as it was, it was all about to go da shape of da pear for Oliva Twist.

Although none of da nippas ever complained, it didn't mean to say they was happy - coz they wasn't. They was always getting da munchies and that was why da workhouse massive decided to do somefing about da sloppy gruel by getting some poor schmuck to ask for more - *even* though it tasted minging. Da only problem they had was knowing which of da workhouse crew was brave enough to take Bumble on. Well, it was decided that they was gonna do da drawing of straws and whoever got da shortest was gonna have to go one on one with da daddy of da workhouse, innit. Everyone was well bricking it, coz they knew that Bumble could take them down, big time. Neverdaless, they was hungry and way past caring and soon they was doing da straw fing.

In no time word spread in da workhouse turf about da sucker what had drawn da shortest straw - Oliva. Although he was well keen to do da two out of free, nobody else was and so at grub time, after he had finished all of da gruel in his bowl, he got up from da table and went over to da fascist what was standing by da massive pot of da stuff. Now, right in front of da whole of da workhouse crew, with da shaking hands, Oliva held out his manky bowl.

"Oi, mate," he said in da littlest voice ever, "Gimme some more!"

"Say *what*?"

"Da gruel, I want some more coz it's *sooo* yummy, innit."

"WHAT! Get over yourself nippa coz you is so gonna regret that!"

And then it kicked off big time with da gruel hitting da fan like never before. No nippa had ever asked for more in da entire history of da workhouse, but as soon as he heard da words, Bumble went ape coz he felt he was being dissed in front of everyone, which just wasn't cool. Fings weren't just looking bad for Oliva; fings were *uber* bad, innit. Well, as soon as da owners of da workhouse turf heard what went down they was close to wasting Oliva for asking for more, even though it was minging.

"Are you having da laugh?"

"No, I was well starving."

"Then you is well out of order you ungrateful scumbag!"

"Er, but then again if now's not a good time, that's cool."

And with that, they ordered Bumble to happy-slap Oliva and eBay da greedy little squirt straight away which he did, when he was sold to da local undertaker geeza for five quid.

At first Oliva was easy like da Sunday morning, coz unlike da rest of his homies he had been sprung from da workhouse turf and - compared to Bumble - da undertaker dude seemed like da well top geeza. However, unfortunately da same could not be said of da undertaker's bitch who kept getting in his face 24-seven. And then dere was Noah, anuvva badass undertaker bruvva what was always trying to stick it to him by coming on like some gangsta dude. On and on it went with da undertaker's bitch never giving him enough grub scraps and psycho Noah going all Jean-Claude Van Damme and busting his chops by calling his dead muvva da turf slapper.

What with everyfing he had been through, Oliva reckoned that Noah was gonna get his for dissing her. But even before he was able to stripe him for being so minging, da whole of da undertaker massive jumped him for taking liberties by showing no respect, innit. Well, after being bundled into da room with da tiny window what had been left open, Oliva decided to get da hell out before he was mashed. So he carefully got himself through da well small gap in da window and legged it to da London turf where da streets, as he was soon to discover, were not paved with bling. But being da new kid on da London block didn't seem too bad after all when Oliva got da break what he had been looking for, and he began to hang with da Artful Dodger. Result.

From da moment they met, he fought Dodger was da most wickedest dude *ever!* He was so street and awesome and when Dodger offered him da chance to meet his main man Fagin, Oliva was well impressed. Coz not only was he totally cool, but Dodger said he'd be able to crash at Fagin's, no questions asked, deffo. Although he fought dis was pukka, Oliva didn't realise that although Dodger was making out he was keeping it real, da truth was anyfing but, you get me.

All he knew was what he was told that Fagin was da top geeza who was always giving nippas like him da place to kip with loads of tasty grub what wasn't da crappy gruel - and all for free. However, what Dodger didn't let on to Oliva was that Fagin was nuffing more than da thieving, lowlife scumbag. Not that he knew it, and not for da first time, but he was deep in da brown stuff and we're not talking gruel.

Oliva was immediately sucked into da gangsta hood, just like all da other nippas what was squatting in da house at da time. He never suspected nuffing, coz he fought Fagin was solid and immediately gave him maximum respect. One minute he was in da workhouse yard being treated like scum, and da next he was living da vida loca with da coolest posse in da hood. Fierce. However, it didn't take long for Oliva to realise that not everyfing was what it seemed when he was sent by Fagin to hang in da City of London turf with Dodger and some of his crew. He wasn't no brain of Britain or nuffing, but even he knew somefing was screwed when he saw they was picking pockets and what was worse still, Dodger wanted him to do it too! Bummer.

Oliva was no thief, but Dodger made him do it which was so awkward turtle. Still, coz he was so gay at da picking of da pockets, it didn't take long for da whole fing to go Pete Tong when Oliva got busted by da filth trying to do over some rich geeza by da name of Mr Brownlow. Well, in da courtroom Oliva was hit with everyfing from an ASBO, to being tagged, to being thrown in da slammer, which Mr Brownlow fought was well out of order. He had da feeling that Oliva wasn't no chav and coz he was well decent, he demanded that he be allowed to take da nippa back to his yard, and that's exactly what happened.

Although dis should have been da end of da nightmare and da start of living da dream for Oliva, it wasn't. Coz just when he was settling into da lush life of kipping in da uber soft bed with da memory foam mattress, eating wicked grub like turkey twizzlers, crab sticks and Pringles, wearing real cool freads and awesome bling, bad fings was being planned what was about to mess with his mojo. Coz although Mr Brownlow and Oliva was happy that everyfing was now cool, Fagin wasn't. In fact Fagin was well unhappy and had been ever since da nippa got cuffed and stuffed and coz he really fought that Oliva was gonna rat him out to da filth, he was seriously bricking it.

Well, before long Fagin was yakking to da big cheese in da

turf, da badass hustling gangsta pimp called Bill Sykes, da well heavy geeza with attitude, anger management issues, and da dog animal called Bullseye. Although they should have left da nippa alone they couldn't coz they weren't sure if Oliva was gonna keep shtoom. So they came up with da plan to snatch and drag him back to Fagin's turf, using Bill Sykes' bitch Nancy as da well fit bait. Harsh. And so it all began after they found out where Mr Brownlow lived and they began to stalk it like they was da SAS. Before long Fagin and Sykes came up with da cunning plan for Nancy to lift Oliva as soon as he left da Brownlow turf alone and guess what? It wasn't long before they got da opportunity when da nippa was sent out on an errand.

Oliva never stood da chance as he was street-jacked faster than da child snatcher in Chitty Chitty Bang Bang and taken back to Fagin's yard. Without da shadow of da doubt, dis was well bad and it was about to get uber worse da moment he saw da butt fugly face of Bill Sykes, who had plans for Oliva. Bummer. Instead of being all safe in da Brownlow turf where he should have been, Oliva knew he was well screwed da moment Bill Sykes decided to take him on da nasty break-in job, which wasn't nuffing to do with no work experience. And even though he had brought his bitch Nancy along, it was clear that dis was not gonna be no romantic night out, especially when da only fing on Bill Sykes' mind was doing over some rich geeza's yard.

But of course, what Bill Sykes didn't take into account was

how pants Oliva was at doing anyfing bad, coz although it should have all been easy peazy lemon squeezy, it wasn't. In fact, it all went south after they was disturbed in da minging act by one angry dude with da gun. Finking only of demselves, Nancy and Bill legged it like da clappers, but da same couldn't be said for Oliva on account of him being shot and left to take da rap. But instead of getting into serious trouble, dis time everyfing went all sweet for him. Nobody fought he was to blame and instead of being busted to da fuzz, he was actually taken care of by da well kind Mrs Maylie. Perhaps it was da female intuition, but da kindly bitch just knew that Oliva was kosher.

But while fings were working out good for da nippa, da same could not be said for Nancy who reckoned Bill Sykes was way, way so not cool for leaving Oliva behind and she was suffering from da really bad guilt trip. Although she knew that her geeza would have issues about it, neverdaless she went back to Mr Brownlow's and grassed her main man up, spilling da beans about everyfing what had happened that night. Now da worm had turned and fings were beginning to look uber skank for you know who.

Well, when Bill Sykes found out what Nancy had done, he totally lost it like he had never heard of women's rights, you get me, and totally violated her space by knocking da crap out of her until she came over all dead, which was well sad. But before he could leg it out of da hood, word spread across da ghetto about what he'd done to his bitch and now everyone was after him. So with nowhere to hide, it wasn't long before he was trapped like da rat in da trap and hung for being da murderous douchebag what he was.

Soon everyone else in Fagin's crew was being busted big time, like da Artful Dodger, who was sent to da Australian turf where da kangaroo animal comes from and Fagin, who not only let Oliva down but also himself, was hung. Good. Meanwhile all was turning uber lush for Oliva, coz it wasn't only Mrs Maylie what fought he wasn't banged to rights. Oh no, coz after she nursed da nippa back to good health fings got even better when Oliva was taken back to da awesome Mr Brownlow geeza who decided to look after him forever.

It was emotional.

DA CHRISTMAS CAROL

Although dis story is da Christmas Carol it should really be called da Christmas Scrooge, named after da geeza what was da meanest and most miserable minger in da whole of da ghetto; Ebenezer Scrooge. He was loaded, but if you didn't know da geeza, you'd never guess. Dis bloke was so minted he could have had – and done - anyfing he wanted, definite. But instead he just loved being miserable and rude 24-seven, and didn't everyone in da hood just know it?

"Yo, Scrooge! How's it hanging?"
"Bah yada yada humbug."
"Dude?"
"Naff off!"

Nobody liked Scrooge coz he had one mean attitude what da turf massive fought was so out of order, coz of da way he was always sticking it to them. Not that it ever bovvered him, coz it didn't. As far as he was concerned they was nuffing more than scum what he had to put up with in much da same way as he had to put up with da scratchy itch in his buttocks, innit. But for all da irritating fings what brought him down, da one fing what really floated his boat was having money and loads of it. He was mad for it coz all he wanted in life was to be da most minted geeza in da turf, which he was. In fact he was so uber rich that if anyone in da ghetto wanted any dosh, then he was da geeza to see, which was just one more reason why nobody liked him. But did he care? Nah.

As far as he was concerned, not only was he da daddy of da hood, but he also had power over everyone living in it. Ebenezer Scrooge was 'Da Man' and how he loved it. However, despite all da dosh and power he never spent nuffing on himself. He could have been da smartest geeza in da turf with really cool freads, dripping in bling and living in da biggest, most awesome-looking yard, but he still preferred da minging look what really suited his miserable attitude, which would explain why he was so Billy no Mates.

Ebenezer Scrooge was no fun. He dissed everything, including Christmas, which was well off da hook in terms of extreme mingingness, innit. As soon as da decorations went up in da turf, da shutters came down in Ebenezer's house of gloom where not only did he never give no presents, but he also never gave nuffing to charity. Scrooge didn't do charity, coz charity was for losers and he didn't see himself as one of those. And as for even finking about anyone getting dere hands on any of his hard-earned dinero, well, he was so not going dere, you get me.

That was da way it was coz that was da way it had always been, from da time he and his main geeza, Jacob Marley, set demselves up as money-lending dragons for da scum what lived in da ghetto, which was anuvva reason why everyone didn't like Scrooge. And business was always good and never suffered no downtown in da economy, even when Jacob Marley went all stiff with da death which meant that da firm now belonged to Ebenezer Scrooge, which was well lush for him. In other words, da moolah-lending business of "Scrooge & Marley" was all his and nobody else's, which meant that he didn't have to share nuffing with nobody ever again. Result! Alright, so Jacob Marley was dead but, hey, every cloud, end of.

But as well as "Scrooge & Marley (deceased)" was doing, Scrooge was finding it well knackering doing all da graft by himself until, finally, he had no choice but to face facts and do da unfinkable which was to take on some geeza called Bob Cratchit to help him with all da counting of da wonga. Though da wages was well minging, Ebenezer still felt da pain of paying anyfing so bad like his balls was being twisted and used for ping pong.

Anyhoo, up to Christmas Eve it was like any other normal day for Scrooge, even though on dis particular day it seemed to him like every douchebag in da hood was coming into his shop on da scrounge, including his nephew Fred.

"Alright Unc?"

"Depends on what it is you is wanting, innit, bah humbug."

"But I don't want nuffing."

"Shu' up! We both know you is after all my dinero, but you is so not getting it!"

"But all I want is to wish you da season's greetings coz we is fam, innit."

"Course you do, now back off before I set me main geeza Bob Cratchit on you!"

All Fred wanted was for his uncle to feel da Christmas vibe, but it made no difference coz Scrooge was having none of it; no sooner had Fred come into da shop than he was told to do one, which well sucked. Da fact was that Ebenezer Scrooge just didn't get what da Christmas fing was all about and by da end of da day, feeling so disrespected by all da charity pimps what kept coming and asking for dosh, he couldn't wait to get back to da home turf where he would be left in all his miserable splendour, which was exactly what he wanted and that's exactly what he got.

Not that dere was much in da house, dere never was but that didn't really bovver Ebenezer Scrooge. Coz as minging as da home turf was, and it *really* was minging, it wasn't as though it was anyfing to do with him on account of da fact that it once belonged to Jacob Marley. Although it was well in need of da 60 Minute Makeover, da only fing that mattered to Scrooge when he got back home after da hard day's counting of da wonga and being so minging to Bob Cratchit, was to grub up his belly and get to bed as soon as he could.

However, da reality for Ebenezer Scrooge was gonna be well different to what he had planned, coz later that night was when somefing screwy began to mess with da miserable old minger's mojo. How bad could it get? Well, he nearly crapped himself when, unexpectedly, da ghostly face of Jacob Marley appeared out of nowhere. Scrooge couldn't make no sense of what was going down, and even less when Marley told him that as far as he was concerned Scrooge had been well out of order by being so gay to everyone. But as spooked as he was, Scrooge tried his best to be cool.

"You is well in da brown stuff, Scrooge, and if you don't get it togevva then you is gonna regret it *big time!*"
"Yada yada yada – next!"
"Screw you Ebenezer dude coz I ain't busting your chops or nuffing - dis is for real, you get me?"
"Whatever."

Interestingly, coz of all da heavy chains what was hanging off him, da first fing that hit Scrooge wasn't how so last year Jacob Marley's bling was, but more how wasted he looked. Dis really was somefing else and was so not normal, which made Scrooge fink that somehow da ham what he had for his tea had been spiked and was well tripping him out. He felt like he was having da heavy hallucination, but Marley just wouldn't let it go.

"Now listen up blud, not being funny or nuffing but if you

don't start behaving, then you is gonna get well busted by free bruvvas of da ghost posse."

"Yeah right."

"Hey, Scrooge, stop giving me attitude coz you is in deep, deep trouble. Blates, babe. Which bit of 'ghost posse' don't you get?"

"Hey, I get it – dese ghost dudes are your big bruvvas yada yada yada, and your point is?"

"They is coming to get you."

Trip or no trip, da fing in da bling what looked like Jacob Marley was seriously giving him da freaks and no way did it make any sense. Coz when he was alive, Jacob Marley was more of da gangsta money-lender than Scrooge ever was, yet now he had da front to come back, trying to stick it to him. But as much as Ebenezer fought that Jacob Marley had lost it, neverdaless, fings were about to become all sweaty underpants for Ebenezer Scrooge in da way he could never have imagined, especially when da first of da free spooks came out of nowhere and put da willies up him. It was none other than da skank ghost of Christmas Past.

Although he had been expecting somefing horrid, smelly and scary, dis ghost dude wasn't actually too bad, as far as ghosts went. He was well cool in da way he tried to get Scrooge in touch with his inner self by taking him on da journey of his yoof which, as it turned out, was well emotional, especially when da ghost brought back all da well sad times when his farva had been so cruel to him when he was just da little nippa. Dis was really screwing with his mojo but it was nuffing compared to being forced to remember his sista; da only one who had ever loved him more than anyone, but still Scrooge had chosen to forget all about her, which was well selfish and sad. But then again, selfish and sad was what Ebenezer Scrooge was all about.

Then it was all over and he was back in da home turf feeling well messed up in da head. All he wanted was to get to bed, crash and not fink about da other ghost dudes what Jacob Marley had said were coming for him. But although he tried to forget about them, da ghosts weren't ever gonna forget about him, coz before too long da dreaded ghost of Christmas Present was by da bed and gagging to bring it on. Now despite dis ghost calling itself 'Present', and although Scrooge didn't do presents, it wasn't like no present he had ever seen before and he so wanted to return it. But unlike M&S, dis ghost didn't run no returns policy and was in no mood let him off da hook. It was on da heavy mission to get Ebenezer Scrooge to see everyfing what was happening all around him but never took no notice of, like da geeza Bob Cratchit what spent all his days counting Scrooge's moolah.

Now although he knew that Bob Cratchit had da tiny nippa called Tiny Tim, and even though he was da turf cripple, Scrooge really couldn't be arsed, end of. But all that was about to change da moment da ghost of Christmas Present made him see how Tiny Tim was not only da well cute nippa, but he was also da well cute nippa with special needs and how Scrooge did not want to go dere.

"Oh c'mon dawg, dis is well out of order!"
"I am da ghost of Christmas Present, it's what I so do, get over it."

Although Ebenezer was beginning to feel like crap, da ghost of Christmas Present hadn't finished and just to stick it to Scrooge even more, he took him to see his nephew. For da geeza what didn't do happy families, Scrooge was amazed how Fred was telling everyone in da hood how much he wished his uncle would stop being so minging, coz deep down he knew that he could be awesome if he put his mind to it. Well, Scrooge couldn't believe it. Somefing real odd was happening coz he was beginning to feel like he cared, deffo.

But before Scrooge got da chance to fink about it, da fird ghost – da ghost of Christmas Future – suddenly appeared. It was like da changing of da ghost shift and Scrooge didn't like it, no way. Coz now instead of being all kind like da others, dis ghost had one mean kickass attitude. Dis ghost, da one for Christmas Future, was da fugliest and da most minging gangsta ghost of them all, which made Scrooge fink da worst. But as bad as he fought it was, it was nuffing to what happened when da ghost took him on one very heavy trip, like he had never been on before in his life.

Scrooge's future was coming at him all at once and it was totally bad coz it brought him up close to da well cute little cripple, Tiny Tim. As much as he tried, Scrooge couldn't get away from seeing da poor nippa looking all whacked and it was affecting him real bad.

"Are you finally getting it, Scrooge dude, coz it looks to me that your eyes are well wet!"
"I don't understand it, coz they are so not tears."
"You reckon?"
"Yeah, coz Ebenezer Scrooge doesn't do tears, end of. Tears are for wimps."

But da truth was that his eyes was so full of tears. Then, before he could get it togevva, he suddenly saw himself lying on da floor, all spaced out and dead to da world. Scrooge knew he was in da Hell turf and he was cacking it. If dis was how it was all gonna end, then he wanted nuffing more to do with it and that was da moment Ebenezer Scrooge decided that as of right now - dis minute - that he didn't want to be no douchebag no more. He had seen da light and wanted to be da geeza what did good fings for everyone, no matter what it took. Dere was no way he was gonna ever high five da Reaper geeza and all coz he had been nuffing less than da first class scumbag all his life.

And from that moment onwards, Ebenezer Scrooge fought only of everyone else in da home turf. Da days of being minging were over, which made him da most wonderful geeza what had ever lived and what he got back was maximum respect from everyone, which was well sweet.

DAVE COPPERFIELD

Not being funny or nuffing but sometimes dere is geezas in da hood what is more worse off than you, end of. Coz sometimes it is just circumstances what makes life suck, and so it was for da geeza in dis story, Dave Copperfield.

It wasn't his fault or nuffing that his muvva, Clara, ended up da single parent after his farva died just before he was busted out of da womb. Although dis was not good for either of them, da fing about Mrs C, though, was that she was one clued up bitch and in theory at least, everyfing could have worked out fine for Dave. Coz despite da way fings were, Mrs C wasn't just da woman doing it for herself, coz she had help from da nurse with da strange name of Peggotty to do all that stinky nappy changing and stuff, which was well fortunate.

Da other fing about Mrs C was that she was still hot to trot, innit. She was da babe with da awesome booty and although she had seen off one husband already, and in spite of da minging circumstances what she found herself in, she *still* managed to get her rocks off with some geeza called Edward Murdstone. So now everyfing was looking real cool coz Edward was gagging for Mrs C; they was in lurve, they was poetry in motion, they was mad for it and they was ready to get it on big time, which was exactly what happened. Now not only was Edward and Clara man and bitch, but Dave had da brand new step-daddy which meant that, finally, they was gonna end up all happy ever after. Or maybe not. Coz sometimes, as Dave Copperfield was about to discover, fings don't always work out exactly as they should.

Even though Mrs C wasn't expecting her main man to be all chocolates and bling, what she did want, however, was for him to be all kind and good to her nippa. Simples. Well, that might have been what she hoped for, but what she got was da miserable geeza who was always getting in Dave's face. Dis was well out of order but if that wasn't bad enough, then dere was Edward's badass sista, Jane, what had crashed da home turf and claimed squatters' rights and wasn't going nowhere. In no time that trailer park trash had become da permanent fixture that not even Cillit Bang was gonna be able to shift, end of. She was one mean sadist what had gangsta tendencies and da knack of messing with Dave's head, which just wasn't cool.

Although dere was no need for it, Jane and her bruvva was bossing da home turf like they was looking to rumble. So it wasn't no surprise when it all kicked off after Dave got bitch-slapped by his step-farva, and that was only for getting crap school grades. Perhaps fings might have been better if he hadn't tried to face his step-farva down by biting da douchebag in da well justified act of self-defence against being bullied. However, in his act of spineless retaliation, Edward Murdstone really stuck it right back to his step-nippa by getting him Borstalled in da Salem House Academy. You could say that Dave Copperfield had been stitched up like da kipper fish and dere was naff all he could do about it. Bummer.

Anyhoo, it could have been loads worse, coz although his step-farva kept busting his chops, not everyone was minging to him, which was just as well, innit. Fortunately he wasn't without friends, like da nurse with da strange name of Peggotty. She saw what had been going down and had always tried her best to make fings better for Dave by trying to make him feel like part of her own fam. She would let him hang with her bruvva and his adopted nippas, Ham and Little Emily, what lived in da wicked upside down boat which was just like da old woman what lived in da shoe but only wetter.

Dis act of kindness was what made Dave keep it real, which was just what he needed to help him chillax, innit. As for da Salem House Academy, well, it wasn't too bad coz Dave actually did good. However, if he was doing alright at da school it was no fanks to his step-farva who was always screwing with him by never telling him nuffing about what was happening in da home turf, no matter what. Good or bad, whenever somefing was going down, Dave would never find out about it until he went back in da holidays.

"By da way, when you was at school your muvva banged out da new step-bruvva which was well foughtful, you get me."

"Wicked."

Sometimes, though, just sometimes, da news was anyfing but sweet, although of course he never had advance warning or nuffing of what was to come.

"Dude, before I forget, when you was at school somefing happened to your muvva and step-bruvva. Now what was it? Oh yeah, that's it, they died. Sucks doesn't it?"

Now it meant he had no fam in da hood except for an aunt what lived in da Dover yard.

But as messed up as it was in da home turf, it could have been better if only his step-farva would have made da effort. Coz now Dave was da sad orphan, dis could have been well good for da building of bridges. However, instead of using dis as da perfect chance for solid geeza-bonding, his step-farva was having none of it. All he wanted was to kick Dave's sorry ass as far away from da home turf as possible, which was well harsh and what was more, he had da cunning plan to make it happen.

Murdstone and his bruvva had da factory in da London ghetto and it was decided to send Dave over and do real challenging stuff, like cleaning wine bottles and that. It didn't make no difference that he didn't want to go, but coz of all da attitude what came from his step-farva, he had no choice. Of course, Dave being Dave, it meant that fings never went smooth coz as usual nuffing ever happened without somefing going belly up. Like when he got to London and some bloke called Wilkins Micawber offered him somewhere to crash. On da face of it he seemed like da well top geeza what had da world sussed. Nuffing ever got him down, or at least that was what it looked like to Dave.

"Yo, Copperfield dude, wassup?"
"Nuffing. I'm cool."
"Not being funny, but da trouble with you is that you is so stressed, when you should be out in da ghetto hanging."
"Whatever."
"Just you remember that no matter what, somefing will turn up coz it always does and that is what I'm saying, you get me bro?"

Wilkins Micawber was always saying somefing would turn up, coz he was da sort of geeza who would always see da can of Stella half full. He was one laidback geeza, unfazed and chilled, and if he said it once then he said it da million times and more. However, da only problem was that while he was waiting for somefing to turn up da only fing that did was da filth what busted him for owing loads of dosh all over da hood. Bummer - especially when he was always banging on about what to do with it, just like he was some RBS financial dude.

"Annual moolah twenty pounds, annual expenditure nineteen and six, result good karma. Annual moolah twenty pounds, annual expenditure twenty pounds naff all and six, then you is gonna have to consolidate with Ocean Finance. Simples."

Well, dis unexpected turn of events was not da kind of fing Dave needed and he knew that he had to make like da banana fruit and split. So bearing in mind da way Micawber got fingered by da fuzz, Dave did da only fing he could; he had it away on his toes and legged it from da factory turf as fast as he could, making for da Dover ghetto where, as luck would have it, his Aunty Betsy Trotwood took him in which was well jammy. Phew!

She was well supportive and made everyfing easy on da mojo, giving Dave da witness protection from his step-farva, by coming up with da new street name for him of Trot, innit. And so began Dave's new life. First he joined da new school ghetto before shacking up with his Aunt's lawyer geeza called Wickfield, and his uber fit daughta Agnes. Well, after everyfing what had happened, it looked like Dave had finally scored it big coz now he was hanging with new bruvvas with cool street names like Uriah Heep. Sweet. Now although Dave had da real crap time growing up as da sad little orphan, it seemed like fings were finally working out for him which was well good. Everyfing was improving, including his schoolwork, and he passed all his exams no probs. Sorted.

Dave was at long last living da dream, which meant that dere wasn't gonna be no danger of him mixing with da wrong crew, getting into rucks, or even getting an ASBO. Da only question now was what would he end up doing for da full time job and of course his Aunt Betsy had her finger on da pulse. What she fought would be well sexy was for him to train to be da lawyer geeza, lawyering for da top firm back in da London turf run by some geeza called Spenlow.

Dis law firm had everyfing da young Dave Copperfield could have ever wanted, including da boss's daughta, Dora, what he fought was well scrubbed and fit. Suddenly everyfing was even sweeter coz not only did he want to be da successful lawyer geeza just like Spenlow but also he knew that Dora was da fox what he wanted to spend da rest of his life with. It seemed like everyfing was looking better than da sliced bread - which it was, innit.

But as fings was all coming togevva for Dave, da same could not be said for da wonderful Aunt Betsy. Although she had given it one hundred percent getting Dave sorted, unfortunately nobody had been watching out for her which was not good. Although she reckoned she was being looked after by her lawyer geeza Wickfield, unfortunately he was only looking after her money for himself. In other words, he was ripping her off big time and leaving her potless which was well skanky, innit. Coz if you can't trust lawyers then who can you trust? Not only that, but to make fings even worse, da double-dealing scumbag Wickfield wasn't acting alone, coz Dave's old school mate with da cool street name of Uriah Heep was in on da dirty deed as well, da swine. It seemed that for poor old Aunt Betsy, life had given her da nasty kick in da teeth, which was just so sad.

Under different circumstances perhaps, Dave would have done somefing to help but unfortunately, and as awful as it was for da well nice but recently mugged Aunt Betsy, he had major issues of his own to fink about. Coz while he was well over da moon and in lurve with Dora, dere was da small problem of her farva, Mr Spenlow, who would not give his approval, end of. It was like da most minging fing he could ever have done to Dave and Dora, as he did his worst to stop lurve's young dream from getting it on.

Fings were looking well bad and deep down they knew that it was gonna take an act of God if they was ever gonna get it togevva. And then one day in da most extraordinary way, da freak act of God accident happened when his carriage was totalled making Mr Spenlow came over dead! Bad news for Spenlow, but da right good result for Dave and Dora. They was made up coz they was finally able to get married without anybody screwing da whole fing up. Sweet.

So with nobody now to get in da way of true lurve, Dave and Dora became man and bitch. They was young, she had da dog animal called Jip and most important of all, they had da rest of dere lives to be with each other. Mind you, that's not to say that everyfing was perfect, coz every relationship has issues what need ironing out to make it perfect. Even though they fancied da pants off each other big time, it didn't mean that Dora wasn't well dodgy at doing housewifely fings like da ironing and da dusting. Neverdaless, while Dave still reckoned that - given time - she could have worked out which end of da duster to use, he couldn't stop her from coming over dead which kind of mashed that marriage.

Dave was well cheesed off, coz besides da sad event of Dora kicking da bucket, he was well gutted when Jip, da dog animal, keeled over and barked da last bark. It was emotional coz Dave really liked Jip. It was then that he decided to get away from da English turf to sort his head out and that's what happened. However, it was well strange coz with all that finking he was doing while he was bumming around, he began to fink all about Agnes Wickford, da daughta of da piece of scum Mr Wickford, da dude what stuck it to his Aunt Betsy and took all her dosh.

Although dere was da heavy guilt trip he gave himself when he fought about da situation - like what Dora would say about him getting all jiggy over anuvva bitch, from where she was in da heaven turf - da one important fing that swung it for Agnes was that Dora was dead, innit. It was crazy but da more Dave fought about her, da more he knew that Agnes was da dogs and that was why he had to get to her. Well, how fortunate for Dave that da feeling was well mutual, coz as luck would have it she always fought he was kind of uber cool, deffo. And in da end Agnes became Dave's new bitch and knocked out several nippas for her geeza which although it was tiring, was well awesome all da same.

WELL GOOD EXPECTATIONS

Hundreds of years ago, dere was naff-all lurve in da hood for dudes and lady dudes what had issues. They wasn't big on getting in touch with dere inner self, which was well sad especially when dere was loads of bros what needed group hugs and that, like Pip, da nippa orphan of dis story. Although he didn't have no muvva or farva, he lived in his sista's home turf with her blacksmiff geeza, Joe. And while no fam is perfect, dis one should have been on Jerry Springer, coz although Joe wasn't no sadist muppet to Pip, da same couldn't be said for his sista, who was one mean ball-busting badass bitch who was always getting in her little bruvva's face.

But even though she was on his case 24-seven, Pip never complained or nuffing, no matter how bad it got. Sometimes, though, when she was really off da hook with extreme mingingness, he would often leg it into da ghetto while he waited for her to take da chill pill and stop being da right stroppy bitch. And dis was what it was like for

Pip until da day when he was hanging in da church turf and found himself unexpectedly face to face with da well dodgy escaped prisoner dude, Magwitch. Dis was one geeza you seriously didn't want to mess with. Not that Pip would have, mind, even if he fought Magwitch would have been da match for his psycho sista if they went one on one, innit. Neverdaless, Magwitch cut da well menacing figure dressed, as he was, in da stinky prisoner freads and chains.

Da other fing that really made him look real scary was that he was so fugly. He looked like he'd fallen out of da fugly tree, hitting every branch before landing face down on da fugly rock. He was da munter without equal, and given that he was da meanest-looking escaped gangsta what Pip had ever seen in his entire life, it was fair to say that da poor nippa was bricking it and stayed rooted to da spot. Everyfing was creeping him out, big time, so when Magwitch told him to get him some grub and somefing to break his chains so that he could leg it out of da turf, who was Pip to argue?

Soon Pip returned and after Magwitch was unchained and grubbed up on cider, left-over kebabs, pizza and curry he bolted, but not before he gave Pip da real heavy warning to keep it zipped. Even though he never laid da single finger on him, Magwitch made it crystal that if Pip breathed even da single word to any ho or bro, then he was gonna be wacked.

41

"What you looking at, nippa?"

"It's your chain bling, innit. Where did you get it?"

"Where do you fink? eBay!"

And still, even when Magwitch was long gone, Pip never said nuffing to nobody. Coz although he might have been small he wasn't no numpty, and did exactly what he was told. Scared yes, stupid no.

But of course Pip and his sista weren't da only dudes what lived in da hood, coz dere was da old and crinkly Miss Havisham and her well fit adopted bitch, Estella, who was living in Miss H's home turf of Satis House. Pip used to hang with Estella although dere was never anyfing in it, which was just as well. Coz da fing about Miss Havisham was that far from being cuddly, she was all bitter and twisted – like da old woman in da shopping line what smells of wee – and she was always giving Estella da grounding in how to be picky when it came to finding geezas and not giving nuffing away for free. In other words, she was training her up to be da 'A-star' tease without having to deliver da goods, innit.

Although dis didn't make Estella da ghetto bike, it was still well dodgy and all coz da crinkly old Miss Havisham had once been dumped at da altar by some geeza called Compeyson, which explained her well skanky attitude to geezas. All dese years on, dis should have been nuffing more than 'boo-hoo, life sucks so get over it bitch', but da strangest fing was that

Compeyson was da real life pukka bruvva of da escaped gangsta Magwitch! As for da nippa Pip, well, as da years passed he grew into da big nippa and was taken on as da apprentice blacksmiff by his nasty sista's geeza, Joe. Not that Pip's new job impressed Estella, coz it didn't.

"Oh my God, why is you interfering with da horse animals though? And not being funny or nuffing but that is *so* gay, innit."

But Pip took no notice, which would only wind Estella up big time. As far as she was concerned, dere was nuffing cool about being no blacksmiff with rough hands and smelling of horse. Da little minx was well minging to Pip and would call him names like 'Horse Whisperer', which would really bring him down.

Although she was always giving him da nurple pipple and busting his chops, Pip just kept his head down and never said nuffing. However, sometimes da fickle finger of fate does somefing real bitching to change fings forever and that was what happened after he met da lawyer geeza called Mr Jaggers in da ghetto pub, where he gave him some news what was gonna really blow his mind. Initially Pip remembered Jaggers from when he was knocking around at Miss Havisham's, so he fought he was safe. Neverdaless, da news really was *so* awesome, coz Jaggers had come to tell Pip that he had scored it big. He had become uber minted and all coz of da generous mystery geeza what was giving him buckets and buckets of wonga. Bring it on!

However, before Pip could get his hands on da cash, dere was two fings what he had to know. First, he wasn't going to be told who his new sugar daddy was, definite, and second, he was being minted up so that he could become da proper gentleman nob. Although Pip didn't know who was behind all of dis, what he did know was that nuffing was gonna be da same ever again. Now, coz of da respect he would be getting for being da big cheese in da hood, he knew he was gonna have to stop being da apprentice blacksmiff geeza, coz even he knew that nobs don't mess with no horse animals. It just wasn't cool.

However, that didn't stop him from giving maximum fought to who da mystery geeza was. Pip reckoned it could have been da bitter and twisted Miss Havisham, but then again coz she was so bitter and twisted, he just couldn't see it, end of. But despite suddenly becoming Numero Uno, Pip said nuffing to nobody, which was well stupid, coz if he had then it might have stopped Estella from screwing with his moxie. Pip just took it, coz deep down he was well in lurve with da saucepot, even if she was always going all Posh Spice on him.

From here on in, Pip was having da most awesome time strutting his stuff in da London turf. He was hanging with some cool dudes; he was wearing only da best freads and blinging himself up with da most wickedest bling what money could buy. But, of course, he was now also learning much more than how to put shoes on da horse animals' feet, on account of da heavy education he was getting from da teacher geeza called Matthew Pocket. Da interesting fing about da teacher was that he was da cousin of Miss Havisham, which only made Pip fink again that it was her what was looking after him, deffo.

Maybe she was or maybe she wasn't, but one fing was for sure, and despite being da newest nob in da hood, instead of blowing it big time Pip was real cool about everyfing, including his education. Respect for da dude what wasn't too cool for school. But even though most of his life was working out real sweet, it's true to say that not everyfing was. While most dudes in da hood was being cool with him, Estella was still treating him like he was nuffing special by being all girlie-girl with so many other geezas in da turf, even though she knew that Pip so wanted to get it on with her. And then perhaps da unkindest cut of all was when she stuck it to him big time after she got all jiggy with some dude with da well stupid name of Bently Drummie and in no time they was married. Da fing about Estella was that she really knew how to twist da blade, and it so ripped at Pip's guts.

But Pip wasn't da only one she was giving bad attitude to, coz before long she was kicking off at Miss Havisham. It was clear that after all da years of living with somebody who was so bitter and twisted, it had made Estella da same, which could only ever end up with them having da most awesome bitch fight ever. Suddenly da gloves was off and da handbags was dropped as Estella got right in Miss H's face and waved da menacing index finger at her like it was da index finger from hell. Not that Miss H was taking that from nobody.

"Know yourself little girl and show some respect or else!"
"Talk to da hand coz da face ain't listening, old lady, coz you is going down!"
"Don't disrespect me, Estella."
"Boring!"
"I'm warning you coz you ain't behaving no better than no ghetto princess and I don't like da attitude!"
"Yada yada yada - *whatever!*"

Man, it was ugly, da way they was dissing each other like they was da worst of enemies and all coz Estella had beef over da way Miss Havisham had brought her up. Da bitch was smoking with rage, but da shame was that later on, when everyfing had all calmed down between them, Estella wanted to check that they was still cool with each other. However, before she was able to make fings right, da bitter and twisted Miss Havisham's clothes caught fire and she was burned to da crisp. Smoking.

But although dis was da awful shock, it wasn't as awesome as da one Pip got. Coz after all da years what had passed since he got da moolah, he finally came face to face with da geeza what scared da crap out of him in da churchyard all those years ago; Magwitch da escaped prisoner. At first Pip was well confused and didn't know what to fink, coz he never fought he'd see him again. It didn't make no sense or nuffing. At first he didn't even recognise da gangsta scum but slowly, and dis time without da heavy menaces, Magwitch came clean. He never did get away like he wanted after he was busted by da filth, and was shipped over to da Australian turf, where da koala animals come from. Even more incredible was that, not only had he escaped again, but he was also da mystery geeza what had given Pip all da cash!

"For real? You mean you're totally not messing with me?"
"Dude, I'm not messing with nuffing coz I'm back to see that everyfing is cool. Are we cool?"
"Yeah, we cool.
"Sweet."

Although Magwitch was calling himself Provis now, but coz he was still da wanted geeza on da run from da filth, Pip had to get him out of sight before he got caught by da fuzz. So coming up with da cunning plan, Pip and Magwitch made for da boat on da river to get him out of da London turf and over to da Hamburg ghetto. And they might have got away with it had it not been for Compeyson, da geeza what had heartlessly dumped da bitter and twisted Miss Havisham at da altar all those years ago. It was also well unfortunate that Compeyson so hated Magwitch, even though they used to go out mugging togevva in da old days. Anyhoo, as soon as he saw Magwitch and Pip legging it, he recognised da escaped gangsta and went for him.

Before long dere was da massive ruck which ended up with Compeyson getting well mashed and dead. Magwitch though, who was also hurt in da battle, was busted by da filth – again. Dis was not how it was meant to be and to make everyfing well worse, dis time he wasn't sent back to da Australian turf but was sentenced instead to da gallows. But every cloud has da silver lining coz although they wanted him to hang from da noose, Magwitch was dying of da minging injuries from da fight, so at least he had da last laugh at da expense of da law – lol!

For Pip, well, he managed to find somefing out about Estella; Magwitch was only her farva! But still dere was one more gotcha, which was that all da moolah that Magwitch had – and dere was buckets of it left – was taken by da court. That was well mean, coz it should have been Pip's and now it was all gone, leaving him potless. It was all too much and he decided to split da English turf and clear his head before fings got any worse.

Meanwhile, and unknown to Pip, Estella had also been having da real crappy time of it. Her marriage to da geeza with da stupid name of Drummie was busted, which meant that her and Pip was both emotionally screwed. But all was not lost coz after years away from England, Pip came over all friends reunited with Estella in da Satis House turf which, and in consideration of all da unhappy events what they had known, was da well nice way to end da story, innit.

NICK NICKLEBY

Given that Godfrey Nickleby was minted, it should've meant that when Nick was sprung from da womb turf, he should have wanted for nuffing but da silver spoon in his gob. However, sometimes fings do not always work out as sweet as they should, especially as Godfrey Nickleby was so crap at looking after all his dosh and investments, innit. So taking into account just how off da hook his financial judgement was, instead of making sure da entire Nickleby crew was safe, Nick, his muvva and his sista Kate eventually found demselves up da creek without da paddle. In fact they was *so* far up da creek that even if they *had* one, they wouldn't know whether to use it to paddle or slap Godfrey in da face with it for being da prize muppet for making them all poor. But of course they didn't. Not coz they didn't want to, but more to do with da fact that Godfrey was already dead.

But as bad as fings were for da Nickleby posse, Nick, who was only nineteen years old himself, had da well sick idea. Although it meant eating da uber sized piece of humble pie, he fought everyfing would work out sweet if he went to see Uncle Ralph Nickleby in da London turf, not just coz he was well loaded but coz he was fam. Mind you, when it came down to it, Ralph wasn't bovvered whether or not da Nickleby's was potless, homeless or even selling da Big Issue, coz he was that kind of douchebag. Of course he could have handed over some dosh to help out his extended family, but he couldn't be arsed, end of.

Neverdaless, that didn't stop Ralph from making himself out to be some kind of top geeza by fixing it for Nick to get work at Dotheboys Hall school as da assistant teacher and as if to make himself look like da most uber cool uncle ever, he even fixed it for Kate to score da dressmaking job. That was da fing about Uncle Ralph, coz he was so far up his own bottom he actually fought it was well cool getting da Nickleby's to fink that he was da man without it costing him.

Although for Kate da dressmaking gig wasn't nuffing too special, for Nick though - being da school assistant teacher dressed up all important – he reckoned it was somefing what would make him look da business and someone to be respected in da school turf.

"Yo Sis, what about da special assistant teacher freads what I'm wearing, eh?"
"But they is so wicked, innit!"
"For sure, coz they is well good, which is why I am being so dazzled by my own awesomeness of da cut of da freads. It does make me fink though – does my bum look big in dis?"

But although at first Nick fought being da well cool teacher was where it was at, and was somefing what could get him maximum respect and that, he was soon to find out otherwise. Coz although he was well up for being all education, education, education he soon realised that not everyfing in da school yard was as he fought it might be. In fact it was well skank and all coz it was being run by some homies of Uncle Ralph, da sadistic Wackford Squeers and his crazy bitch Mrs Squeers.

They was like da Adolf and Eva of da school turf coz they was both one hundred per cent mental, 24-seven. They was scum, da pair of them, coz they was always beating da crap out of da nippas, big time, with da Wackford Squeers cane of pain. They was both well out of control, leaving Nick feeling gutted for da nippas. Most times he would say nuffing but not always.

"Yo, Wackford, leave them kids alone, dude. Them nippas have done nuffing, yet you is always so badass, innit!"
"Talk to da cane, coz dis aint got nuffing to do with you."
"Look, not being funny or nuffing, but what you do to those kids just ain't cool, blud."
"Oh, boo hoo, Nickleby you muppet. Now get outta my face before I bounce you out of da school turf, you get me!"

Nick Nickleby knew Wackford Squeers needed to be sorted with da heavy slap, but coz he needed da wonga what he earned for da family, he did nuffing for fear of getting busted. He was like da silent witness and it really ripped at da guts big time. He knew what da thumbscrew sadist Wackford Squeers was doing to all da kids was bang out of order, and especially so to da handicapped nippa called Smike, but dere was no stopping him. He was getting in his face over nuffing and what made it worse was that Smike couldn't fight back coz he was so special. Da evil Squeers never stopped da minging punishments until da day when Nick finally snapped, coz he knew that he had to rescue Smike before he finally got wasted, never to be seen again. It wasn't big and it wasn't clever, but Nick lost it big time.

"Dawg, you is gonna get yours for every manky fing what you've ever done in da school turf, and especially to Smike!"
"Nickleby, what is you doing? Have you been on da Stella?"

And as he stuck it to da sadistic Wackford Squeers by giving him da taste of his own Nazi mentalness by beating da crap out of him with da dreaded whacking cane, Nick knew that he had to leg it before he got busted to da filth by da well scary Mrs Squeers. So grabbing Smike, he bolted out of da school turf to get as far away from Dotheboys Hall as he could.

They headed towards da Portsmouth ghetto where he fought it would be well funky for them to hitch all da way to da docks, finding da ship what was looking for sailors and join up. But before they even got as far as sticking out da thumb, on da way to da port, they got yakking to some theatre geeza called Vincent Crummles. Perhaps it was da roar of da greasepaint and da smell of da crowd, but Nick was well impressed by what da dude had to say about what it was like to be da actor on da stage. Suddenly they wasn't going to be sailors no more, coz Nick and Smike was gonna be actors. Fierce.

But for every yin dere has to be da yang, coz while fings were beginning to look real lush for Nick, da same couldn't be said for his innocent little sista Kate. Although Uncle Ralph had made promises to da bitch, da truth was that far from being safe she was being well violated by not only Ralph but also his homies, who were trying to stick it to her like she was nuffing more than da WAG at da roasting. It was minging. But Kate was no slapper, no way no how, and she was not putting out for no geeza what was looking for any jiggy-jiggy against her will, which only wound up Ralph. As far as he was concerned da Nickleby's was becoming da right pain in da booty, especially after he had heard all about what went down at da Dotheboys Hall turf and now with Kate not giving it up to da posse, he was getting da right hump.

Although fings were definitely not looking good for Kate, what she didn't know was that after da bit of time treading da boards, her big bruvva Nick was back in da London turf with Smike, not only to check up on how she and his muvva were doing but also to meet some geeza called Newman Noggs who worked for Uncle Ralph as his clerk. Sometimes though, as Nick was about to discover, life comes and kicks you straight in da buttocks with all da power of da Reebok trainer with da very sharp pointy spike on da toecap, and messes up da mojo real bad.

Quite by chance, when Nick and Smike stopped for some grub, Nick overheard some geezas yakking and getting gobby about being all jiggy with some bitch who was gagging for it. Not only was it well sexist but even worse, da more Nick heard about her being mad for it, da more he realised that da bitch what they was disrespecting was none other than Kate. And as they carried on giving it large, da more angry Nick became until finally he decided that somebody was gonna get slapped for dissing his little sis and violating her space. Well, da way it worked out, that somebody was Sir Mulberry Hawk who got his right in da kisser with da well nasty horse whip. Unfortunately for Nick, and as if to make matters worse, dis geeza was one of Uncle Ralph's massive.

Anyhoo, by da time he finally met with Norman Noggs, Nick was well emotional coz of da way Kate had been yakked about. But when Newman Noggs told him all about all da minging scams what his Uncle Ralph had been up to, he felt that he had to do somefing and fanks to Noggs, he had da documents to prove it. One way or anuvva he was gonna take Ralph down, but da only question was how?

Fortunately for Nick, da opportunity to stick it to his Uncle was about to present itself.

By chance, anuvva of Uncle Ralph's crew – Arthur Gride, da creepy 70-year-old numpty – was stalking da well-fit babe called Madeline Bray. Now, although she fought he was nuffing more than da manky old dinosaur, it didn't make her any more safe. Although it had nuffing to do with her, but coz her farva owed Ralph Nickleby loads of dosh, da slimeball Gride told him that everyfing would be sorted if Madeline's farva agreed that it was cool for him to get his rocks off with da bitch and marry her, as you do. Even though dis was taking liberties but coz he was over da barrel, her farva said it was cool.

Sometimes, though, luck is at hand coz all was not lost, fanks to Nick getting da vibe off da street about what da dirty old geeza Arthur Gride was planning to do to Madeline. He legged it over to Gride's yard and got right in his face, warning him to back off Madeline or he was going to so happy-slap da crap out of him and he did. Good. Well, although it was only meant as da friendly threat with menaces, da next day, da day of da nuptials, Arthur Gride did what any geeza would do in his position – he grassed Nick up to his Uncle Ralph.

Well, feeling what he did about his nephew, dis was all da reason he needed to waste him. After all da aggro that Nick had caused him, da last fing Ralph was gonna do was let Nick get away with anyfing and that was why him and Gride got over to Madeline's to make sure that everyfing was still cool. But always expect da unexpected, coz hot on da heels was Nick, out to do all he could to screw up da wedding plans. Then, somefing well jammy happened when Madeline's farva - suddenly and without warning - came over all dead. Although it was sad, it was solid for two well good reasons. Firstly, coz her farva was now stiff, Madeline didn't have to go through with da wedding rave and secondly, Nick was in lurve with her which was just so unexpected and awesome.

However, dere still was da problem of keeping Uncle Ralph away from Madeline. Although her farva was gone that didn't mean to say that she was out of da brown stuff, innit, and that was why Nick had da well good idea of getting his muvva and his sista to look after her. However, what goes around comes around and coz Uncle Ralph had been spreading uber bad karma about da turf, he was gonna find out da hard way about paying da heavy price for being so minging. And that's da fing about karma, coz you never know how it's gonna mess with da mojo.

Coz when da two-faced scumbag got back to da home turf dere was da grim news that he had lost loads of dosh on account of his financial investments going belly up. In other words, Uncle Ralph was feeling da effect of da credit crunch. Perhaps he should have left well alone, but now fings had got too personal and that was reason enough for him to get Nick by da short and curlies and bounce him around, innit. So togevva with his main man Wackford Squeers, they decided da best way to get to Nick was to bust da unfortunate Smike back to Dotheboys Hall school where they could kick da crap out of him.

However, what they hadn't reckoned on was da sheer determination of Smike. Dere was no way they was ever gonna get hold of him and he managed to escape back to da safety of Nick's yard before they could do dere worst. But although Nick was so pleased to see him again da joy soon turned to pain when he suddenly died from da acute shortage of breath and tuberculosis which, after everyfing he had been through, was well sad. Still, through da sadness came some joy when, finally, Uncle Ralph got his and it was all fanks to Newman Noggs; remember, he was da geeza what worked for Uncle Ralph as da honest clerk – who gave Nick all da incriminating paperwork what proved that Uncle Ralph was nuffing more than da 100 per cent, bona-fide financial crook.

However, if da fought of financial ruin and criminal prosecution wasn't bad enough, da final piece of news what hit him was nuffing short of tragic; Smike, da handicapped nippa what had been so abused all his miserable and sad life, was nuffing less than his very own son. Well, after finding out Smike was his, Uncle Ralph decided to do da most honourable fing what he had ever done in his entire miserable life – he hung himself.

But for Nick and Madeline life was much brighter and happier coz they finally got it togevva which - after all da crap what they had to deal with - was well beautiful, innit.

BARNEY RUDGE

Picture da scene. Night time and da weather was minging. It was cold and windy and was no night for wusses what didn't like getting dere hair wet, definite. But for some homies what didn't mind chancing da conditions it was da perfect opportunity to get togevva to yak about geeza fings like da latest pimped up carriages, bling, bitches and..... murder! Coz huddled togevva at da Maypole Inn somewhere on da frontline in da Chigwell ghetto, was free geezas yakking big time about da well grizzly death of what happened 22 years previous to da exact day.

All of them was bros of John Willet what bossed da Maypole turf. Soloman Daisy was in da chair, giving it loads about what happened to some geeza by da name of Reuben Haredale what had come over all murdered in da most mysterious of all circumstances, innit.

"Look, not being funny or nuffing but it was da steward what done it, end of."
"Dude, dere was only ever two bruvvas in da frame, blud, and they was da ones what worked for Reuben; da gardener

and da steward and da word from da street was that it was da gardener what wasted him. Like he was well dodgy, you get me."

"Yada yada yada – whatever!"

"It's blates man, coz it could have only been da gardener what done da Reubenator in, coz although da steward ended up whacked – and we know it was him coz of da steward freads he was wearing when they found da body – da gardener was never seen again and that is what I am saying."

Reuben Haredale was known in da ghetto as one minted geeza what owned da well nice property in da home turf called Da Warren, where his daughta Emma and his bruvva Geoffrey lived. After da murderous ruck, da steward and da gardener geezas became da chief suspects in da gory goings-on after Reuben suffered da fatal shortage of breath what left him well disadvantaged by being dead, innit. When da body of da steward was found, da heavy finger of suspicion was pointed at da gardener.

Mind you, and despite all da aggro going on about da murder, all was not so cool in da Maypole Inn booza for John Willet on account of him being well minging to his own nippa Joe. He was always getting in his face 24-seven until finally Joe stuck it to his old man by giving him da finger and splitting da home turf, but not before saying goodbye to his own ghetto princess, Dolly, da well fit locksmiff's daughta of Gabriel Varden. Although they was both well up for it, it wasn't just Joe and Dolly who were feeling all lurved up in da hood, coz Reuben's niece Emma was getting it togevva with some geeza called Edward Chester, and it was full on, although not everyone was so keen.

Edward's farva, da well Catholic John Chester, and Emma's Uncle Geoffrey was sworn enemies, and they was doing dere best to muck everyfing up. Well, dis made Edward go all moody and he fell out with his farva before taking off for da West Indies, innit. However, if it had gone all Pete Tong for Edward, then that was nuffing to da strange fings what had started to happen to da Rudge family.

Barney's muvva, who was da widow of da dead steward what was originally in da frame for da hit on Reuben Haredale, was being stalked by da shadowy highwayman geeza. But instead of trying to get him done for violating her space, she took pity on dis weirdo by giving him care in da community. Dis was obviously not da actions of somebody who was all da ticket although, in fairness, dis must have been where her nippa Barney got it from. I'm not saying he was special or nuffing but when you know his best mate was da pet raven bird called Grip, you get da picture. Even though she was being looked after by getting da allowance from Reuben's bruvva, Geoffrey, it wasn't enough to make her feel safe so she and Barney suddenly had it away from da home turf to escape da weirdo stalker.

And so life went on in da turf until five years later on da

27th anniversary of da grizzly murder of Reuben Haredale, when on yet anuvva minging night John Willet, da boss of da Maypole booza and Hugh da handyman came across three homies – Lord George Gordon, da secretary geeza called Gashford and da servant what was known as John Grueby - who was all on da way to da London turf but needed somewhere to crash for da night so they could escape da crappy weather. Never one to miss da opportunity to make some dosh, John Willet took them back to da Maypole Inn booza where they was all given rooms.

After da solid night's kip, da free geezas went on dere way to da London ghetto and took with them da really bad anti-Catholic attitude what meant that in order to be da uber cool Protestant then you really, *really* had to happy-slap Catholics, which was so gay. Well, they was getting real tasty coz not only was they taking all dere minging racism to London, but they was also packing muscle. Dere was Simon Tappertit, who was da apprentice to da locksmiff Gabriel Varden and farva to da well fit Dolly what got all jiggy with Joe, and Ned Dennis, da hangman of Tyburn. Da free geezas also got Hugh da handyman to join them. Not that he was no racist, but after reading da leaflet at da Maypole booza about what it was like to be fun *and* Protestant he fought he'd have some of that, innit.

Meanwhile Barney Rudge and his muvva had been hanging in da country ghetto trying to avoid da shadowy highwayman geeza who had stalked them away from da London turf in da first place. But far from being safe, da truth was they weren't, coz now da shadowy highwayman geeza decided to send in da heavy mob to get some dosh from Mrs Rudge. He was mean and moody but who was he, dis superbad geeza?

"Some say he was da desperate villain who didn't care what he had to do to mug some poor, defenceless old bitch, but to da shadowy highwayman he was simply called - da Stagg."

However, not only was da Stagg mean and moody, but he was also blind! Neverdaless, and even with his disability, it was uber nice to know that when it came to getting work, da Stagg wasn't discriminated against. Blind or not, da Rudge's weren't looking for no trouble and dere was no way they was going to get demselves duffed up, so they legged it back to da London turf. Although dis seemed like da good idea at da time, da reality was anyfing but.

Coz soon after they got to da Westminster yard they saw da Protestant massive heading for da meeting near da river. Dere was going to be da heavy ruck, deffo, coz they was looking to kick some Catholic ass all over da hood before marching on to da Parliament turf. Well, all dis excitement was enough to turn da head of any geeza, especially one as special as Barney and don't forget how special he was; he's da one whose best mate was da raven bird called Grip. His muvva could see da danger even if Barney couldn't and tried to warn him off.

"Barney Rudge, what have I told you about mixing it with dodgy geezas what are looking to rumble?"

"Whatever."

"Don't *you* go giving me no attitude or else you is gonna be so grounded!"

"Shu'up coz that is *so* unfair! I hate you coz I ain't done nuffing and nor have da posse!"

"Then why is they carrying torches?"

"Hey Momma, be cool coz me and me new homies are only making toast, innit."

"But you ain't got no bread, so what is you using?"

"Catholics."

Although she tried, Mrs Rudge couldn't stop Barney from getting duped into joining da racist posse of Catholic bashers. It was well bad as it kicked off big time with da Protestant massive led by Hugh da handyman and Ned Dennis, da Tyburn hangman, heading for da Chigwell turf to give Geoffrey Haredale da right good going over. Barney Rudge was left to guard Da Boot, which not only was da turf booza, but was also da new gangsta headquarters.

Now da Protestant mafia was giving it large as they looted and torched da Maypole Inn on da way to Da Warren, which was da home of da murdered Reuben Haredale and where his bruvva Geoffrey and his daughta Emma hung out. Da mob snatched Emma Haredale and Dolly Varden – da locksmiff's daughta and da well fit babe what was once doing it with Joe Willet – and they was taken captive.

However, it wasn't only da bitches what were in trouble coz Barney Rudge was also well in da brown stuff. Although he wanted to be one badass racist just like his new bros, he couldn't coz he was so crap at it. He didn't stand da chance as he got busted and taken prisoner by da filth who carted him off to da dreaded Newgate prison which, coincidentally, was what da Protestant massive was planning to torch.

But what of da shadowy highwayman, da mysterious stranger what had been stalking Mrs Rudge? Well, he was about to make da classic mistake of being in da wrong place at da wrong time after he turned up at da now smouldering ruins of Da Warren so he could get his kicks by joining up with da arson-crazy Protestants. However, what he did not know was that Geoffrey Haredale had returned. Oops. If only da shadowy highwayman had stayed where he was, stalking Mrs Rudge, coz then he wouldn't have been taken down by Haredale. Ah well, stuff happens.

And then it all came out. Da shadowy highwayman geeza wasn't just da random stalker of Mrs Rudge coz he was, in fact, Barney Rudge Senior, da *real* farva of her nippa Barney! What are da odds? But not only that, coz he was *also* da geeza what murdered Reuben Haredale *and* da gardener, which meant that Barney Rudge Senior was actually da steward what was assumed dead. It seemed that da only reason he had got away with da grizzly murder at all was that he had switched freads with da gardener and that was why everyone fought he had done it.

But all dis was of no concern to da Protestant posse who planned to break in to da Newgate prison and release all da gangsta prisoners by kidnapping da master locksmiff Gabriel Varden to open up all da doors. Da only snag in dis plan was that da master locksmiff wouldn't do it, which was somefing they so didn't want to hear. But before they could talk him round with da heavy slap of reason, da locksmiff was rescued by some geezas what he had never seen before. One of them, strangely, had only da one arm which just goes to show that being disabled didn't mean that you had to end up on da scrapheap of life, innit.

Anyhoo, most – but not all – of da prison massive managed to escape as da Protestant posse went about doing da torching of da prison. Unfortunately Barney Rudge and Hugh da handyman were captured by da prison fuzz who were helped by none other than Ned Dennis, da turncoat Tyburn hangman who, on seeing da opportunity to use his talent for hanging dudes, switched sides due to da amount of people that were going to be recaptured, tried and hung. Clever boy. But who was da mysterious one-armed hero what rescued da locksmiff Gabriel Varden? Well, it turned out to be none other than Joe Willet! But how?

Well, after he had da massive row with his farva coz he wouldn't allow him to marry da well fit Dolly, Joe went off with da right hump and ended up largeing it in da American Revolution with his bro Edward Chester, who came back from da other side of da pond to help with da rescue. Da timing of Joe's return was perfect coz he was able to rescue Emma Haredale and also da lurve of his life, Dolly Varden. But as sweet as that was for Joe, da same could not be said for Ned Dennis, da traitor Tyburn hangman who finally got his when, despite his best efforts of switching sides, he and Hugh da handyman was captured and sentenced to death. Unfortunately so was Barney Rudge, which was well unfair on account of him being special. But all was not lost, coz fanks to da locksmiff Gabriel Varden, Barney was excused death, tagged, let off with da ASBO and pardoned. Phew!

Now with Joe all returned fit and well but without da arm, obviously, dis time dere was nuffing to stop him and Dolly from getting it togevva just like Edward and Emma who went off to da West Indies, which was cool. However, not everyone lived all happy ever after when da chicken birds came home to roost for da Protestant mafia what was doing all da rioting and kidnapping and that. Dudes like Simon Tappertit, Varden's apprentice locksmiff, got his legs busted in da riots; and as for Hugh da handyman, well, he came over dead when Geoffrey Haredale killed him in da duel. Good.

But what of Barney Rudge and his muvva? Well, after all da excitement of da stalker and da riots, they kept dere heads down and lived happy ever after.

MINGING TIMES

Thomas Gradgrind was da daddy what ran da Coketown school of hard facts. He was all education, education, education with da kickass attitude what would make all da nippas in da school turf poop dere pants. Nobody messed with him in case Gradgrind went all John Claude Van Damme with anyone he caught dissing him, innit. But although he was well good at brainstorming words and number crunching and that, when it came to da ways of da street, dis was one geeza what needed to take da chill pill coz he was so uptight. He didn't do fun, coz fun was for wimps and that was why when da Sleary Circus came to da Coketown turf, he couldn't have cared less.

"Sir, if we is good in school today can we go to da circus though?"
"Like that is gonna happen – not!"
"Oh my God Prof, I *so* don't believe we is gonna miss all da animals and clowns, coz that is *so* unfair!"
"Hey, talk to da cane, you get me?"
"Fascist!"

But although da class nippas were kept in order, da same could not be said for da Gradgrind crew. Coz as soon as they saw da circus posse hit da Coketown frontline two of his kids, Tom Junior and Louisa, legged it over and hung with da circus massive which was well defiant, although they should have known better, coz dis was like giving dere farva da finger. And so just as soon as he knew what they had done, he busted them straight back to da home turf, coz as far as he was concerned they was so in trouble for dissing him, innit. Still, it could have been worse if da other nippa, Jane, had joined in, but she didn't. On da one hand maybe she was well scared of what her farva would do or maybe, just maybe, clowns didn't float her boat or nuffing.

Back in da Gradgrind home turf, his main man, da self-made yuppie mill owner and banker geeza, Josiah Bounderby, was yakking with Mrs Gradgrind. Da vibe in da yard was chilled and would have stayed that way if her bro hadn't come back with da well heavy attitude.

"Yo, TG, why is you acting so Emo?"
"Get out of my face coz dere are fings what you do not understand what is messing with my mojo!"
"Hey, dude, to be honest, just chillax or you is gonna give yourself piles in da bottom and that just ain't cool, blud."
"No, I'll tell you what ain't cool and that's finding Tom and Louisa over in da circus hood doing fings with dwarf geezas!"
"Is it coz they is short?"

For Gradgrind dis was da straw what broke da camel animal's back but his main man Bounderby was well clued up. To him it had everyfing to do with da nippa of one of da circus posse, Sissy Jupe, who had somehow got enrolled into da Coketown school by her farva. But instead of busting her out of da school turf, Gradgrind decided to check out what was going down and dis was when everyfing became crystal. He just couldn't believe that Sissy's farva had done one leaving her all alone, da swine, or so da circus owner Mr Sleary had said.

Well, although he was one badass teacher, Gradgrind was cool and coz he felt sorry for her, he decided to look after Sissy himself. Respect. Da only condition was that Sissy was never to say nuffing about ever being one of da circus crew. Perhaps he fought it might hold her back or maybe he also had clown issues of his own.

Anyhoo, Thomas Gradgrind and Josiah Bounderby was real homies which would explain why Bounderby had over da years been finking about his best mate's nippas. Coz while he reckoned that Tom Junior would do good as da apprentice worker in his bank, he had somefing else in mind for da well fit Louisa, you get me.

Tom Junior, though, could see what Bounderby was after but even so, he stayed well shtum, finking that if he kept it zipped then it would score him monster brownie points. But as for Sissy, well, she was finding that being in da Gradgrind turf sucked. Whether it was cleaning up after da elephant animal when she was with da circus posse, or changing nappies of da youngest Gradgrind nippa, Jane, but whatever way she saw it, it was still poo.

Meanwhile, back in da Bounderby yard, dere was trouble at da mill. Stephen Blackpool, one of da weaver geezas, was all lurved up with da uber fit Rachel and was desperate to get all jiggy jiggy with her. However, coz he was still married, da bitch wasn't putting out until he dumped da current Mrs Blackpool who, bedsides being so last year, was also da full time drunk what was always getting well hammered. It was emotional and he wasn't handling fings too well when he turned to Josiah Bounderby for help.

"Dude, dis is serious and I don't know what to do and that is what I am saying."
"Hey, don't touch da freads."
"But I is desperate!"
"Your desperation is not da issue. And *don't* touch da freads or else you is gonna enter da world of pain, you get me."

Feeling like he had been bitch-slapped big time, Blackpool went back to da home turf but he just couldn't stop finking about da way he had been dissed, especially when some wrinkly old hag called Mrs Pegler got right in his face asking all sorts about Josiah Bounderby. Well, not knowing who she was, Blackpool told her to get out of his face and do one. He just couldn't be arsed and who could blame him? However, where life for Blackpool was da pits, da same could not be said for Josiah Bounderby where everyfing was going well sweet. Not only was Tom Junior now his apprentice, but he was well up to getting it togevva with Louisa, although she didn't want nuffing to do with it, fank you very much. But at da end of da day what she wanted didn't count for nuffing, especially when her farva said it was cool and that was it. In no time Bounderby and Louisa had became man and bitch.

So everyfing was looking solid when some geeza called James Harthouse came knocking with da letter of introduction from Louisa's farva. They did not know him, but coz of da letter, it meant everyfing was cool – or maybe not. Although Harthouse started to hang in da Bounderby home turf, what he couldn't help but notice was that Mr and Mrs Bounderby wasn't all that tight and it actually made him fink that, given da right circumstances, he might well be in for da bit of extra marital jiggy with Louisa, as you do. Not that Bounderby was any da wiser coz of what was going down at da mill on account of da union geeza called Slackbridge, who was like da well militant leader of da work massive and was busting his chops big time, for dissing da union.

It was Stephen Blackpool, though, what was getting all da hassle coz he was told to sort it or else. But what with not being able to dump Mrs Blackpool, da last fing he needed was da sack and guess what, even though it was Josiah Bounderby what bossed da turf, Blackpool was out. As if dis wasn't minging enough, fings were about to get uber bad for him and all coz of Tom Junior and his gambling habit. Coz when it came to betting he was pants and owed loads of wonga all over da yard and that was why he came up with da cunning plan of robbing Josiah Bounderby's bank and letting Stephen Blackpool take da rap by making everyone fink that it was him what did it instead.

Knowing Blackpool's days were numbered, Tom Junior got him to hang about in da bank turf long enough for everyone to fink he was casing da yard after da bank was hit. Although none da wiser, Stephen Blackpool was screwed, with Tom Junior reckoning that Josiah Bounderby would fink it was Stephen Blackpool who had turned da bank yard over. Ah well, stuff happens, innit. And although everyone fought he was banged to rights, Louisa had found out from James Harthouse that Tom Junior had maxed out his credit cards and was up to his neck in debt which made her fink that not everyfing was kosher.

Although grassing up her bruvva wasn't cool or nuffing, coz nobody likes grasses, Harthouse reckoned that it would be his ticket to true lurve with da girl what he fancied da pants off. And it was, coz before long they was holding hands and getting it on. But although they was well happy, some old wrinkly called Mrs Sparsit wasn't. She was Josiah Bounderby's ex-housekeeper with attitude, who really didn't care much for Louisa. Well, as soon as she found out about what she and James had been up to, Mrs Sparsit was determined to grass her up – see, they was all at it. Anyhoo, before dis bitch from hell could do her worst, Louisa had already told her farva that she was done with being Mrs Bounderby and was hot to trot for anuvva geeza. Surprisingly, Gradgrind was cool about it. Respect. And then she fainted.

With Louisa doing all da swooning stuff, it messed with da mojo of both her farva and James Harthouse. Coz while Mr Gradgrind was giving himself loads for being too hardass on his daughta, Harthouse was left feeling like Lenny da Loner. He and Louisa had arranged to meet before she passed out, but coz of what happened he was well out of da loop. But not for long, coz just as soon as circus girl Sissy found out about Louisa's new geeza, she went and faced him out.

"Yo, Harthouse, you is wasting your time though, coz Louisa ain't coming and you've been so dumped."
"Say what?"
"Oh my God, hello! What bit of dumped do you not understand?"
"For real? Bummer."

Well, although she couldn't get to Mr Gradgrind, da ex-housekeeper Mrs Sparsit ratted to Josiah Bounderby that his bitch Louisa had become da turf bike and that left him feeling well gutted. Well, knowing for sure that all da magic with Louisa was gone he fought "scer-reeew *you* missy!" He had well and truly been gutted by da two-timing eye-candy bitch and Bounderby was in da mood to stick it to someone. And then he fought about Stephen Blackpool and da robbery at da bank. What was dere to fink about? Louisa busted his balls and now he was gonna squeeze Blackpool's. Now who's da daddy?

Anyhoo, just as soon as she heard what was going down in da hood, da well fit Rachel – da bit on da side what Blackpool wanted to dump Mrs Blackpool for – was well upset by what she found out had happened to him. And although he was laying low in anuvva ghetto, she sent word that he had to get his ass back to da turf to clear his name. But she never heard nuffing, which seemed well odd. So after yakking with Sissy, they went looking for him. However, when they got as far as da country turf they made da surprising discovery of da Burberry cap - what they knew belonged to Blackpool - laying on da ground near to an old mine shaft. Well, it must have been da girly intuition what made them fink that he had fallen down it coz, horror of horrors, that was exactly what had happened.

Without anuvva fought, da bitches went and got help from some of da Coketown massive, including Mr Gradgrind, and dis is where everyfing went da shape of da pear for everyone. Although they was busting all da health and safety rules, some of da posse got lowered into da shaft to get Stephen Blackpool back to da top. But they couldn't do nuffing for da geeza coz of all his injuries from da fall. However, before da grim reaper came to get him, he told

Mr Gradgrind that he didn't rob da bank. He was just da patsy, coz it was Tom Junior what did it, before Stephen Blackpool came over all dead, like you do.

It was emotional. Suddenly da net was closing in on Tom Junior who did da only fing he could. He legged it, but only as far as da circus turf, yet for all his cunning he didn't fink about Sissy. Coz she was once part of da circus crew, Sissy knew exactly where Tom Junior was holed up, and it didn't take long before he was busted for being da thieving minger that he was. And he would have been shipped off to da American ghetto had it not been for da help of da circus owner Mr Sleary, who somehow managed to help Tom get away from da turf, which was lucky. Well, actually, not so lucky as it turned out, if only coz he got da fever and snuffed it.

But what of Josiah Bounderby who really mucked up everyfing for Stephen Blackpool? Well, fanks to da ex-housekeeper Mrs Sparsit, da cat animal was out of da bag after she found Mrs Pegler, da old woman who had approached Stephen Blackpool asking about Josiah Bounderby at da time when he wanted to so dump Mrs Blackpool. Well, coz Mrs Sparsit was da real nasty piece of work, she took Mrs Pegler back to da Bounderby home turf where Bounderby's past came and gave him da well heavy bitch-slap.

Although Josiah Bounderby had always yakked to everyone about how he was da self-made big-shot business-geeza who had been dumped when he was just da poor little nippa, it was all nuffing but lies. Mrs Pegler, da mysterious old woman was, in fact, his loving muvva which proved, without da single doubt, that Josiah Bounderby was her very own pride and minger.

As for Sissy, well, maybe coz of all da time she helped Mrs G with da nippas, in da end she had nippas of her own and was able to bring happiness to everyone including Thomas Gradgrind who, after a lifetime of trying to teach nuffing but hard facts, decided it just wasn't worth it no more. Let's face it, life's too short, innit.

MARTY CHUZZLEWIT

Marty Chuzzlewit Junior was da top geeza what had been brought up by his filthy rich but well paranoid grandfarva, who was called Marty Chuzzlewit Senior. However, da fing about da rank old dinosaur was that he fought everyone was after his wonga even if they weren't. As far as he was concerned every geeza and his bitch in da hood and especially his family, was well suss and nuffing was gonna change his mind, end of. Da other fing what occupied his mind, besides his well OCD attitude to his moolah, was not wanting to come over dead and that was why he had da cunning plan to stay one step ahead of da Grim Reaper dude.

He decided to make dis orphaned bitch what he knew, Mary Graham, an offer what she could not refuse and it was dis. If she was by his side 24-seven looking after his minging old body and making sure that da Reaper geeza couldn't take no liberties with it, then she would be allowed to live with him in da home turf. Da arrangement, however, was all quid pro quo just as long as she made sure that he didn't suffer from da shortage of breath. If she managed to do dis little fing for him, then Marty Senior would make Mary da solid promise to look after her, definite. However, if it all went belly up and she failed to keep him safe then she would get her booty busted out of da home turf without nuffing to show for it.

Anyhoo, as for Marty Junior, well, life was well good coz he wasn't nuffing like da rest of da Chuzzlewits who wanted his grandfarva all RIP so they could inherit everyfing, and that was exactly why Marty Senior made him da heir to da entire Chuzzlewit fortune. He was gonna cop for da lot. Everyfing was looking cool for Marty Junior, coz not only did he know that he was gonna be well minted in da future, but he was also in lurve with da orphaned Mary Graham which for some reason really gave his grandfarva da right hump, big time. Although it shouldn't have made no difference, they decided to sit and talk about it like two reasonable geezas.

"Junior, is you trying to get it on with me Mary?"
"Yeah coz she is well fit."
"Well forget it coz that is so not gonna happen, end of, coz dere is no way you is gonna get all jiggy with her body when she is meant to be looking after mine."
"But that is *so* unfair and I'm so not gonna do that!"
"Well then consider yourself cut of da will as of now, you get me!"

And just like that, Marty Chuzzlewit Junior was out of da inheritance loop. Neverdaless, he kept it real and without further fought for da dire and minging consequences of being bounced out of da house, disinherited, he didn't waste no time in getting himself sorted after he saw da apprenticeship opportunity with da architecture geeza Seth Pecksniff. Now, although being da architect was da well respected job in da turf, Marty Junior's boss was nuffing but da lowlife douchebag what made his staff do all da work while he took da credit. Mind you, all da Pecksniff family was like that, including his daughtas, Mercy and Charity, who went around as if they was ghetto princesses instead of da trailer park trash they really were.

In truth it would have been well wicked if Marty Junior had been taken on by da Pecksniff geeza for having da architect X-factor, but it wasn't like that or nuffing. Da only reason he had been taken into da architect turf at all was to get Seth Pecksniff closer to all da moolah what belonged to Marty Senior, coz unknown to him, Seth Pecksniff was really one of da grasping Chuzzlewit posse.

Marty Chuzzlewit Junior soon settled into da architect way of life and began mixing it with dudes like Tom Pinch. But just to prove how minging Marty Senior actually was, and coz he was still well miffed over da business with da orphaned Mary Graham, Marty Senior decided to turn da screw of mingingness by getting Pecksniff to bust him out of da architect turf. And that's exactly what he did, given that Pecksniff would do anyfing Marty Senior wanted him to do in order to get closer to his wonga, da swine.

But even though dis was well awkward turtle for Marty Junior, seeing that he had no dosh and no job, it didn't stop Chuzzlewit Senior messing with Junior's moxie even more. Coz as if to really stick it to his grandson, Marty Senior decided that now Junior was out, him and Mary was gonna bunk up in da Pecksniff turf, which really was so uncool, on every level. Mind you, Marty Junior wasn't without mates, coz even though his bro Tom Pinch was in lurve after meeting da fragrant orphan Mary Graham, he still didn't make no move on da bitch. Dis geeza was uber cool by giving her da wide birth and all coz he knew that Marty Junior was hung up on her. Respect.

Meanwhile, anuvva greedy Chuzzlewit, Anthony, da bruvva of Marty Senior, was in da hood and up to no good coz at da end of da day, he was just as bad as all da other grasping Chuzzlewits, innit. Not that he really needed anyfing, coz he was doing alright for himself as it was. Anthony was in business with his nippa Jonas and although they was well minted they was so tight-fisted that they lived like they was dossers. But he who lives like da Chuzzlewit, acts like da Chuzzlewit, which meant none of them was ever up to any good. Coz while Anthony was sniffing about for da huge slice of his bruvva's fortune, Jonas was finking about his farva and how long it was gonna be before he kicked da bucket so he could get his greedy mitts on da family dosh.

Ah well, what goes around comes around, coz before too long Anthony Chuzzlewit actually came over all dead, which meant that Jonas got all of his farva's moolah. Suss or what? After all, he *wanted* him dead and now he *was*, well, da dude was uber minted. Dis was da well good result for him coz now it meant that he could have da choice of any babe in da hood to be his WAG. So after much consideration, da babe what he chose to get it on with was Charity Pecksniff.

But of course, da path of true lurve was not all that it was cracked up to be for da poor deluded Charity, coz despite Jonas dissing her sista Mercy, da dirty rotten douchebag suddenly dumped Charity and married da sista! Now, although he fought he was like da cat animal what got da cream, it wasn't long before da cream went sour. Mercy was well gobby who got tired of being treated like she was nuffing special and gave Jonas loads of lip back. However, da shame was dis only made him slap up his bitch, which was well heavy. Her sista Charity, though, felt well good about da situation on account of having had da dirty done on her by Mercy. So you could say that dis was one sista who was doing it for herself, definite.

Not that Jonas cared, coz he didn't and in any case, he was spending more and more time hanging with Montague Tigg, some badass dude who fought he was da man on account of him wearing all da coolest freads and da most expensive bling even though, in truth, he was nuffing more than da minging con-geeza, innit. Montague Tigg was bad news though, and before long he got Jonas involved in some of his well dodgy dealings, which was only ever gonna end in tears.

But as for Marty Chuzzlewit Junior, well, he was chilling with some geeza called Mark Tapley, who worked in da booza close to da Pecksniff turf. Now da fing about Tapley was that he was always acting like da cheerful chappie, which Marty Junior fought was well sick. They was getting on like real homies, like they was having da true bromance, so when Marty said he was going off to da American ghetto to make some serious moolah, Mark Tapley decided to go with him to see if he could still be cheerful, no matter what continent da turf was in. Although they was both up for da adventure, da truth was that trying to settle in da American hood wasn't all that. In fact it ended up going Pete Tong from da moment they arrived, on account of being stitched up into buying some crappy land called Eden.

Well, instead of it being da best that dosh could buy, it turned out to be nuffing more than swamps full of da killer malaria disease which almost made Marty Junior toast. So taking into account da fact that da Americans didn't like da English travellers, it was no great surprise that before long they returned home to da English turf, even though they was potless after everyfing they had been through from da trip across to da other side of da pond.

Jonas Chuzzlewit, meanwhile, had got himself even more involved in da well dodgy insurance scam, and with da even more dodgy Montague Tigg, who had been blackmailing Jonas by implying that he knew he was well involved in his farva's death, which he so wasn't. Not that blackmail was da excuse for Jonas doing in Montague Tigg, but then again being blackmailed wasn't either, and soon he was dead. But if it had gone south for Jonas, fings were finally about to come well undone for Seth Pecksniff after Marty Senior came clean about da way he had been behaving.

Coz although Seth Pecksniff had fought he had got him under his control after he had moved in to his turf, he couldn't have been more wrong. Da fing about da mean-spirited, hare-brained, grandson-rejecting Marty Chuzzlewit Senior, was that he had only pretended to be one Stella short of da six pack what had lost his marbles and had came under da heavy Pecksniff influence. In fact it was just one big trick to see for himself how bitter and twisted da Chuzzlewit family was. And they were, big time.

Although da Chuzzlewits were da rank bunch of mingers, one fing that came out about Jonas was that, despite everyone suspecting, he didn't actually do his farva in. Da poor geeza died of da broken heart after he found out that his own nippa wanted him dead, which was well sad. Anyhoo, although that was da right good result for da Chuzzlewit One, unfortunately though, what fate gives with da one hand, it takes with da other, coz da fact that Jonas had stuck it to Montague Tigg meant that he really *was* da murdering douchebag after all. Now that's what I call karma.

Marty Senior, though, was now seeing fings all different. It seemed that he had really gone off at da deep end, coz at da time all he wanted was to get him and da orphan Mary Graham togevva, but got well narked when he found out they was doing it without his help and that really got up his hooter. Families, eh, who'd have them? But all's cool that ends cool, coz Marty Junior and da orphan Mary Graham finally became man and bitch and had demselves da most wicked wedding rave ever.

Even Tom Pinch, da lurve-struck geeza what still was holding da candle for da new Mrs Chuzzlewit, kept his feelings to himself and never said nuffing more about it, which was well cool. And although it really ripped at da guts like nuffing else, and despite never marrying no bitch of his own, he still remained da well solid mate to Marty Junior and Mary, like, forever which made Tom Pinch da real diamond geeza, innit.

DOMBEY AND SPROG

On da face of it, Paul Dombey was da real big cheese in da hood and was da geeza what had everyfing he could ever want. He had it all; da mansion turf, da mega shipping company, da bling and da freads. He also had da little girl nippa what him and Mrs Fanny Dombey called Florence. However, although he should have been well chuffed with what he had, he wasn't, coz what he wanted more than anyfing was to have da boy sprog. He wanted an heir to carry on da Dombey name and inherit everyfing what he had, and blow me if that wasn't what happened after Mrs Dombey only went and got herself up da duff.

So by da time Fanny Dombey had knocked out da baby, Paul Dombey was already in da zone as he waited to hear da news from da Doctor geeza what had brought da nippa into da world.

"Wicked news Mr D."
"Talk to me."
"Well dere is da awesome news and da not so awesome. Da awesome news is that Mrs D finally whacked out da boy sprog."

"That is *so* G - bring it on for Paul Junior! Alright, so what is da not so awesome news?"
"Your Fanny is dead, innit."

With Mrs D gone, suddenly it was da tale of two sprogs. Although Florence was da first born, her farva kept dissing her, coz all he cared about was Paul Junior. And so while Florence was getting da crappy end of da farvahood stick, da same could not be said of her bruvva, who was getting everyfing da Dombey moolah could buy. But despite all da wonga and having da fit daughta to fink about, it didn't alter da fact that Paul Junior had serious health issues, which was well sad.

But no matter how much Florence tried to make fings cool, it made no difference to da way her farva treated her. In fact, da more she tried to be da well loving daughta, da more minging he was towards her. But as for da son, well, being wussy didn't stop his farva doing whatever he could to give Paul Junior da very best of everyfing, and that was why he sent him to Doctor Blimber's school for nobs. Dis wasn't da kind of yard where any of da nippas were allowed to do any touchy-feely stuff, not if they wanted to be proper hardcore, bitch-slapping, hardass gangsta geezas, innit.

Unfortunately for Paul Junior though, he was so out of da loop and just couldn't cut it. No matter what he did, da poor nippa was always left feeling so cream crackered that it made him da weakest link in da school turf. He was well wasted and despite being taken from da Blimber's yard and looked after by his big sis Florence, Paul was on his way towards da light. Well, he must have been on one wicked trip, coz he reckoned his muvva was hanging at da end of da tunnel waiting for him. "Da light about her bonce is all shining for me, innit," he said and then as he did da shutting of da eyes, little Paul Dombey was gone to da heaven turf. It was emotional.

Well, dis was all awkward turtle for Paul Senior, coz what was da point of having da business called Dombey and Sprog without da sprog? But, no matter how much Florence tried to be dere for her farva, he just told her to do one, which was well harsh. However, dis act of paternal mingingness wasn't going unnoticed by Walter Gay, some geeza what worked in da Dombey business who couldn't help but feel sorry for da way Florence had been dissed by her farva. Walter was an alright dude who lived with his uncle, Solomon Gills, da geeza what made ship instruments in da yard what was called da Wooden Midshipman. They also hung with some other dude called Captain Cuttle who had dis wicked hook on da end of his arm instead of da hand; it was so now and da ultimate in pointy bling.

Anyhoo, Walter had dis fing for Florence coz he reckoned she was da tasty bit of alright what made him go all gooey whenever he saw her. Mind you, they also had history. Years previous when she was just da small nippa, Florence got herself all lost in da London turf and he was da one what found her; from that day they was always good homies. But what was really so lush about Walter and Florence being so solid was that da friendship had got him in with Paul Junior before da Grim Reaper did. Dis was just as well, innit, given that all was not going too good at da Wooden Midshipman turf what had run out of dosh.

Dis was da sweaty pants situation when it looked like Uncle Sol's yard was going to be all repossession, repossession, repossession and if Paul Junior hadn't been around to put in da good word with his farva, then da whole Wooden Midshipman posse would have been busted from da home turf. But da nippa did da business, coz although his farva wasn't normally no Dragon, Paul Junior actually made him listen and come to da decision what was about to change da future of Solomon Gills and da rest of his so solid crew.

"Alright, I like da proposal and I fink we can turn da Wooden Midshipman around and save it from going down and for that reason - I'm in!"

Result! Now Uncle Sol had da wonga it meant he was still in business. Da boy done good, definite.

Well, everyfing now was looking well phat for Walter. Not only was he spending more time with Florence, but he was also getting tight with her farva and maybe it would have stayed that way if it hadn't been for some smarmy geeza called James Carker who worked at Dombey and Sprog. Dis bloke was bad news from da start and was always brown-nosing Paul Senior like his hooter was stuck to his buttocks, you get me. He was da company 'yes' geeza and although James Carker was nuffing less than da scheming douchebag with da fake smile and cheesy grin, he was slowly but surely taking over da business without Paul Dombey suspecting nuffing.

Mind you, somebody else who also didn't fink that Carker was suss was Walter Gay. Shame really, coz had he smelt da big stinky rat, then he would have been able to stop Carker busting him out from Dombey and Sprog and over to da West Indies ghetto. On da one hand, Walter might have seen dis as da well good opportunity to visit da strange but exotic turf, but on da other, well, he might have fought to himself it was too risky on account that he could end up shipwrecked, presumed drowned. He was.

Florence was gutted by da news, not that it bovvered her farva who was getting himself out and about with some widow called Edith Granger. Although she was forever busting his balls with all da nagging, it never seemed to put him off, no matter how stroppy and moody she was. Dere was somefing about Edith what made Dombey fall for da little minx coz no matter how much attitude she gave him, it only seemed to float his boat, big time. And even though it was clear that Edith was only after da Dombey moolah and whatever else she could get her greedy little claws on, he still wanted to marry da calculating bitch and that was exactly what he did, da schmuck.

But of course, fings didn't get no easier for da dude, coz not only did she always have da massive strop on, but she also wound Dombey up big time by becoming best girlie mates with his daughta. Boy, did dis bitch know how to mess with his head! It's true, though, that every geeza has his breaking point and maybe for Paul Senior it was Edith being all Facebook with Florence which was da final straw what broke da camel's back. Paul Dombey had had enough and decided to stick it right back to da piece of trailer-park trash what he had married.

However, no matter how clever he fought he was, Edith was always one step ahead coz she had been working on da cunning plan to bring her geeza down big time. Coz unknown to Dombey, da scheming Edith had been sucking up to da well creepy James Carker and was playing him like an old fiddle by filling his head with all sorts of fings what made him fink he was on some kind of promise with da conniving Mrs Dombey.

Togevva, Edith and Carker sloped off to da Paris ghetto making Paul Dombey feel like da right numpty, making him take out his frustration and humiliation on his daughta, da swine. But while it all looked pretty skank for Florence it was looking da whole lot worse for Edith and Carker. Sometimes it's brilliant when somebody gets dere comeuppance and that's exactly what happened to da unfaithful bitch when she realised that just like her husband, Carker wasn't no sex on da stick after all. In fact he wasn't much of nuffing and so she dumped him, just like that. Job done. End of.

Everyfing was coming well undone for James Carker faster than Edith Dombey's sexy freads and he was now bricking it, not knowing what to do next. Edith had left him feeling well crushed as she got herself back to da English turf just before everyfing went belly up. Now he had been left on his own to face da humiliated Dombey geeza who had tracked down da pair of unfaithful mingers to da Dijon lurve nest what they had been shacked up in.

Faced with dis crappy situation, he did da only sensible fing he could do; just like Edith he bolted as quick as he could back to da English turf. But dere was no hiding place for Carker, coz it was only da matter of time before Dombey found out that da spineless, cheating scumbag was holding out close to da railway station and he was now moving in on da rat. But as soon he saw da shadowy figure of Paul Dombey approaching, Carker tried to leg it across da railway tracks but lost his footing and got splattered all over da sleepers by da oncoming train. Good.

Although James Carker got what he deserved, da same couldn't be said for Florence, coz no matter how much she tried to make fings better for her farva he just wouldn't have it. Da poor cow just didn't know what to do with herself, especially when he was so violating her space by knocking da crap out of her. So, realising that she was worth more than just being some punch bag, she split da home turf which was well sad, if only coz it meant that she was now on her own. Florence wandered da hood looking for shelter until she came to da old familiar yard of da Wooden Midshipman, da turf what used to belong to Uncle Sol but was now being run by Captain Cuttle, da sailor geeza with da hook for da hand.

At last Florence felt that she was safe and being looked after, but if everyfing was finally beginning to look more settled for her, da same couldn't be said for her farva. Even though James Carker was now clinically train dead, da fact was he had been stitching Dombey up good and proper by being well naughty with da accounts and didn't Paul Senior now know it! Carker had been taking liberties for ages with da business, which meant that Dombey and Sprog was about to feel da full force of da credit crunch, innit.

Well, although life was calmer for Florence at da Wooden Midshipman she nearly weed herself when Walter Gay, da dude who was meant to be all drowned, walked into da yard like he had never been away. Wicked. But as for Dombey, well, with his business on da brink, dere was nuffing but bad vibes in da air coz everyfing in his life was collapsing around him like da house of cards. He was now da broken geeza what had lost everyfing. Or had he?

Although she had every right to give him da finger, Florence didn't turn her back on him or nuffing. He didn't deserve her good karma, but she actually decided to look after him for da rest of his life, nursing him all better. But while she was doing that, dere was still time for her to get it on with Walter, which was well pukka. They was both mad for it and it wasn't long before they became man and bitch. They was happy, they was in lurve and they even had some sprogs of dere own what they named Paul and Florence.

For Paul Dombey Senior, da geeza what once owned da business what was called Dombey and Sprog, he was able to live out da rest of his days in da bosom of his family all happy ever after.

DA WELL OLD ODDS AND SODS SHOP

Little Nell Trent's grandfarva was so G, da real laidback dude who was so awesome that he could have gone to da University of Cool and scored da first class degree in coolness. But besides being like da Fonz of da hood, he was also da guardian of his grand-daughta, Little Nell, after her muvva pegged out and split for da Heaven turf when Nell was just da very small nippa. So in as far as it went, they did alright living in his Odds and Sods shop what sold just about everyfing.

But as good as it was, Little Nell did have beef, coz apart from some boy called Kit who worked in da Odds and Sods turf what she had been trying to help read and write and that, she had no crew to hang with. She was all Billy no Mates and it kind of brought her down, big time, but that was just da way fings were, innit, coz as difficult as it was for Little Nell, her grandfarva had issues too.

Da fact was that Little Nell's family had left her potless and her grandfarva knew that if anyfing happened to him, then what he wanted more than anyfing was to leave her shed loads of dosh. Da only problem, though, was that he never put any of his wonga into no ISA's or nuffing, preferring instead to invest it in playing cards with some of his homies. Now that might have worked but for one fing; he was so not good at it, which meant that he lost da lot and that sucked. Although he never said nuffing to Little Nell about how screwed da financial situation was, she wasn't stupid.

She was fourteen and soon worked out for herself that somefing was up, coz instead of keeping it togevva, her grandfarva had suddenly become all stressed out on account of being pants at whatever he gambled on. No matter how many times he played cards he would come over all Kenny Rogers by never knowing when to hold them or fold them. Little Nell was well concerned and that was why she needed someone to yak to, like da sympathetic Mrs Quilp. Alright, she was no Oprah or nuffing, but at least she fought that Mrs Q might come up with somefing what could help.

"Well, if he's all maxed out, then maybe he should try one of them moolah consolidation geezas, you get me?"
"But it's not just that, coz he is *so* not coping and that is what I am saying and I am well concerned."
"Is he smelling of wee?"
"What do you fink. He's old - duh!"
"Oh my God, not being funny though, but is he on da Stella?"
"Naa, to be honest wife beater makes him puke, innit."

Although Little Nell fought it was well in order being probed by da kind and sensitive Mrs Q, what she didn't know was that she was being overheard by da most minging dwarf scumbag in da hood, her main geeza Daniel Quilp. Dis was bad news, coz far from being just some nosy dude with ears as big as da elephant animal he was, in fact, da douchebag what her grandfarva had been borrowing all da wonga from and owed loads to. Quilp couldn't believe his big ears, coz now he was getting well clued-up about everyfing what was going down in da Odds and Sods turf, as Little Nell was spilling her guts out to his bitch.

Fings were looking well grim for da grandfarva, definite, coz now Daniel Quilp was all Wikipedia'd-up about da kind of trouble and stuff he was in, his twisted, dwarf brain began working like da clappers, finking about da best way to stitch him up like da kipper fish. Dis was better than sex for da poisoned dwarf, coz in all da time that he had been loaning him da dosh, Quilp reckoned that da grandfarva was minted and could afford it. How wrong he was - not that he was too bovvered, coz one way or da other he was gonna get da lot back and more.

Da moment he invaded Little Nell's space by poking his well curious dwarf nose into where it shouldn't have been, Daniel Quilp knew for sure that her grandfarva was well broke. Not that he didn't already know he stunk at cards, but now he knew that da wonga had all run out, he reckoned dis was da time to foreclose on da well old Odds and Sods Shop.

He wanted everyfing including, believe it or not, revenge on Kit, da kid what helped out in da shop who Little Nell was helping to read and write and that, and all coz Daniel Quilp didn't like da way Kit had been dissing him behind his back. For ages he'd been calling him names like Shortarse, Munchkin and Oompa Loompa and now it was payback time. Quilp was out for revenge and was gonna frame Kit by accusing him of being da snitch what grassed up how bad da grandfarva was at gambling.

Well, although they was down and da karma was in short supply, Little Nell and her grandfarva knew they wasn't gonna be treated like filth by da likes of da vertically challenged Daniel Quilp, end of. So with all da cool they could muster, they decided to do da moonlight flit and leg it out of da London turf as quick as they could, innit. So began da long journey away from da hood and into da countryside ghetto and soon they was thumbing da lifts on da back of da horse and cart. That night they managed to bum da bed at da local inn and while they was dere they met some Punch and Judy geezas, Short and Codlin, who Little Nell fought were well suss. After all, geezas playing with dolls was just too dodgy and so she decided it was time to hit da road again, as you do.

Anyhoo, coz of all da walking they was doing, they was both getting well knackered. Although they could have, they didn't give up or nuffing and before long they found demselves in da school playground turf where, luckily, dis well kind teacher geeza fought nuffing of letting dem hang in da school yard for da night. However, by da next day Nell and her grandfarva was back on da road where they came across da travelling show of waxworks. Dis was cool, especially as Mrs Jarley, who was da manager, gave Little Nell da job doing whatever people do with waxworks. All in all, Little Nell fought dis was da most wickedest fing what had happened since they was bounced out of da Odds and Sods Shop by da evil dwarf Daniel Quilp.

Perhaps fings might have worked out better if da grandfarva hadn't begun hanging with some shifty geezas what liked to play cards. Perhaps if he had gone to da Gamblers Anonymous it would have been alright, but he just couldn't help himself - not only to da temptation of da cards, but also da gold coin what Little Nell was keeping safe for emergencies. Well, it wasn't long before da smell of da gold coin hit da grandfarva's hooter and he actually decided to take it. And he might have got away with it, too, if he hadn't messed up by waking her in his well loud search for da dosh what didn't belong to him. Well, you know what junkies are like when they need to feed dere habit, even grandfarva junkies.

However, Little Nell knew that her grandfarva was still well decent, so she had to fink of somefing quick to get him to behave before he really did end up doing somefing stupid. And that was why she came up with da story to make him fink that she had da awful nightmare of seeing geezas like her grandfarva robbing other geezas while they was all sleeping. Alright, so it was da desperate act by da desperate grand-daughta but, neverdaless, it so worked coz he never tried nuffing like that again.

Soon they were back on da road continuing on da journey away from da London turf, which seemed like it had gone on forever. But just when they fought it was getting too much, they was well surprised when they saw da teacher geeza from da school turf they were at before. Well, as soon as Little Nell recognised who it was, she was so overcome with emotion.

"Hey, is you alright, bitch?"
"Prof, I feel I'm gonna crash and burn, you get me."
"For sure, coz I can see you is looking well wasted!"
"Shu' up! Are you saying I'm tripping blud, coz that is so not true! I don't do that stuff, coz not only does it screw with da head and da septum, but it is well illegal too."

Unable to move anuvva step coz she was off her face with da tiredness, Little Nell crashed out from all da walking what seemed just to go on, like, forever.

Perhaps fings might have turned out all different if her grandfarva didn't suck so bad at cards and maybe life would have been more funky if they hadn't been shafted by da evil dwarf geeza Daniel Quilp. But da fact was, they had. End of. They was in deep, deep trouble coz everyfing had gone da shape of da pear for Little Nell and her grandfarva. What they needed was somefing solid to happen, and it did when da teacher came good for them. Da fing about da teacher geeza was that from da first time he met Little Nell, he fought that she needed taking care of and now they was all back togevva, he was so up for keeping her close so he could make sure she would get better.

He was now living in da village turf where he had got da new teaching job, and he decided to look after Little Nell without da fear of getting any hassle from da social services, innit. Top bloke. And now, coz she was in da hands of dis caring dude, she was able to recover her mojo. Respect to the prof, coz as fings were turning out, it was so right letting her and her grandfarva be part of his school posse.

It took time, but when she was finally getting better, Little Nell got da job as da caretaker of da church and together with da grandfarva, they ended up living in da yard next to da teacher geeza. So at last, after everyfing what they had been through, Little Nell reckoned that once her health was pukka, everyfing was finally gonna be well good.

Meanwhile, fings had finally managed to work out for Kit - da kid what Nell had been helping to read and write and that - all that time ago when he was working in da well old Odds and Sods Shop, but it wasn't any fanks to da minging dwarf Daniel Quilp who had been getting in his face, 24-seven. What with one fing and anuvva, it didn't take too long for everyfing to kick off on account of Quilp's miserable behaviour towards Kit, which meant that da writing had been on da wall for ages, not that Kit could have read it, innit.

Maybe it was coz of da way that Kit had dissed him so much in da past, but Daniel Quilp tried to stitch him up big time by getting him busted to da filth for allegedly nicking stuff and then get him transported over to da Australian turf. It wasn't true of course. Neverdaless, sometimes karma happens to those who really deserve it, coz after he avoided being transported to da bush yard, Kit found da top job working for some decent oldies called Mr and Mrs Garland. Result. Mind you, Kit never stopped finking about whatever had happened to Little Nell and her grandfarva. Funnily enough, and dis was well mind-blowing, da same fought occurred to anuvva strange geeza who suddenly turned up out of da blue who also wanted to know da exact same fing. Spooky.

As it turned out, da strange geeza wasn't as strange as all that coz he was none other than da grandfarva's younger bruvva what had been living in anuvva country for years and now he was minted, he'd come back to share all his moolah with his bruvva, but couldn't find him. Just fink, all that dosh and nobody to share it with. Bummer. But all was not lost for da long-lost bruvva, coz togevva with Kit and da Garlands, they actually managed to find out where da Odds and Sods Two was hanging out, which meant they was so close to scoring it big. However, what should have been da well good happy ending was anyfing but, and all coz da rescue posse arrived too late.

Somefing bad had happened to Little Nell, coz by da time everyone had turned up on da night, da grandfarva had begun to crack up big time and was hiding da truth from them all. Although he had told everyone that she was akip, da poor nippa had come over dead and had been like that for days, coz dere was never enough grub to eat, and all that walking had got her so cream-crackered that she was finally taken down by da Grim Reaper geeza. Despite being looked after by da teacher, in truth, Little Nell never stood da chance.

Although in da final days she had found fings to be da happiest what they had been, neverdaless, it wasn't enough to stop her becoming all stiff with da death, innit. But if that wasn't crappy enough, da grandfarva curled up on da grave of Little Nell and also came over dead. So you could say that as far as family reunions go, dis one really sucked, innit.

WELL SMALL DORRIT

As far as it went, Well Small Amy Dorrit wasn't so much born with da silver spoon in her gob, but more da hard wooden one with splinters, and all coz of da fact that she was banged up in da well skank Marshalsea Prison for debtors. Not that she should have been dere at all, but it wasn't as if she had da choice. It was all to do with her farva geeza who had been busted by da filth for owing loads of wonga all over da hood. Although debtors' prison was minging for them, it was also well bad for da rest of da Dorrits what found demselves living dere. Back then if one went down, then everyone in da fam went too, like it was some kind of care in da community programme, innit.

But as bad as it was, at least they were all in it togevva, living da "Prisoner Cellblock H" life, eating da nasty prison grub and slopping out as nuffing more than one big happy family. OK, so it wasn't perfect but boo-hoo, get over it. Stuff happens. So dere they all was doing time - Amy, her stuck-up big sista, Fanny, and her bruvva Tip, whose real name was Edward, not that he ever used it coz it just wasn't street, you get me. However, da only one of da Dorrit crew what wasn't in da clink was da muvva, who was well out of da doom and da misery by being dead, and had been ever since Amy was just da very small nippa.

But for everyone else, life in da Marshalsea turf was real minging, especially for Amy, as growing up in da slammer really brought her down. Coz instead of being dis fit twenty-somefing girlie, she looked nuffing more than da ten year old with da eating disorder. Although she would have been well entitled to go on da whinge-binge bender about how bad fings had been inside da prison ghetto over da years, she never complained or nuffing. Instead she kept everyfing real for da Dorrit massive by being da domestic goddess and doing everyfing her muvva would have done had she not come over all stiff, like cooking and that. What's more, she was well good at it too.

Da fing about da debtors' prison was that, although her farva had to stay 24-seven, da rest of da Dorrits didn't, and Amy made sure to get everyone into da work groove.

"Edward, what is your sorry ass still doing here?"
"Are you talking to me little sis, coz I don't see no Edward - dere is only da Tip Meister here, so check yourself and show some respect!"
"Well, *Tip Meister*, you better get yourself togevva and bring home da bacon, or else you is gonna get *so* happy-slapped right here right now, you get me. I *said* - you get me?"
"Whatever."

But as for Amy and Fanny, well, they got demselves in da city hood working as seamstress bitches and soon they was working da sewing fingers to da bone - especially Amy, who was stitching like da clappers for da really badass Mrs Clennam. She was trouble and was always coming it with da minging attitude to Amy, which would explain why dis boss from hell didn't have nuffing to do with her own son, Arthur, who had been away with his farva working in da overseas turf.

Now dis arrangement had been cool for years until his farva came over dead, leaving him to return to da loving bosom of his muvva. However, da fing about Arthur Clennam was that he was nuffing like his muvva and instead of coming over like he was ready to rumble, he was well chilled. Anuvva fing about Arthur was that he didn't have no beef with nobody, he just got on with fings coz that was da kind of awesome dude he was. Respect.

And maybe it was coz he was so mellow that he noticed da Well Small Amy Dorrit working hard, stitching like crazy. Without question, dere was somefing special about her in da way she caught his attention, which he fought was well nice. Coz although Arthur wasn't usually da type of geeza what could get in touch with his feminine side, he actually picked up on da vibe and began to take da real interest in everyfing to do with da family of da little seamstress what worked for his hardass muvva who treated everyone like they was scum.

Anyhoo, da more he and da Well Small Dorrit yakked, da more interested he became in what was going on with da family what was squatting in da prison yard. Da more he heard, da more da whole fing sounded well dodgy and perhaps that was why he decided to go for it and get da Marshalsea One sprung. Well, considering da circumstances, it wasn't no big surprise that Amy Dorrit began to fink that Arthur Clennam was some wicked looking dude. So wicked, in fact, that she even began to get da heavy crush on him what was well mushy, innit.

And so he began trying to get to da bottom of all da debts, trying his best to get William Dorrit out of stir as quick as he could. He was determined to find out why da poor geeza had been stuck in da Marshalsea slammer all those years. Perhaps it shouldn't have come as too much of da shock, but da truth *was* out dere. Coz after he had da nose around and then had an even bigger nose, Arthur soon discovered da bitching truth about what led to da sorry downfall of William Dorrit.

Coz far from being nuffing more than da geeza with da busted pockets and massive debts who had been sent down on account of his credit crunch situation, Amy's farva was, in fact, minted – only he didn't know it. Dis was awesome, coz what Arthur discovered was that he was actually da heir to da massive fortune! Well, on hearing dis incredible news, everyfing suddenly changed for William Dorrit. It was like he had won da lottery and had arrived, big time.

Suddenly he had cash on da hip and coz he was able to pay everyfing off meant that he was finally da free geeza. Job done. Result.

Everyfing had worked so sweet for da Dorrit massive coz if it hadn't been for all da effort of Arthur Clennam, nuffing would have happened, end of. Not only had William Dorrit walked out from Marshalsea Prison but now, instead of being treated like scum, all da Dorrits was dressed to impress and dripping in bling. It was mad, it was crazy and they was living da dream. And so, given all da circumstances of what Arthur had done in rescuing da Dorrits from being broke and in prison, anyone would have fought that William Dorrit would have made Arthur his main man, right? Wrong. Coz despite everyfing what he had done, nearly all da ungrateful Dorrit massive told him to do one, end of, which was pants.

Da only Dorrit who fought different was Amy, coz not only could she see Arthur was da real deal, that he was solid, but she could also see he was sex on da stick and that he was everyfing she had been saving herself for, naughty girl. Anyhoo, it was da whole new beginning for da Dorrits. Coz now they was more loaded than ever, they was well determined to forget all about da past, party like dere was no tomorrow and spend it like da Beckhams, innit. So as soon as they was able, they was splashing da cash and mixing it in da Euro turf by hanging with all da wealthy nobs who never knew nuffing about dere past. Dis was exactly how da Dorrits wanted it and was well careful not to let da truth come out. Mind you, if it had then possibly fings might have turned out all different for Amy's sista, Fanny, after she was given da come-on by some geeza called Edmund Sparkler, da step-son of some banker by da name of Mr Merdle.

Now, although they was young enough to chizzle da nizzle, what really floated dere boats was da smell of dosh, and it made them well perfect for each other in every respect. Coz although Fanny didn't fancy da pants off Sparkler or nuffing, what she was well up for was getting it on with all his family wealth, including Edmund Sparkler's uber rich step-farva Mr Merdle, who happened to be just as greedy. Da fing what got Merdle all fired up was da Dorrit wonga and he couldn't fink of anyfing better than getting his family married to it as quick as he could - and that's exactly what happened.

Well, it wasn't long before da newlyweds got back to da London turf where da greedy banker Merdle began to invest William Dorrit's dosh without going to da trouble of ever saying anyfing about investments going up as well as down. Not that William Dorrit was too bovvered, coz now he was da big cheese he didn't fink anyfing could go wrong and never fought nuffing about da risks - da schmuck - just like da rest of da brood. Coz now they was shaking it with all da snobs and nobs, what they didn't want was for anyone to fink they was stupid by asking questions about dere own moolah.

Of course dere biggest fear was still anyone finding out about all da time they spent in Marshalsea Prison yard, and so they all kept shtum so they wouldn't draw no attention to demselves. However, da only one who didn't care about any of that was da Well Small Dorrit who didn't give nuffing for all da dosh, coz she just wasn't like that. Da only fing she cared for was Arthur, coz although everyone in da family dissed him big time, Amy didn't, and she never forgot how solid he had been when they was all broke and busted.

Well, as they say, what goes around comes around, coz although life should have been well sweet for da Dorrits, da good times were about to crash and burn on account of da greedy Mr Merdle. He just couldn't leave it alone and all coz he was an out and out banker with no morals and he took William Dorrit for everyfing. It was like taking candy from da baby, coz although he was meant to be dis big-shot banker, da fact was he never looked after all da moolah like he promised. And coz William Dorrit never asked, everyfing went da shape of da pear.

But if fings looked well bad for him, then it was looking even worse for Arthur Clennam. Not that it was his fault or nuffing, but coz he was da one who suggested da greedy douchebag banker Merdle should handle all William Dorrit's financial doings, everyone fought he had somefing to do with what went down with da lost wonga and he was so screwed. But such is da fickle finger of fate that despite being nuffing less than da well decent geeza what tried his best to help others, and coz of da right mess-up with da Dorrit's finances, Arthur Clennam was now well skint. After everyfing he did, he ended up with nuffing, which really brought him down big time - especially when he got busted into da Marshalsea Prison - which was well unfair.

Maybe it wasn't no big surprise that, with all da stress of everyfing what happened to Arthur, da poor sod came over seriously ill. Without doubt da situation was not cool but all was not lost. Coz although he'd been caught up in somefing what was beyond his control, dere was at least one person what didn't forget about him; Amy, da Well Small Dorrit.

"What is you doing here, Well Small Dorrit? Look away coz I don't want you seeing me like dis - it is so uncool!"
"But I am da angel of mercy, blud. You is so unwell and I is here to get you all fixed and chillaxed with some of me special herbal remedies."
"Cool."

How strange it was, but da really odd fing was that for all da time he had known her, it wasn't until that moment that Arthur even realised that Amy was really into him. Even stranger was da feeling that, despite what da rest of da Dorrits did that led to him being busted into da prison turf, he was feeling da same fing for Amy too. But as lurved up as they was, da fact was that between da two of them they was well penniless, and coz of circumstances beyond dere control, it looked like they was destined to stay in da

Marshalsea Prison turf forever. But sometimes fings have da well nice way of working demselves out and especially so for really nice geezas and bitches like Arthur Clennam and Amy Dorrit.

Coz just when everyfing seemed lost, in da nick of time an old bro from da ghetto, Daniel Doyce - who had found out about what went down with Arthur - came up with da spondulix and sprung him from da debtors' prison. Now after everyfing they had been through, dere was nuffing to stop da Well Small Dorrit becoming da Well Small Mrs Clennam, which is so Mills and Boon, innit.

OUR MUTUAL BRO

Da fing about well minted geezas what are tighter than da duck animal's bottom is that when they come over dead, they can't take none of dere wonga with them when they is high fiving da Reaper. It's always da same when they go ashes to ashes, innit, which is exactly what happened with da uber rich miser bloke called Harmon, da geeza what made all his dosh from all da stinky rubbish in da London turf. Or, to put it anuvva way, he was like Stig of da Dump, only richer, you get me.

Harmon was so not nice that da only dude what gave him any respect when he was alive was da rubbish foreman geeza, Nicodemus Boffin. He was well loyal, but he was da only one. However, da really big surprise was that his son, John, had been left da lot even though they hadn't seen each other for ages on account of them having issues with each other. But even though he had been living far away in da South African ghetto his farva still decided to leave most of his dosh to him which was well unexpected. Respect. However, before John Harmon could get to party on and fill his boots with all da lovely dosh, his farva had done somefing well cunning what meant that if he really wanted to get his hands on da moolah, then he had to return to da home turf and become man and bitch with da mysterious Bella Wilfer.

Although he fought his farva was really sticking it to him by making him get it togevva with someone who might be nuffing more than some old munter, in da end da fought of being uber minted meant that he decided to go for it. However, before he got within sniffing distance of Bella or da moolah, da word on da street was that John Harmon had got himself drowned sailing back to da home turf, which was well stinky. But if dere had been any doubt that some geeza was having da laugh, da sad news was confirmed when Harmon's soggy and wrinkly body was found in da river Thames by Gaffer Hexam, whose job it was to go sailing about looking for dead geezas floating in da water and reeling them in, as you do. Well, as far as work went, it wasn't much but he did have da well lucrative bunce of going through da watery pockets of all da bodies what he found and nicking whatever was dere.

However, when John Harmon's squelchy body was brought back to da turf for proper identification, dere was dis mysterious young geeza, Julius Handford, hanging about and watching everyfing. It was well suss coz nobody knew who he was. But before questions could be asked he'd legged it without even leaving da forwarding address or nuffing. But for every cloud dere was da silver lining, and dis was especially true for Mr and Mrs Boffin who must have been carrying around loads of good karma, coz fanks to da unfortunate watery death of John Harmon, they got everyfing.

Now they was minted kings of da rubbish empire, they did somefing for da broken-hearted Bella Wilfer, who they knew was meant to be John's bitch, and took her into da home turf and treated her like she was da ghetto princess what they never had. As for da Boffins, well, now they was loaded, Nicodemus was starting to enjoy only da best fings now he could afford them. Strangely, one of da fings he did was to hire da one-legged Silas Wegg to read some of his soppy lurve ballads, coz when you is da well minted dealer of rubbish, you can have anyfing you want, obviously. But although dis one-legged geeza seemed on da level, perhaps it was too good to be true although if that was da case, Nicodemus Boffin was none da wiser.

Neverdaless, da Boffins was da very trusting couple who never judged nobody but even so, when da strange and mysterious geeza by da name of John Rokesmith unexpectedly turned up on da doorstep offering his services as da Boffins' confidential secretary, they still had questions.

"Get over yourself dawg, why is you really wanting da job?"
"Two reasons, dude. First coz I'm well cool at organising fings and that, and second, I'll do it for nada."
"Say what?"

"I'll do it for zilch - zippo – nuffing, you get me."
"Fierce."

So now da strange and mysterious geeza had got inside da Boffin home turf - although had they known that he was really da even more mysterious Julius Handford, who had been hanging about da river when John Harmon was fished out - then they might have fought him well suss. Anyhoo, as time went on, John Rokesmith began clocking everyfing da Boffins and da broken-hearted Bella Wilfer was up to, which was uber creepy, you get me.

But while dis stalking situation was unfolding, life for Gaffer Hexam, da geeza what found da soggy corpse of John Harmon, had become da proper sweaty pants situation and he was feeling da pressure. All he did was hook da soggy body out of da Thames, but now an old homie called Roger 'Rogue' Riderhood was putting da squeeze on, big time, by accusing Hexam of being da one what did Harmon in. Dere was da time when everyfing between da two of them was cool, but that was until Hexam told Rogue to beat it. Now it was payback time and he was loving it. Well, Rogue by name and rogue by nature, coz what he was after was da reward what was being offered for information about John Harmon's watery death. He was well up for it, no matter if he had to take Hexam down to get what he wanted.

Now everyfing was going da shape of da pear for da innocent Hexam, coz it seemed like he was being given da bums rush from everyone in da hood, which wasn't good. He was barred from da local booza which meant he couldn't even go and get himself wasted on da Stella with da posse which left him with nowhere to go and nobody to do it with. It seemed like every ho and bro in da hood was blanking him for somefing he so didn't do, and da situation was minging. It was only his daughta Lizzie who was giving him any support which was more than could be said for his other nippa Charlie, who was off faster than da rat animal up da drainpipe. So that was it for Gaffer Hexam, who only went and drowned himself which was well sad and very, very wet.

For others, however, dis unfortunate series of events meant somefing else to geezas like da barrister Eugene Wrayburn, who was da bro of da solicitor Mortimer Lightwood, who was pointing da heavy finger of guilt at Gaffer Hexam before he stopped doing da treading of da water and sunk like da stone. Da problem for Wrayburn, though, was that he went all weak at da knees from da moment he clapped eyes on Lizzie Hexam and he was smitten. In fact he was in deep smit but, neverdaless, and unknown to da lurved-up solicitor geeza, some other dude had come over all gooey for Lizzie; his name was Bradley Headstone.

Bradley Headstone was da schoolmaster of Lizzie's bruvva Charlie, who was nuffing but da bullyboy fascist thug who wanted to get it togevva with Lizzie. Well, although she should have been well flattered and that, all she knew was that her space was being so violated and after carefully weighing up all da options, Lizzie legged it out of da London turf just as soon as she could. Neverdaless, it wasn't long before Eugene Wrayburn and Bradley Headstone tracked her down, but instead of trying to win Lizzie over with da chocolates and roses, Bradley Headstone – or should that be Headcase – went for Eugene Wrayburn and happy-slapped da crap out of him, just so Lizzie would be all his.

He went mental, knocking seven bells out of him and leaving da poor geeza well wasted. Dis was bad, coz if Lizzie Hexam hadn't got to him in time, then da Reaper would have, definite. But da fact was she did, and although they fought he was gonna be going to da great courtroom turf in da sky, Eugene Wrayburn proposed to Lizzie and she was so up for it. Result, especially when he started to make da cool recovery which made everyfing perfect. Anyhoo, dere must have been somefing in da water coz da strange and mysterious John Rokesmith had come over all Mills and Boon with da grief-stricken-didn't-quite-make-it-to-da-altar Bella Wilfer, although she really didn't want nuffing to do with him. As far as she was concerned - now she was well minted fanks to da Boffins - she didn't do poor. He was potless and she didn't want to know, end of.

However, fings sometimes happen what can change da point of view of anyone like Nicodemus Boffin, who had begun to get up his own bottom with all da power and wonga what he inherited. Coz like John Harmon's mean-spirited farva, he seemed to be going da same way when he dissed John Rokesmith. Although he was da dude what had been working for nuffing, suddenly he was told to do one from da Boffin turf or else. However, and as minging as it all was, dere was still da 'up' side to all dis, which was to do with Bella Wilfer who, against all da odds, decided she wanted to be John Rokesmith's bitch after all. OK, so he had no dosh or nuffing, but da fing what she realised was that he was where it was at and she so wanted to be dere with him.

One fing was for sure, life has da way of working itself out and if it was true for Bella and John, then it was even more so for Bradley Headstone and Roger 'Rogue' Riderhood, da geeza what had grassed up Gaffer Hexam. Such was da mingingness of Bradley Headstone that he tried to finger Roger Riderhood for beating da crap out of Eugene Wrayburn. It was only da matter of time before they got in each others' faces and had da monster ruck. Dis wasn't no happy-slapping situation, coz they was giving it large right by da canal. It was well dirty but, neverdaless, everyfing worked out brilliant when they both fell into da canal and drowned. Result!

Meanwhile back in da Boffin home turf, Silas Wegg - remember he was da one-legged geeza what Nicodemus Boffin took on to read some of his soppy lurve ballads - had been poking his nose into matters what he shouldn't have. And coz he couldn't keep his hooter out, he came across information what he hoped was going to smash apart Boffin's world, big time. What Wegg had found was anuvva will, what meant da Boffins was in serious trouble, coz if it was real then everyfing would be taken away and go to da Crown, and all coz it didn't mention nuffing about Harmon's nippa, John.

"Blackmail is well crap, innit, Nicodemus, but if you is as clued up as I fink you are, and as long as you come up with da deniro, then I can lose da will, you get me."
"Talk to da hand dawg, coz I don't do blackmail and dere aint no way no geeza is gonna mess with da Boff!"

Nicodemus Boffin was too cool to have his mojo screwed with, coz unknown to da one-legged blackmailing scumbag, he suddenly whipped out yet anuvva will, which clearly showed that everyfing was exactly as it was in da original, which meant that da Boffins kept everyfing, which really stuck it right back to Silas Wegg. Although dis was awesome news, da really good vibe was only just happening. Coz what was well sick was when John Rokesmith removed his cunning disguise to show that he was really John Harmon, which meant he so wasn't dead and *could* tread water after all!

In fact he hadn't even got his toes wet, coz on da voyage back to da English turf he had been mugged of all his freads and stuff by da bloke what Gaffer Hexam had found floating in da water. But coz he had been wearing da freads what belonged to John Harmon everyone fought it was him what had drowned but they was so wrong, and now he was back. Although he had been well naughty to pretend to be some other geeza, da reason John Harmon decided to be John Rokesmith was to find out if Bella Wilfer was fugly or not. Coz knowing that if he was going to get his farva's inheritance, he'd have to go through with da wedding rave and he just had to know if she was da beauty or da beast. It was either munter or bust.

Well, coz everyfing was now all cool, Bella was weeing herself with all da excitement, coz not only was dere finally gonna be wedding cake, but best of all, da geeza what she wanted to get it on with that she fought was all skint - wasn't - which just made everyfing perfect.

DA PICKWICK PAPERS

Dere was somefing well good about Samuel Pickwick, but it wasn't on account of his looks what wasn't nuffing special, or even da fact that he was da tubby little bloke with da shiny bonce what wore goggles. No, what separated him from da other geezas in da turf was that not only was he well minted but he also owned his own club what he called after himself. Cool or what? Now da fing about da Pickwick Club was that everyone what joined had da one fing in common, namely they was all nosey geezas what had hooters da size of da elephant animal.

So, togevva with other Pickwick Club nerds, Nathaniel Winkle, Augustus Snodgrass and da geeza with da girlie name Tracy Tupman, Samuel Pickwick reckoned him and da Pickwickian posse should do somefing real geeky to make demselves even more smug.

"Blud, it is time for dis posse to split da London ghetto coz we are da Pickwickian massive, hot to trot and we is going to hit da road."
"Road trip - road trip – road trip!"

"For sure, coz we is gonna bust da English turf so we can tell da rest of da club posse what's going down on da street!" "Respect dawg, coz like me bitch is always saying, why don't you weirdos get yourself out more?"

And that was how they found demselves going to da Rochester hood coz let's face it, it was as good as anywhere to start da journey of self-important smugness.

But before they had even got on da coach, da Pickwick massive got into da huge ruck with da crew of gangsta cab driver geezas what began giving them da real heavy kicking. They was getting well mashed and if it hadn't been for da help of some bloke called Alfred Jingle what happened to be in da right place at da right time, then they would have been done over, big time. Although he looked like somefing da cat animal brought in, he was da sight for da sore eyes - and da sore arms and da sore fists – but neverdaless, he was da geeza what saved da day. Respect. But also, da well good fing was that with Alfred Jingle on da coach, da Pickwickian geezas knew that they wasn't gonna be messed with, which was well lucky, innit.

Da fing about Alfred Jingle was that he seemed to be da geeza what knew all da right places to hang in da Rochester turf. Well, what with that being da case, he had passed da word to Tracy Tupman about da well cool rave what was going down later that night in da local booza. According to him dere was gonna be loads of Stella and fit bitches which all seemed well good for Tupman, who was so up for getting down with da ho's.

However, when they arrived, Alfred Jingle hadn't reckoned on his luggage going missing and without his smart freads he knew he wasn't going nowhere. But all was not lost, coz in consideration of everyfing he'd done for da Pickwickians (and also coz he was wanting to get it on with some foxy chick at da rave), Tracy Tupman did what only a true bro would do. He let Alfred borrow Nathaniel Winkle's decent freads.

Now da geezas were all booted and suited for da night out on da pull, Alfred wasted no time in coming on to dis well nice babe who was already with anuvva bloke, and that's when it kicked off, big time. Da geeza what he had dissed was her main man Doctor Slammer and he went ape, challenging Jingle to da duel for trying to get it on with his bitch. Dis was well heavy and Alfred did da only fing he could; he legged it before da doctor dude could find out who he was. However, da doctor was well determined to know who da scumbag was and it wasn't long before he'd found out that it was none other than Nathaniel Winkle. Nathaniel Winkle?

Well, although he wasn't even dere, his suit was and that was what put him in da frame after some servant geeza had recognised da freads instead of da geeza what was wearing them. So even though Nathaniel Winkle wasn't da one what messed with da doctor, he now found himself challenged to da grizzly duel. He was so bricking it and all coz he had got himself well hammered da night before and couldn't remember if he did what he was being fingered for.

So da next morning he was on da field with his fellow Pickwickian Augustus Snodgrass, waiting for da duel to start or not, as he was about to discover when he came face to face with da doctor.

"Dude, what is you doing here?"
"Er, coz you wanted to duel, duh."
"But you wasn't da snake what wanted to get all jiggy with me bitch. So what's going down coz I is well confused!"

Fortunately, da doctor realised that Winkle wasn't da one what had crossed da line and luckily for him, he called da duel off which was well lucky. Well, you can only imagine how stupid da geeza would have felt if he had gone and whacked da wrong bloke.

So putting dis one small misunderstanding behind them, da Pickwick massive decided to party on at da parade what was going down in da Rochester turf, which got them mixing it with da geeza by da name of Mr Wardle, who was hanging with his sista Rachael, who Tracy Tupman fought was well fit, innit. Anyhoo, as time went on, everyone was getting on like they was all long lost bros and when Wardle made da invitation to come and hang in his home turf, Manor Farm at

Dingley Dell, everyone was well up for it. So finking about da lush booty of da lovely Rachael, Tracy Tupman accepted for all da rest of da Pickwickians. Ding dong.

Well, da next day, da Pickwickians was taken out on da wicked rook hunt and it would have been well good if Wardle hadn't been so crap with da gun and accidentally shot Tracy Tupman in da arm. Still, it didn't ruin nuffing coz now he was hurt, he got da attention of Rachael Wardle to rub it better. While dis was all going on, Samuel Pickwick managed to bump into da well suss Alfred Jingle. Although he had been responsible for getting one of da Pickwickian massive involved in da deathly duel, Pickwick didn't have beef with da geeza and even invited him back to Wardle's turf.

Well, dis was like winning da lottery, coz being in da Manor Farm yard allowed Jingle to do what he did best by screwing fings up big time for everyone else. It didn't take long for him to discover that da Wardles were well minted, and so he hit on da cunning plan of stitching Tracy Tupman up by making Wardle's sista Rachael fink that he was nuffing more than da prize numpty.

"Listen sista, what is you doing hanging with some muppet with da girlie name?"
"What, you mean Tracy? Oh-my-God, no way, he's cool."
"Hello! What you mean is 'loser'."
"I cannot believe you said that coz that is so not true though!"

"Blates babe, but just chillax coz da geeza is history, and that is why you and me is gonna split da turf."

"Wicked. But who is you dude?"

"Da geeza what you have been waiting for all your life."

And she was suddenly swept away in lurve as da two of them eloped into da night.

Although Jingle fought he had got one over everyone he was well wrong, coz in no time at all Samuel Pickwick and Mr Wardle was hot on da trail of da miserable scumbag, searching da London turf to stop Jingle getting it on with Rachael. They went all over trying to track da elopers down until, eventually, they got da red-hot lead as to where da miserable creep was. But they was too late, coz Jingle had da marriage licence to prove it which meant that as they was now man and bitch, dere was nuffing anyone could do about it. But then again, maybe dere was. Although they could have given him da right good slap they appealed to da greedy nature of da dosh-grabbing swine by offering him one hundred and twenty big ones to naff off. And being da true romantic he was, that's exactly what Alfred Jingle did.

And so with da Jingle situation sorted, all da Pickwickians got demselves to da London yard, although it seemed that for Samuel Pickwick fings were about to go belly up for dis well-intentioned geeza, and all coz of da stupid misunderstanding with his housekeeper after he got back to da home turf. Da problem with da widow, Mrs Bardell, was that she reckoned that Pickwick had proposed to her when he hadn't. Although he fought nuffing of it, da same couldn't be said for da now well miffed housekeeper, and that was why she decided to sue da pants off him for da heavy breach of promise of making her da new Pickwick Club WAG by becoming Mrs Pickwick.

Well, she must have got one of those no-win, no-fee legal geezas, coz not only did she take him to court but da bitch won and scored seven hundred and fifty quid in damages. Not that Samuel Pickwick was bovvered coz, in truth, he couldn't be arsed. As far as he was concerned he wasn't gonna give da Bardell widow nuffing, not even if that meant getting busted, being sent to da slammer and becoming da Pickwick One. Anyhoo, what with all da aggro of da court case and coz he hadn't been tagged or nuffing, all da Pickwickians decided to make dere way over to da Bath ghetto. And why not, as they was still trying to find out more about what life was like outside of da Pickwick Club.

Da fact was that they was still up for da bit of fun and jiggy jiggy and especially so Nathaniel Winkle, who seemed to be up for it just that bit more than da others, definite. And so when Samuel Pickwick asked him to meet da lush looking Arabella Allen, he didn't need asking twice. Da fing was that da Pickwickians had already met da fragrant Arabella when they was hanging with da Wardles in da Manor Park turf. But right at dis moment she wasn't feeling over da moon or nuffing coz her bruvva was hoping to get her all shacked up with his main man, Bob Sawyer, and she was having none of it which, incidentally, meant that Bob wasn't neither.

Da way Winkle had heard da story was that Arabella was gagging for anuvva geeza, what he fought was *him*. But just as fings were about to get real interesting, it all went south for Samuel Pickwick when he found himself well busted by da filth and all coz he wouldn't hand over da single penny what he owed to his housekeeper. Well, as soon as he got back to da London turf he found himself all banged up in da Fleet Street prison, which was so minging.

But if fings weren't looking all that for da unfortunate Pickwick, fings were looking even more dodgy for da bitter and twisted Mrs Bardell. She was having issues on account of being done over by her lawyer geezas, and all coz they was out of pocket from da Pickwick case. Da problem for her was that as they couldn't get nuffing out of Pickwick, they decided to stick it to Mrs Bardell big time by also getting her sent to da Fleet Street prison which was what you would call bad karma for da bitch, innit. Good.

But of course da fing about da Pickwickian massive was that they was all well loyal and before long Nathaniel Winkle and his new wife, da fragrant Arabella, was in da prison turf trying to get Samuel Pickwick to pay up what he owed. However, dere was also anuvva reason for all dere care and concern. Da newlywed Winkles were getting heaps from her bruvva and his farva for getting it on with each other and what they needed was da cool-headed Pickwick to stop da bad vibes and smooth everyfing over. And being da top geeza what he was, Samuel Pickwick coughed up da moolah to help out his bro.

Well, it seemed that dere wasn't nuffing Pickwick couldn't do, coz not only did he get da result for da Winkles, but he was also able to sort Mr Wardle after telling him to chill after he found out that one of his daughtas, Emily, wanted to become Mrs Augustus Snodgrass. Not da coolest name in da hood, perhaps, but she was well in lurve with da geeza, Anyway after Samuel Pickwick said that he was one pukka dude, Wardle was cool with da idea of having da son-in-law with da silly name of Snodgrass, after all.

So with everyone sorted, Samuel Pickwick decided it was time to close up da Pickwick Club. Although dere had been some wicked times he decided to give it all up and retire to da country turf. Ok, so da ending wasn't no big deal but even so, it ended up all happy ever after.

EMO HOUSE

To everyone in da ghetto, Sir Leicester Dedlock and his much younger bitch, Honoria, was da Posh and Becks of da turf. They had da bling and da freads what made them da hottest and da fittest pair of nobs in da hood. But behind all da glamour and da wonga of living life to da max, dere was da dark secret of Honoria what dare not speak its name, or at least not to her main geeza anyway. Coz although she wasn't no turf slapper or nuffing, da fact was that before her and Sir Leicester got it togevva, she had only gone and got herself knocked up by some other geeza called Captain Hawdon.

But as far as Sir Leicester was concerned, his Honoria was da most awesome babe on da block and not some bike what had been round it. However, he might have fought different had he actually known that she once gave it large to anuvva dude, definite. Not that Sir Leicester was any da wiser, coz at da end of da day da golden rule was that what went on in da past, stayed in da past, and while it kept that way Honoria was safe.

At da time da nippa was busted out of da womb, Honoria was given da well sad news that it was dead but in truth that was rubbish. Despite what she was told, it was actually all healthy, but coz Honoria had been so naughty by being da single muvva, it was taken away without her even knowing she had bashed out da girl nippa what was given da name of Esther. So far so cool, except for da fact that she was bundled over to one badass muvva called Miss Barbary who always went around with da gangsta attitude and da well nasty strop, innit.

Da bitch kept getting in Esther's face like she owned da piece of her ass, even though da poor nippa hadn't done nuffing wrong, yet it kept coming 24-seven which was so not cool. But as minging as it was, Esther might have been toast if Miss Barbary hadn't done da decent fing by coming down with da nasty dose of death, which was well good. So while it was all ashes to ashes for da bitch, fings was certainly looking better for Esther when da much nicer John Jarndyce took her to live with him in da home turf of Emo House.

Although meeting new homies could be well intimidating for any dude, fortunately for Esther dere was Richard Carstone and Ada Clare to hang with, who was cousins and who was already in da house. However, while Esther fought everyfing wasn't too bad, da truth was that dere was bad vibes what was causing real smoke on da water and all coz of somefing what was happening in da Chancery Law Court.

Dis was da well heavy situation of who was gonna get da wonga in da Jarndyce and Jarndyce inheritance case what had been going on, like, forever, and it was really bringing everyone down, coz it was so pants. Well, everyone that was except for Richard and Ada, coz they was da ones who was gonna score all da moolah as and when da case was finally over. Dere was also one other fing about da cousins what would explain dere sense of karma, coz although they was related they was pretty well gagging for each other - which was so awkward turtle, if only *coz* they was related.

But while fings were looking well interesting for da kissing cousins, all was not so cool for da Lady Honoria Dedlock who was about to regret da moment she asked her well dodgy lawyer geeza called Tulkinghorn to check out somefing what she should never have yakked about. Of course, she should have kept her gob zipped to stop da words from coming out, but when she came across some legal documents in da handwriting of her old big boy geeza Captain Hawdon, she had to find out more.

But for reasons best known to her, she started to yak to Tulkinghorn, who then decided to Facebook it round da London turf. Well, as luck would have it, he found out somefing what led to information about da document and some pauper geeza called Nemo. But if that was da 'up' side, da 'down' side was actually *finding* Nemo, which was jinxed from da start coz he was dead.

Neverdaless, and as luck would have it, all was not lost. Dere was dis road-sweeper geeza called Jo who used to hang with Nemo and was said to have some info what might have been useful, and that was why Lady Dedlock fought it was well worth meeting up with da road-sweeping Jo. But of course she realised that she couldn't be too careful just in case somebody recognised her. After all, she was da respected Lady Honoria Dedlock, and no way could she risk being seen mixing it with no common road-sweeper geeza, deffo. So taking everyfing into consideration she decided to disguise herself as her French maid called Hortense, as you do. But all da time dis was going on, every move she made was being watched by Tulkinghorn, which was well creepy.

Mind you, somefing else well odd happened to Lady Honoria Dedlock, coz quite by chance she had come face to face with Esther, da daughta she fought was toast. It was real spooky coz they just happened to be in da same place at da same time and were actually yak, yak yakking to each other when they was both in da church turf doing fings what people do in church. Well, it wasn't long before da moolah dropped and Lady Dedlock realised that da sprog what she dropped all those years ago was actually in da pew sitting next to her!

Well, dis should have been when da bitches went all friends reunited and put each other on da Christmas card list, but coz she just didn't wanna go dere, Lady Dedlock began having da hot flushes and bricked it, which was well sad. While it could have meant wicked times getting wasted, catching up on all those special moments like muvva's day and that, da simple fact of da matter was that Lady D so didn't want to go dere and didn't want nuffing to do with her long lost daughta what reminded her of da past.

Well, dis really made Esther mad, coz although she was well up for doing all da catching up with her muvva, what could she do after being told to naff off by da bitch what had brought her into da world? It left her feeling so dissed, but if she was looking for da spare tissue from Richard Carstone back at Emo House, then she was gonna be well disappointed, coz she wasn't da only one who had issues.

"Wassup?"
"Oh my God you are so not going to believe dis blud, coz I was well disrespected in da church turf by my own muvva and it was *well* emotional."
"That's nuffing, coz to be honest I got beef what is really bringing me down."
"So you got beef?"
"For sure."
"Lol."

Richard Carstone should have been off da hook, coz he and his cuz, Ada, had finally become man and bitch, which meant that not only did they have each other, but they also had all that dosh to look forward to from da inheritance what they had been waiting for – or so they fought. Unfortunately, and as hard as it is to believe, it was only when Richard found out that all da wonga had gone on da fees for da lawyers what was working on da Jarndyce and Jarndyce court case, that he realised that dere was nuffing left. Now they was potless, busted and gutted.

For Esther though, and despite being told to do one by her muvva, at least dere was somefing else going down what was helping her to deal with fings, you get me. Coz although dere was no connection between her and her muvva, da same could not be said for some geeza what she fought was da George Clooney of da turf. Da truth was that for ages she had been getting well turned on to Doctor Woodcourt who, luckily enough, had been carrying da torch of lurve for her for so long. However, and as is usual in da course of matters of da heart, fings had got seriously out of whack.

Coz although he had really wanted to get it on with Esther and make her his significant bitch, John Jarndyce had also fought she was well fit. Dese geezas was like da bee insect around da honey pot and coz da Doctor had been away from da hood for some time, Jarndyce was smooth enough to ask her to get it on with him first, and she said "Cool". However, now Doctor Woodcourt was back everyfing had changed, but what could she do to stop herself from making da really bad choice? But it seemed that while Esther was having to make da really big decision of da heart, it was like nuffing compared to da mess what her muvva, da Lady Honoria Dedlock, had found herself in and all on account of her unscrupulous lawyer geeza.

If only Tulkinghorn could have left it alone, then fings might not have turned out so minging, but he was one crafty lawyer who, togevva with Lady Dedlock's ungrateful maid Hortense – da one what Lady Dedlock disguised herself as – he just couldn't help himself from trying to mix it big time after he found out da truth about Lady D getting up da duff all those years ago. As for da maid, well, da only reason she was hanging with Tulkinghorn at all was to see for herself that Lady Dedlock was really gonna get hers.

"Yo, Mr T, is we gonna stick it to da bitch coz she is so asking for it!"
"Hortense, babe. What is it about da Lady D you don't like?"
"She was wearing my freads, innit."
"And?"
"Oh I so don't believe that you haven't seen Single White Female! Da bitch was trying to be me and that is *so* not cool."

Maybe dis should have told Tulkinghorn that da relationship with Hortense was so not going anywhere, if only coz she might be nutso. But instead of using his brains, Tulkinghorn told her to naff off, which was not da smartest fing he could have done, definite. You don't have to be no Einstein dude to work out that dere was nuffing more dangerous than da maid what had been dissed and in da moment of madness, Hortense decided to give it large to da lawyer geeza by shooting him dead, as you do.

Although dis was unfortunate for Tulkinghorn, da way fings had gone made it feel much worse for Lady Dedlock after da filth started snooping around da hood, and she felt she was deep in da brown stuff, even though she had nuffing to do with da well grizzly murder. So now, feeling well screwed, she decided to leg it without saying nuffing to nobody which was well tragic. Coz although in da end she was cleared by da fuzz of being involved in da grizzly murder, nobody knew where she was until she was eventually found proper dead, lying outside da cemetery where Esther's farva, her bit on da side, Captain Hawdon, was six foot under. It was emotional.

But although dis was not da most perfect ending for her muvva, it didn't end up too bad for Esther, and all coz of what John Jarndyce did - not just for her, but Ada too. Despite da Jarndyce and Jarndyce case finally being sorted, but coz of everyfing going to da lawyers, her main man Richard was never da same again until it all got too much and he came down with da terrible death from da tuberculosis illness. However, coz John Jarndyce was well decent, he decided to look after her and da nippa what she and Richard had. Respect again to JJ.

But although he could have been well bitter and twisted towards Esther for choosing da Doctor geeza over him, he was cool, and to put da icing on da cake, he even gave da happy couple da well smart house in da Yorkshire turf where they both lived all happy ever after, which was well lush. As far as decency went, John Jarndyce was da man, innit.

DA WELL SUSS MYSTERY OF EDWIN DROOD

Sometimes da course of true lurve is just somefing what happens when da point of Cupid's arrow is whacked straight into da hearts of well fit young dudes and bitches. But in da case of Edwin Drood and Rosa Bud, Cupid's well sharp pointy bit was given da assistance of da heavy promise made by dere parents when they was just nippas, and well before they was both unexpectedly orphaned. Although dis was well unfair it meant, no matter what, that Edwin and Rosa was destined to get it on with each other when they was older, whether they wanted to or not, end of. Or was it?

Coz da fact of da matter was that as they got older, growing up in da Cloisterham turf, da last fing they wanted was to get all jiggy with each other. They *so* didn't want to go dere. Not that it made any difference coz it was still gonna happen anyway, especially while Edwin's uncle, John Jasper, had been keeping da very watchful eye on what had been going down. Da Cloisterham yard belonged to him and coz he was da daddy or, rather, da uncle, he had da special responsibility to his nephew coz not only was he fam, but he was also his guardian and that was why Edwin had already yakked to his uncle about him and Rosa.

As far as Edwin was concerned, Rosa just didn't float his boat, end of, and no matter what his uncle said, he just didn't want to get it on with da bitch, no way no how. Well, coz he was da uncle and guardian, John Jasper was well solid about da situation and told Edwin to take da chill pill. Dis could have been coz he was well understanding, or maybe he had anuvva reason. Da fing about him was that as he was Rosa's choirmaster in da Cloisterham Cathedral, and besides showing her what to do with all da high notes, double quavers and that, he also fancied da pants off her, big time, oh yeah. Anuvva fing about John Jasper was that he was well into doing da opium drug what he would often score in da London turf. So what with his fing for Rosa, da opium and doing all da music, John Jasper was all sex, drugs and rock 'n roll, man.

Meanwhile dere was some new dudes what had arrived in da Cloisterham yard, Neville and Helena Landless, and while Neville had got da short straw of being looked after by da Reverend Septimus Crisparkle, his twin sista Helena was bunking up with Rosa. But while all that seemed sweet, Helena had issues with John Jasper on account of da fact that he creeped her out, big time. Anyhoo, if settling into strange new turf was proving difficult for Helena, it was proving nuffing like it for Neville after he saw Rosa and fought that she was fit as da butcher's dog. However, what he also noticed was da way Edwin was being so minging to her, which he reckoned was well out of order, but he couldn't have been more wrong.

Coz although Edwin and Rosa was always busting each other's chops, they didn't mean nuffing by it coz they was always well cool with each other, despite Edwin still not wanting to touch her with da fifty foot barge pole. Neverdaless, it didn't stop Neville from finking that if Rosa was his bitch, he would seriously deck Edwin for disrespecting da ghetto princess. As far as he was concerned, Neville didn't like da way Rosa was being violated 24-seven, end of, and so that was why, before long, they was squaring up to each other like they was real badass gangstas.

"Yo Drood you muppet, you is well out of order for da way you is always dissing Rosa, you get me."
"Whoa, are you talking to me or chewing da brick?"
"Yeah, I'm talking to you Drood and guess what, you is going down big time!"
"Oh yeah? Well bring it on blud!"

Before long they was well knocking da crap out of each other and bitch-slapping just like they was on da Jerry Springer Show, innit. It was monster bad, coz it was crystal that somefing had to be done to stop da two of them rucking like they was chavs. Well, maybe it was somefing to do with it being so close to Christmas but when news hit da street, Reverend Crisparkle decided that dere was too much attitude coming over da Cloisterham frontline.

Dere was no way he was gonna let it become some kind of no-go turf and so he decided to get da two of them togevva in John Jasper's yard to finally sort it over some grub and Stella on Christmas Eve. Let's face it, coz if anyfing, not only was it bad karma to be rucking at Christmas but also, well, Santa knows who's been naughty or nice, innit. Respect for da Claus geeza.

But before then dere was still stuff to sort between Edwin and Rosa, on account of da fact that they still wasn't cool about becoming all hitched to each other, which was why Rosa was well chuffed to hear from her guardian geeza, Hiram Grewgious, with some well good news. It was all to do with da massive inheritance what was gonna come her way from her dead parents and was gonna make her one uber minted orphan. Dis was bitching news and even better was that it didn't come with no strings or nuffing, which meant she wouldn't lose none of it if she and Edwin didn't get it on with each other. However, and as good as it was, it wasn't just Rosa what was getting some surprise news from Hiram Grewgious, coz unknown to her, Edwin had also met up with da geeza and da news that he got really blew his mind, big time.

Although Rosa had been told one fing, Edwin was being

told somefing else what was about to mess with his mojo. Coz da reason for meeting up with Hiram Grewgious was all to do with da bit of finger bling what Rosa's farva had originally given to her muvva and now it was all his, just so long as he did one fing. Although da bling was his, deffo, no question, before he could actually get his hands on it, if he wanted it, then all he had to do was get engaged to Rosa, whack it on her finger and make everyfing kosher by making her his bitch.

Dis really was heavy stuff, but in his heart he knew that – as sick as da whole inheritance fing was - dere really was no choice. And by da time Edwin had got himself back to da Cloisterham turf and met up with Rosa, they both reckoned it was time to finally cool it and split. Dis was da huge fing for da both of them to do and they fought that they had to be well grown-up about it. So after taking everyfing into account and knowing what da responsible and grown-up fing to do was, they decided to let Hiram Grewgious break da news to tell Edwin's uncle, John Jasper. Oh yeah, very grown-up.

Anyhoo, elsewhere in da hood and maybe coz of what happened earlier with Edwin, and possibly also coz of da Stella-summit what was going down at John Jasper's later, Neville Landless decided to chillax and get away over da Christmas break. He was feeling mellow and had got himself da pimped-up walking stick for da journey ahead. Well, if da geeza couldn't treat himself at Christmas, when could he? Although nuffing was mentioned about Edwin and Rosa splitting, da get-togevva at Jasper's was cool and didn't turn into no ruckfest or nuffing. It could have been all awkward turtle, but by da time it was over, peace had broken out with everyone acting like they was real homies, which was well good.

And so with everyfing chilled and sorted, when it was time to go, and despite da minging weather – coz it was well lashing it down – Edwin and Neville decided to split da Jasper turf and head off togevva towards da river. Coz dere was nuffing but positive karma, everyone was feeling well good with each other, which meant that from here on in, everyfing was gonna be cool in da hood between Neville Landless and Edwin Drood. Well, da next day was Christmas Day when everyone in da ghetto should have been getting down and doing da Christmas fing, but dere was dark clouds on da horizon instead of white snowy ones, and all coz word had spread across da turf that Edwin Drood was missing.

Not that he knew it, but fings was not looking good for Neville Landless, coz by da time everyone found out, he was well away from da turf on his hike so, taking all factors into account, not only was Neville Landless turning into Cloisterham's most wanted, but he was already looking more stuffed than da Christmas turkey. Of course it didn't have to be that way, but fanks to some uber stirring from John Jasper, everyone in da hood knew that Neville

Landless was da last geeza to see Edwin alive, which made his chances for da merry Christmas less than optimistic, innit.

Of course, him being gone didn't mean that Neville Landless actually had anyfing to do with Edwin's disappearance; however, fanks to John Jasper's big mouth, everyone fought that he was da geeza what did Edwin in, even though he was only missing. Fings weren't looking good for da poor geeza, especially when da Cloisterham massive managed to catch him up and bring him back to da home turf. Now dis was well bad for Neville, who was looking more and more like da Cloisterham One than da innocent dude. But despite everyone finking that he had been banged to rights, dere wasn't enough evidence to lock him up and so – and as much as everyone fought that Neville Landless was as guilty as anyfing - he was released into da care of Reverend Crisparkle.

What with everyfing what was going on, obviously dis might not have been da best moment to tell John Jasper about da break-up between Edwin and Rosa, but guess what, that was exactly what Hiram Grewgious did, da insensitive minger. Of course Jasper was well gutted and it only seemed to make him even more determined to find out for sure what really happened to his nephew and as importantly, fink about how Rosa was coping with da situation. Anyhoo, with everyone in da hood now yakking nonstop about da well suss mystery surrounding da disappearance of Edwin Drood, fings became even more random when some of his bling was found by da river. Without doubt, dis was certainly turning into da well heavy situation for Neville Landless and he was bricking it like never before.

Well in da six months since da fickle finger of suspicion had been pointed at him, everyone in da Cloisterham hood had sent him to da Coventry turf. They was treating him like he was nuffing more than da geeza with da very guilty secret although, in reality, dere was no secret coz everyone knew it was Landless what had whacked Edwin Drood. And dis was why da Reverend Septimus Crisparkle decided to do somefing about da situation by getting Neville out of da Cloisterham hood and off to da London turf near Hiram Grewgious' yard at Staples Inn.

Meanwhile, and probably coz he was only trying to be all sympathetic about what had happened to Edwin, John Jasper hadn't forgotten how well stacked Rosa Bud was and wanted to do somefing to prove how much he cared for her.

"Rosa, you is da fine looking bitch and I'm hurting for you big time."
"Fank you."
"And if dere is anyfing I can do to make it all better, then just tell me. It can be anyfing, coz you scrub up well nice and are so worth it. And so if you want I'll arrange da hit on

Neville Landless for what he did to Edwin Drood, da scum!"
"Fank..... Say *what?*"

And although he probably meant well by declaring his undying lurve for her and promising to whack Neville for what he fought he did to Edwin, all that happened was that he scared da living daylights out of Rosa who didn't waste no time in legging it over to Hiram Grewgious. Dis guy was well bonkers and she didn't want nuffing more to do with da psycho.

Meanwhile, back in da Cloisterham yard, da mysterious Dick Datchery had begun to take da unhealthy interest in da comings and goings of John Jasper. It was well intense in da stalking sense, coz not only had dis geeza got himself somewhere to kip in da exact same building where Jasper lived, but he also got da nippa called Deputy to keep da close eye on everyfing John Jasper did.

"OK, you is my ears and my eyes, you get me, and I want you to tell me what dis dude is up to 24-seven."
"So you is wanting me to let you know where he goes and what he does, right?"
"That is what I'm talking about Deputy, dawg."

It was well odd but, neverdaless, what with John Jasper being kept under da stalking eye of Dick Datchery and Deputy, it was clear that fings in da well suss mystery of Edwin Drood was about to get even more suss.

But it is well unfortunate that we'll never know what da outcome was, coz before he finished da story, Charles Dickens died.

Bummer.

Dark Matter

Invisibility
in
Drama, Theater, & Performance

Andrew Sofer

The University of Michigan Press
Ann Arbor

Published in the United States of America by
The University of Michigan Press
Manufactured in the United States of America
⊗ Printed on acid-free paper

2016   2015   2014   2013   4   3   2   1

A CIP catalog record for this book is available from the British Library.

Library of Congress Cataloging-in-Publication Data

Sofer, Andrew, 1964–
    Dark matter : invisibility in drama, theater, and performance / Andrew Sofer.
        pages   cm. — (Theater: theory/text/performance)
    Includes bibliographical references and index.
    ISBN 978-0-472-07204-0 (cloth : alk. paper) — ISBN 978-0-472-05204-2 (pbk.
: alk. paper) — ISBN 978-0-472-02968-6 (e-book)
    1. Offstage action (Drama)   2. Presence (Philosophy)   3. English drama—
History and criticism.   4. American drama—History and criticism.   I. Title.
PN1696.S65   2013
792.01—dc23
2013026614

Cover: 3-D map of the large-scale distribution of dark matter, reconstructed from
measurements of weak gravitational lensing with the Hubble Space Telescope
(NASA/ESA/Richard Massey).

To Enoch Brater

Perception is not first a perception of *things,* but a perception of *elements* . . . of *rays of the world,* of things which are dimensions, which are worlds.

—Maurice Merleau-Ponty,
The Visible and the Invisible

Acknowledgments

I have benefited from the help and advice of many friends and colleagues in pursuing this project. Among them are Alan Ackerman, Wendy Arons, Emma Katherine Atwood, Philip Auslander, David Bevington, Rhonda Blair, John Russell Brown, Marvin Carlson, William Carroll, Mary Crane, Scott Cummings, J. K. Curry, Tracy Davis, Jody Enders, Penny Farfan, Verna Foster, Elinor Fuchs, Spencer Golub, Linda Gregerson, Kenneth Gross, Barbara Grossman, Atar Hadari, Kyna Hamill, James Harding, Dayton Haskin, William Hutchings, Coppélia Kahn, Katherine Kellett, Ric Knowles, Donna Kornhaber, David Krasner, Jill Lane, Steve and Ellen Levine, John Mahoney, Suzanne Matson, Cary Mazer, Bernadette Meyler, Andrés Pérez-Simón, Martin Puchner, Brendan Rapple, Alice Rayner, Charlotte Reiter, Christopher Ricks, Joseph Roach, David Roby, David Saltz, Catherine Schuler, Richard Schoch, Mike Sell, Laurence Senelick, Jennifer Sinor, P. A. Skantze, Michael Sowder, Matthew Wilson Smith, Enrique Urueta, Adam Vines, Elizabeth Kowaleski Wallace, Don Weingust, Chris Wilson, Christina Woodworth, W. B. Worthen, Harvey Young, Kevin Young, and Ted Ziter.

The participants in my 2001 San Diego American Society for Theatre Research (ASTR) seminar Materialism and the Material helped me conceptualize this project at an early stage: Rhonda Blair, Chase Bringardner, Donnalee Dox, Jon Erickson, F. Elizabeth Hart, Kimberly Jannarone, Peter Novack, James Peck, Nicholas Ridout, and Matthew Wagner. My graduate students in the seminars Performance and Representation, What Is Performance?, and Beckett on Stage and Screen asked all the right questions and deepened my understanding of this material. I thank my wonderful colleagues in Boston College's English Department and Dean David Quigley. Special thanks are due to LeAnn Fields, for her patience and faith in this project, and to the University of Michigan Press and its outside readers. Kerry Burke and Michael Swanson at Boston College Media Technology Services assisted with the images. Ellen Kaplan-Maxfield provided the index.

For inviting me to present some of the material that follows, I thank the University of Michigan's Arthur Miller International Symposium, Boston College English Department's Graduate Colloquium, Harvard University's Shakespeare Studies Seminar, Tufts University's Department of Drama and Dance, Loyola University Chicago's McElroy Shakespeare Celebration, Northwestern University's Interdisciplinary PhD Program in Theatre and Drama, the Southeastern Theatre Conference Theatre Symposium, and the University of Alabama at Birmingham's Department of English. Thanks also to ASTR; the Association for Theatre in Higher Education; the Mellon School of Theater and Performance Research at Harvard University; and the Association of Literary Scholars, Critics, and Writers.

Versions of chapters 1, 4, and 5 appeared in *Theatre Journal, Modern Drama,* and *Arthur Miller's America: Theater and Culture in a Time of Change,* ed. Enoch Brater (Ann Arbor: University of Michigan Press, 2005). Sections of my introduction appeared in *Theatre Journal* under the title "Spectral Readings." I am grateful for the editors' permission to reprint this material.

My brother, Paul Sofer, and mother, Elaine Sofer, died during the writing of this book. Their intellectual and creative spirit continues to inform everything that I write.

Loving thanks, as always, to Bonnie Tenneriello and Julian Sofer.

This book is dedicated to my teacher and mentor, Enoch Brater, who continues to inspire.

Contents

Dark Matter

An Introduction

We know very little for sure about dark matter.
—Frank Wilczek, Nobel Prize winner in physics

Sometimes you see ideas in the way an astronomer sees stars
in the far distance. (Or it seems like that anyway.)
—Ludwig Wittgenstein

At the heart of English medieval liturgical drama lies the Visit to the Sepulchre by the three Marys on Easter morning, with its revelation of Jesus'
Resurrection at the empty tomb. Various versions survive, but all incorporate the famous *Quem quaeritis* (Whom do you seek?) trope, originally
sung in tenth-century monastic churches as part of the Easter service. The
clergy was actively encouraged to develop the trope in the direction of performed drama. For example, in *The Regularis Concordia* of St. Ethelwold,
a liturgical script prepared at Winchester for Benedictine use in England,
three brethren dressed in copes are instructed to haltingly approach the
"tomb" area of the church, bearing thuribles with incense to suggest the
three Marys. There they discover a fourth cleric, wearing an alb and holding a palm in his hand in imitation of the angel seated on Christ's tomb.
"Whom do you seek in the sepulchre, O followers of Christ?" chants the
Angel (in Latin). The three answer with one voice, "Jesus of Nazareth, who
was crucified, O heaven-dweller." The angel responds, "He is not here, he
has risen as he had foretold . . . Come and see the place." In what can only

be called stage directions, the scene reaches its climax as the Angel reveals the empty tomb with a flourish.

> Saying this, let him rise and lift the veil and show them the place bare of the cross, with nothing other than the shroud in which the cross had been wrapped.[1]

The scene ends with the three Marys taking up the shroud and spreading it out before the assembled clergy (chanting "The Lord has risen from the sepulchre"). They then lay the shroud on the altar as the bells peal in unison, and the community unites in a joyful hymn. Communal faith is reaffirmed by a double metonymy: the cloth stands in for the absent cross that was previously wrapped in it, and that ghostly presence in turn stands for Christ's invisible, miraculously resurrected body.

Centuries later this enacted scene climaxed the Passion Play portion of England's medieval Corpus Christi Cycles. Performed in English verse by lay actors under the sponsorship of trade guilds, the cycles publicly celebrated the Festival of Christ's Real Presence in the Eucharist. Here the Visit to the Sepulchre is not proto-drama but full-blown theater. In the *Play of the Resurrection of the Lord* (Wakefield version), the three Marys approach the sepulchre and are met by two angels, and the "Whom do you seek?" exchange recurs. The First Angel intones:

> He is not here, the sothe to say.
> The place is voide therin he lay.
> The sudary [burial cloth] here se ye may
> Was on him laide.
> He is risen and gone his way,
> As he you saide.[2]

The ocular proof of Christ's resurrection—eagerly awaited by the crowd—is again twofold. The bloody cloth, which the audience has followed through the cycle, symbolizes Christ's Passion and the salvific power of Christ's blood. But the true proof of Christ's divinity is the equally flourished *absence* of his physical body ("He is not here").[3] The real presence of Christ is paradoxically guaranteed by his felt absence—an absence designed to move the crowd from theatrical wonder to reaffirmed faith.

Inscribed in liturgical rite at the foundational moment of postclassical

Western drama, Christ's absent body is a striking example of what I call *dark matter.* In physics dark matter refers to nonluminous mass that cannot be directly detected by observation. Thanks to infrared astronomy, we can now see so-called cold matter—that is, the clouds of dust and gas between the stars. But because it does not emit light, x-rays, or any other radiation, dark matter can only be inferred by its gravitational effects on the motion of ordinary matter. According to physicist Frank Wilczek, "Galaxies of ordinary matter are surrounded by extended halos of dark matter. The halo weighs, in total, about five times as much as the visible galaxy. There may also be independent condensations of dark matter."[4] We infer that dark matter exists because without its gravitational pull observable galaxies would fly apart.[5] Unlike so-called dark energy (which makes up the rest of the universe's missing mass-energy), dark matter "clumps" rather than being uniformly distributed through space.[6] This invisible matter is believed by scientists to constitute somewhere between 80 and 95 percent of the matter in the universe.[7] Dark matter is, quite literally, the secret ingredient whose mass holds our visible world together, although scientists do not yet know what it is.

Translated into theatrical terms, dark matter refers to the invisible dimension of theater that escapes visual detection, even though its effects are felt everywhere in performance. If theater necessarily traffics in corporeal stuff (bodies, fluids, gases, objects), it also incorporates the incorporeal: offstage spaces and actions, absent characters, the narrated past, hallucination, blindness, obscenity, godhead, and so on. No less than physical actors and objects, such invisible presences matter very much indeed, even if spectators, characters, and performers cannot put their hands on them.

Faced with the unseen, theater scholars tend to discuss offstage persons, spaces, and objects in terms of the indexical sign first posited by Charles Peirce.[8] Thus, according to Marvin Carlson, "The fictive space of almost all theatre . . . is composed of both onstage and offstage components, and the latter, in much theatre of at least equal importance to the onstage space, is constructed almost entirely of indexical signs."[9] An index points to something else connected to it not by resemblance (iconicity) but by cause and effect. An offstage siren indexes a police car, for instance, just as smoke indexes fire or a knock on the door a visitor. But to observe that fictive stage space, action, and/or character are pointed to by narrative (or audible) indices—the messenger's story of Oedipus's blinding, the breaking string in *The Cherry Orchard,* the gunshot in *Hedda Gabler*—does not yet account for their pull within the fictive world or their power over an audience, the gravitational effects that are my subject here.[10]

Just as reducing offstage presences to indexical signs risks downplaying their importance, we should be wary of reducing dark matter to metaphysical absence, as certain poststructuralist versions of the critique of presence might suggest.[11] On the analogy of Saussurean linguistics, in which *signifieds* (meanings) flow along a chain of hollow *signifiers* (words) in an endless game of telephone, poststructuralism considers any transcendent "presence" outside discourse a chimera.[12] Yet dark matter is neither ghostly sign nor rhetorical flourish. When terrified Elizabethans hallucinated one devil too many during performances of *Doctor Faustus,* they somehow thought they *saw* what was not there. A fresh method and vocabulary can help account for theater's capacity to alter our perceptual field through means besides the visual—to alter others' consciousness at will.[13] This ability is no mere epiphenomenon, an indexical pendant to the iconic stage. Dark matter is woven into the fabric of theatrical representation.

Alongside material bodies and objects, then, invisible phenomena continually structure and focus an audience's theatrical experience. These daggers of the mind remain incorporeal yet are crucial to the performed event. My thesis is straightforward: *invisible phenomena are the dark matter of theater.* Materially elusive though phenomenologically inescapable, dark matter is the "not there" yet "not not there" of theater.[14] Much as the vast majority of the universe's mass is constituted by what remains transparent, most of the event we call theater depends on what might be called felt absences. This is no less true of realism than of other, less naturalistic modes.[15] The late General Gabler looms over his daughter's tragedy, just as offstage men haunt the action in Maria Irene Fornes's *Fefu and Her Friends* and Lorca's *The House of Bernarda Alba.* Distinct from the free play of an audience's imagination, in which every bush is supposed a bear, dark matter subtends any theatrical performance. Dark matter, not unlike sex in the Victorian realist novel, is intangible yet omnipresent.[16] Exerting irresistible force over our imaginations in the playhouse, it pulls the visible elements of theatrical representation into a pattern. Dark matter comprises *whatever is materially unrepresented onstage but un-ignorable.* It is not a finger pointing at the moon but the tidal force of gravity that pulls at us unseen.

Synecdoche is the modus (pr)operandi of postclassical Western theater. A beach chair stands for a seaside; a living room stands for the world. Theater continually encourages us to take parts for wholes, but it also encourages us to take holes for parts. The complementary aspect of this synecdochic accretion—imaginatively filling out the stage based on visible evidence—is excision. An absence stands in for a presence ("He is not here, the sothe to say"). In the Wakefield play, both aspects support each other: the cast-off shroud metonymically invokes real presence, while the missing body conjures felt absence. This double aspect of performance, held in continual tension by dramatist, stage, and performer, operates every time theatrical performance is witnessed. It is dark matter that produces the difference between horror and terror, for example. Horror is what we see; terror is what we know is there though it remains unseen. As if to underscore the difference, Rupert Goold's 2007 Chichester Festival production of *Macbeth* (with Patrick Stewart) staged the banquet scene twice, with Banquo's ghost (Martin Turner) first visible and then invisible.[17]

How can theater and performance studies illuminate dark matter, which sheds no light of its own? This is not the same problem as reconstructing the material traces of once-visible objects and performances that have dimmed in historical memory (*kinamnesia*).[18] In the following chapters I model a critical approach that I call *spectral reading*. The term is a deliberate pun. Not only are we looking for ghosts we can see right through, invisible presences that cast no light themselves.[19] We are expanding our investigative spectrum beyond material bodies and objects in order to discern hidden wavelengths beyond the reach of the naked (critical) eye. Philosopher Colin McGinn calls this imaginative operation *mindsight*.[20] Spectral reading traces the effects of those invisible forces at work in the world of the performance or play, such as characters who never appear, events that take place offstage, noises off, the narrated past, onstage hallucination, or any related phenomena. Practitioners (including dramatists) in every theatrical period treat dark matter as a constitutive element, whether it is the shaman summoning the ancestral spirit or Shakespeare conjuring an offstage union between clown and queen that may never, in fact, occur. Spectral (or spectroscopic) criticism allows us to read across the complete spectrum of dramaturgies: *classical,* in which our everyday laws apply to the world of the play; *quantum,* in which indeterminacy governs the dramatic world; and *prismatic,* in which the play spatializes variations on a theme rather than tracing cause and effect. Spectral reading thus complements what I have elsewhere called "reading in five dimensions," a critical approach that seeks to recover the hidden spatial and temporal trajectories of theater's mobile, material objects.[21]

Spectral reading does not produce an ontology of dark matter, saying what it is or what it is not.[22] Nor does it reduce dark matter to an effect of indexical language, so that what remains unseen onstage becomes just a figure of speech. Rather, spectral reading opens up a phenomenology of the unseen. Broadly speaking, phenomenology rests on Kant's distinction between the world as it is in itself (*noumenon*) and the world as it offers itself to sense perception (*phenomenon*). Phenomenologists describe our shared experiential world, which for perceiving subjects is filtered by time and space (Kant's forms of perception), before that world is translated into concepts or symbols for something other than itself.[23] Phenomenological descriptions of theater address "the perceptual impression theater makes on the spectator" and emphasize "the site of our sensory engagement with its empirical objects."[24] A phenomenologist is less interested in what the gunshot in Suzan-Lori Parks's *The America Play* "means" than in what it does to an audience's nerve endings. Phenomenology avoids solipsism by positing shared experiences—of the color "red," for example—by those who possess the same empirical equipment, so throughout *Dark Matter* I refer to "we" and "the audience" interchangeably. This is not to deny that individual spectators may have idiosyncratic responses to a given performance; naturally they do. But it is to make the assumption that a given performance provokes common responses, and that the kinds of theater I consider here turn spectators into something we can reasonably call *an* audience for the duration of a given performance.

Recent interest in theater, literature, and philosophy's phantasmal aspects has been so widespread that Jeffrey Weinstock has identified a "spectral turn" in cultural theory and criticism.[25] Narratologists like Wolfgang Iser have long been concerned with narrative gaps.[26] Jacques Derrida coined the pun *hauntology* to describe Marxism's uncanny haunting of the present from beyond the grave.[27] Marvin Carlson's *The Haunted Stage* describes theater as a vast recycling machine in which "ghosting presents the identical thing [audience members] have encountered before, although now in a somewhat different context."[28] Joseph Roach's *Cities of the Dead* traces surrogation, "the enactment of cultural memory by substitution," a particular variety of ghosting in which a stand-in pinch hits for an absent original.[29] Peggy Phelan observes that "[f]rom the ghost of Hamlet's father to the ghost in the machine of contemporary theatre's special effects, Western theatre has had a sustained conversation with the incorporeal," and that mourning absent bodies may be theater's central preoccupation.[30]

Alice Rayner's *Ghosts* sees theater as a form of consciousness in which the problem of representation is not so much sidestepped as transcended.[31] Such crucial instances of cultural haunting are but one dimension of dark matter, for what is invisible *always* holds what is visible in place, just as cosmic dark matter provides the scaffolding for visible galaxies. If theater is a memory machine, as much current thinking in theater and performance studies insists, it is also an invisibility machine. Hidden in its wings we find not only actors, props, and sets but directors, producers, designers, publicists, stagehands, carpenters, and lighting technicians.[32] Part of theater's task is to make the invisible visible, as when ghosts or devils occupy the stage. But theater must also keep some phantoms up its sleeve.[33] Whereas old Hamlet is as corporeal a presence as his living namesake, Laertes' fencing master, the aptly named Lamord, remains a mordant signifier.[34]

What distinguishes dark matter from the free play of the spectator's mind as he or she watches a performance? In short how can one pin down something so seemingly ethereal? We can argue about what *Richard II*'s crown signifies, but at least we can agree that the prop is (or was) *there* in performance.[35] But what, for instance, of Macbeth's hallucinated dagger? The invisible prop, so vivid in its absent presence, invites spectral reading. On his way to murder King Duncan in the dead of night, the regicidal thane is arrested by a horrifying apparition floating in midair:

Is this a dagger which I see before me,
The handle toward my hand? Come, let me clutch thee:
I have thee not, and yet I see thee still.
Art thou not, fatal vision, sensible
To feeling as to sight? or art thou but
A dagger of the mind, a false creation,
Proceeding from the heat-oppressed brain?
I see thee yet, in form as palpable
As this which now I draw.
Thou marshal'st me the way that I was going,
And such an instrument I was to use.
Mine eyes are made the fools o' th'other senses,
Or else worth all the rest. I see thee still;
And on thy blade and dudgeon gouts of blood,
Which was not so before. There's no such thing:
It is the bloody business which informs
Thus to mine eyes. (2.1.33–49)[36]

Macbeth's dagger is visible to him but invisible to the audience. For Macbeth the dagger's palpability is the source of its horror, yet he cannot instrumentalize it as a prop; the air-drawn weapon eludes his grasp. Macbeth's eyes tell him one thing, his other senses another. In McGinn's distinction, the dagger is a percept rather than an image. He argues (contra Hume) that mental images are not "weak" percepts but distinct phenomena, although both perception and visualization are kinds of *seeing*: "We might say that the image is *created* by the act of attention, while the percept is generated by an outside stimulus."[37]

From the audience's perspective, also, the phantom dagger is not a prop like Richard's crown. Nor is it a hallucination, quite, as it is for Macbeth. We conjure it in our mind's eye as an image (or sequence of images—now beckoning, now bloody) rather than a percept. But although it is conjured by language, the dagger is not *reducible* to language.[38] Pointed to by the dialogue, it is no mere trope or figure of speech—although Lady Macbeth certainly wishes it were.[39] For Macbeth the dagger is as nightmarishly real as any bad dream.[40] It tugs the doomed couple even farther apart and intensifies Macbeth's expressionistic isolation, which in turn fuels his homicidal paranoia. Macbeth's dagger is neither there nor not there; we "see" it and do not see it at the same time. The dagger is at once in the text, in Macbeth's perception, in our imaginations, and (not) *there* onstage. Unlike the presence of the eldritch witches, the dagger's presence can be inferred only by its gravitational effects. Those effects transcend Macbeth's deictic (pointing, indexical) figures of speech to produce those effects beyond language to which spectral reading attends: horror (Macbeth), antimetaphysical skepticism (Lady Macbeth), and uncanniness or even terror (for the audience).

Spectral reading also invites the Macbeth actor into the phenomenological scene. For him the imaginary dagger must occupy a similar "not there . . . not not there" space as for the character. The actor must play an imaginative "as if" game in which the dagger hovers *between* percept and image. If the dagger is just a figment, then the scene loses its power; if the dagger is "real," it is not hallucinatory but a mime.[41] Ralph Richardson expressed this knife's edge clearly when he remarked of his own failed performance, "I found, when I came to play Macbeth—'Is this a dagger I see before me?'—I just damn well didn't see the dagger and neither did anybody else."[42] Unlike Richardson, the successful actor must build a verbal carapace around the invisible dagger that allows us to visualize it as charged *negative space*. It is at once the epicenter of the scene and a black hole, and when Macbeth draws his own material sword, as Shakespeare's verbal stage direction insists, theater's visible and dark matter meet. Yet at the corporeal level *there is nothing there* except the actor, his words, and his props. Through *Macbeth*'s uncanny poetics of felt absence, Shakespeare slyly enacts, theorizes, and deconstructs dark matter at the same time.

Aside from invisible props like Macbeth's dagger and offstage figures like Godot, spectral reading illuminates the impact of phantom presences whose substance is not, in the first instance, rhetorical. In such wordless spectacles as contemporary dance theater or performance art, for example, the invisible is no longer indexical in the same way.[43] Thus *Sleep No More*, Punchdrunk Theatre's site-specific, phantasmagorical remix of *Macbeth* as filtered through Hitchcock and *The Shining,* is both nonmimetic and nonverbal. Far from synecdochically representing an elsewhere, the cavernous performance space is the total space of action. The "Manderley" bar remains a working bar where the audience can order a drink (even if it is cunningly ghosted by a double or doubles embedded elsewhere—a Platonic joke). The audience dons white masks before entering a warren of performance spaces through a pitch-black corridor. As we wander through a series of creepily detailed environments that, as W. B. Worthen has shown, transform *Macbeth*'s rhetoric of horror into scenic elements, we encounter not only performers but also our masked doubles.[44] Accompanied by an eerie soundtrack, the experience is like walking into a movie—or a nightmare. Meanwhile, manic performers erupt into designated spaces and enact wordless, highly disturbing vignettes (loosely based on *Macbeth*) to which we become mute, complicit witnesses. Not there, yet not not there, the masked spectator becomes *Sleep No More*'s dark matter. We are conjured into visibility whenever a performer draws us into the scene, only to be consigned to oblivion once the performer abandons us and moves on. Paradoxically, we remain visible to the other masked spectators even when placed under erasure by the performers; our phenomenological status with respect to the action is a conundrum. No Peircean analysis can do justice to the ontologically dislocating effect of such immersive performance art, in which we can feel rendered somehow more shadowy and insubstantial than the vivid performers.[45]

Given my claim that in the playhouse dark matter transcends mere rhetoric, a reasonable question might be whether my analogy is anything more than poetic license: an admittedly suggestive trope, but one that does not tell us anything we did not already know. Why appropriate a metaphor that can fairly be called, if not quite metaphysical, then unabashedly cosmic? My answer is that the analogy can help students, critics, and practitioners see theater afresh in at least three usefully precise ways.

First, *dark matter allows for the existence of visible matter.* The Swiss astronomer Fritz Zwicky first postulated dark matter in the 1930s to explain why rotating galaxies did not fling themselves apart.[46] Scientists have since discovered that dark matter "acts as a skeleton around which bright matter—galaxies and clusters of galaxies—assembles."[47] In the same way, invisible theatrical phenomena, whether contiguous (the bedrooms off the kitchen in *Miss Julie*) or distant (Moscow in *The Three Sisters*), hold visible ones in place. In the modern theater's most famous example, the offstage Godot, elusive and indifferent, may or may not offer salvation to Vladimir and Estragon, but the belief that he *might* ties Beckett's tantalized clowns to their merciless tree indefinitely.[48]

Second, *dark matter's presence observably distorts the visible through its gravitational effects.* In the words of Eric V. Linder, "In a manner akin to the Polynesian seafarers who sense islands out of their sight through the deflected direction of ocean waves, cosmologists can map a concentration of the universe's unseen mass through the gravitational deflection of light coming from sources behind it."[49] In Susan Glaspell's *Trifles* (1916), the protagonist, Mrs. Wright, never appears. Along with the onstage characters, we must interpret each clue she left behind in order to solve a murder mystery, which baffles the play's (male) sheriff: "Nothing here but kitchen things."[50] Unbeknownst to him, though increasingly apparent to the shrewd female chorus, Mrs. Wright's gravitational field has bent every domestic detail into forensic evidence of mariticide. Glaspell models spectral reading for an audience that is taught how to see.

Third, *dark matter's ability to bend visible light allows observers to look back in time and space.* When placed in the foreground, halfway between the observer and a very distant galaxy, a concentrated mass of dark (or even bright) matter deflects light from that galaxy, both magnifying and distorting the galaxy's visible image.[51] Acting as a gravitational lens, dark matter bends light that would otherwise be too far away to detect, and by measuring that light's "doppler" shift to the red end of the spectrum—a phenomenon known as redshift—cosmologists can calculate how fast that galaxy is speeding away from us.[52] By analogy the distortion of any given theatrical performance's effects across historical time and geographic space might well be called that performance's *semiotic redshift*—a useful measure of kinamnesia.[53] Harnessing theater's dark matter as a lens, we can reconstruct distant performance effects that would otherwise remain hard or impossible to detect. Thus, in the Wakefield play, the actor's absent body (dark matter) lenses the Real Presence of Christ in the Eucharist, whose miracle the play celebrates.[54]

How fanciful, then, is theatrical dark matter? Its ontological fuzziness may trouble positivist readers.[55] But for my purposes, dark matter is less a substance than a concept designed to draw our attention to a crucial and universal dimension of performance experience that transcends semiotic analysis alone, useful as such analysis has been. I am not performing science here, but making use of analogies drawn from science to bring aesthetic phenomena into phenomenological focus.[56] Of course, in seeking nature's hidden patterns, science itself makes use of heuristic conveniences like the wittily named "quarks" first posited by Murray Gell-Mann (with an allusion to James Joyce), which were later discovered to exist. Science also sometimes proceeds by aesthetic leaps, such as Maxwell's elegant theory of electromagnetism. Karl Popper famously claimed that scientific advances depend on bold conjecture, followed by attempts at falsification, rather than on inductive proof (which he believed impossible).[57] Einstein, who relied on thought experiments rather than lab work, suggested the word *Heuristchen* for work that is not a rigorous solution but a suggestion for further development.[58] In that spirit I proffer dark matter and spectral reading as, respectively, heuristic and lens for reconstructing how felt absences conjure theater itself into being.

Rather than providing a taxonomy of dark matter, I want to suggest the range of issues—historical, practical, aesthetic, and ideological—that spectral reading can address in practice. To this end I have organized *Dark Matter* as a series of independent case studies, each of which analyzes a specific site of dark matter through the lens of particular plays or playwrights, in order to address a particular representational issue that might otherwise evade detection. Along the way I introduce some broadly applicable concepts and terms, which are gathered in the glossary. Because my intended readership includes theater specialists, generalists, and students alike, I discuss both familiar and less familiar plays; my aim is to balance familiarity and freshness. (Conspicuously absent, *Hamlet* and *Waiting for Godot* nonetheless exert a spectral, gravitational pull throughout these pages.) Each chapter stands alone as an individual study whose theoretical and methodological terms are set by the issue at hand. Taken together, the variety of approaches demonstrates the hermeneutic potential of spectral reading for literary scholarship and theater and performance studies. My intent is neither comprehensive coverage nor historical survey but to clarify how dark matter helps shape audience experience in different periods of theatrical history. As my subtitle emphasizes, dark matter obtains not just in scripted drama—which, when read privately, takes place *only* in the imagination—but in theater and performance more generally.[59]

Chapter 1 explores the supernatural—a ghostly realm that continually threatens to burst through into visibility—on the Elizabethan stage. Why did certain Elizabethans attending *Doctor Faustus* apparently hallucinate one devil too many and flee the playhouse as if their imaginations were too much for them? Approaching the play through J. L. Austin's speech-act theory, I trace black magic's unnerving performative potential. Stage conjuring models a performative speech act that threatens to blur the distinction between theater and magic. Far from dismissing black magic as charlatanism, *Doctor Faustus* equates conjuring with the dangerous verbal magic of performativity itself. The potential for *inadvertent* magic on the part of the players thrilled and alarmed spectators, causing them to "see" devils that were not literally there. *Doctor Faustus* at once enacts and critiques performative speech, challenging Austin's distinction between efficacious (successful) performatives and hollow (unsuccessful) theatrical quotations of them. Theater's ever-present potential to conjure something real out of thin air explains the play's hallucinatory power.

Chapter 2 investigates another important locus of dark matter on the Elizabethan stage: offstage sex. Taking Bottom's inscrutable sexuality as *A Midsummer Night's Dream*'s central riddle, I ask why the central sexual encounter between transmogrified weaver and fairy queen remains not only unstaged but *undecidable*. In the dream-logic of the mysterious wood, Shakespeare complements classical dramaturgy, whose offstage elements follow defined arcs in stage space and time, with what I call *quantum dramaturgy*, in which unobserved characters and events exist in various states of indeterminate probability held open by the text. Shakespeare's quantum mechanical lacks a definitive trajectory between (sexual) acts as he makes his cloudy, untraceable way through the wood. Poised between two dramaturgies, one of which obeys conventional rules of fictive space-time and the other of which confounds those very rules, Bottom's sexuality eludes definition.

Chapter 3 considers the ubiquitous mask adopted by both actresses and (female) spectators in the Restoration playhouse. In a theater that relentlessly commodified women as sexual objects, what were the risks and benefits of exposing the female body onstage? Aphra Behn's *The Rover,* perhaps the era's most popular comedy, presents the masked face as an object lesson in the difficulties of women's self-representation. Far from liberating its wearer, the mask distorts female identity and threatens women's autonomy. Behn's critique of the mask invites us to replace its flattening sexual signification with three-dimensional images of performing women who retain agency and individuality. Just as a spectroscope can determine the precise level of cosmic light deflection produced by an intervening mass of matter—whether dark or luminous—between us and some very distant object, Behn dramatizes the mask's signal distortions yet allows us to reconstruct the female presence behind it, bodying forth for the first time on the professional English stage.

Chapter 4 takes up a recurrent thread of dark matter: the central character that never appears onstage.[60] Tennessee Williams's *Suddenly Last Summer* textualizes its absent protagonist, the doomed and decadent poet Sebastian Venable, until we can no longer say for certain where the body ends and discourse begins. Not unlike Behn's masquerading heroines, Williams's characters move through a perilous transpersonal medium that could be termed (after Foucault) *power/sexuality.* Fantasizing a performativity that finally, ecstatically transcends the flesh, Williams's doomed protagonists are self-consuming artifacts whose performances use up their own bodies. Performance becomes a life-and-death strategy for arrogating, deflecting, and resisting power's depredations until the self is literally consumed. Each element of *Suddenly Last Summer* feeds off itself; cannibalistic performativity engulfs theatrical rhetoric. Williams writes a self-devouring play without a subject for an audience starved for realism yet excluded from its frame of representation.

Shifting the focus from offstage, masked, and absent bodies, Chapter 5 examines invisible technology. In Arthur Miller's *The Archbishop's Ceiling,* a listening device may or may not be concealed in the ceiling of a former archbishop's residence, now frequented by local and foreign writers in an Eastern European police state. Beneath a superficially conventional plot, which involves a dissident writer's choice between saving himself or his art, *The Archbishop's Ceiling* critiques linear dramaturgy in order to embrace nonlinear structure. Miller repudiates a dramatic form he had earlier championed and shifts from the use of theatrical devices that drive the plot forward to a single image, "the bugged ceiling of the mind," which transforms linear action into existential predicament.[61] Miller's increasingly sophisticated engagement with technology transforms linear drama into *prismatic drama*, which refracts rather than resolves a dramatic problem. Through its unsettling ability to double, fragment, and disperse the subject, modern technology challenges the very possibility of moral accountability that grounded Miller's former poetics. And if the protagonist's very self vanishes in *Suddenly Last Summer*, what seems at stake in *The Archbishop's Ceiling*—not unlike *Doctor Faustus*—is nothing less than the soul.

My final chapter considers how contemporary playwrights represent personal and collective traumas in the light of recent theorizing, which views trauma as thwarting narrative chronology, comprehension, and cure. Indeed, trauma haunts the contemporary stage less as a bounded event than as a toxic environment, perhaps the very air we breathe. The New Trauma playwrights—among them Suzan-Lori Parks, Adrienne Kennedy, Caryl Churchill, and Martin Crimp—depart from the standard model of theatrical trauma as the return of the repressed. Instead, they stage trauma's aftereffects as a psychic gap, rejecting psychological verisimilitude, linear plot, and Aristotelian catharsis alike. Skeptical of both dramatic closure and performative cure, the New Trauma playwrights forge new connections between trauma and theatricality. I conclude with performance artist and playwright Anna Deavere Smith's documentarian project to let America's trauma literally speak *through* her. By reproducing Smith's interview subjects' discourse with utter fidelity, including the gaps in language where trauma bleeds through the social performance of self, Smith's palimpsestic performances reclaim what Cathy Caruth terms "unclaimed experience" for the polis.[62]

Like those currently mapping dark matter in the skies, I have chosen magnification over panoramic coverage. These six studies uncover quite separate invisible worlds, over a fairly broad historical span, thereby suggesting the range of dark matter in postclassical Western theater without attempting an (impossible) overview. As astronomers have discovered, dark matter is lumpy and discontinuous rather than smooth and evenly spread out; I have found myself drawn to several of its densest theatrical concentrations, but many others await spectral investigation. While my chapters pursue a variety of approaches, my organizing question remains: How have playwrights in the postclassical Western tradition exploited dark matter as constitutive of theatrical performance? My focus is dramaturgical because playwrights are among our very best theorists of dark matter. Every playwright, whatever his or her chosen style or genre or agenda, must decide what to put onstage and what to leave out. Indeed, what playwrights choose not to show is as telling as their mise-en-scène.

Here one can draw a useful distinction between the *unrepresented* and the *invisible*. In *A Midsummer Night's Dream,* for instance, Hermia's mother is a blank; unlike dark matter, she is utterly absent from the play's imagined world and never registers on the audience. Conversely, the *Dream* revolves around a mysterious object of desire, the Indian boy who never appears onstage but bends the action around him. Moreover, Athens' fringes are haunted by unseen redoubts of female autonomy: the nunnery, Amazonia, and Lysander's aunt's house. Woven into the play's fabric, these negative spaces are, along with the Indian boy, dark matter. Spectral reading attends to such ghostly presences and asks what phenomenological work they do for the audience. As in the popular assignment in which art students are asked to draw the gaps between objects until those objects' outlines magically emerge, *Dark Matter* limns the transparent—but never empty—spaces that allow theater to materialize before our very eyes.

Continuing my theoretical investigation into the fundamental materials from which theater is built (begun in *The Stage Life of Props*), *Dark Matter* highlights the unseen as a crucial complement to theater's visible dimension. Like the material props considered in my earlier book, daggers of the mind cannot be reduced to rhetoric alone; their phenomenological effects, both within and beyond the world of the stage, are too multifarious for that. Godot is more than a mere sign.[63] Both visible and dark objects matter in performance, and they do so in ways that invite distinct ways of reading. In these pages theater of course remains the "seeing place" (*theatron*).[64] But it is also a place of not seeing, or rather not not seeing, as Oedipus's blindness, that quintessential theatrical emblem, reminds us. My hope is that by stimulating the imagination, this book will help the reader see theater in a new light—or even, perhaps, in the dark.

How to Do Things with Demons

Conjuring Performatives in
Doctor Faustus

'Tis magic, magic that hath ravished me.
—Faustus in *Doctor Faustus* (1.1.112)

I can't fix the roof by saying "I fix the roof" and I can't fry an
egg by saying "I fry an egg," but I can promise to come and
see you just by saying "I promise to come and see you" and
I can order you to leave the room just by saying "I order you
to leave the room." Now why the one and not the other?
—John R. Searle

What did it mean for an Elizabethan actor to perform black magic on
the early modern stage? When Edward Alleyn stepped onstage as Faustus,
dressed in a white surplice and cross and carrying his magical book, the
air was charged with dangerous electricity.[1] True, Alleyn was clearly an actor, reciting lines that had been set down for him in a play whose comic
scenes made light of the blasphemous act of conjuring demons. Noted
one skeptical witness at the Fortune, "A man may behold shagge-hayr'd
Devills runne roaring over the Stage with Squibs in their mouthes, while
Drummers make Thunder in the Tyring-house, and twelve-penny Hire-
lings make artificiall Lightning in their Heavens."[2] But once the magical
formula escaped Alleyn's lips, anything could happen—and apparently
did. Stories of "one devil too many" appearing onstage at performances
of *Faustus* became legendary.[3] Decades later the antitheatricalist William
Prynne relished

the visible apparition of the Devill on the stage at the Belsavage Play-house, in Queene Elizabeths dayes, (to the great amazement both of the Actors and Spectators) whiles they were there prophanely playing the History of Faustus (the truth of which I have heard from many now alive, who well remember it).[4]

As David Bevington comments, "The hope of such an event was possibly one fascination that drew audiences to the play, in somewhat the same fashion as spectators flock to the circus wondering if the high-wire artist will fall and be killed."[5]

If the infernal realm constitutes the dark matter of Renaissance con-juring plays, much of the fascination conjuring held for Elizabethan audiences can be traced to its unnerving performative potential. More precisely, in plays such as *Doctor Faustus*, conjuring models a performa-tive speech act that threatens to blur the distinction between theater and magic. Mirroring the ontological ambiguity of performance itself, conjur-ing is poised on the knife-edge between representing (*mimesis*) and doing (*kinesis*). How could spectators have been so convinced of the efficacy of Faustus's conjuring that they "really" saw dark matter—a case of involun-tary spectral reading?[6] My answer is that the play's power in performance relies on keeping the ontological stakes of black magic deliberately uncer-tain. Far from dismissing black magic as mere charlatanism, *Doctor Faus-tus* equates conjuring with the dangerous verbal magic of performativity itself. Faustus's spells enact theater's potential to escape from the character's (and actor's) control and unwittingly bring into being that which it names. *Faustus* traffics in performative magic not in the service of skepticism, as some critics have argued, but to appropriate speech's performative power on behalf of a glamorous commercial enterprise, the Elizabethan theater itself. It was precisely the potential for *inadvertent* magic on the part of the players—the belief that Faustus's spells might operate independent of actor and character—that thrilled and alarmed Elizabethan audiences, causing them to see devils that were not literally there.[7]

Doctor Faustus, especially in its A-text version, at once enacts and cri-tiques performative speech (much as *Hamlet* both enacts and critiques revenge tragedy). While my principal interest is in the phenomenology of Elizabethan stage conjuring, my interpretation of magical speech acts revisits the theoretical debate over the difference between performance and performativity. *Faustus* continually challenges J. L. Austin's distinction between "efficacious" (successful) performatives and "hollow" (unsuccessful) theatrical quotations of them. Austin's distinction breaks down whenever a speech act in the world of the play makes a material difference in the world of the playhouse. But what constitutes a "material difference"? As my epigraph from John Searle suggests, performativity's transformative magic lies less in measurable changes in objective states of affairs (an actor cannot build a bridge by saying "I build a bridge") than in its phenomenological effects (an actor might blaspheme by blaspheming, just as he might laugh by laughing or eat by eating).[8] Stage conjuring enacts the slipperiness of performativity itself.

Black Magic and the Riddle of Performativity

Necromancy held an ambiguous space in the Elizabethan imagination.[9] At a time when Queen Elizabeth consulted her own court astrologer, John Dee, Elizabethan thinkers continually probed the crucial yet blurry distinction between white and black magic.[10] When did an Elizabethan scholar pass from a quasi-respectable scientific investigation into the occult arts (such as astrology) to damnable practices? According to Marlowe biographer David Riggs:

> The passage from this so-called "natural" magic to idolatrous or "black" magic occurred when the practitioner employed talismans, symbolic utterances or ritual practices in order to operate a demon (spirit, intelligence or demi-god) that embodied an occult force. The boundary was imprecise, but somewhere along this spectrum the "white" magician became an idolater practicing a pagan religion.[11]

Public interest in magic may have peaked during the mid-1580s, just before the time when *The Tragical History of Doctor Faustus* staged the by then notorious story of German magician Johann Faustus, who trafficked with the devil. The play dramatizes how Faustus's thirst for occult knowledge, whetted by humanist skepticism of traditional sources of authority, tempts him into the practice of black magic—precisely the slippery slope that vexed Marlowe's contemporaries.

What characterized the extraordinary "symbolic utterances" that constituted black magic, at least in the Elizabethan popular imagination? Any utterance that conjured a demon into the corporeal presence of the utterer and, thereafter, forced the demon to obey the conjuror's instructions obviously counted as magical. These utterances were *imperatives*—a demon could not refuse the injunction to appear. Another salient characteristic of magical utterances was that they were formulaic. No conjurer could bring a demon running through improvisation; magic did not work that way. In order to be efficacious, then, a spell had to be *citational*. Conjuring was in essence a literary endeavor for literates only; Riggs indicates that "English scholars learned how to operate demons from Continental books on magic, from John Dee's *Preparatory Teachings* and *Hieroglyphic Monad* and from the works of the Italian Immigrant Giordano Bruno, especially his *Expulsion of the Triumphant Beast*."[12] Indeed, the title page of the 1616 edition of *Doctor Faustus* (reprinted in 1619) shows the magician standing in a circle marked by hieroglyphs, book in one hand and magic staff in the other, conjuring a grotesque demon, which squats just beyond the limits of the circle (fig. 1). Last, the magical utterance was *autonomous*. For Elizabethans the power to conjure inhered in the utterance itself—what Riggs calls its "occult force"—rather than in the will or intention of the speaker. Magic spells were perlocutions (the performance of an act *by* saying something) rather than illocutions (the performance of an act *in* saying something). From this perspective, the utterance constructs the speaking subject *as* conjuror; the spell makes the magus, rather than vice versa. Bang your thumb with a hammer and mutter an ill-advised curse and you just might have a demon on your hands.[13]

Imperative, citational, and autonomous, Elizabethan conjurations belong to that class of speech acts first defined by Austin in his 1955 William James lectures at Harvard, later published as *How to Do Things with Words*. Austin distinguishes between constative utterances, which describe an already existing state of affairs ("the cat is on the mat"), and performative utterances, which bring into being the act that they name. Austin's examples of performatives include "I name this ship the *Queen Elizabeth*," "I bet you sixpence it will rain tomorrow," and the marital "I do."[14] Austin clarifies:

> In these examples it seems clear that to utter the sentence (in, of course, the appropriate circumstances) is not to *describe* my doing of what I should be said in so uttering to be doing or to state that I am doing it: it is to do it . . . When I say, before the registrar or altar, &c., "I do," I am not reporting on a marriage: I am indulging in it.[15]

Figure 1. Faustus conjures a demon. (Woodcut from the title page of the B-text 1619 quarto.)

Performativity, then, is a kind of magical altering of reality through the power of the word, one that channels what might well be called an occult force. It follows for Austin that performatives, unlike constatives, cannot be true or false statements; rather, they are either "efficacious" or "inefficacious." In the latter case, "the utterance is then, we may say, not indeed false but in general *unhappy*."[16] One way in which a performative can turn awry is to be merely theatrical. Austin notes that

a performative utterance will, for example, be *in a peculiar way* hollow or void if said by an actor on the stage, or if introduced in a poem, or spoken in soliloquy . . . Language in such circumstances is in special ways—intelligibly—used not seriously, but in ways *parasitic* upon its normal use—ways which fall under the doctrine of the *etiolations* of language.[17]

A marriage ceremony that takes place within a play, even one that uses the exactly prescribed formula, will not conjure a marriage between actors into being.[18]

If, for Austin, those performatives sabotaged by the conditions of their utterance (such as being spoken onstage) are exceptions to normal speech acts, for Derrida the possibility of infelicity is built into the material structure of language, since to be recognizable *as* language, any utterance must be in some sense a quotation.[19] If so, to performatize successfully is always to cite an accepted formula ("I bet," "I promise"). For Derrida all performative utterances are therefore "in some peculiar way" parasitic—perhaps not unlike the way theatrical performatives onstage ("I do") are parasitic on nontheatrical ones, or the way Elizabethan charlatans cited legitimate magical formulae in their hocus-pocus.

The problem deepens once performativity is understood to stretch beyond parasitic discursive practices and colonize human experience. In Judith Butler's influential extension of Austin's term, the citational aspect of performativity acquires the sinister connotation of a ruse practiced on subjectivity itself. For Butler performativity is the mechanism by which we accept the fiction that we, as individuals, precede the discursive acts that conjure us into being as subjects. Gender, Butler's exemplary instance of performativity as ruse, is "a stylized repetition of acts" that creates the illusion of a continuous self that precedes those acts: "Gender reality is performative, which means, quite simply, that it is real only to the extent that it is performed."[20] If all performative utterance threatens to collapse into hollow quotation, human behavior *tout court* may be a species of performativity, a demonic conjuring trick.

What, then, distinguishes theatrical performance from compulsory performativity? Refuting those who took her earlier characterization of transvestite drag as evidence that one can pick and choose one's gender performances, Butler rejects the equation of performance and performativity, since the former implies a performer that ontologically precedes and then fabricates his or her gender effects.

[P]erformance as bounded "act" is distinguished from performativity insofar as the latter consists in a reiteration of norms which precede, constrain, and exceed the performer and in that sense cannot be taken as the performer's will or "choice"; further what is performed [performatized?] works to conceal, if not to disavow, what remains opaque, unconscious, unperformable. The reduction of performativity to performance would be a mistake.[21]

Once again we are perplexed. Theater harnesses performativity as its basic mechanism: *all* dramatic characters are performative in Butler's sense—for what is a character if not a series of speech acts, materialized by an actor's body and voice, masquerading as an essence that precedes their materialization?[22] And if no autonomous agent precedes performative acts, by Butler's own logic, performance *cannot* be a bounded act "freely" chosen.[23] The riddle of performativity and its relation to theatrical performance persists; attempting to diagram their relationship, we are confounded.[24] If Austin casts hollow, theatrical performance outside the magic circle of efficacious performatives, Derrida erases the Austinian circle by viewing *all* efficacious utterances as similarly parasitic. And if Butler in turn banishes "voluntarist" theatrical performance outside the magic circle of performativity, performance scuttles back into the performative circle once one realizes that no freely chosen, bounded acts are in fact possible. Performance untainted by performativity seems a chimera, as is performativity untainted by performance.

Performing Ontological Uncertainty

A cognate riddle faced early modern theorists of performance. In the early decades of the professional London playhouses, commentators struggled to develop a vocabulary to describe what they thought actors actually did onstage. Terms ranged from the sometimes derogatory *play* to *enact, present, represent,* and the somewhat later term *personate.*[25] Defenders and critics agreed that the actor possessed a powerful charisma, together with the uncanny ability to blur the boundary between seeming and being—at least in the spectator's imagination. Thus the author of "An Excellent Actor" (probably John Webster describing Richard Burbage in 1614–15) marveled that "by a full and significant action of body [the actor] charmes our attention: sit in a full Theater, and you will thinke you see so many lines drawne from the circumference of so many eares, whiles the *Actor* is the *Center. . .* for what we see him personate, we think truely done before us."[26] A charismatic actor like Burbage or Alleyn evidently played at the edge of *mimesis.*

As Mary Thomas Crane has shown, the ambiguity inherent in the early modern usage of the word *perform* captures the confusion between performance and performativity that has vexed recent theorists, for "the very concept of performance was, itself, both contested and in flux."[27] In her survey of the word's various uses in the period, Crane observes that "'Perform' in this period had the primary meaning 'to carry through to completion; to complete, finish, perfect.'"[28] One could "perform" a door. According to the *Oxford English Dictionary*, the first use of *perform* to mean "to act, play (a part or character)" appears in *The Tempest* (ca. 1611), but Crane argues that Ariel "performs" the tempest and harpy in the sense of *executing* rather than *representing* them. And because plays were seen as "material practices that could effect real change in the world," we distort Elizabethan drama by supposing that its consumers necessarily equated theatrical representation with fraudulent imitation: "[E]arly modern conceptions of performance include embodied, non-representational aspects of drama as well as its implication in discursive systems."[29] The Chorus's promise that the players will "perform" Faustus's story implies, then, not only representing the story but *conjuring it into being* (Prologue l.6). Thus "'Perform' in all its early modern senses already incorporates a concept of performativity, in that it involves turning something immaterial (a duty, a promise, a contract, the pattern of a ceremony) into a material thing."[30]

Confirming Crane's sense of a "true uncertainty about the ontological status of performance" in the period, Faustus himself confuses the two meanings of *perform*.[31] After the visitation by the good and bad angels, Faustus commences a reverie of power set in the future tense, in which *perform* takes on the sense of to complete, rather than feign, an action: "Shall I make spirits fetch me what I please, / Resolve me of all ambiguities, / Perform what desperate enterprise I will?" (1.1.81–83). Faustus imagines the spirits "performing" not theatrical impersonation but material stuff: gold, pearl, fruits, delicacies. Lost in his Epicure Mammonish fantasies, Faustus summons his fellow scholars: "Come, German Valdes and Cornelius, / And make me blest with your sage conference!" (1.1.100–101). And yet it remains uncertain whether performed magic can offer anything more than appearances: "The miracles that magic will perform / Will make you vow to study nothing else," promises Cornelius (1.1.138–39). Faustus himself seems uncertain about whether he craves the show of magic or the real thing: "Come, show me some demonstrations magical, / That I may conjure in some lusty grove / And have these joys in full possession" (1.1.152–54). A "demonstration" is at once a proof, something material and incontrovertible, and an exhibition or display—just theater.

Elizabethans had another term for what I am calling the riddle of performativity, whereby some utterances are both constative and performative, both *mimesis* and *kinesis*, both willed and autonomous, both "peculiarly hollow" theater and dangerously efficacious. That term is *conjure*, and it makes its first appearance in *Faustus* in the passage just quoted. While for a modern audience *conjuring* connotes prestidigitation, Philip Butterworth reminds us that the common Elizabethan terms used to denote deceptive tricks used for entertainment or criminal purposes (sometimes both) were *tregetry*, *legerdemaine*, *prestigiation*, *juggling* or *jugglery*, *feats*, *feats of activity*, and *sleight of hand*. According to Butterworth, "The most consistently used words to describe the production of magic [tricks] throughout this period are *juggler* (for the exponent) and *juggling* (for the activity)," and so these are the terms adopted by Butterworth throughout his study, which does not deal with witchcraft at all.[32] Conversely, "*Conjuring*, as a term employed to describe the act of performing magical tricks, was not used in its current sense in England until the nineteenth century. The words *conjuration*, *conjure*, *conjurer* and *conjury* first come into use with related meaning in the eighteenth and nineteenth centuries."[33]

In Elizabethan England, to conjure meant both to "[c]all upon solemnly, adjure" and to "[c]all upon, constrain (a devil or spirit) to appear or do one's bidding by incantation or the use of some spell, raise or bring into existence as by magic."[34] Like performing itself, conjuring was a Janusfaced endeavor whose ontological stakes were uncertain. When, for example, in *Othello* Emilia informs us that Othello "conjured" Desdemona that she should guard the handkerchief he gave her, we cannot be sure whether the Moor has actually practiced the witchcraft of which Brabantio accused him in act 1 or has merely admonished his wife not to lose a favorite trinket. In a famous crux, the napkin is variously a magical charm given by Othello's mother to his father (3.3.294) and an "antique token" given by Othello's father to his mother (5.2.216).[35] On the Elizabethan stage, the word *conjure* always carries a whiff of danger about it, for to adjure something—to address or call on it solemnly—is to risk calling that thing into existence, just as to perform any act onstage—a laugh, a belch, a curse, a consecration—is to risk actually doing it. In a still widely illiterate culture whose oaths and promises (such as betrothal *de praesenti*) were considered legally binding, and where exorcisms were practiced by both Roman Catholic priests and Puritan exorcists, Elizabethans were keenly aware that words bore perlocutionary powers beyond the illocutionary intent of the speaker, and that they potentially unleashed the occult force Riggs identifies with magical conjuration. It was left to Marlowe and his contemporaries to appropriate that force on behalf of a newly invigorated professional theater, which, although censored by the Master of the Revels, found itself freed from the orderly bureaucratic surveillance of a clerical hierarchy.

Unstable Magic, Unwitting Performatives

Nowhere on the Elizabethan stage is the tension between conjuring as hocus-pocus and conjuring as black magic—or, as speech-act theory recasts the distinction, between hollow performance and efficacious performativity—explored more searchingly than in *Doctor Faustus*. The play considers whether a difference obtains between performing as feigning and performing as doing, precisely the distinction theater seems uncannily able to blur. Conjuring is the crux of that meditation, and of the play's double perspective on magic. In its contrast between Faustus's sometimes terrifying spells and his jejune parlor tricks—not to mention the inane antics of its clowns—*Doctor Faustus* debases magic even as it celebrates theater's power to conjure something from nothing. *Faustus* intimates that perlocutionary force might at any moment exceed or thwart the intentions of the speaker, as language takes on a devilish life of its own.

Doubleness of vision colors almost every aspect of *Doctor Faustus*. The play exists in two versions, the so-called A-text of 1604 and the B-text of 1616, which adds some 676 new lines and cuts 36 while introducing thousands of variations. Both editions were published quite some time after the play was written (*ca.* 1589–90). Each printed version reveals the hand of Marlowe and at least one other author, with the earlier text probably prepared from Marlowe's manuscripts and including comic scenes interpolated by a collaborator, and the later text incorporating additions by Samuel Rowley and William Birde, commissioned by Philip Henslowe in 1602, as well as other possible accretions.[36] Both versions lurch between comedy and tragedy, with the B-text's additions accentuating slapstick, theatricality, and Protestant nationalism at the price of diluting the A-text's focus on Faustus's psychology.[37] As literary documents, each surviving text of *Faustus* may conceivably present a coherent ideological position on necromancy (although how and why such an agenda might have been coordinated between two or more commercially motivated artistic collaborators remains problematic). But as an evolving theatrical event, the play invited interpretation by Elizabethan spectators who brought to bear a variety of belief systems, attitudes toward magic, and levels of theatrical sophistication, much as it continues to invite reinterpretation in our own day with each new production.[38] What some textual critics identify as a stable, authorial position on magic becomes a more open question in performance, especially given the palimpsestic, collaborative nature of this play (or plays).

Given this fundamental instability, it is not my intention to summarize once more the critical debate over Marlowe's, or the play's, theological orthodoxy.[39] As Gareth Roberts persuasively argues, no coherent theory of magic lies behind the play, just as no "authentic" ur-text lurks behind the A- and B-texts: "*Doctor Faustus* may rather be seen as the site of the interplay of different and sometimes competing, contestatory and contradictory perceptions of magic, which may also be perceived in the early modern world outside the play."[40] To illustrate his emphasis on plural understandings of magic in the period, Roberts ingeniously imagines three very different spectators, each representing one of three circulating discourses about magic: Samuel, a countryman whose London friends take him to the playhouse; Orthodoxus, a Cambridge graduate interested in demonological works; and Master Lordinge, a conjurer influenced by the noted magician Cornelius Agrippa.[41] Each views the magic differently, because "Robin and Wagner's popular beliefs coexist in the same play(s) as Faustus' initial high magic confidence in the power of words and Mephistophilis' [*sic*] impeccable exposition of [orthodox] demonological theory which declares that confidence empty." Roberts's helpful insistence on the "heteroglossic plurality of magical belief and opinion in *Doctor Faustus*" invites us to accept those inconsistencies between and within the A- and B-texts that scholar-editors have tried to reconcile or clarify.[42]

Diverging from Roberts's conclusions, Daniel Gates likens magical utterances in *Faustus* to failed performatives. Gates begins by acknowledging the immense power ritual utterances held in early modern Europe and compares Faustus to the real-life case of Francesco Spiera, an Italian Protestant compelled to abjure his faith by the Roman Inquisition. Spiera subsequently felt himself damned by his insincere recantation. Because in the popular imagination Spiera was damned by an utterance ironically performative in spite of itself, his case epitomizes "the unpredictable consequences of complex speech acts and the inevitable uncertainty regarding their authenticity."[43] By contrast Gates views *Faustus* as a Protestant debunking of the terrifying power of magic in general and of performative language in particular: "Marlowe's version of the case of Faustus seems to present in the demonic pact a speech act of seemingly ultimate power while it also challenges its audience's faith in magically powerful utterances."[44] By portraying Faustus as a credulous believer in supernatural language, "Marlowe's play illustrates the impotence of necromantic spells, mocking by implication the potential theatricality of such orthodox institutions as divinity and law."[45]

But if *Faustus* acknowledges that institutions such as divinity and law depend on social power for their performative efficacy, why should the commercial theater not then arrogate such magical power for its own uses—in much the same way as it appropriated (and literally purchased) the formerly talismanic props and vestments of the church?[46] I have argued elsewhere that critics who view the London playwrights of the 1580s and 1590s as modeling a skeptical, Protestant gaze misunderstand the commercial pressures on and opportunity for those playwrights to fill the imaginative void left in the wake of the suppression of the mystery plays and the Old Religion.[47] If magic is, ultimately, a *phenomenological* practice—the art of changing consciousness at will, that is, of persuading others to accept one's version of reality by renaming it (as when a green piece of paper *is* rather than symbolizes twenty dollars)—then theater's power to affect audiences, for example, by making them "see" immaterial spirits, suggests that it deserves a place alongside divinity and law as a site of performative efficacy. After all, the fact that the law takes its authority from self-citation does not make it a fiction; nor does the fact that the US tax system requires enforcement by the Internal Revenue Service render it a hoax. *Any* successful performative requires social consensus, by any other name a credulous audience. A private performative would be pointless; I cannot knight myself, or give myself a doctorate. Even Gates, who believes that *Faustus'* spells "only" gain (social) power through belief, concedes "the uncanny power of performative language," the magic in the web of *Faustus*.[48]

Gates argues that Marlowe's iconoclastic vision demystifies the idea that words have intrinsic magical power. Instead, "the force of the successful performative speech act is created through belief" and guaranteed, if need be, through coercive violence.[49] Yet, from a phenomenological perspective, it is precisely contagious belief that constitutes theatrical magic. Indeed, the two are quite possibly synonymous, as Shakespeare hints in *Othello*—a profound meditation on the deadly performative effects of beliefs that, from a constative perspective, are patently false. In terms of the tragic plot, it does not matter whether or not Desdemona is *truly* unfaithful, just as it makes no difference whether the handkerchief is *truly* magical (it produces panic in Desdemona whether or not Othello believes his own "magic in the web" speech). Once aroused, Othello's jealousy becomes both self-perpetuating and deadly, and Desdemona's guilt performative situation rather than constative fact. Othello's jealousy mirrors the way magic works to alter consciousness at will; in fact the mechanism is identical.[50] The point is not that magic is fraudulent but that its effects, once unleashed, are dangerously out of control, as when the Exeter *Faustus* players' panic spread to the audience. Misreading a performative situation as a constative statement is a category mistake.[51]

We mischaracterize *Doctor Faustus*, then, if we view it as a play confidently in charge of its own performative effects on an audience or as staking the claim that necromancy is pure illusion. Rather, *Faustus* unleashes the energies of conjuring precisely by blurring the boundary between representing magic and performing it. Although its devils labor to equate magic with theater so as to distract Faustus from his self-damnation, the play never closes the door on the performative threat. Just as we can never be sure whether Faustus is or is not damned before the story begins to unfold, so we cannot be sure whether Faustus is a real magician, a credulous victim of his own megalomania, or a man whose words have the magical power not to summon demons from hell but only to damn himself. This ambiguity recurs on the level of theatrical representation. Alleyn's conjuring of Faustus for contemporary audiences was at once an impersonation (an actor's trick) and a *personation* (a literal making of a fictional or legendary character into a person).[52] The play's charm depends on its keeping the ontological stakes of demonic conjuring uncertain and its audience off balance.

Flirting with Periperformatives

Once we acknowledge that the play does not prejudge the efficacy of Faustus's black magic, how might the play have walked that knife-edge between *mimesis* and *kinesis* in performance? When Faustus enters his "solitary grove" to conjure Mephistopheles for the first time, he casts his magic circle and vows to "try the uttermost magic can perform" (1.3.15). As Crane reminds us, *perform* for an Elizabethan audience would likely signify an activity closer to performativity than theatrical performance.[53] Faustus utters a Latin incantation, sprinkles holy water, and makes a sign of the cross to conjure a hideous Mephistopheles. He then issues an explicit performative: "I charge thee to return and change thy shape. / Thou art too ugly to attend on me" (1.3.24–25). When Mephistopheles exits to the tiring-house in order to don the robe of a Franciscan friar, Faustus congratulates himself on a job well done in lines laced with unwitting irony: "I see there's virtue in my heavenly words . . . Such is the force of magic and my spells. / Now, Faustus, thou art conjurer laureate" (1.3.28–33).

Yet Faustus's speech act is more complex than Faustus himself grasps, for Mephistopheles claims to have materialized of his own free will.

MEPH: I am a servant to great Lucifer
    And may not follow thee without his leave.
    No more than he commands must we perform.
FAUSTUS: Did not he charge thee to appear to me?
MEPH: No, I came hither of mine own accord.
FAUSTUS: Did not my conjuring speeches raise thee? Speak.
MEPH: That was the cause, but yet *per accidens* [incidental]. (1.3.40–46)

The logic here is complex and contradictory.[54] Mephistopheles seems to be saying that Faustus's conjuring is theatrically hollow in Austin's sense yet somehow efficacious despite itself. On the one hand, the disingenuous Mephistopheles may have had no choice but to appear once the magical formula was uttered. This would seem to accord with widespread popular beliefs regarding the magical efficacy of spells (and with the clowns' later conjuring of an irate Mephistopheles in 3.2). On the other hand, Mephistopheles tells us he appears *per accidens,* which would seem to confirm the suspicion of magical language voiced by those late-sixteenth-century demonologists for whom blasphemy, not words, conjures the devil. On the third hand, it is Lucifer's "occult force," *speaking through* Faustus's utterance, that conjures Mephistopheles, the latter's free will paradoxically circumscribed by Lucifer's ur-performative.[55] *Something* has conjured Mephistopheles onstage, but it is very difficult to locate any agent behind the act other than the playwright's dialogue.

Stretched on the dilemma of horns, Mephistopheles underscores the volatility of conjuring for early modern audiences. Faustus's summoning of a demon may be the triumphant performative of which he boasts, or it may be just a stage cue, with Lucifer as the (perhaps visible) prompter. Yet Faustus's conjuring is no failed performative in Austin's sense; rather, its ambiguous occult force exceeds the conjurer's will. For in Mephistopheles' explanation, it is Faustus's blasphemous, or near blasphemous, language that summons the demon, a threat Mephistopheles turns on the audience.

> For when we hear one rack the name of God,
> Abjure the Scriptures and his Savior Christ,
> We fly in hope to get his glorious soul,
> Nor will we come unless he use such means
> Whereby he is in danger to be damned.
> Therefore, the shortest cut for conjuring
> Is stoutly to abjure the Trinity
> And pray devoutly to the prince of hell. (1.3.51–55)

Whether or not the A-text sides with the skeptics who believe that words alone lack the power to conjure demons, Mephistopheles insists that in efficacious performative speech acts—magic by any other name—perlocution trumps illocution. While Faustus's conjuring words are necessary for *something* to happen, the utterer does not control what that something is. If we trust Mephistopheles, the speech act that truly lures the demon is the theological one we can never be sure Faustus actually utters—the one that incontrovertibly damns his soul to hell.[56]

Marlowe thus creates dramatic suspense in the minds of his audience. Will Faustus utter the damning words? Has he already? And if Alleyn the actor utters blasphemy, might he not damn himself *merely by quoting Marlowe's notorious dialogue?* Instead of a conclusive performative, *Faustus* teases us with a series of what Eve Kosofsky Sedgwick usefully calls "periperformatives." These are utterances that "*allude* to explicit performative utterances" without actually being them.[57] *Doctor Faustus* is shot through with such periperformatives, as in this passage.

> FAUSTUS: Seeing Faustus *hath incurred* eternal death
> By desp'rate thoughts against Jove's deity,
> Say *he surrenders up to him his soul,*
> So *he will spare him* four-and-twenty years,
> Letting him live in all voluptuousness,
> Having thee ever to attend on me,

To give me whatsoever I shall ask,
To tell me whatsoever I demand,
To slay mine enemies and aid my friends,
And *always be obedient to my will.* (1.3.90–99, emphasis added)

Faustus's speech casts the damning bond as either in the past or in the con-
ditional future, rather than in the first-person present indicative. Because
Faustus is always about to utter the decisive formula but seemingly never
quite does so, despite the apparent performative "Ay, Mephistopheles, I
give it [my soul] thee" (2.1.48)—or else why repeat the action of signing
his name in blood?—the devils have a problem.[58] Should Faustus decide
to repent at the last minute, they will have wasted twenty-four years of
servitude. Thus the devils repeatedly use magic as a *theatrical* distraction
to take Faustus's mind off his impending damnation—staging the masque
of the seven deadly sins, for example, and exhibiting "*a devil dressed like a
woman, with fireworks,*" as Faustus's wife (2.1.149 s.d.).[59]

For the bulk of the play, then, the devils equate magic with theatrical
entertainment and conjuring with jugglery. They are able to do this in part
because Faustus is such an unimaginative man (why demand a wife when
you can conjure a harem?) and keeps confusing devils with the characters
they impersonate. By the middle of the play, Faustus's thirst for absolute
power and knowledge of occult mysteries has dwindled into magical tourism (he visits Rome) and the performance of conjuring tricks designed to
pander to an anti-Catholic audience, such as turning invisible in order
to box the pope on the ear. Having once dreamed of becoming "great
emperor of the world" (1.3.106), Faustus finds himself employed as the
emperor's court magician, using a roster of conjuring tricks to curry favor
with the powerful—in short, like his creator(s), devising theatrical entertainments to please moneyed patrons with a short attention span.

Especially in its slapstick scenes, the A-text repeatedly demystifies acts
of magic as conjuring tricks (for instance, the horse-courser's new horse
dissolves into hay when wet) even while reminding us that Faustus is always on the brink of damning himself in language. Demons pop up on the
stage with unsettling regularity, sometimes conjured by elaborate ritual,
other times when they feel like it, confounding Faustus's delusions of lin-
guistic control. The increasing banality of his magic acts (such as fetching
grapes for the pregnant duchess of Vanholt in 4.2) has been maligned by
critics and scholars as an etiolation of the play's dramatic power and/or as
the mark of Marlowe's inferior collaborator. Yet the irony here is not that

magic is always and only theater but that Faustus himself cannot tell the difference. He continually settles for theatrical performance because he confuses representation with reality: watching demonic actors impersonate Alexander and his paramour or kissing a (male?) succubus disguised as Helen of Troy instead of the real Helen (trickier to engineer and possibly less enjoyable). Yet the play warns us against the very trivialization of magic in which it traffics. We are aware that the clock is running out on Faustus's life and that he is frittering it away on what the antitheatricalists called "vain shewes."

The play's debasement of Faustus's necromancy can be linked to an implicit contrast between the *imagined* potency of black magic and the *actual* potency of performative speech acts—which, in the wrong mouths, possess a dangerous, real-life magic of their own. Consistently staging the ability of unwitting performative speech acts to hijack mere word-games— with self-damnation as the ultimate speech act of Damocles hovering over the protagonist (or is it just a speech act of the mind?)—*Doctor Faustus* undoes Austin's equation of theatrical representation and hollow performativity. And whereas Gates emphasizes "the uncanny ability of a failed performative to exceed or thwart the intentions of its speaker," *Faustus* dramatizes unwittingly *successful* performatives' ability to do this as well.[60]

In this vein, act 3, scene 2, begins with the two comic stableboys, Robin and Rafe, entering with a conjuring book they have stolen from Faustus.[61] "Ecce signum!" Robin crows semiblasphemously, holding the book aloft as he fantasizes using magic to fill his belly. But the two clowns are interrupted by a vintner who pursues them concerning a stolen goblet. After some horseplay with the goblet, Robin attempts to distract the vintner with some hocus-pocus, reading the book's Latin gibberish. Suddenly Mephistopheles appears, spouting not fire but indignant blank verse. Far from coming of his own accord, as he asserted earlier, Mephistopheles finds himself inconveniently conjured from Constantinople by a performative that, like Spiera's false recantation, is efficacious despite the intentions of its speaker. Arrogantly taking charge, Robin treats Mephistopheles like a hireling: "Will you take sixpence in your purse to pay for your supper and be gone?" Mephistopheles responds with some stagey magic of his own: "Well, villains, for your presumption I transform thee [to Robin] into an ape, and thee [to Rafe] into a dog. And so, begone!" (3.2.38–40).[62] The debased conjuring of the clowns—the gibberish that works in spite of itself—is answered by the revenge-magic of the demon, which is itself a piece of harmless theater.

That the clowns' conjuring works at least as well as Faustus's, and for such debased ends, implies that the play views performative speech acts and black magic as equivalent conjurings. Flirting with perlocutionary efficacy through its deft deployment of periperformatives, the play makes it very difficult to say where performative speech ends and real magic begins. Intriguingly, Faustus tends to speak in imperatives rather than in what Sedgwick labels "explicit performative utterances," which for Austin are "exemplified in a cluster of sentences in the first-person singular present indicative active."[63] By contrast the Good and Bad Angels tend to speak in what I would call "hollow imperatives," which tempt Faustus to the sin of pride: "Be thou on earth as Jove is in the sky" (1.1.78). Periperformatives proliferate as if to establish that the imperative stage cue—which Austin might consider as theatrically hollow—is no less magical than the conjuring of a demon (who is himself, of course, an actor responding to a stage cue).[64]

As parodies of black magic, both imperative address and stage cue appropriate performative power for the theater. The first two scenes of the A-text, which precede the famous conjuring scene, *already* present theater as having the power to conjure through words—although the dramatic characters seem unaware of the fact. Before the A-text introduces black magic, the Chorus alerts the audience that the power of words to conjure reality into being is at stake: "Only this, gentlemen: we must *perform* / The form of Faustus' fortunes, good or bad" (Prologue 7–8, emphasis added). The uncertainty over whether to "perform" is to impersonate or actually effect material change continues once the Chorus reveals—or, in effect, produces—Faustus, possibly by drawing aside the discovery-space curtain to reveal the magician in his study. Faustus speaks of himself in the third-person imperative, a speech act whose verbs at once command, describe, and enact themselves.

> *Settle* thy studies, Faustus, and *begin*
> *To sound* the depth of that thou wilt profess.
> Having commenced, *be a divine* in show,
> Yet *level* at the end of every art,
> And *live and die* in Aristotle's works. (1.1.1–5, emphasis added)

Here the imperative form of address becomes a mode of magical self-fashioning. Faustus conjures himself into being through actions made material through words alone.

Ironically, in summoning his servant Faustus demonstrates himself able to conjure beings onto the stage *without* the help of black magic: "Wagner!" (1.1.66). The imperative stage cue, akin to alchemy in Jonson's *The Alchemist* or to Prospero's magic in *The Tempest,* emblematizes theater's own powers of conjuration, its ability to do things with words. Wagner is at once an impersonated being (like the gods and goddesses in Prospero's masque) and the flesh-and-blood actor (or "spirit") who embodies him. Wagner is "performed" in both of Crane's senses and, like a devil, is materialized by a performative speech act. This point is reiterated when in act 1, scene 4, Wagner conjures Balioll and Belcher without the benefit of magic incantation but simply by using their names (1.4.45). As Butler avers, naming is always a kind of magic, whether in or out of the theater: "[T]o be addressed is not merely to be recognized for what one already is, but to have the very term conferred by which the recognition of existence becomes possible."[65]

Conclusion: *Playing With Words*

By proposing the stage cue and imperative address as verbal conjurings analogous to black magic, *Doctor Faustus* refuses to side with its own devils and reduce magic to (fraudulent) theater. Indeed, the play insists that the stakes behind Faustus's quasi-blasphemous speeches are not only ontological but eschatological. At issue in the play is not just the status of speech acts but a far more pressing question for an Elizabethan audience: the state of Faustus's soul. Faustus inhabits what seems to be a Calvinist universe, in which, according to the doctrine of election, some souls are predestined for salvation and others for damnation.[66] From this perspective, the play dramatizes the cruel paradox of *God's* performative. If Faustus is reprobate—if he *cannot* repent, as he keeps telling us, even at the moment he sees Christ's blood stream in the firmament—then is he not Prometheus rather than Icarus? The prologue announces that "the heavens *conspired* his overthrow" (my italics), a word that implies that Faustus's free will may be illusory. Reading aloud from Jerome's Bible in act 1, scene 1, Faustus is unwilling or unable to complete the quotations from Romans 6 and I John 1 that disillusion him against divinity, when doing so could have reassured him that Christ stands ready to forgive sin. That his eyes are blinded suggests that Faustus may be a Calvinist reprobate helpless to alter his fate. In a Calvinist universe, salvation or damnation seems not to depend on our choice of good or evil acts—acts that may confirm our reprobate or elect status respectively—but on the occult force of a divine performative that calls us into being through a series of acts that only *appear* to issue from our own wills.

If Butler is correct, performativity is no mere curiosity, a peculiar accident of language (like rhyme). It is the very mechanism whereby we accept the fiction that we precede the discursive acts that retrospectively conjure us into being as subjects. *Doctor Faustus* is cunningly constructed so that we can never say for sure at any given moment that Faustus is or is not damned. It may be that Faustus suffers less from the fear of Hell ("I think hell's a fable" [2.1.127]) than from the aporia of Augustine's supposed dictum, as recalled by Samuel Beckett: "Do not despair, one of the thieves was saved; do not presume, one of the thieves was damned."[67] Stretched on the rack of uncertainty, Faustus seems determined to settle the question once and for all by having intercourse with a succubus in the guise of Helen of Troy and repeatedly swearing allegiance to Lucifer and renouncing Christ. As a reiterated series of periperformative speech acts, Faustus's damnation hovers between the constative and the performative: "My heart's so hardened I cannot repent" (2.3.18). Watching the play, we cannot tell whether the dialogue is *describing* a damned soul or forcibly *producing* one.[68]

In its ambiguity regarding Faustus's damnation, as elsewhere, *Doctor Faustus* probes the uncertain boundary between hollow performance and magical performativity. Such probing occurs in both tragic and comic modes, and from multiple perspectives that are not easily reconciled either between or within printed versions. I do not deny the inevitable presence of skeptics in Marlowe's audience; Elizabethans were fully aware that "inchanting words" were used as distracting patter by con-artists posing as masters of the black arts.[69] But Elizabethan drama appears to have been caught between the urge to demystify black magic on the one hand—the ignorant horse-courser calls Mephistopheles "hey-pass" (4.1.143)—and to appropriate its vocabulary and spectacle for theatrical ends on the other (a tug-of-war later dramatized in *The Tempest*'s dialogue with *The Alchemist*).

Doctor Faustus critiques the presumption of *mimesis*—the notion that the theatrical is automatically parasitic on reality—just as the Elizabethan words for dramatic exhibition (*exercise, play, enact, act, present, personate*) hover between doing and feigning. Theater's imitations arouse genuine emotions in an audience (terror, jealousy, rage, erotic desire), rendering theater disturbing and appealing at the same time. According to Gates,

"*Doctor Faustus* reveals the words of necromancy not to have power in themselves, but only in their persuasive effect on an audience."[70] But, as Susanne L. Wofford observes in her penetrating essay on performative language in *As You Like It,* at stake in staged performative speech acts is, precisely, the power of theater as a social institution. Theater seeks to arrogate the rights of church and state to determine what counts as a binding performative (just as proponents of lesbian and gay marriage do so today). "One might speculate that with these performative utterances onstage the theatre as institution also claims for itself a performative power, a power to shape or create social norms simply by performing them."[71]

To invoke the play's double vision once more: one could say that from a skeptical perspective, *Faustus* is mere *theater*—a conjuring trick played on the audience and, perhaps, on Faustus himself. But it is also *mere* theater, in the Elizabethan sense of pure performativity: a celebration of the art of conjuring states of being into existence by words alone.[72] As popular entertainment, *Doctor Faustus* stages the act of conjuring not in service of skeptical Protestant orthodoxy, but in order to appropriate the magical power of performative speech—the monarch dubbing a knight; an exorcist casting out a demon; perhaps even, blasphemously, the priest's consecration—on behalf of the commercial London theater. *Faustus* highlights the phenomenological stakes behind the *act* of onstage conjuring for the Elizabethan audience. Whereas the B-text seems more interested in portraying Faustus as the demons' gull (they are onstage more often, for instance, without being summoned by the magician), the A-text of *Faustus* reveals an unresolved tension in the Elizabethan imagination between conjuring as an act of "jugglery" and conjuring as a particular kind of speech act—one with potentially magical effects. To hold the position that Faustus' magic spells do not really work, and that the play thus denies the very possibility of magic, is to slight the play's certified power to terrify Elizabethan audiences *even as it entertained them.*[73]

A thoroughly skeptical audience would have little use for the Elizabethan theater. If we view *Doctor Faustus'* magic as a rhetorical trick masking coercive power relations, we underestimate its sly ability to make fun of its (theatrical) magic and have it too. *Faustus* appropriates the power of speech acts to alter the audience's consciousness at will and provides an object lesson in the power of performativity. Without question *Faustus'* diabolism disturbed its Elizabethan spectators, who could never be sure whether they were watching black magic or a simulacrum of it—Prospero or Pinch. Riggs reports, "Early performances of [*Faustus*] were notoriously successful at blurring the distinction between performance and reality," as attested to by the reports of one devil too many joining the performance.[74] At the same time extremist Puritans saw in the anecdote confirmation of the playhouse as a devil's chapel and theatrical performance as a blasphemous playing with words. The historical appearance of a "real" devil at performances of *Doctor Faustus*, then, is best understood as manifesting the potential embedded in *all* performative speech to conjure dark matter into visible reality. As Faustus cautions his audiences, "Be silent, then, for danger is in words" (5.1.24). Unlike skeptical twenty-first-century scholars, Elizabethans understood that the distinction between performance and performativity threatened to dissolve whenever an actor conjured a demon onstage.

2

Quantum Mechanicals

Desiring Bottom in
A Midsummer Night's Dream

All for your delight
We are not here.

—Quince as Prologue,
A Midsummer Night's Dream (5.1.114–15)

It is easy to get lost in *A Midsummer Night's Dream*. Like most of Shake-speare's comedies, the *Dream* concerns misprision: a misunderstanding in which one thing is taken for another.[1] A quartet of lovers blunders around a threatening wood; a troupe of actors misplaces its star; Bottom the weaver temporarily loses his head; Puck, alias Robin Goodfellow, lays the love juice on the wrong swain's eyelid; and fairy Queen and King battle for custody of a changeling child.[2] Bushes are supposed bears, and monsters paramours. Even the self-appointed rationalist Duke Theseus, never having read Chaucer, let alone North's Plutarch, misses the hilarious incongruity of his own presence in a comedy that ostensibly celebrates marriage. References to eyes and eyesight continually remind us that Shakespeare's muddled characters are in the dark. Often performed in broad daylight, *A Midsummer Night's Dream* invites us to celebrate our own superiority over its love- and law-addled Athenians, and to congratulate ourselves on our own (English?) clear-sightedness.[3]

Yet all is not as it appears. As Dennis Kay remarks, "The play is full of unresolved matters requiring the active engagement of an audience's interpretative response . . . The perennial stage success of the *Dream,* its apparent capacity to be made and remade in each succeeding generation, seems to me to be bound up with the conscious incompleteness of the script. It is in many ways the least authoritarian of Shakespeare's plays."[4] And yet all the play's roads lead eventually to Bottom, the play's most colorful character, whose dramatic function, other than augmenting the comic relief well supplied by the other characters, remains a puzzle.

Bottom features in *Dream* criticism as a touchstone for interpretation of the play as a whole. In C. L. Barber's influential interpretation, Bottom remains "uproariously literal and antipoetic" despite his metamorphosis and ultimately helps to reaffirm a hierarchical social structure.[5] In Jan Kott's equally influential reading, theriomorphic Bottom is pizzle rather than puzzle, a literalized fantasy of bestiality.[6] Reading Bottom in the context of cultural fantasies surrounding Queen Elizabeth, Louis Montrose unsexes Bottom: his encounter with Titania is a fantasy of male infantile, narcissistic dependency on "a powerful female who is at once lover, mother, and queen."[7] For Dympna Callaghan, Bottom-as-actor reduces Titania to a parody of a female spectator, seduced by an economy of "all-male mimesis."[8] Gail Kern Paster's Bottom oscillates between carnal satiation and pregenital infantilism. Paster wittily speculates that, given his reference to laxatives, it may be not intercourse but purgation that Bottom avails himself of between acts.[9] John Joughlin respiritualizes Bottom, who holds open a space for wonder within the everyday.[10] Bottom is a Rorschach mechanical, congenially open to whatever desires we wish to project onto him.

Indeed, the key term for understanding Bottom is *desire.* Bottom's desire is the dark matter of *A Midsummer Night's Dream,* emitting an invisible gravitational force that bends the visible action around it. Winking out of sight following his first encounter with Titania in 3.1, Bottom reappears before our eyes in 4.1. In doing so, Bottom invites us to adopt a different perspective on dramatic character itself. To explain this I will use the heuristic analogy of the contrast between classical and quantum mechanics: two thus far incompatible mathematical understandings of the physical world, the former governing large bodies (peas, tables, chairs) that we can touch and measure, the latter applying to the very small atomic and subatomic world, which we cannot. The two worlds obey mystifyingly different laws. The world of classical physics is causal and predictable and deals with facts. The world of quantum physics is random and unpredictable and deals with probabilities. Whereas classical physics describes a clear and determinate world, quantum reality is fitful. By analogy, while "classical" dramaturgy imagines fictive characters as carrying on offstage lives that follow definite trajectories, what I shall call quantum dramaturgy introduces fuzziness: a probabilistic wave-function in which an invisible character simply *has* no precise location or trajectory when unobserved.[11] Like a subatomic particle, the unseen character can be "everywhere at once" until the very act of observation pins him or her down. A quantized character, to adopt Natalie Angier's poetic description of a whizzing electron's probability distribution, is thus "a spoonful of cloud."[12]

From this perspective, a quantized character becomes (to use physicist Richard Feynman's formulation) a sum of probabilities rather than a history—smeared, as it were, across the hidden landscape of the play rather than fired like a particle from A to B. In Ibsen's well-made play, we have no problem tracing Hedda Gabler's location and momentum through stage time and stage space; her trajectory is as fixed and inexorable as that of her pistols.[13] But what happens to Bottom in between (erotic) acts depends on whether we adopt a classical or quantum perspective—on how we "see" Bottom's invisible desire. Like light itself, offstage Bottom can be either particle or wave—even if he cannot be both simultaneously.[14] Plumbing the dark matter of Bottom's absent desire requires a very specific kind of spectral reading indeed.

Presenting Bottom

Nominally Athenian, the very English Bottom and his entourage seem far removed from the Athens to which we are introduced at the beginning of the play. At first sight their appearance is dramatically inexplicable; Montrose notes, "The immediate reason for the presence of Bottom and his companions in *A Midsummer Night's Dream* is to rehearse and perform an 'interlude before the Duke and Duchess, on his wedding-day at night.'"[15] Yet Bottom transcends his role as unwitting butt for his withering, courtly audience at *Pyramus and Thisbe*. Uniquely privileged, Bottom alone passes between mortal and fairy worlds, and he is the only mortal (besides the audience) to whom the fairies are visible. Unlike the mortal lovers, amiable Bottom seems comically unperturbed by his adventures in the wood. He is immune to the self-doubt, madness, loathing, and jealousy experienced by those caught in the grip of romantic folly and delusion as they traverse the wood of infatuation.

Moreover, Bottom's personality, unlike that of the wood-crazed lovers, does not really change: "Despite his translations into an ass-headed monster and a fabled lover, Bottom remains immutably—*fundamentally*—Bottom."[16] While Bottom is the victim of Puck's mischievous metamorphosis from man to ass (Puck takes his cue from William Adlington's 1566 translation of Apuleius's *The Golden Ass*), the donkey's head "translates" (3.1.119) but does not transform him.[17] Far from undergoing an identity crisis, Bottom remains sweetly ignorant of his own asininity. Stranger still, Bottom seems to have patented his own magical formula, for he possesses the magical ability to make (almost) everyone fall in love with him—his fellow mechanicals, Titania, the audience—seemingly without effort. In an Athens where friendship seems in short supply, Bottom alone can take the love of friends for granted; they adore him despite, or maybe because of, his desire to play all the parts. Bottom is his own love-juice, although his charm is potion free. Perhaps most astonishingly of all, the play's dunce emerges as its sole contented character. Shakespeare's *Dream* is full of intelligent but unhappy people who suffer from their wish to possess what they lack. Yet Bottom can accept the love of a fairy queen at one moment and her disappearance the next and lose neither his equanimity nor his robust self-confidence.

Certainly Bottom himself could never articulate the secret of his contentment. Nick Bottom may be a weaver by trade, but he is not a weaver of texts (from *textere*, "to weave").[18] Illiterate at least to some degree, he must ask Peter Quince's help in setting down his dream in ballad form. For better or worse, Bottom lacks the skill of the artist whose soul he possesses. Yet Bottom alone among the mortals feels compelled on waking to translate dream into art.

> I have had a most rare vision . . . The eye of man hath not heard, the ear of man hath not seen, man's hand is not able to taste, his tongue to conceive, nor his heart to report, what my dream was. I will get Peter Quince to write a ballet of this dream. It shall be call'd "Bottom's Dream," because it hath no bottom. (4.1.204–16)

Hardly a poet, Bottom's synaesthetic mangling of Saint Paul (1 Corinthians 2:9) embodies the negative capability that Keats famously defined (in a nod to Shakespeare) as "when man is capable of being in uncertainties, Mysteries, doubts, without any irritable reaching after fact & reason."[19]

How, then, was Bottom's negative capability personified onstage for

Elizabethan audiences? The role was almost certainly written as a cameo part tailored for the Lord Chamberlain's Men's clown, Will Kemp, who played Peter in *Romeo and Juliet* and Dogberry in *Much Ado About Nothing*. He is thought to have played most or all of Shakespeare's clowns before being replaced in 1599 by the more refined Robert Armin, who created Shakespeare's professional fools. Kemp could dance, improvise, and mangle words comically; as an actor he would have been ideally suited to play Bottom.[20] Shakespeare's clowns are not usually defined by frustrated sexuality (Silvius in *As You Like It* is an exception), as are so many Richard Burbage protagonists. So it seems reasonable that Shakespeare would have expected innocent Bottom to be ghosted (in Marvin Carlson's term) by Kemp's previous characterizations, in which desire was subordinated to clownage.[21]

In his dual role as actor and dancer, Kemp may have left more of an impression on the audience than is apparent from Shakespeare's text. In the early 1590s, performances in London's public playhouses usually ended with a bawdy jig. According to Bruce R. Smith, these jigs were in tension with romantic comedy: "The subject of most surviving jigs is anything but a celebration of marriage. Typically, the chief dancer—in Shakespeare's company through the 1590s he was the clown Will Kemp—succeeds in seducing someone else's wife . . . On paper Shakespeare's comedies, with their teleological drive toward marriage, may look like instruments of the patriarchal state apparatus, but in performance they gave passion wide room for play."[22] David Wiles observes that Bottom's promise to the audience that he will sing a ballad in the latter end of a play for the Duke anticipates Kemp's transformation from clown to jig-maker following the play's finale.[23] If so, the original audience was left with a double exposure: Bottom/Kemp as sweet clown; Kemp/Bottom as bawdy dancer. Bottom was a composite image, a possibly vexed collaboration between Shakespeare and Kemp (both equal sharers in the company's profits). That said, the role transcends any single actor, as the parade of memorable Bottoms in Kemp's wake attests. Rather than attempting to reconstruct Kemp's performance, then, I will focus on Bottom's essence—the dark matter that subtends his physical appearance onstage.

My starting point in solving Bottom's riddle is that he is, like the invisible Indian boy, a figure for *desiring*—or, rather, for being desired. (It cannot be a coincidence that beast and boy end up in Titania and Oberon's respective bowers.) As William C. Carroll reminds us, "The primary force behind the comic plots of the romantic comedies is erotic desire, and the primary action is the overcoming of obstacles to the fulfillment of such desire."[24] Susan Zimmerman emphasizes that "the production of [Renaissance stage] eroticism involved every aspect of theatrical production, including the casting and composition of the companies (the transvestite acting convention providing an inescapable and distinctive erotic element); staging, costuming, and the use of props and other theatrical apparatus; language, gesture, and interpretation," as well as audience response.[25] The professional London stage was a desire machine.

Yet if Carroll and Zimmerman single out erotic desire as the motor of English Renaissance drama and theater, much materialist criticism questions whether Elizabethan-Jacobean desire is readily discernible from our historical vantage point. Bruce Smith cautions us against projecting the notion of fixed sexual identity based on object choice onto early modern genital experience: "In terms of our own nomenclature, the passions played out in Shakespeare's plays and poems are not heterosexual, not homosexual, not bisexual, but *pan*sexual."[26] Valerie Traub reminds us that "Shakespearean drama represents erotic desire as *constituted* within a complex and contradictory social field." It cannot be seen as an internal, bodily given: "Characters in these plays do not so much possess sexuality as inhabit it."[27] And for Celia R. Daileader, the erotic locus of Renaissance drama is always offstage and theatrical eroticism itself paradoxically constituted by the very impossibility of materializing actual female bodies onstage (though not, of course, in the audience).[28] Desire in recent Shakespearean criticism is at once present and absent; historicized yet gamely poststructuralist; psychoanalyzable and yet respectably pre-Freudian (and therefore pleasingly anti-essentialist). No wonder sex is so hard to pin down.[29]

For the Lord Chamberlain's Men and its rivals, staging desire was as much practical challenge as materialist conundrum. Materializing desire posed various challenges. First, in a censored theater licensed by the Master of Revels, the sexual act could not be presented or simulated onstage (although some plays came remarkably close). Second, onstage bodies were uniformly male.[30] Nudity and/or sexual activity threatened to collapse the illusion of heterosexual relations into homoeroticism—precisely the charge leveled at the public theater by Puritan antitheatricalists. Many plays exploit this ambiguity. For example, *Othello*'s "willow song" scene between Emilia and Desdemona, one of the relatively rare scenes of intimacy between two female characters in the period, involves one boy actor undressing another. And when Sebastian Wengrave kisses his cross-dressed beloved, Mary Fitzallard, in Middleton and Dekker's *The Roaring Girl* (1611) and comments, "Methinks a woman's lip tastes well in a doublet" (4.1.50), we cannot tell whether he relishes kissing the boy, the girl beneath the boy, or the boy beneath the girl beneath the boy.[31]

Third, the playwriting of the period obsessively figures the unknowability of women's desires, often to the point of misogyny. Jacobean drama is replete with sexual paranoids: Othello, Leontes, Alsemero in *The Changeling,* Corvino in *Volpone,* and the rest. "Down from the waist they are Centaurs, / Though women all above: / But to the girdle do the gods inherit, / beneath is all the fiend's," warns King Lear (4.6.126–29). How, then, could female desire ever be channeled by male actors' bodies in a culture that viewed that desire as essentially inaccessible to the male gaze? Since publicly performed early modern drama was male authored and male acted, a case can be made that female desire never appears on the Renaissance stage except as cultural fantasy or parody.[32] Conversely, the convincing presentation of male desire poses its own problems. How does one communicate male sexual arousal, for instance, beyond its expression in dialogue? The codpiece models an ingenious material solution in this context: a mask that foregrounds the very endowment it disavows. Indeed, we might think of the codpiece as a material marker for the (im)possibility of materializing bodily desire onstage.[33]

The codpiece foregrounds desire without literalizing it onstage. Sexuality itself becomes the *negative space* of early modern theater. Eroticism—neither quite inside nor outside the human subject, but in play among author, character, actor, and spectator—slips in and out of visibility, its absent presence marked by the charged language of deferred desire, which promises the audience something it will never actually get to see. The cross-dressed theatrical entertainment for Marlowe's King Edward II imagined by the king's lover, Gaveston, exemplifies this strategy.

> Sometimes a lovely boy in Dian's shape,
> With hair that gilds the water as it glides,
> Crownets of pearl about his naked arms,
> And in his sportful hands an olive tree
> To hide those parts which men delight to see,
> Shall bathe him in a spring, and there hard by
> One like Actaeon peeping through the grove

Shall by the angry goddess be transformed,
And running in the likeness of an hart
By yelping hounds pulled down and seem to die. . . . (1.1.60–69)[34]

Like the antitheatricalists, Gaveston realizes that the androgynous boy actor's charms are all the more eroticized for being hidden from view.[35] And, like Gaveston, the early modern playhouse substitutes the titillation of fantasized pleasure for the merely physical gratification of the neighboring brothel, banking on the fact that *not* giving the audience what it wants will ultimately bring them back for more. Sexuality is a game of deferred gratification; we are all Jonson's Sir Epicure Mammon, cheerfully paying out coin in return for alchemical fantasy—and arguably getting our money's worth despite the con artistry.

Shakespeare's seductive yet mysterious clown embodies this delicate balance between visible and invisible desire. For desiring Bottom not only means desiring his body (like Titania) or his presence (like his fellow mechanicals) or his absence (like the aristocratic audience at *Pyramus and Thisbe*, which just wants to get to bed). Shakespeare suggests that it means our envying Bottom, or even, conceivably, our desiring to *become* Bottom. Yet *A Midsummer Night's Dream* cloaks what and whom Bottom himself desires. Is Bottom a desiring subject, and if so, who and what does he desire? A solution to the riddle of desiring Bottom presents itself spectrally in and between the two love scenes between Bottom and Titania in the wood.

Difficulties in Translation: Wooing Bottom

Act 3 finds an invisible Puck surprising the mechanicals in the grove where they have gathered to rehearse *Pyramus and Thisbe*.[36] The action is continuous from act 2, in which the enchanted Lysander pursues Helena offstage and the panicked Hermia wakes from a nightmare to find herself abandoned. Drugged Titania lies asleep, perhaps within the curtained discovery space that projected from the rear stage of The Globe, and she remains asleep onstage for the first 129 lines of the act. The rehearsal scene is played for laughs as the mechanicals' failure to grasp theatrical representation leads them to hilarious solutions (such as an inserted Prologue to explain mimesis to the audience). Bottom exits offstage to see a noise that Pyramus has heard, reenters with the ass's head, and speaks his part on cue.[37] His friends flee in terror, perhaps a parody of those actors who reportedly fled mid-*Faustus* when one devil too many appeared onstage.[38] The miffed Bottom remains alone onstage singing to himself (he alone can turn to art for solitary respite), and his mellifluous braying awakens Titania, who has been sleeping on her "flow'ry bed" for the previous 102 lines of dialogue.[39]

In light of Apuleius, it is tempting to read Bottom's transformation as a dirty joke in the making.[40] But just how bestial is the play's implied coupling between woman and donkey within Shakespeare's terms? According to Kott's sinister reading, "The *Dream* is the most erotic of Shakespeare's plays. In no other tragedy, or comedy, of his, except *Troilus and Cressida*, is the eroticism expressed so brutally."[41] The wood presents itself as a psychic space in which sadomasochistic desires find comic expression, as when Helena invites Demetrius to beat her like a spaniel and he threatens to sexually assault her (2.1.188–243). Kott sees "passing through animality" as the play's key symbolic journey: "This is the main theme joining together all three separate plots . . . Titania and Bottom will pass through animal eroticism in a quite literal, even visual sense."[42] Spurred to revenge by his wife's humiliating sex-strike, which is public knowledge, Oberon has prepared us in the most lurid terms for Titania's debasement: "Be it ounce, or cat, or bear, / Pard, or boar with bristled hair . . . Wake when some vile thing is near" (2.2.30–34).[43]

For the Elizabethan playgoer, the putative union between ass and fairy queen represents more than the scandal of bestiality.[44] Gail Kern Paster and Skiles Howard remind us:

> Insofar as Titania was played by a boy actor and Bottom was played by an adult male . . . envisioning them together sexually is to imagine an act of same-sex, male-male intercourse . . . But even beyond flirting with an allusion to criminal sexuality, the play subverts the customary sexual dynamics of dominance and attraction. Instead of an older man loving a beautiful young man, the play gives us a "boy" Titania making love to the man Bottom. Insofar as the union would have to take place while Bottom is, technically speaking, only part human, their liaison could also be seen as bestiality . . . But Bottom, captured and dominated by the fairy queen, is not only Titania's beloved, he is also symbolically her changeling child . . . In the popular religious imagination of early modern Europe, any forbidden act of sexual intercourse would be—or should be—punished with a monstrous offspring. Thus doubly monstrous in his overlapping roles as lover and baby, Bottom is the object of a forbidden love like that of Queen Pasiphaë for the bull, and he is the monstrous offspring too.[45]

On this historicized reading, translated Bottom is polymorphous perversity incarnate.

Yet if Shakespeare has prepared us for a ribald scene in which Bottom's augmented genitalia provide his principal appeal—"My mistress with a monster is in love," exults Puck (3.2.6)—the love-scene that follows fails to measure up to expectations (even despite the erotic augmentations of director Peter Brook and others). Unlike the unpleasantly fixated Demetrius and Lysander, drugged Titania finds not only her libido but her fundamental generosity and sweetness awakened.

> I'll give thee fairies to attend on thee;
> And they shall fetch thee jewels from the deep,
> And sing while thou on pressed flowers doth sleep.
> And I will purge thy mortal grossness so,
> That thou shalt like an aery spirit go. (3.1.157–61)

Titania's lines might be bawdy double entendre—is this a sexually cathartic purge?—but they also reflect her genuine desire to *purify* Bottom. Far from sexually slumming, Titania wants to raise the Athenian ass to her level. There is no doubt about Titania's carnal intentions, however, and the scene concludes with her bidding her servants to lead Bottom to her bower. Titania invokes the play's bellwether of female mood, the moon.

> Come wait upon him; lead him to my bower.
> The moon methinks looks with a wat'ry eye;
> And when she weeps, weeps every little flower,
> Lamenting some enforced chastity.
> Tie up my lover's tongue, bring him silently. (3.1.198–201)

In Titania's lovely image, the dew (conventionally understood by Elizabethans to be produced by the moon) laments "some enforced chastity." But does this phrase mean "violated chastity," in the sense that the flowers lament sexual violence of the kind visited on Procne by Tereus (and, perhaps imminently, by Theseus on Hippolyta or Demetrius on Helena)? Or does Titania mean "prescribed chastity," like that of the nunnery with which Theseus threatens recalcitrant Hermia? Titania may be lamenting her own chastity, or Bottom's, or else she might simply be reveling in her sexual designs on her mute plaything. As elsewhere in the *Dream*, the moon, like Bottom himself, proffers a double image of desire.

The conceited weaver shows no surprise at being wooed by this fairy queen. Aphoristic for once, Bottom takes Titania's sudden infatuation in stride: "Methinks, mistress, you should have little reason for that. And yet, to say the truth, reason and love keep little company now-a-days" (3.1.142–43). For one moment Bottom becomes the wise fool, although his sententious line is somewhat out of character. Bottom seems hilariously ignorant of the once-in-a-lifetime opportunity that has come his way. "Thou art as wise as thou art beautiful," coos Titania, to which Bottom replies: "Not so, neither; but if I had wit enough to get out of this wood, I have enough to serve mine owe [own] turn" (3.1.149–51).[46] Bottom prefers familiar Athens to seduction by a fairy queen, but he is too polite to refuse the queen's blandishments. Nonetheless he is more intent on painstakingly making the acquaintance of Peaseblossom, Cobweb, Moth, and Mustardseed than on joining Titania in her bower—so much so that Titania interrupts and insists that they tie up his tongue. The scene ends with the stage direction "*Exit*" in both Q1 and F; we cannot say if the fairies lead Bottom offstage or simply into the discovery space from which Titania emerged on being awakened. If the Elizabethan actors retreat to the upstage discovery space, they remain ensconced there—producing an invisible action space with a big sexual question mark hanging over it—until the curtain is drawn aside once more at the start of act 4.

No textual evidence within the scene suggests that Bottom is tempted by Titania's body; rather, he wishes to serve his own turn. Indeed, faced with the chance to make love to a fairy queen, Bottom prefers to make friends with the help. While polite to his inamorata, Bottom is instinctively more at ease with Titania's servants, addressing them as "your worships" (3.2.179). Bottom's gift is for friendship, not romantic love, and he would rather play a scenery-chewing tyrant than a lover (1.2.27–28). Even through her scrim of love-juice, Titania recognizes what she accurately calls Bottom's "fair virtue" rather than dwelling on his gross anatomy (3.1.140). The gentle comedy of this love-scene seems far removed from Kott's leering animality.

At the point when mute Bottom and besotted Titania exit the visible stage, Shakespeare draws a discreet veil over the duo's actions for 464 lines. Once they depart for Titania's bower at the end of 3.1, we do not meet Bottom and Titania again until 4.1. The intervening scene returns to the juice-crossed lovers as Demetrius and Lysander strive to convince the women of their fealty to Helena. At the scene's close, Oberon sends Puck off to restore the lovers to their "wonted sight" (3.2.369) and announces:

Whiles I in this affair do thee employ,
I'll to my queen and beg her Indian boy;
And then I will her charmed eye release
From monster's view, and all things shall be peace. (3.2.375–77)

Oberon exits at line 395, and the lovers' scene goes on for 87 more lines. In the play's narrative, it must be during this crucial gap that Oberon accosts Titania offstage.

If so, this implies that Bottom and Titania somehow physically separate, at least temporarily, between their two love-scenes. And if an intermission occurred between acts 3 and 4, Shakespeare's original audience would have found it harder still to determine whether enough stage time had elapsed for Bottom and Titania to consummate her love. We can imagine the Bottom-Titania affair as either continuous or interrupted action; and, in some counterintuitive sense, *it may be both.*[47] Shakespeare offers us a crux. Just where is Bottom between 3.1 and 4.1? Might he be in two (or more) places at once—both making love to Titania in her bower, and, somehow at the same time, not? Bottom's indeterminate whereabouts invite a detour into quantum mechanics.[48]

Marv'lous Hairy: Quantum Fuzziness in the Dream

The *Dream* hovers between two ways of looking at Bottom, which one might mischievously call the classical mechanical and the quantum mechanical. As we know, classical physics governs the large-scale world human beings inhabit and quantum physics governs the strange atomic and subatomic realms. Whereas in the large-scale world physical properties vary smoothly and continuously, the quantum realm is discontinuous and lumpy—going from A to C does not necessarily mean passing through B.[49] According to physicist Werner Heisenberg, "The world thus appears as a complicated tissue of events, in which connections of different kinds alternate or overlap or combine, and thereby determine the texture of the whole."[50] Quantum ideas undermine the notion of atoms, nuclei, and subatomic particles as tiny balls of matter—the solid world writ small. Instead, the quantum landscape is fuzzy and indeterminate, a veiled world of probabilities rather than certainties. Quantum mechanics undermines the notion that physical objects exist independent of observation, at all times, and with fixed physical properties. In the words of one recent commentator, "If classical mechanics is George Eliot, quantum mechanics is Kafka."[51]

One consequence of quantum theory is that we cannot tell how the subatomic world behaves when it is not under observation. Heisenberg's uncertainty principle states that a subatomic particle has either a position in space or a well-defined speed, but it cannot possess both at the same moment. The more accurately we can know an electron's position, the less certainly we know that electron's momentum, and vice versa, because an electron's collision with a photon uncontrollably disturbs its motion (for the electron to be visible at all, it has to deflect at least one photon into our microscope). As physicist John Polkinghorne puts it, "Observables come in pairs that epistemologically exclude each other."[52] Moreover, Niels Bohr's principle of complementarity states that matter and radiation can behave as both waves and particles, and that these particle and wave aspects cannot be dissociated. This is not necessarily because of intrinsic reality but because of the nature of observation and the measuring apparatus: an observer is part of the interdependent process that produces an observable phenomenon (just as no act of theater can take place without an observer).[53]

When it comes to the microcosm, acts of observation introduce unavoidable quantum fuzziness. Because no elementary particle is a phenomenon until it is registered, it becomes weirdly impossible to track subatomic particles through space and time. We can speak only of a cloud of probability, in which a given particle exists in multiple places at once until pinned down by observation. Physicist Richard Feynman invites us to understand this unpicturable state of quantum affairs by imagining that an electron does not travel in a straight line from A to B. In the absence of observation, the electron somehow explores all possible routes at once, and these all contribute to the reality. When the electron ultimately arrives at a target, all possible paths have somehow simultaneously contributed to this singular event. The *observed* wave-function comes from factoring in all these possibilities, even if in some sense they cancel each other out to arrive at what Feynman calls a "history" (the shortest distance between A and B) rather than a "sum" (all possible roads that eventually lead to Rome, or Athens).[54] Though disputed, Feynman's path-integral, sum-over-histories formulation of quantum mechanics accurately describes the bafflingly illogical quantum world when it is expressed mathematically.[55]

On an analogy to quantum physics, then, we might say that within quantum dramaturgy an unobserved character can be path integral. Like an electron, he is at once a bullet, tracing an inexorable arc offstage, and a probability wave, spread out in all directions through invisible space like the ripples made by a pebble in a pond. A quantized character is not a *thing* but an *event*—and that event is itself made up of the sum of all possible histories of that character between observations by an audience. In just this way, Bottom seems to hover between wave and particle, macrocosmic and microcosmic scales of behavior. For something strange happens to Bottom when he undergoes translation from classical Athens to the microscopic fairy world. Some sort of portal is crossed, and mortal and fairy worlds can temporarily overlap despite apparent differences of scale. Indeterminacy of size teases the audience with the possibility that Bottom enters a new relationship to "fairy time" (5.1.364). When Quince blesses translated Bottom at 3.1.118, the two men seem to be the same size. And yet once Bottom awakens Titania, the queen and her tiny entourage appear to be on the same scale as the formerly full-size weaver.

In his playful thought experiment, Shakespeare hints that the laws of physics—and theater—work differently on extremely tiny scales. He was evidently encouraged in his indeterminacy by popular imagination, in which fairies could apparently belong to different orders of scale simultaneously. Marjorie Garber comments, "In the folklore of Shakespeare's time figures like Puck were well known, but many were considered to be of normal human size . . . Oberon and Titania are fairies, but they are clearly envisaged on a human scale. Their attendants—Cobweb, Moth, Mustardseed—are, just as clearly, imagined as miniscule (although they are played on the stage by human actors)."[56] Robert Greene's *The Scottish History of James IV* (published 1598 but likely written ca. 1590) describes Oberon as smaller than the King of Clubs. In the French romance *Huon of Bordeaux* (translated by Lord Berners, 1533–42), King Auberon is crook shouldered and three feet high.

The *Dream* repeatedly insists on the tininess of its fairies.[57] Oberon tells us that a snake's skin is a garment big enough to enwrap Titania (2.2.255–56). Peter Holland notes that "it seems safest to accept that fairies varied in size from rare appearances at full adult height through frequent manifestations as small children to occasional sightings as tiny creatures down to the size of ants . . . [Shakespeare's] fairies' size seems to shift unpredictably and fluidly. They are small enough to wear snake-skins, creep into acorn cups, and risk being covered with one bee's honeybag. Their names, similarly, suggest their small size: Peaseblossom, Cobweb, Mote, Mustardseed. At the same time Titania is large enough to hold an undiminished Bottom in her arms."[58] But who is to say that Bottom is "undiminished" rather than miniaturized?[59]

Determining whether boys or men originally played Puck and the fairies would not clarify how tiny Shakespeare meant his fairies to be.[60] As Matthew Woodcock indicates, instead of cutting fairies down to size, Shakespeare "mocks the kind of literalist readings of the stage that underlie attempts to measure fairies."[61] Perhaps Bottom has shrunk, the fairies have magnified, or both, or neither. Denied any yardstick for scale in the Bottom-Titania love scenes, we are free to imagine, if we choose, that Bottom has magically shrunk to the point where Titania is not only visible but embraceable. Shakespeare transports us from an Athenian world of classical dramaturgy, in which characters possess graspable size, location, and trajectory, to a fairy world in which such coordinates are imaginatively up for grabs. In the poetic dream-world of quantum fuzziness, where the rules of classical dramaturgy do not apply, ass-eared Bottom can be both larger and smaller than life.

Furthermore, Bottom can be in two places at once. The counterintuitive notion that an unobserved particle can be in more than one place simultaneously is known as the superposition principle. In classical physics there are only two possibilities: a state where a particle is "here" and a state where it is "there." But in the quantum world, "there are not only states of 'here' and 'there' but also a whole host of other states that are mixtures of these possibilities—a bit of 'here' and a bit of 'there' added together. Quantum theory permits the mixing together of states that classically would be mutually exclusive of each other."[62] Alternative possibilities are thus held open; the electron's probability wave remains spread out until the physicist's observational experiment pins the electron down. An indivisible electron can mysteriously pass through two separate apertures (slits in a screen) at the same time. This defies logic, but even if scientists cannot explain it, they can *show* it. For if one tries to determine the path of the electron through either slit A or slit B through direct observation—a particlelike question—the electron becomes particlelike (demonstrating impact at point X or point Y). But if one looks at the accumulated interference pattern caused by the impact of a stream of electrons—a wavelike question—the electrons become wavelike. Once observed, the electron is no longer in a state of probability (here and there), but instantly *here,* in a state of sudden and discontinuous change. This so-called quantum jump collapses the wave-packet (the distribution of probabilities).

These weird experimental findings undermine the solidity of the microcosm. Because particles exist as facts only in the eye of the beholder, Erwin Schrödinger states, "It is better not to view a particle as a permanent entity, but rather as an instantaneous event. Sometimes these events link together to create the illusion of permanent entities."[63] Quantum reality is fundamentally unpicturable; the notion of a trajectory, claimed Heisenberg, does not even exist.[64] According to the Copenhagen interpretation of quantum physics, atoms "form a world of potentialities or possibilities rather than one of things or facts."[65] Atoms, particles, and the rest are merely heuristic images designed to make sense of observable experiments. In Bohr's words, "In our description of nature the purpose is not to disclose the real essence of phenomena but only to track down, so far as possible, relations between the manifold aspects of our experience."[66]

I am arguing here for a Copenhagen Interpretation of Shakespeare's quantum mechanical. Through quantum illogic, unobserved Bottom can be here, not here, and in any number of superpositions simultaneously. Unlike, say, Jean and Miss Julie in Strindberg's *Miss Julie,* whose sexual intercourse takes place just offstage and in real time behind a closed door, Shakespeare's quantum mechanical exists between 3.1 and 4.1 in various states of indeterminate probability held open by the text.[67] He is not unlike Schrödinger's unfortunate quantum cat, which is both alive and dead until the observer collapses the superposition of the two wave functions into a single outcome. Offstage, Bottom has neither fixed position nor momentum, as the flesh-and-blood actor playing him does. Rather, he enjoys a different kind of reality. Bottom may not be as "locally real" as Einstein might wish him to be, but a partially veiled reality is the price paid once intelligibility rather than objectivity comes to define quantized phenomena.

As a fictional construct, then, Bottom lacks a definitive offstage trajectory between (sexual) acts as he makes his untraceable way through the wood. But when *this* Bottom in *this* production as played by *this* actor pins down his coordinates, the wave of probabilities collapses. Manjit Kumar reminds us, "Unlike a particle, a wave is not localized at a single place, but is a disturbance that carries energy through a medium"—a wonderfully evocative description of drama.[68] Bottom's waviness between acts 3 and 4 is not like a coin toss, in which anything can happen but only one thing ever does, and where the odds are always 50/50. All possible paths through the wood contribute to the Feynmanian sum that is visible Bottom. We cannot pin down Bottom's precise whereabouts between 3.1 and 4.1 without queering his pitch.

What of the equally quantized fairy queen? A further weird aspect of quantum reality is so-called entanglement between two particles, "such that they can instantly coordinate their properties, regardless of their distance in space and time."[69] Bottom and Titania remain inseparably linked. It makes no sense to see them as unconjoined particles, since clearly one cannot make love without the other present. Offstage, or perhaps merely hidden behind the discovery space's curtain, Titania and Bottom exert an invisible gravitational presence on the mortal lovers' ensuing erotic adventures in act 3. Transgressive sex is in the air, not least because Bottom and Titania are played by male actors. Bottom and Titania are entangled metaphysically as well as bodily. We cannot tell if they are making love or not making love offstage—and to observe them in the act (as some productions do) is instantly to tumble them out of quantum into classical dramaturgy.

Quantum theory suggests alternative ways of understanding Bottom and Titania's entanglement. I have already summarized Feynman's path-integral approach, in which a given outcome is a combination of every possible history leading up to that state and in which each possible history contributes according to its quantum amplitude (wave-function). But it is also possible that Shakespeare designed the *Dream* so that, imaginatively speaking, *parallel* Bottoms and Titanias coexist between acts. According to Hugh Everett's controversial Many Worlds Hypothesis, the illogic of superposition and entanglement can be explained by the notion that *every* possible state that a particle can be in is in fact realized—but in parallel but segmented universes. On this ingenious view, superposition is just parallel tracks in parallel universes.[70] Instead of any given electron being here, there, or anywhere all at once, "the universe divides into as many nearly identical copies of itself as there are possibilities for the position of the electron . . . This scenario argues that all possible outcomes of events must happen, each in its own universe."[71] While a minority view in physics, the hypothesis recuperates realism from the Copenhagen Interpretation's unsettlingly probabilistic description of the world.

By analogy Everett's Many Worlds concept can reconcile contradictions between conflicting versions of Shakespeare's plays. For instance, act 5's master of ceremonies is Philostrate in the Q1 *Dream* but Egeus in F, thereby puzzlingly giving Egeus two separate, contradictory dramatic trajectories (alienation from the court, reconciliation with the court). It is as if Shakespeare was in two minds and produced parallel universes with different outcomes for the same character. Similarly, in one fictional world Hamlet delivers his "How all occasions do inform against me" soliloquy after meeting Fortinbras's army (Q2), and in two others he does not (Q1 and F). Unaware of the others' existence, the three Danes are separated by a thin textual membrane, perhaps analogous to that supposedly separating our universe from parallel ones in other dimensions. Variant texts may be irreconcilable according to the others' logic, but they do not cancel out the others' validity; the recent editorial trend to print variant texts alongside each other, rather than conflating them into a (mythical) original or final intention on Shakespeare's part, implicitly recognizes this.[72] Likewise, every performance of the *Dream* creates a new, collaborative history for Bottom, undermining the notion that a single authority (called "Shakespeare") authorizes or delegitimizes such interpretations.[73]

Many directors of the *Dream* are of course tempted to decide the question of Bottom and Titania's putative lovemaking once and for all. But deciding that clown and queen either do or do not consummate their relationship is to collapse a wave-packet that Shakespeare wishes to leave beclouded. For when we do rejoin Titania and Bottom in act 4, enough time *seems* to have passed for offstage intercourse of various kinds, and yet for Bottom no time seems to have passed at all. Bottom obeys macroscopic laws in the wood when he is with his fellow mechanicals, but another, dreamier physics explains the strange sense of continuous action between Bottom and Titania's two love-scenes, which are apparently discrete for Oberon and Titania (who exchange the Indian boy in the interval), although perhaps not for the enchanted if bewildered Bottom.

What does it mean to treat Bottom as a quantum mechanical? This dramaturgical frame precisely requires us *not* to visualize a precise offstage trajectory for Bottom between acts 3 and 4. Rather, in something akin to a quantum leap, Bottom winks out in 3.1 only to beam down in 4.1, where "[t]his flow'ry bed" (4.1.1) *both is and is not* Titania's sleeping-bower of 3.1.[74] Because we have not yet heard Oberon's account of his encounter with Titania gathering favors behind the wood (4.1.47–70), we have no sense of time having passed for Bottom between love-scenes. Visibly unchanged since being led offstage by Titania's train, Bottom seems to have shifted location instantaneously. Indeed, Bottom is in the same amiable mood as in 3.1.196 and treats one scene as the continuation of the other. Poised between two complementary dramaturgies, one of which obeys conventional rules of stage space-time and the other of which confounds those very rules, quantized Bottom is both particle and wave, entangled and held in superposition. Like his inscrutable measurements—"Methought I was, and methought I had" (4.1.208–9)—Bottom's endearing fuzziness charms and eludes us.

Serving One's Own Turn: Desiring Bottom

Bottom's offstage interlude with Titania equally invites a path-integral interpretation (one Bottom, many paths) and a Many Worlds Interpretation (many Bottoms, many paths). But as act 4 begins, quantum uncertainty collapses back into classical Athenian dramaturgy.[75] At the close of act 3, Oberon has instructed Puck to drive the homosocially maddened Demetrius and Lysander to exhaustion and then to administer the antidote to Lysander in order to restore his love for Hermia.[76] Oberon leaves the stage at line 3.2.395 in order to demand the Indian boy in exchange for releasing Titania from the charm. Sixty-seven lines pass, during which Puck orchestrates the four lovers' collapse from exhaustion on different parts of the stage, where (according to a stage direction in F) they sleep through the first 138 lines of the following act. Possibly following a musical interlude, at least in the Chamberlain's Men's performance, the scene shifts to Titania's bower, where Titania and Bottom enter attended by the fairies, with Oberon invisibly behind them.[77] Oberon has no reason to penetrate the bower, a space figured maternal as much as erotic, except voyeurism; perhaps his observation alters the experiment.

Once Bottom and Titania rematerialize, we can again follow their position and movement. Yet Shakespeare continues to play games with the audience's sense of time. *In retrospect* Oberon's sixty-seven-line absence toward the end of the previous scene *must* cover the time when he demanded the fairy boy and extracted Titania's submission to his authority. Oberon tells Puck later in this very scene that he has "of late" met with Titania and humiliated her, after due taunting, into giving up the boy (4.1.3–61). Time has moved for Oberon between acts with no quantum jumping; a logical interval has passed, which leaves him in victorious control of wife and pageboy. But in the unidirectional experience of watching the play, an audience has no way of knowing this. Titania herself never alludes to the missing scene, which seems to be outside her experience (part of the dream). Instead, we presume that Oberon just happens on Titania and her lover *for the first time* at the top of the act. After all, he has just shared with us his intention to seek her out and release her with the help of the antidote (3.2.374–77)—and here she is, obviously still charmed.

Is this second love-scene pre- or postcoital? If the former, the action for Bottom and Titania appears continuous from 3.1, in which case their love is still unconsummated (even though the action cannot have been continuous for Oberon). If the latter, Bottom's request for his ears to be scratched is the languid equivalent of asking for a cigarette. Sex may be in the air, but once again it isn't on the stage. Titania wants to turn Bottom into another changeling to be petted and cosseted.

> Come sit thee down upon this flow'ry bed,
> While I thy amiable cheeks do coy,
> And stick musk-roses in thy sleek smooth head,
> And kiss thy fair large ears, my gentle joy. (4.1.1–4)

Teasingly ambiguous, Titania's quatrain hovers between foreplay and afterglow.

Bottom's second love-scene shows him to be as immune to Titania's charms as he was in the first. While he has no objection to Titania's cheek-stroking and ear-kissing, his preferred pleasures as newfangled royal consort are decidedly nonsexual: he asks Titania's servants for honey, scratching, music, dried peas, oats, and hay, before falling asleep in Titania's arms.[78] The donkey head has taken over Bottom only from the neck up.[79] Translated Bottom never once expresses physical desire for the fairy queen. Unbuffeted by the erotic frenzy that afflicts the play's mortal lovers, who are "wode within this wood" (2.1.192), the clown accepts his magical transformation, his fairy paramour, and his retranslation into Nick Bottom the weaver without regret.

Oberon comes forward and gestures to the sleeping couple with irony, and perhaps no little self-disgust, at seeing his lurid fantasy realized in tableau.

> Her dotage now I do begin to pity.[80]
> For meeting her of late behind the wood,
> Seeking sweet favors for this hateful fool,
> I did upbraid her, and fall out with her.

For she his hairy temples then hath rounded
With coronet of fresh and fragrant flowers;
And that same dew which sometime on the buds
Was wont to swell like round and orient pearls,
Stood now within the pretty flouriets' eyes,
Like tears that did their own disgrace bewail.
When I had at my pleasure taunted her,
And she in mild terms begg'd my patience,
I then did ask of her her changeling child;
Which straight she gave me, and her fairy sent
To bear him to my bower in fairy land.
And now I have the boy, I will undo
The hateful imperfection of her eyes. (4.1.47–63)

Meeting Titania in the wood (and perhaps also her entangled beloved), Oberon collapsed the wave-packet, at least *for him*. Oberon's authoritative narrative retroactively fixes Titania's location and momentum offstage. And yet Oberon's account remains fuzzy in its details. We do not know when "of late" was. And what could "*behind* the wood" possibly mean— backstage in the tiring house, perhaps? And if Titania was abroad seeking favors, where was Bottom? Did Oberon actually see Bottom's hairy . . . temples?

Also peculiar is Oberon's suggestive line "When I had *at my pleasure* taunted her," which implies that Oberon may have avenged his frustration at Titania's sex-strike (1.2.62) by asserting his conjugal rights then and there behind the wood. Shakespeare makes it impossible to treat fairy-time as coterminous with human-time: "We the globe can compass soon, / Swifter than the wand'ring moon" (4.1.97–98). We cannot accommodate the fairy-time of Oberon's narrative to the phenomenology of stage-time as it elapses for the audience, because fairydom does not really exist unless we are looking at it. For these are spirits of a quantized sort: fairies can be everywhere at once, moving faster than the speed of (moon)light, both entangled and in superposition.

Remarkably, Shakespeare leaves unstaged the dramatic confrontation between Oberon and Titania that should logically climax their story— humiliation, reconciliation, and the resolution of their custody battle. Shakespeare's decision to tell rather than show is all the more peculiar given that female rebellion against patriarchal authority drives both mortal and fairy plots. Oberon's speech illustrates the dramatic strategy that William Gruber calls "attempts at storytelling that seem deliberately to bypass conventional mimetic enactments."[81] Oberon narrates the resolution of the Oberon-Titania plot with maximum economy, and then a dance in which the husband leads (4.1.86), together with Titania's resumption of "my lord" as an address (4.1.99), signals the couple's marital concord and resumption of traditional gender roles. The couple's restored amity provides a model, as well as a blessing, for the mortal triple-wedding to follow. There is no divorce in Athens; mortal couples are "eternally knit" while they live, and the phrase has even more lasting resonance for the immortal monarchs of fairyland, who must remain bound forever (4.1.181).[82]

Why does Shakespeare keep the crucial scene of Titania's submission to her lord—so ripe with dramatic possibility—dark matter? We now arrive at the heart of Bottom's secret. In a tradeoff between classical and quantum dramaturgies, Shakespeare wishes to leave ambiguous whether Bottom and Titania have made love. He embeds two crucial offstage scenes (Bottom and Titania's lovemaking and Titania and Oberon's reconciliation), one of which may never have happened. As Tony Tanner observes, "It is a gap, a silence, an unrecuperable missingness—a mystery. It is a vital blank we can never fill in—and nor should we try."[83] Shakespeare renders Titania and Bottom's affair undecidable so as to make Bottom's sexuality *invisible*. Bottom's sexuality is the dark matter of the *Dream*. The other mortals must pass through the wood of adolescence and erotic intoxication, and even the fairies seem to embody free-floating desire.[84] Yet Bottom is magically exempt from the law of desire, hence untouchable in the wood. In picking him out for translation, Puck somehow intuits that Bottom alone is impervious to damage from bestial metamorphosis, immune to fantasies of power and sexual possessiveness alike (in Bottom's position, Demetrius might well become a sort of fairyland Macbeth). Bottom emerges unscathed from the madding wood because its sharp law cannot touch him. It is not that Bottom definitively does or does not make love to Titania; in a quantum world, both possibilities are in superposition. The point is that it makes no difference. Bottom has not so much rejected sexuality as transcended it.

Bottom is not the only character exempt from the law of desire, of course. Puck acts as something of a chorus, delighting in the folly of mortal love and desire. But while we enjoy Puck, we do not share his indifference to the lovers' erotic suffering, however ridiculous that suffering appears from the outside, because we ourselves are (have been, will be) them. As evidenced in his waggish exchange with the First Fairy (2.1.1–58), Puck comes across as mischievously childlike, and this limits his understanding. Unlike Puck, Bottom is unambiguously a sexually mature adult. He is not so much *pre*sexual as *a*sexual. We do not know if he is married or has children; the play is careful to mention "Bottom's house" (4.2.1) and leave it at that. Bottom's wife, if he has one, is Schrödingerian; she exists in superposition until observed (by someone other than us).[85]

Bottom's exemption from the law of desire becomes explicable in the context of his emblematic personality, which never alters when it alteration finds. In a play about lovers whose object of desire seems ever elusive, *only Bottom is in love with himself.* Despite enjoying the company of others, Bottom needs nothing from them except applause, since nothing can stir his high estimation of himself. Perhaps perversely, this lack of neediness is exactly what draws people to him. Bottom's electric current reverses Helena's: her need for Demetrius drives away her beloved, whereas Bottom's cheerful narcissism magnetizes him. The law of desire thwarts same-sex amity: compulsory heteronormativity sours Helena and Hermia's bosom friendship on the one hand and short-circuits Lysander and Demetrius' homosocial bond on the other (the young men can play out their attraction only through heterosexual rivalry). But Bottom's adoring friends indulge his conceitedness because it is free of graspingness, malice, and even condescension.

Shakespeare makes it impossible to determine whether Bottom's sexuality even exists. Despite Kott's and other critics' best efforts, it simply *never comes up* in the play. Even if we adduce Bottom's reference to serving one's own turn in the wood as a bawdy quibble, the joke becomes yet another indication that Bottom's desires tend toward innocent self-gratification. One never has a sense that Bottom suppresses his desires; he unselfconsciously indulges them. Rather than an avatar of continence, like the Athenian nuns who achieve independence from Athenian law at the price of "Chaunting faint hymns to the cold fruitless moon" (1.1.73), Bottom is shameless in the best sense of the term. He is in fact perfectly in touch with his own needs and desires, unlike virtually everyone else in the *Dream.* Bottom's desire is not there, but it is not not there, either. Not even jealous Oberon can penetrate a force field as strong as Bottom's self-love (and significantly, only Oberon is impervious to Bottom's charm). Although Bottom remains hilariously ignorant of his good fortune, Shakespeare suggests that self-delusion may be a small price to pay for evading the pain of erotic desire. Shakespeare also slyly hints that erotic autonomy—the ability to serve one's own turn, to die upon one's own hand—is the antidote to infatuation.[86]

Bottom's magical exemption, his free pass through the wood of desire, extends to the *Dream*'s parallel tyranny, the sharp patriarchal law. For Hermia forced marriage to a man she does not love is tantamount to legalized, state-sanctioned rape (1.1.79–82), and the silent presence of the defeated Amazonian queen sharpens her point. The shadowy pockets of resistance to Theseus's authority—Lysander's aunt's house, Amazonia, the nunnery, the fair vestal who dodges Cupid's bolt—remain dark matter. Pressing up against patriarchal Athens without quite being able to burst through into representation, these negative spaces promise true female autonomy. Conversely, the wood is not a respite from patriarchal law but an extension of it. Oberon directs the circuit of erotic attraction through the love-juice and its antidote, just as his double, Theseus, directs female coverture through the "sharp Athenian law" (1.1.162). The point is reinforced when Oberon simply steps through the fairies' *ineffectual* charmed circle to daub his rebellious, helpless wife's eyes with the love-potion. Theseus at first insists that even he is subject to the law he enforces (1.1.120). Yet discovering the befuddled lovers in the forest, Theseus abrogates the very law he earlier claimed was immutable (4.1.178). Perhaps fearing that Hermia's tears will mar his wedding day, the Duke willfully twists the law against the capricious paternal whim the law initially supported—except "will" (with its phallic pun) is of course what the law represented all along. By extenuating the law of Athens, Theseus reaffirms it. The only difference between Egeus's "no" to Hermia and Theseus's ultimate "yes" is that in Athens Theseus *is* the law. Comedic resolution is bought at the price of exposing patriarchal law as beneficent tyranny.[87]

Theseus need not concern himself with Bottom's marital status; luckily, the weaver is small fry. The Athenian law contains a loophole wide enough for the clown to slip through because, unlike Hermia, Hippolyta, or Titania, Bottom does not threaten it. Bottom cheerfully evades the teleology of romance. The law of Athens is also the law of Plautine comedy: in order to maintain the institution of marriage, the occasional *senex* must have his will thwarted (husbands are interchangeable; the important thing is to have one by the end of act 5). The superflux of patriarchy is stirred but not shaken by Hermia's choice of either colorless young man. The law of comedy drives all except the clown to the marriage bed—except the occasional bachelor, like *As You Like It*'s Jacques, who beats the bounds of heteronormativity through his embrace of cynical bachelorhood.

Bottom's sexuality is the *Dream*'s most privileged site of invisibility, and it thematically justifies the unrepresented scene of consummation between queen and clown.[88] As with the presumed original doubling of Theseus/Oberon, a practical necessity—the impossibility of staging the sexual act in a censored theater—has been turned to dramaturgical advantage. Valerie Traub describes Shakespearean sexuality as riven by contradiction: "On the one hand, an elevated, naturalized, transcendent 'sexuality' coincident to and synonymous with a historically incipient ideology of romantic love; on the other side, a politicized 'sexuality' simultaneously physical and psychological, often bawdy, and constituted as much by anxiety as by desire."[89] The *Dream* pits Lysander and Hermia's idealized love-match against the political dictates of Athens only to reconcile them. From these constrictions and contradictions Bottom passes on in bachelor meditation, fancy free, modeling a solution to erotic unhappiness almost Buddhist in its simplicity. Harold Brooks comments, "In Bottom, the artisan world has its uncrowned king, and he is cast for the part of a lover whose love is never to be consummated."[90] Unconsummated love may be a tragedy for Pyramus but one devoutly to be wished by the clown who plays Pyramus with such gusto.

A Midsummer Night's Dream offers us a "parted image" of sexual desire in which "everything seems double"—both mountain and cloud. Shakespeare's clown both is and is not a desiring Bottom, his sexuality an absent presence that holds open the riddle of desire itself. Always invisible yet perhaps never quite absent, Bottom's desire represents the dark matter that structures all our experience in the playhouse. Bottom's offstage adventure (if it is one) reminds us that theater unfolds as a dance between the withheld and the disclosed; it frames and defines the phenomenology of theatrical pleasure, which both satisfies and frustrates our desire.

Widening the stakes beyond Shakespeare's comedy, I have argued against the critical impulse to reify dramatic character by pressing quantum physics into poetic service. In so doing I have relied on physicists' own equation between quantum cloudiness and poetic dream. As we saw, Schrödinger warned us against an overmaterialist view of physics, while Bohr conjectured that physics merely provides a language for making sense of subatomic observation. "There is no quantum world," Bohr once wrote—astonishingly—to a friend. "There is only abstract quantum physical description. It is wrong to think that the task of physics is to find out how nature is. Physics is concerned with what we can say about nature."[91] Adopting a quantum perspective—surely no less absurd than collapsing three Hamlets into one, accepting the convention of the soliloquy, or endowing imaginary characters with past histories and Oedipus complexes—we can understand how indivisible Bottom may pass through two (or more) slits at once. As the exasperated Wittgenstein complained, "[Shakespeare] is completely unrealistic. (Like a dream.)"[92]

Perhaps we might see classical dramaturgy as a sort of virtual hologram in which three-dimensional people (like atoms) are constructed out of words (or images) and take on lives of their own independent of the words set down for them. Bottom does not, strictly speaking, exist as a coherent psychological being, and he may not have done so for his creator. Lina Perkins Wilder points out that while the clown has been called Bottom in speech prefixes since the eighteenth century, in the earliest printed texts he is identified by three different names: Bottom, Pyramus, and Clown.[93] As Random Cloud asserts, the editorial standardization of speech tags and the creation of lists of dramatis personae create the illusion of preexistent essence, whereas what we call characters are relational and interactive "illusions built up out of the simultitudinous dynamic of *all* the ingredients of dramatic art, of which character is only a part."[94] The norms of classical dramaturgy are no less fanciful for being conventional, and Shakespeare was unafraid to flout them—aware that his audience's imaginations were likewise fluid, especially in such an oneiric play as the *Dream*.

Is quantum dramaturgy too much of an imposition on Shakespeare, who after all predates not only quantum physics, but classical physics as well? However fascinated by the idea that miniscule entities can move at light speed, clearly Shakespeare was not reading Einstein or Bohr.[95] But my point is not that we (or Shakespeare's audience) need quantum physics to understand Bottom's role, nor do I claim Shakespeare for science. Rather, quantum theory's overturning of classical physics nicely mirrors how *A Midsummer Night's Dream* performs ontological uncertainty, destabilizing our assumptions about invisible character and offstage action alike. Like Norman Rabkin, I take complementarity to be less scientific dogma than a transhistorical mode of vision.[96] If twentieth-century speech-act theory helps explain how Elizabethan spectators believed that actors could unwittingly conjure devils onstage, as I argued in chapter 1, quantum theory similarly models how Bottom can be in two contradictory states at once. This approach is surely no more anachronistic than applying, say, Lacanian psychoanalysis to early modern subjectivity, or Michel Serres's theory of polychromic time to English Renaissance matter.[97] Historicist critics freely use modern and postmodern theory to illuminate historical phenomenology without letting Shakespeare's obvious ignorance of that theory stand in the way. And as theater historian Marvin Carlson has observed, we are doomed to be post-Heisenberg whether we like it or not.[98]

Elizabeth Spiller notes, "For early modern writers, the existence of science depends on the possibility of fiction . . . Critics of the early modern period have recognized how closely allied the 'inventions' of literature are with those of science."[99] Far from dividing the two modes of understanding, in fact, the technique of heuristic analogy unites scientific practice and literary criticism. Einstein, Schrödinger, and their colleagues found thought experiments indispensible in reimagining physics, bodying forth the forms of things unknown and turning them into shapes—quarks, protons, gluons, and the rest—that held explanatory power despite lacking empirical verification. Einstein modestly cast his revolutionary 1905 theory on the quantized nature of light, which eventually earned him the Nobel Prize, as *Heuristchen*.[100] In recent superstring theory, a particle is poetically understood as just the pattern of vibration of an internal string in hidden dimensions. Different particles are just different "notes" played by the same string vibrating at different frequencies.[101] This wonderful image revives the poetic-mathematical idea of the music of the spheres; literary and scientific imaginations beautifully converge. As Joseph Roach writes, "Theatrical performance is the simultaneous experience of mutually exclusive possibilities—truth and illusion, presence and absence, face and mask."[102] These contradictory possibilities bridge literature and science in ways precluded by a strictly positivist view of scientific method and encourage us to indulge our own negative capabilities.[103]

Like *A Midsummer Night's Dream*, quantum mechanics takes us from common-sense realism (the metaphysics of savages, according to Bertrand Russell) to dream-logic. Although quantum theory accurately describes subatomic matter's movement through time and space, it makes no sense. Faced with science's own metaphysical confusion alongside the accuracy of its results, one is inevitably reminded of the old Soviet apparatchik joke: "That's all very well in *praxis,* but how does it work in theory?" I am far from the first observer to note quantum theory's surreal aspect. Physicist

Charles Bennett describes quantum information as "like the information of a dream—we can't show it to others, and when we try to describe it we change the memory of it."[104] If quantum mechanics teaches us anything, it is that what we take to be fundamental reality is as much creation as discovery. Theseus does not believe in fairies; Heisenberg does not believe in atoms. And it is Shakespeare himself, in *Romeo and Juliet,* who has Mercutio refer to miniscule Queen Mab's fairies as "little atomi" (1.3.57).[105] At once clouds and atoms, Shakespeare's "small and undistinguishable" fairies have been quantized all along.

3

Unmasking Women

The Rover *and Sexual Signification on the Restoration Stage*

> What is the essential nature of a fully-developed femininity? . . . The conception of womanliness as a mask, behind which man suspects some hidden danger, throws a little light on the enigma.
>
> —Joan Riviere

> [M]en act and women appear.
>
> —John Berger

In Aphra Behn's popular Restoration comedy *The Rover* (1677), set in Naples at Carnival time during the English interregnum, three spirited young Spanish women decide to evade the control of their noble family and rove the streets in masquerade and vizard. The heroines seek romance with some English cavaliers, followers of the banished Prince Charles, who are visiting the city. Florinda has her eye on an English colonel, Belvile, who saved her from ravishment at the Siege of Pamplona. Her saucy younger sister Hellena, intended for a nun by the sisters' brother Don Pedro, prefers Belvile's companion-in-arms, the devil-may-care Willmore, an impecunious rake. Valeria, the sisters' cousin, falls by default for the less colorful cavalier Frederick. While the women seek romance, the roving men (with the exception of the priggish Belvile) are out for easy sex and, if they can get it, money as well. As if this were not enough excitement, for a woman to don vizard and masquerade during Carnival is to advertise herself as a

66

prostitute for hire—and thus to risk propositioning, or worse, from sexual tourists on the prowl in Naples.[1] The promise of anonymous "rambling" excites Behn's young and sheltered heroines. As Behn's intricate plot unfolds, however, the women get more than they bargained for—including narrowly averted rape at the hands of the Englishmen; narrowly averted incest (at one point Pedro attacks a masked Florinda); and, by play's end, three more or less tamed cavalier husbands.

The heroines' boldness in venturing out in masquerade mirrors that of the gentlewomen in the audience who came to see Behn's play at the Dorset Garden Theatre, where William Davenant's Duke's Company, one of the two professional companies patented by the king, had moved in 1671.[2] Katharine Eisaman Maus reminds us, "Not only the [Restoration] actresses disguised themselves; the women in the boxes and the pit took to wearing masks that covered the whole face. In fact, two groups of women wore masks—aristocratic ladies and prostitutes."[3] Part of the thrill for the aristocrats was the ensuing confusion as intrigued men sought to penetrate the mask, and "a woman of quality who went to the play in a mask was for all practical purposes choosing to compete with [prostitutes] for the attention of men."[4] Behn's sophisticated drama anticipates a pressing question in feminist theater and film criticism.[5] In a representational economy that works to commodify women as sexual objects, what are the relative risks and benefits of exposing the female body to the male gaze?

The Rover's central motif is a masked woman presenting herself before an audience of intrigued men. Thus, in act 1, scene 2, the Englishmen encounter a group of masked women dressed as courtesans and carrying baskets of roses. When the cavaliers' companion Blunt asks for an explanation of the papers pinned on their breasts advertising "roses for every month," Belvile answers, "They are, *or would have you think,* they're courtesans, who here in Naples, are to be hired by the month" (1.2.81–82, emphasis added).[6] Masquerade levels the playing field between respectable women and common prostitutes. Spanish and Englishmen alike insist they can tell the difference but are repeatedly mistaken, a major source of the play's bawdy comedy (Blunt mistakes the prostitute Lucetta for a slumming aristocrat). And while the game is exciting for the women, too, it involves playing with fire.

As the heroines don and shed their disguises, Behn dramatizes both masking and unmasking as risky enterprises. *The Rover* nevertheless critiques the mask's frisson and invites women to seize the reins of representation. Such coming into visibility is not only a matter of literal unmasking—the play's courtesan, Angellica Bianca, rarely wears a mask and yet never signifies outside of her role as object of desire—but of performative *motion*.[7] Behn's dramaturgy models a path for women in which they must strive to control sexual signification without the mask's protection, which comes at the price of translating individual personhood into commodified femininity. Behn's heroines cannot find *themselves* in the mask; nor can they see the mask while they are wearing it. Again and again, the women look out "normally" onto a society that, staring back, sees them as prey—a faceless object of desire that drives men by turns to romantic idealization, misogynistic violence, and sexual cynicism. Hellena must put aside the thrill of anonymous allure and instead become a body that visibly *matters.*

Critics have traditionally seen Willmore both as the play's titular rover and as the mouthpiece of the play's values. The charming yet inconstant rake wittily resists the institution of marriage, which constrains the genre of romantic comedy in which he finds himself. Willmore offers his two paramours, the prostitute Angellica and the spirited virgin Hellena, free love outside the economy of "portion and jointure" that (for Behn) enslaves women (5.1.432). The royalist Behn, who served Prince Charles as a spy in Antwerp, clearly prefers the values of the unconstrained cavaliers to those of the rigid Spaniards, whose practice of marrying off their gentlewomen to the highest bidder the play equates with prostitution (with the ironic caveat that the prostitute can at least choose her own clients). But *The Rover* is neither a spirited defense of free love nor a lusty celebration of libertine attitudes whose heroines are "ruffled" but ultimately unharmed.[8] Rather, Behn exploits a radical and recent (for England) technology in order to interrogate sexual signification anew: the staged female body. But what did it mean to present female bodies within a signifying system—the professional London theater—from which women had been historically excluded?

Staging the Actress

A woman speaking onstage was not unheard of before the Restoration. Queen Anne took nonspeaking roles in Ben Jonson's masques, and Henrietta Maria and her ladies notoriously participated in entertainments at court. But before Parliament closed the theaters in 1642, all female roles on the professional English stage were played by boys or, occasionally, men. Elizabethan plays exploited the homoerotic potential of this all-male stage by adopting cross-dressing motifs in which female characters donned male clothing, foregrounding the male body beneath the female guise.[9] Antitheatricalists of the era such as John Rainoldes, Philip Stubbes, and William Prynne accused the public stage not only of encouraging idleness but of inciting homosexual desire for boys. Despite the extraordinary variety of female roles created by the male playwrights of the day, there were no female bodies on the stage, only representations of them written and performed by males (albeit for a mixed audience of men and women).[10]

Constrained by the ban against actresses, English Renaissance playwrights turned limitation to advantage. Plays such as *Othello, The Duchess of Malfi,* and *The Changeling* focus on male anxiety over female sexual choice, while comedies frequently consider what might be called the Hermia complex: spirited women seeking to make their own marital choices, sometimes in male drag. Settings in such plays as *Othello* and *The Changeling* are a patriarchal phantasmagoria in which the male need to control women (sometimes embodied by a literal citadel) expresses itself rhetorically as an obsession with reading women's bodies as sexual palimpsests. At once ubiquitous and invisible, female sexual desire haunts the early modern theatrical imagination.[11]

The impossibility of materializing not only female desire but female anatomy within a transvestite theater becomes a running joke in plays such as Middleton and Dekker's comedy *The Roaring Girl* (1611), itself based on the infamous, real-life cross-dressing Londoner Mary Frith (Moll Cutpurse). The eponymous Moll crosses gender boundaries without seeking to erase them. Far from threatening the patriarchal economy, Moll helps match up the play's dully conventional lovers even while spurning marriage herself—not because she rejects the institution as oppressive but because by her own admission she lacks the submissiveness needed to be a good wife. Although Moll attacks the double standard that labels any free-thinking woman a whore, she herself polices the boundaries of gender behavior, testing the faithfulness of citizen-wives among her many oddball activities, which include shopping and tour-guiding (the play doesn't know quite what to do with her in terms of plot). For their part, the play's male characters are fascinated by the felt absence beneath Moll's swaggering codpiece.

It [Moll] is a thing
One knows not how to name; her birth began
Ere she was all made. 'Tis woman more than man,
Man more than woman, and—which to none can hap—
The sun gives her two shadows to one shape.
Nay, more, let this strange thing walk, stand, or sit,
No blazing star draws more eyes after it. (1.2.129–35)[12]

Sir Alexander's outraged yet prurient description of monstrous Moll mimics that of any playhouse attendee "shocked, shocked" by the spectacle of a squeaking boy impersonating a roaring girl on the public scaffold.

Because Moll was played by a boy, her phallus is at once absent (for the character); present (for the boy actor playing her); and, for the original audience, somehow neither and both, depending on the extent, as it were, to which its attention is drawn to the boy player's anatomy. Sexless Moll truly *does* usurp the phallus, as the male characters seem to fear—but only once we acknowledge that "Moll" isn't really there at all.[13] Middleton and Dekker's audience witnessed a staged figure that highlighted the maddening indecipherability of women's bodies. That the fictional Moll seems to lack libido of any kind, having transcended sex in favor of shopping, shows that *The Roaring Girl* is more interested in transgressed gender roles than dangerous female desire. Whatever threat a transvestite theater posed for Puritan imaginations, the all-male stage provided a safe environment in which metropolitan culture could stage and contain that threat, on the level of both plot (where cross-dressed heroines, like *The Roaring Girl's* plucky Mary Fitzallard, usually get their man) and phenomenology. No actual women disrupt male impersonation onstage, although women did of course pay to attend the theater and so must have liked, if perhaps not identified with, what they saw.[14]

Immediately following the reopening of the London theaters by Charles II in 1660 at the Restoration, male actors such as Edward Kynaston temporarily continued to play female parts.[15] The first professional actress on the English stage apparently appeared as Desdemona for the King's Company, under Thomas Killigrew, on December 8, 1660 (possibly Anne Marshall), and the practice quickly became normative.[16] In his 1662 patent granted to Thomas Killigrew, manager of the King's Company, the king decreed that women's parts would henceforth be played by women. Tongue presumably lodged firmly in his cheek, Charles cloaked a blatantly commercial practice in the guise of moral reform. The merry monarch would himself "resort" to taking at least two Restoration actresses, Nell Gwyn and Moll Davis, as his lovers.

The arrival of the first actresses on the licensed public stage revolutionized English theater. Until 1660 the natural way to play a woman was to have a boy impersonate her. But the Restoration stage's "natural woman" literally looked quite different, and in the process of assimilating the actress to English drama, Restoration playwrights were compelled to reassess an entire tradition of staged femininity, just as the professional actresses themselves needed to define a new social space for women outside the domestic sphere. Now that women were to play women in a professional environment almost entirely scripted and controlled by men, would the dramatic conventions that had operated in the transvestite era, enshrined over decades of playwriting, fossilize or evolve?

Based on eyewitness sources, theatrical records, and textual evidence, theater historians converge on the relentless sexualization of the Restoration actress both onstage and off. The connection in the public's mind between prostitution and the theater was so strong that "'playhouse flesh and blood' [Dryden's phrase] translated effortlessly into sexual terms."[17] As one epilogue of the period waggishly put it:

> Item, you [the male spectator] shall appear behind our scenes
> And there make love with the sweet chink of Guinees
> The unresisted Eloquence of Ninnies.
> Some of our women will be kind to you,
> And promise free Ingress and Egress too.[18]

Elizabeth Howe points out that the introduction of professional actresses "was simultaneously radical—in allowing women a voice on the public stage for the first time—and conservative: within a predominantly courtly, coterie theater the women were almost entirely controlled by male managers and playwrights and were exploited sexually on stage and off."[19]

The Restoration actresses' material circumstances were perhaps more nuanced than Howe implies. In 1695 two actresses, Ann Bracegirdle and Mary Saunderson Betterton, became shareholders of the new Lincoln's Inn Fields Company, with the right to a certain percentage of the profits. The most celebrated English actress of the early Restoration period, Elizabeth Barry, began in the shadow of her protector-lover, the notorious Earl of

Rochester, who famously trained her as an actress on a wager that he could make an actress of her in six months.[20] After earning fame and a measure of financial independence as the Duke's Company's leading lady, Barry served as a financial officer for the United Company (formed 1682), receiving payments from the Lord Chamberlain's office for plays performed before royalty. Barry eventually comanaged the company with Thomas Betterton. Unlike her less fortunate peers, Barry was able to choose her paramours (her daughter by Rochester died at the age of twelve or thirteen, and she did not marry). She possessed a magnetic charm onstage and "dazzled audiences with a beauty she did not have" (see fig. 2).[21] An even more remarkable career belonged to Aphra Behn—not the first English woman to have a play produced but "the first recognized professional woman writer in English," a Restoration self-fashioner responsible for perhaps twenty plays, among them some of the most popular of their day, along with poems, novels, and much else.[22]

Although actresses were indeed vulnerable to sexual coercion and assault (famous for her representations of imperiled virtue, Bracegirdle suffered a notorious offstage rape attempt), the staging of women in the late seventeenth century need not be understood merely as a story of exploitation and victimization onstage and off. Rather, the debate over a woman's role in Restoration theater—as dramatic character, actress, audience member, shareholder, and in Behn's case, playwright—should be theorized as an ongoing negotiation over the sexual politics of the female body and its representation. In *The Rover* Behn dramatizes an authoritarian sign system that turns women into emblems of sexual availability. At the same time, she models acts of agency in which women unmask themselves as individuals and threaten to signify in their own right.

Mapping the Dark: A Tomographic Approach

As a veil between the visible and the invisible, the Restoration mask invites spectral reading. The vizard is physically visible onstage but, like the Renaissance codpiece, directs our attention to what lies behind it. It does not signify in isolation; indeed, if the mask is sufficiently neutral rather than expressive, it takes on the emotional character indicated by the bodily gestures of the person who wears it (fear, happiness, flirtatiousness, and so on). Unless removed onstage, it is more prosthesis than prop, and its impact cannot be separated from that of the performer who wears it. Al-

Figure 2. Elizabeth Barry, after Godfrey Kneller. (Garrick Club, Art Archive at Art Resource, New York.)

though as a material object the mask is not, strictly speaking, dark matter, it functions as a lens that simultaneously focuses our imagination on the hidden face and—since facial features are the locus of individuality as well as expressivity—distorts the wearer's semiotic signal. We might say that the mask substitutes the idea of a face for the face itself; it is a machine for producing dark matter, along with our desire to bring that matter to light. And because the worn mask in some sense fuses with the actor in performance, we "see" and don't see it at the same time.

Poetically speaking, the mask resembles the matter (both dark and luminous) whose mass bends distant starlight by warping the space and time in its vicinity.[23] From our observation point on Earth, we see the light rays from a background source, such as a galaxy, visibly bend around an intervening massive object, such as a black hole, which magnifies the background image while itself remaining invisible. Cosmologists have noted the odd optical illusions (such as the doubling of a quasar) that accompany such gravitational lensing, which magnifies, as well as distorts, the distant light signal.[24] When it functions as such a lens, cosmic dark matter enables us to view the light from extremely distant objects that would otherwise be much too far away to see.[25] Thanks to recent technological advances, cosmologists can even correct for the distortion of the original light signals (some of which go far back in time) and then use statistical analysis to map the scrim of dark matter in the foreground—a kind of spectral reading in its own right.[26] In fact the night sky shimmers with a veil of dark matter that intervenes between us and the heavens (astrophysicist Richard Ellis has poetically compared stargazing to sitting in the bottom of a swimming pool looking up).[27] The Restoration mask similarly intervenes between the object (the face) and the observer. But what the male character "sees" when he looks at the mask is an *imaginary* projection: the fetishized sign of femininity. Collapsing the categories of prostitute and woman of quality, the mask at once intensifies the desire to penetrate it and warps the signal issuing from behind it—even if the woman's identity somehow "leaks out" around the edges and blows her cover.[28]

Feminist critics emphasize the Restoration mask's double nature as ally and foe. Anne Russell notes, "In *The Rover* masks are often both subversive and liberating for the women characters; on the other hand, they also place some of the women in dangerous situations because of the association of the mask with the prostitute."[29] According to Jessica Munns, *The Rover*'s emancipatory impulse helped open up "a new sexual space" for women, which was then forced to contract amid the conservative backlash in the 1670s.[30] For Catherine Gallagher, however, Behn's masks reflect moments of crisis "when the veiled woman confronts the impossibility of being represented and hence of being desired and hence of being, finally, perhaps, gratified."[31] Susan Green registers the mask's semiotic instability: "[T]he female body moves between designations in theatrical place to designations in language within a semiosis that uses up the logical possibilities for the representation of women at the same time as it semantically opens up possibilities for transformation and reevaluation of those conditions of representability."[32] Lesley Ferris distinguishes between the masked actress, who is neutralized by patriarchal signification, and the masked female spectator, who *could* experience masking as a subversive act: "Since the physicality of a woman's face—her beauty or lack of it—so centrally influenced her success in life, then eradicating and neutralizing this face was equally anarchistic."[33] Conversely, for Mark S. Lussier, the mask is a Lacanian mirror held up by Behn's female characters before the audience's gaze as a protest "against the symbolic order itself."[34] There are as many ways of reading the mask as there are of reading Restoration sexual politics; the only critical consensus is that, as it circulated from pit and gallery to stage and back again, "the mask became a central symbol of Restoration theatre"—passing from life to art and back again.[35]

Once we read the play as Hellena's education in the privileges and pitfalls of the mask—informed by Angellica's journey (from prostitution to free love to desperation) on the one hand and Florinda's journey (from chaste love to attempted rape to marriage) on the other—we cut through the play's dizzying twists of plot and confront the semiotic stakes behind masquerade. Must women remain somehow invisible—the victims not only of patriarchal control but of male projection (Willmore), romantic idealization (Belvile), and sexual sadism (Blunt)? That the observer of the masked woman sees a *blank* where the face should be symbolizes the way that Behn's male characters cling to fantasy. "I long to see the shadow of the fair substance," claims Willmore, explicitly preferring a two-dimensional image—Angellica's picture—to the real McCoy (2.1.19). The mask intensifies, magnifies, and distorts female identity itself, and only by laying down the mask can women present themselves as desiring agents in their own right.

Willmore and his companions remain lost in fantastic projections, continually misreading "woman" even as the mask sharpens her anonymous allure. Behn suggests that our task is to correct for distortion by employing what I call *tomographic criticism*. The word *tomography* derives from the Greek *tomos* (part or section) and *graphein* (to write).[36] Tomography combines a series of cross-sectional views (such as Willmore's glimpse of his gypsy at 3.1.187 or Angellica's portraits) into a three-dimensional image: in this case, a flesh-and-blood actress/character moving through stage time and space for embodied spectators. The tomographic approach reanimates stage figures rather than reverting to a succession of "stills," like the notoriously erotic portraits of Nell Gwyn by the likes of Simon Verelst and

Gerald Valck (which circulated in the 1680s). Tomography turns shadows (projections) back into substance—as when, in an early instance of the method, the ancient Greeks correctly reconstructed Earth's spherical reality from its disclike projection on the lunar surface during an eclipse. And just as astrotomography allows cosmologists to look back in time (by measuring redshift) and to map dark matter (by measuring gravitational distortion), so can spectral reading reconstruct female identity itself, bodying forth for the first time on the professional English stage.[37]

The Rover continually asks us to reconcile several competing perspectives: the heroine looking out from behind the mask at her male observer(s); the observer(s) looking on in a series of erotic misprisions; and our own gaze, in which we watch the masked woman watching her watcher (who himself may be observed by various onstage figures).[38] Meanwhile, behind the vizard lies yet another lens: the fictional character that stands between us and the actress who impersonates her. Tomographic criticism, then, attempts to reconstruct the spectral presences missing from the scene—the character behind the mask and the actress behind the sign "Woman."

Reconstructing Hellena: The Rover's Play of Gazes

Because female roles were so identified with the actresses who played them, Dorset Garden audiences no doubt wished to stargaze on the young Elizabeth Barry, who was still new to the company when *The Rover* premiered in March 1677 (she probably debuted as Draxilla in Otway's *Alcibiades* in late September 1675). As Hellena's creator, Barry was not yet "ghosted" (in Marvin Carlson's term) by her subsequent performances.[39] In addition to her great tragic roles, these would come to include Willmore's love interest La Nuche in *The Second Part of The Rover* and even Angellica herself in a late revival shortly before Barry's retirement. Nor was Barry yet ghosted by visible pregnancy at *The Rover*'s premier; her daughter by Rochester was born shortly before December 17, 1677. When we imagine Hellena's first appearance, then, we must imagine her as a kind of mask or veil lightly thrown over Barry's persona as a witty ingenue. The charismatic star's halo surrounds (and perhaps occasionally eclipses) the fictional character, which itself acts as a sort of magnifying glass for the starlight behind it.[40]

Fittingly for a play so concerned with female visibility, *The Rover* begins with the threat of a vanishing act. Young Hellena is intended for the nunnery, a female space divorced from the male gaze.[41] Unlike *Measure for*

Measure's Isabella, Hellena rejects the Ophelia strategy of withdrawing in protest from the economy of representation altogether.[42] Hellena chides her bashful sister Florinda, whose face is an open book, for her semiotic transparency: "why do you frown and blush?" (1.1.64–65). Masking would seem the perfect antidote. Hellena hopes that the vizard will strike the perfect balance between liberty and objectification (erotic attention on the one hand, freedom from sexual assault on the other). For Hellena the masquerade forestalls the prospect of forced marriage and forced nunhood, and everything that transpires follows her decision to enter the space of representation incognita. Hellena's irresistible proposition deliciously challenges patriarchal authority: "let's ramble" (1.1.176).[43]

Hellena's desire to "take all innocent freedoms" under the cover of mask and gypsy costume, accompanied by her sister and cousin, both launches the play's plot and foregrounds the politics of representation (1.1.178).[44] The vizard magically combines anonymity and mobility even as it produces facial invisibility. Exciting for the women and titillating for the men, the mask incites desire based on erotic fantasy. Hooked by the masked prostitute Lucetta, Blunt believes that she is a woman of quality, much to the derision of the other Englishmen. And once the heroines, disguised as gypsies, encounter their three English gallants, male misprision fuels the comedy. Hellena's education in the mask commences when, after a witty exchange, Willmore bluntly propositions her. Chagrined to discover that her masked disguise has advertised her body as fair game, Hellena attacks the double standard: "Why must we be either guilty of fornication or murder if we converse with you men—and is there no difference between leave to love me, and leave to lie with me?" (1.2.188–90). "Faith, child, they were made to go together," quips Willmore, and the lovers duly agree to a postprandial rendezvous.

As the cavaliers flirt with their respective masked partners, Behn accentuates her comedy of misprision.[45] Throughout the act the men divide women into two categories, "virtuous maid" (1.2.234) and "cheap whore" (1.2.42), the very distinction deconstructed by the mask. Belvile fails to recognize his beloved Florinda in her "charming Sybil" disguise, although he later recognizes her handwriting when she leaves him a note suggesting an assignation that night (1.2.218). If Belvile's idealization of Florinda renders him incapable of recognizing her as a gypsy, Willmore is smitten by his faceless paramour's wit and humor: "Hang her, she was some damned honest person of quality, I'm sure, she was so very free and witty" (1.2.295–96).

The mask distorts the (class) signal produced by Hellena's voice; Willmore cannot be sure of his impression. Ignorant of Lucetta's profession, Blunt disdains prostitution, not realizing that Naples embodies sexual commodification.[46] In Naples both well-born virgins and prostitutes are for sale to the highest bidder. The men's bumbling attempts at sexual tourism (all lack money save Blunt) will take on darker tones when a drunken Willmore and a vengeful Blunt each attack Florinda, and "the threatened violence of [a] brother" (1.2.241) becomes an unwittingly incestuous assault. Although the heroines experience a rush of erotic power in act 1, the link between female adventure and male aggression will be made alarmingly clear once Florinda's virtue repeatedly comes under attack.

Act 1 sharpens the voyeuristic male gaze and leaves open whether the (mixed) Dorset Garden audience will identify with the ogling cavaliers, laugh indulgently at their misreadings, or both. Act 2 belongs to the courtesan Angellica, who *replaces* the mask as a lens for magnifying male desire. Setting her own price at a thousand crowns, Angellica embraces her commodity status because, unlike wives and daughters, she controls the means of production. But Angellica's self-image relies on a male desire that reflects her own pride: "[Men's] wonder feeds my vanity, and he that wishes but to buy gives me more pride than he that gives my price can make my pleasure" (2.1.120–22).[47] Angellica trades from a position not of strength but of vulnerability.

Instead of disguising her features through masquerade, Angellica reproduces her image by prominently displaying several portraits that advertise the real thing. Willmore steals a picture as a masturbatory keepsake for the long voyage, arousing the courtesan's ire and curiosity. Angellica exposes herself to Willmore's gaze in a long "railing scene" that culminates with her giving herself to him sexually despite her former vow that "nothing but gold shall charm my heart" (2.1.135). Willmore's gaze cuts her to the quick, and she is powerless before his scathing criticism: "Poor as I am, I would not sell myself" (2.2.50).[48] Willmore cannot see the *who* of Angellica—a woman seeking financial independence in a cutthroat sexual economy—but only the *what* (the sign "whore"). And because she has no identity aside from her professional masquerade, Angellica melts before Willmore's critique and succumbs to amorous enslavement. Angellica's illusory power depends on another's desire for an *inaccessible* erotic object rather than (yet another) possessive, flesh-and-blood mistress. Having internalized the mask of femininity before the play even begins, Angellica remains an object rather than subject of the gaze—the play's cautionary tale for women.[49]

Hellena, too, is tempted by an imaginary identification with the mask, "the vanity and power to know I am desirable" (3.1.59). But unlike Angellica, Hellena wishes to woo as well as be wooed. Hellena embodies the yearning for heterosexual mutuality in a world that reduces women to wives, daughters, prostitutes, nuns, rape victims, and icons. Naples recasts these roles as identities, what one *is* rather than what one *does*. When Hellena sees the satiated Willmore descend from Angellica's room after lunch, the sexual double standard is rubbed in her face; men like Willmore can get sex *and* money without marriage.[50] It is a bitter lesson, and yet Hellena—masked once more as the gypsy—decides to keep her debauched lover on the hook despite his faithlessness. Flirtatious Hellena mirrors Willmore so as to reflect his own narcissistic desire: "we are both of one humour; I am as inconstant as you" (3.1.170).[51]

At this key moment, Hellena adopts a new representational strategy, moving from *rambling* to *flashing*. She whips off her mask and exposes her face, briefly, to Willmore's—and the audience's—gaze before immediately replacing the vizard. The mask becomes an erotic prop that complicates the play of gazes. Hellena's strategic unmasking is a flirtation akin to "accidentally" dropping her fan. Once the veil drops, does Willmore see Hellena clearly, or does he emblematize her as he did Angellica? Willmore is instantly besotted by the glimpse of beauty beneath.

> By heaven, I never saw such beauty! Oh the charms of those sprightly black eyes! That strangely fair face, full of smiles and dimples! Those soft round melting cherry lips! And small even white teeth! Not to be expressed, but silently adored! Oh, one look more! (3.1.187–91)

Willmore's rhetorical transports illustrate male projection in action. His praise of Hellena's "parts" could not be more generic. It is neither Hellena's nor Barry's individualized face to which he responds, but an idea of beauty. Here Willmore's gaze performs what might be called a *debased* or *failed* tomography. Willmore scans a selected plane of Hellena's face that is literally and figuratively superficial rather than penetrating.

How, then, does the spectral reader recover a more three-dimensional Hellena from a flat projection equivalent to a movie still or pinup? Although Willmore glimpses his gypsy only in bursts and flashes, we track Hellena's progress through the play. Theatrical performance, which unfolds in time as well as three-dimensional space, allows us to integrate various "snapshots" of Hellena, taken as it were from different angles (in this particular case, Willmore's and Angellica's), so as to build a fuller picture of her.[52] For Willmore, Hellena's face is an image instantly to be framed as a generic portrait (*tomos*); Willmore iconizes Hellena's beauty just as he earlier appropriated Angellica's picture. Hellena's afterimage remains seared into Willmore's retina as a disembodied blazon of parts—eyes, face, mouth, teeth (3.1.268). And depending on his or her view of "Elizabeth Barry," the spectator is left free to critique Willmore's fetishized projection or identify with it.

Having exposed Willmore's affair with Angellica, Hellena makes Willmore swear constancy on his knees, and he agrees to rendezvous with his "dear pretty angel" the following day (3.1.261). Meanwhile, Belvile once again fails to recognize masked Florinda, who in her guise as an erotic adventurer tempts the penurious cavalier to accept a jewel that contains her picture (a constancy test). In these parallel scenes, both men begin with a masked woman and end up with her two-dimensional image as a substitute for the real thing. For Willmore, his nameless gypsy's face, revealed in a flash, becomes an *extension* of the mask rather than its antidote. For Belvile, Florinda's jewel-portrait betokens her chastity rather than her perfidy—two sides of the same semiotic coin.

The gaze goes both ways, for the audience also watches the women watching their paramours through the eyeholes of their vizards.[53] Hellena enjoys her flirtatious power, but Behn is careful to include the jilted Angellica's pain as visual counterpoint. Should Hellena push her delicious masquerade too far, warns the playwright, she, too, will become addicted to it. The darker consequences of Hellena's stoking of Willmore's desire become apparent when Willmore assaults Florinda later that evening as she waits for Belvile in her garden.[54] If, by the close of act 3, masked Hellena embodies pert desirability, then exposed Florinda signifies sexual vulnerability. Under cover of night, the drunken rake easily substitutes one "errant harlot" for another (3.6.20). Florinda enters the garden scene "*in an undress*" and barely escapes Willmore's clutches (3.5.s.d.). For his part Belvile remains blinded by idolatry, unable to conceive how Willmore could have mistaken Florinda for a harlot: "Could'st not see something about her face and person, to strike an awful reverence into thy soul?" (3.6.23–24). Belvile is a prisoner of romance; Florinda's mask (here, night itself) mirrors his own blindness.

Taking place the following day, act 4 traces Willmore's turn from Angellica, whose abject devotion bores him, to his wealthy, nameless gypsy.

Now male identity, too, is in masked confusion. Spared by his rival Antonio following an unjust arrest for murder, Belvile finds himself honor bound to take Antonio's place and duel Pedro on the Molo for Angellica's favor. Florinda cannot penetrate Belvile's Antonio disguise; one of the play's recurrent metatheatrical jokes is that Mr. and Mrs. Betterton cannot recognize each other's fictional counterparts. Belvile disarms Pedro in the duel but spares his life, and a rapid sequence of "discoveries" turns farcical. Pedro reveals his identity to "Antonio" and offers him Florinda in marriage immediately; Belvile unmasks to a startled Florinda behind Pedro's back; and, just when Pedro has unwittingly delivered up his sister to her Englishman, Willmore accidentally unmasks Belvile, prompting Pedro to hastily reclaim his sister. A stalemate resumes between Spanish and Englishmen over their female property, played out under the sign of masculine honor.

At this juncture Behn inserts the expected Restoration twist on the cross-dressed heroine motif familiar from Renaissance drama: the so-called breeches role.[55] When Willmore takes the stage, Angellica accuses him of forsaking her for Hellena's two hundred thousand crowns. During this lovers' quarrel, Hellena enters disguised as a young male page. Instead of a boy actor playing a woman (Rosalind, Viola) playing a boy, we see an actress (Barry) playing another woman (Hellena) playing a boy. Like the mask, the breeches role summons a range of critical responses.[56] Is Hellena's cocky male attire another mask, or does it "reboot" her sexual signification? The former seems more likely, for by Restoration stage convention, the donning of masculine dress further eroticized the female form, "suggestively outlining the actress's hips, buttocks and legs, usually concealed by a skirt."[57] If male dress, like rambling, represents the heroine's wish to assume male prerogatives, then here that attempt backfires.[58]

Hellena's motive is mischief. She comes to warn Angellica about Willmore's inconstancy and claims to speak on behalf of his jilted mistress—that is, herself (Willmore still does not know her name). But Hellena's disguise proves ineffectual, for Willmore sees *through* Hellena's male disguise to the gypsy beneath as "*he gazes on her*" in another act of visual framing (4.2.320.s.d.). Unlike the startled glimpse of Hellena's unmasked features at 3.1.185, this is a recognition scene: "Do I not know that face" (4.2.322). But if Willmore's aggressive gaze earlier penetrated Angellica's essence (2.2.67), his scrutiny of Hellena remains superficial. Willmore does recognize the gypsy behind the boy, but thanks to Angellica's revelation of Hellena's fortune, his gypsy has now become what Prague structuralist Petr

Bogatryev calls a sign of the object's sign (wealth).[59] Erotic signification has become commodified in another sense.

At the same moment Behn invites us to look more deeply than the libertine, seeing Barry *behind* Hellena *behind* the gypsy *behind* the boy. How many layers did Behn expect the audience to pierce—is there a "real" woman behind the parade of signs? Behn was no doubt aware that Barry herself must have stood for the sign "whore" for many in the Dorset Garden audience.[60] Barry was ghosted by her reputation as Rochester's lover, but also by her earlier roles, in which she played virginal and virtuous young heroines in plays by Behn, Ravenscroft, Rawlins, Durfey, and Otway. *The Rover* exploited celebrity ghosting elsewhere by having Belvile and Florinda played by the married Mr. and Mrs. Betterton, whose offstage union foreshadows that of their conventional characters; unlike Barry, Mary Betterton (formerly Saunderson) retained a reputation for untainted virtue.[61] Here Behn models the tomographic challenge: a series of receding planes that can be either sliced into constituent portraits (boy, breeches, gypsy, Hellena, Barry, actress, whore, woman) or integrated into a single composite image of unmasked female identity (Hellena/Barry).

Within the plot the masquerade lesson for Hellena is kinder than it was for Angellica. If Willmore's gaze conquered Angellica in act 2, Willmore here teases Hellena but chooses not to expose her. He merely discomfits her by insulting the gypsy to her (and Angellica's) face. Hellena's male disguise disadvantages her in the merry war between the sexes. Easily penetrated, it places her at Willmore's mercy until she flees the stage. The plot thematizes a choice that plays out in semiotic terms: Hellena must decide whether to remask as the seductive gypsy or reveal herself as a virgin heiress in love with an inconstant rake.

The mask's dangers are thrown into sharp relief as rambling devolves into attempted rape.[62] Escaping her brother, Florinda flees to Blunt's lodgings and surprises him, still in undershirt and drawers, in his chamber. Determined to avenge his humiliation at the hands of Lucetta, Blunt threatens to rape and beat her. With the entrance of Frederick, the scene turns still uglier. Blunt interprets the masked intruder as a prostitute, Frederick as a gentlewoman in search of rough trade (4.5.71–72). Blunt rends the veil of male idealization to reveal the misogyny beneath; by this logic kissing, beating, and *seeing* become equivalent acts of violence (4.5.49). Masked Florinda's pleas to "pity a harmless virgin" (4.5.39) and to be "use[d] . . . kindly" (4.5.109), with its obscene pun, only aggravate Blunt. For him the vizard emblematizes woman's hypocrisy—and for the purposes of vengeance, one faceless woman is as good as another.

Still more disturbing is the hitherto colorless Frederick's decision to frame the situation as comic (teaching womankind a lesson) rather than heroic (rescuing the maiden in distress). But despite his eagerness to partake in sex, Frederick is given pause by Florinda's diamond. Are the men merely keen to "ruffle" a harlot, or are they raping a woman of quality, for which they will be held liable as foreigners (4.5.123–25)? Under patriarchal logic, an identical sexual violation becomes two quite different acts (sport, rape) depending on the victim's social class. Act 4 ends with Frederick locking up Florinda, her fate hanging on Belvile's arrival. The mask's lesson has become frighteningly clear: by rendering women interchangeable for purposes of sexual violence, the vizard short-circuits female self-representation.

At this point in the action, genre exerts its inexorable gravitational pull on the plot. Since Behn casts *The Rover* as a (problem) comedy whose end is marriage, act 5 must tie up the plot's loose ends even if thematic issues such as Angellica's future or Willmore's sex addiction remain unresolved. How are the men's libertine values to be reconciled with marriage? What will become of vengeful Angellica, an inconvenient leftover of the marital traffic in women? And how will the mask's transgressions be neutralized once Carnival space returns to business as usual? Significantly, the act's continuous scene is confined to Blunt's chamber, the space of male sexual rage. Blunt's chamber embodies the logical conclusion of the ramble, and all three heroines improbably wind up there.

Pushing the boundaries even by the permissive standards of Restoration comedy, Blunt's private revenge becomes a threatened gang rape once Belvile, Willmore, Frederick, and Pedro break down Blunt's door to jeer at their gulled friend. Belvile recognizes Florinda's diamond and must improvise a plan to rescue her without revealing her identity to her brother. Behn equates sexual violence and the desire to unmask women's essence once and for all: "We'll see her, let her be what she will; we'll see her," crows Willmore, a would-be rapist once more (5.1.81). Confident in his ability to tell a woman of quality from a whore, Pedro chillingly makes reference to the unseen captive's being provided "for your diversion" (5.1.82–83), a metatheatrical reference to the sexualized Restoration actress. Once the men cast lots for Florinda, and Pedro (in what can only be called a sight gag) draws the longest sword, Florinda enters running, still masked, with

Pedro after her. Pedro's ideology has led him (unwittingly) to attempt incestuous rape—perhaps the ultimate emblem of the patriarchal control he and his absent father have exerted throughout. A prisoner of her honor, Florinda would rather suffer her brother's assault than drop the vizard and reveal her identity, thereby humiliating her name and family. The mask has put Florinda in an impossible position. She cannot expose herself without social ruin, yet to remain masked is to court incest.

Saving the play from tragedy, Florinda is rescued by an unmasked Valeria ex machina, who brings Pedro fictional tidings of Florinda's flight that drive him offstage in the nick of time. Florinda then *unmasks* to the assembled company—her single boldest move in a play that has continually disempowered her. The removal of the distortive lens instantly shifts the play's genre from quasi pornography to romantic comedy. In what amounts to tableau, the men can now *see* Florinda for the first time (Willmore reminds the company that when he last accosted Florinda, it was nighttime). Will the men's erotic projections now resolve into a three-dimensional image of a "real" woman?

Unable to make the tomographic leap, Willmore once more frames feminine pulchritude as a generic image: "'tis a surprising beauty" (5.1.147). The audience sees not only Florinda but Mrs. Betterton—reunited with her real-life husband and about to repeat her marriage vows offstage. In an oddly rushed, perhaps ironic denouement, Florinda forgives the cavaliers— friends of her soon-to-be husband, after all—their capture and attempted violation of her (twice), while the page runs to "fetch a father instantly" (5.1.148).[63] Suddenly playing Hymen rather than Daphne, Florinda commands the penitent Frederick to marry Valeria (with Valeria's fortune as sweetener) in exchange for forgiveness.[64] Surprisingly, even the egregious Blunt is included in Florinda's generosity, and Florinda and Valeria prepare to wed their respective cavaliers.[65]

Just in case the audience has missed the thematic import of Florinda's unmasking, Behn provides a sobering coda. While Willmore guards the door behind which the couples are making their vows, Angellica enters in a masquing habit and vizard. Willmore, ever on the prowl, mistakes her for his gypsy until she draws a pistol and threatens to shoot him. Angellica melodramatically doffs her mask in a visual echo of Florinda's genre-shifting gesture: "Behold this face" (5.1.202). But it is too late; by identifying with male desire, Angellica has given away her power. Without Willmore's desire for her, she has nothing to fall back on. Angellica is enslaved to passion in a way she never was by prostitution. In this sense Blunt *is* unknowingly revenged on womankind for his mortification; the play's female scapegoat suffers humiliation in addition to whoredom, a double denigration. Angellica now recognizes Willmore as her "undeceiving glass" (5.1.273). A mirror is the opposite of a mask, since the latter allows the play's women to observe how *others* misprize them rather than having to contemplate their own reflection. As a fallen idol, Angellica emblematizes semiotic desperation. She is easily disarmed by the symbolically emasculated Antonio, whose arm remains in a sling. The phallic pistol passes safely from female to male hands without destroying Willmore, and Behn's object lesson is complete: any woman who overidentifies with the mask's glamour will likely sacrifice her identity, agency, happiness, and freedom. Angellica exits the space of representation entirely, leaving only her malediction behind.[66]

Has Hellena learned from Angellica's mistake? She enters, unmasked yet once more dressed as a boy, and pulls Willmore aside to engage in a witty bargaining scene over whether there should be sex before marriage. Her male disguise no longer functions as a mask, if it ever did; once more Willmore happily sees through the disguise to his gypsy beneath. Hellena's boy costume seems merely piquant, part of an erotic game designed to tease Willmore to madness (and the altar). The jovial lovers square off in their final round. Willmore delivers the libertine's credo to free love that earlier seduced Angellica, but clear-sighted Hellena wittily rejects a "cradle full of noise and mischief, with a pack of repentance at my back" (5.1.439–40).

Hellena's insistence on the marriage vow has troubled some critics. According to Hutner, for instance, marriage defeats the enterprise of female autonomy with which the play began.[67] Yet Hellena reminds us that her desire all along has simply been to level the playing field: "[M]y business is the same with all living creatures of my age, to love, and be beloved, and here's the man" (5.1.479–81). To enlist Hellena for feminist subversion is to warp *The Rover*'s fabric, for patriarchy's dark matter (in the person of unseen or absent fathers) holds *every* character, whether male or female, in its gravitational field. More modestly, Hellena's values win out over Willmore's, at least in this round. Hellena marries the man of her choice on her own terms, and, by eluding the nunnery, she even keeps control of her inheritance.[68] It is not Hellena's masks but her "humour" that ultimately captivates Willmore; indeed, Hellena's witty, ironic, clear-sighted gaiety is her signature trait. And once we read the play spectrally, Hellena's rounded personality, expressed through Barry's engaging voice, trumps the mask's flattening significations. In a delightful verbal variant of unmasking, the engaged couple at long last share their Christian names. Willmore and Hellena now see each other clear—or, at least, as clearly as men and women ever see each other in *The Rover*.[69]

Conclusion: Aphra through the Looking Glass

The Rover champions female visibility. In the course of her ramble from the protected world of patriarchal control through the carnivalesque world of male desire, Hellena achieves the best that a woman in her position (virginal, attractive, intelligent, educated for the convent) can hope for: to speak her own desire, control her sexuality, choose her partner, marry clear-sightedly, and retain her fortune. All of Behn's heroines struggle to establish a representational foothold within an economy that commodifies them. Behn is well aware that exposing playhouse flesh and blood risks renewed sexual exploitation onstage and off, yet masked anonymity is no antidote to female victimhood. As dark matter the masked female face warps female identity even as it captivates the male gaze; the actress's various masquerades threaten to efface female presence once and for all. While the mask tempts women as both recreation (Hellena) and occupation (Angellica), its significations easily spin out of the wearer's control, as Florinda discovers. Within the play's semiotic structure, Florinda and Angellica embody the Scylla ("angel") and Charybdis ("whore") of patriarchal fantasy. Spirited Hellena must navigate between these twin dangers in her odyssey from daughter to gypsy to boy to wife.

The Rover seeks to make women's faces matter once more—to recover female identity from behind an intervening scrim that dazzles the gaze. In reconstructing Hellena's journey, I have used the mask as a lens to look back in theatrical time and space and to map the dark matter of the Restoration stage. In doing so I have tried to correct for the semiotic redshift that has obscured Barry's presence behind the role as her original performance recedes from view.[70] I have focused attention on a series of staged moments in which the male gaze arrests an idealized femininity to fit its own fancy, because it is precisely at those moments that we are invited to correct for the mask's distortions.

Tomographic criticism's attempt to round out the stage image echoes Restoration stagecraft itself. Plays like *The Rover* make ample use of "dis-

covery scenes," in which painted shutters roll back to reveal successive perspective scenes that are framed by the proscenium arch.[71] The action then
spills out of this upstage "picture frame" onto the forestage, a long plat-
form that reached out into the pit and close to the boxes and galleries. The
effect is that of a framed picture coming to life before our eyes—precisely
the tomographic leap Behn invites us to make while watching *The Rover*.[72]
Jane Spencer emphasizes Behn's innovative stagecraft, in which "forestage
scenes [are] increasingly interspersed with acting in the scenic area behind
the arch. Her characters weave in and out of the scenery, moving between
scenic area and forestage, and carry on more than one action simultaneously, using different areas of the stage."[73] Upstage and downstage acting
areas model two- and three-dimensional gazes respectively—as when Frederick and Valeria mutely flirt in the scenic area, while the more rounded
Hellena and Willmore audibly dally on the forestage in act 1, scene 2.
Although we cannot be certain just how the play unfolded spatially at
Dorset Garden, Behn's stagecraft encourages us to read the action in three
dimensions.

My spectral reading of *The Rover* rests on an analogy drawn from science: the mask as a kind of (in)visible lens that magnifies even as it distorts
sexual signification. A spectographer of sexual politics, Behn was fascinated
by cutting-edge astronomy and had a keen interest in optics. The telescope
was a relatively recent invention: Galileo's original design was realized in
1609 and Kepler's improvement in 1611. Behn translated Fontanelle's *A
Discovery of New Worlds* in 1688, along with an "Essay on Translated Prose"
containing her own remarks on Copernican theory. Both Kepler and Galileo make cameo appearances in her musical farce *The Emperor of the Moon*
(1687), along with a twenty-foot-long telescope brandished by a lunatic
scientist-astrologer, Doctor Baliardo.[74] Fooled by young Charmante into
believing that he will be able to view the denizens of the moon through
its lens, Baliardo eagerly peers into the telescope. Meanwhile Baliardo's
servant Scaramouch provides Charmante with a "glass" (mirror) with a
picture of a nymph on it. Charmante presents the glass to the audience
with a light behind it—possibly a candle—so that it sees the erotic image
clearly. Charmante then inserts the glass into the mouth of the telescope,
driving Baliardo into transports at the "beauty young and angel-like, leaning upon a cloud" (1.2.85–86).[75] Thanks to the interposed lens, Baliardo
comically mistakes a two-dimensional picture for a three-dimensional
reality—precisely the situation I have traced in *The Rover*. And once again

a scrim obfuscates the view: "Now a cloud veils her from me" (1.2.89). Parallel lenses of the patriarchal imaginary, mask and telescope magnify misprision to comic effect.

So what might the women spectators in the original Dorset Garden audience have made of *The Rover*'s masquerade? Did they identify with Hellena's semiotic autonomy or see through it, dismissing Hellena/Barry as an emblem of sexual patronage? Here the theater historian can only speculate; the inevitable drift in audience responses over time—semiotic redshift—obscures our view of sexual significations.[76] We know that *The Rover* remained popular for decades but not whether Hellena's example inspired women to take up or put down their vizards. Intriguingly, an eye-witness report comes down to us of a production of *The Rover* at Covent Garden in 1757, some eighty years after its premiere, allowing us a glimpse back in theatrical time. When Blunt undresses down to his shirt and drawers in Lucetta's chamber, the ladies at the playhouse "are first alarmed; then the men stare: The Women put up their Fans."[77] Here women once more eschew visibility and take refuge behind a screen (for are the men staring at Blunt or at *them?*)—but whether it is to enjoy a private moment free from the male gaze or out of scandalized bashfulness remains obscure. Whatever the case, this was the last recorded performance of *The Rover* in London until the late 1970s.[78]

It is no doubt possible to read Behn's preference for unmasked women as joining her male colleagues in exploiting female flesh for all it is worth in the service of a commercial hit (she received the third-night proceeds as her fee). The master-mistress of ambiguous authorship, Behn seems to have wanted it both ways, at least in print: the first, anonymous issue of *The Rover* featured a prologue, written by "a Person of Quality," which addressed the author as "He" and "him," although a postscript appeared subsequent to the first issue implicitly acknowledging that the author was female. But reading *The Rover* solely as an act of authorial identification with what Behn calls "my Masculine Part" underestimates her gimlet-eyed meditation on sexual commodification. The self-possessed Hellena, embodied by the ambiguous sign "Elizabeth Barry," invites the audience to critique the culture's relentless conversion of the actress to sexual semaphore.

Unmasking women was a dramaturgical experiment whose outcome was far from certain. At the time of *The Rover*, almost exactly a century after the first professional playhouses appeared in London, actresses had occupied the professional English stage for less than two decades. Behn was the first publicly female professional playwright England had ever known, and she needed commercial success, since she lived by her pen. A realist rather than a feminist, she may have suspected that liberating women from objectification was an impossible task given the economy in which she operated. But Behn's acts of unmasking nonetheless imply that women might wrest control of sexual signification even as they burst out of the picture frame onto the stage.[79] Perhaps that is why the title page of the third issue of *The Rover* announces that the play's author was, in fact, a woman.

4

Unbecoming Acts

Power, Performance, and the Self-Consuming Body in Tennessee Williams's Suddenly Last Summer

> It's a simple but hugely effective theatrical conceit, this idea
> of a main character who never materializes, and I suppose
> it's the same idea that "faith" is built around in any of your
> organised religions—God is out there, he or she just hasn't
> decided to reveal themselves quite yet.
>
> —Neil LaBute

> . . . What had that flower to do with being white,
> The wayside blue and innocent heal-all?
> What brought the kindred spider to that height,
> Then steered the white moth thither in the night?
> What but design of darkness to appall?
> If design govern in a thing so small.
>
> —Robert Frost

Suddenly Last Summer is unique in the Williams canon in that its protagonist is dark matter. The poet Sebastian Venable dies before the action takes place; he is at once a blank text, like the empty pages of the notebook his mother Violet brandishes in triumphant fury as proof of his inability to write his last *Poem of Summer,* and a palimpsest "awesome in his ambiguity."[1] Although Sebastian is literally absent, his afterimages repeat and refract until the play becomes a dizzying hall of mirrors: Cousin George

90

appears sporting Sebastian's wardrobe, Catharine wears a suit Sebastian bought for her, and Doctor Cuckrowicz wears all white, just as Sebastian did on his dying day. No Williams play is more haunted by the body's directives and disguises, yet in no other play is the body in question so elusive.[2]

Produced Off Broadway in 1958 while Williams was undergoing psychoanalysis, *Suddenly Last Summer* belongs to the middle period of his so-called punishment plays, and is arguably the bleakest.[3] Praised for its construction and reviled for its content in equal measure at the time, *Suddenly Last Summer* cuts to the heart of Williams's matter by constructing the (absent) body in relation to power on the one hand and to performance on the other. Violet's and Catharine's narratives alternately flesh out and strip away the figure of Sebastian Venable, raising questions crucial to a long-overdue rereading of the Williams canon. What claims can discourse make to represent the truth of the body? Is there a space for the body outside discourse, or a space for discourse uninflected by power? Does power have the last word to decide where truth lies, or does performance? More tautly than any other Williams play, *Suddenly Last Summer* weaves its subject into a glittering skein of language until we can no longer say for certain where the body ends and discourse begins.

Suddenly Last Summer takes place in the Garden District of New Orleans, on the patio of Violet Venable's Victorian mansion and in her son Sebastian's adjacent garden. Williams's stage directions limn an atmosphere of lush, sickly decay, "steaming with heat after rain."[4] Sebastian's garden (and, by extension, the world of the play) is both postlapsarian jungle and ruthless Darwinian experiment. As Violet explains to her guest, "Dr. Sugar," her son fed fruit flies originally bred for experiments in genetics to his Venus flytrap—a subtle invocation of Nazi medical experiments. The flytrap is kept under glass from early fall to late spring and emerges only in summer, like the carnivorous Sebastian himself. Sebastian has in fact created his garden in his own image, so that every inhabitant feeds off another: "There are massive tree-flowers that suggest organs of a body, torn out, still glistening with undried blood" (9). This rupture rehearses Sebastian's own dismemberment, while the aural tumult punctuating the action suggests a savage rite offstage.

Before the action even begins, Williams rejects what W. B. Worthen terms the rhetoric of realism, which "claims to stage an objective representation by integrating dramatic and performance style into the pictorial consistency of the material scene onstage. The purpose of this consistency is not, in the end, simply mimetic: the aim of realism is to produce an audience, to legitimate its private acts of interpretation *as* objective."[5] Worthen cites the garden in Belasco's *The Return of Peter Grimm* (1911) as an example, for Peter Grimm's garden implicates him "in a complex of social, economic, domestic, and even psychological histories." Yet Williams explodes the compact between playwright and audience by which "a character so fully identified with its productive environment is more completely contained within the stage."[6] Indeed, Williams's setting parodies such realism, for the garden's godlike creator is nowhere to be seen. Displaced by his own voracious metonym, Sebastian is an absent cause. The play offers the audience no safe or privileged point of view from which to judge him.

Undoing the rhetoric of realism is Williams's first move in the exposure of a self whose unity is illusory. Worthen argues that the false "transparency" of realistic production enables both an "objective" interpretation and the "unconstructed" freedom of an audience unaware of its own implication in the machinery of representation.[7] But Williams demystifies his audience. Instead of explaining the dramatic action as a function of the characters' psychology and development, plays like *Suddenly Last Summer* "stage this self as self-delusion, a fiction or evasion, as a commodity for others' consumption that masks an inner emptiness."[8] Character is no longer mimetic, "part of a dramatic ecology the audience can observe but not enter," but "a medium of theatrical exchange between actor and audience"—as it was in Shakespeare's day, before a proscenium contained the actor's image.[9] In this play the rhetoric of realism is superseded by what we, following Stanley Fish, may duly term a rhetoric of self-consumption. The symbolic trajectory of *Suddenly Last Summer*'s antirealism is clear. Violet's mansion presents a facade of gentility in which every object (like Violet herself) is carefully lacquered or laced, but it cannot contain the bodily eruptions Violet seeks to repress. Even as Violet gives birth to and seeks to inscribe Sebastian as a maligned and martyred saint within her own fiction, she herself is consumed by her offspring's legacy: the body that attacks and devours itself.

The self-consuming body is Williams's central motif, but one that has attracted less attention than his characters' celebrated performativity, which, in Judith Butler's definition, acts by "constituting the identity it is purported to be."[10] The two are in fact inseparable, for performativity is the theatrical mechanism by which Williams's self-consuming body is realized onstage. According to Butler, both gender roles and "sex" itself are tenuously constituted in time "through a *stylized repetition of acts*" rather than emanating from a stable bodily identity.[11] Butler construes the body itself as "a process of materialization that stabilizes over time to produce the effect of boundary, fixity, and surface we call matter."[12] The performativity of bodies is, for Butler, regulated by the discourse that produces them—a discourse that is, of necessity, always a citation of earlier performances, a doing continually disguised as a moment-by-moment being. One cannot escape the body's discourse entirely; the only alternative is to seek to resignify the body by reiterating its discourse with a subversive twist.[13]

Butler's notion of performativity unravels the connections among power, performance, and the body so carefully imbricated in *Suddenly Last Summer* and in Williams as a whole. C. W. E. Bigsby has noted that Williams's protagonists are "compulsive fictionalisers," and that Blanche DuBois "turns her life into an art work."[14] Performance allows Williams's creations to come alive, both onstage (as incarnated by actors) and, more important, at the level of their own subjectivity. By transforming the real at the level of the imagination, Williams's characters use fictions of themselves and of their sexuality to carve out a site of resistance, a haven from implacable forces that seek to destroy them. Some, like the Princess Kosmonopolis in *Sweet Bird of Youth,* succeed in jump-starting their theatrical "careers."[15] But most fail, and the penalty is madness, mutilation, and death.

Performance in Williams thus becomes a life-and-death strategy for arrogating, deflecting, and resisting power.[16] In the signifying economy of Williams's drama, the body is the site in which the energies of power and performance circulate and vie for dominance. This struggle is then literally inscribed on the body in the form of cancer (*Cat on a Hot Tin Roof*), rape (*A Streetcar Named Desire*), and sterility and castration (*Sweet Bird of Youth*), to name only a few striking examples. The subject in Williams is caught between a self-reiterating performance, fueled by the body, and a lethal "reality" imposed from without that seeks to switch off the footlights once and for all.

Williams's characters are master-performers—"It wouldn't be make-believe If you believed in me," sings Blanche—but their self-fashioned *personae* have one catch.[17] Like the cigarettes they so often wield as props, Williams's characters are *self-consuming artifacts*. I borrow this phrase from Stanley Fish, but with a twist. Fish uses his term in a purely rhetorical sense, applying it to certain seventeenth-century works he classifies as "dialectical." The dialectician-author is "the good physician," and the reader becomes his patient, moving from a discursive, rational understanding to an antidiscursive, antirational, all-embracing unity with the elusive object of his inquiry. In reading a work like *The Pilgrim's Progress*, "the reader's self . . . is consumed as he responds to the medicinal purging of the dialectician's art, and that art, like other medicines, is consumed in the workings of its own best effects."[18] The work, as an object, seems to disappear; it is self-consuming in two directions, "as an object, which is to be used rather than enjoyed, and as a strategy."[19]

In the case of Williams, Fish's phrase can be taken literally. It is the *self*, which seeks to impose its own version of itself on the world, that is literally consumed in the praxis of performance. Williams's characters continually try on versions of themselves for public display, mapping an increasingly desperate performance onto the resistant and shrinking matter of their bodies, which threatens to go dark at any moment. This performance is always uncertain, since at any moment the bodily ground can give way beneath (or above) one's feet. Blanche "does" Blanche impeccably until her affected speech accidentally lapses into naturalness, and for a moment she literally forgets herself. Far from illustrating Fish's benign "aesthetic of the good physician," then, Williams's self-consuming artifacts choke on their own medicine.[20] They have no recourse other than continual self-depletion; should they falter for more than an instant, more powerful performers will move in for the kill. Power feeds off the body of the other: as Big Daddy's body gnaws away at itself in *Cat on a Hot Tin Roof*, his greedy family hovers like buzzards around carrion. Typically, Big Daddy suffers from malignant uremia, aptly defined by his son Gooper as "poisoning of the whole system due to the failure of the body to eliminate its poisons."[21] Big Daddy's disease manifests what in Williams can only be termed the aesthetic of the self-consuming patient.

While self-dramatizing offers the one respite from a rapacious world, and may succeed in holding the vultures at bay (at least for a while), even the most accomplished of Williams's performers cannot resist time's inevitable triumph over the body. As self-consuming artifacts, Williams's performers are thus left with an impossible choice: to be consumed from without by human predation or to be eaten from within by a performance that inevitably feeds off its bodily surface. Either way the body eventually attenuates to the point where no further discourse is possible. Or does it?

The fantasy in Williams's theater is of a performativity that finally, ecstatically, transcends the body. When Blanche leaves Elysian Fields for the insane asylum, she escapes into the total freedom of madness; her incarcerated body no longer holds her back from her phantom assignation with Shep Huntleigh, a union perfect in its incorporeality. As the body gives way, exhausted by the toll of endless self-citation, the subject in Williams flees from sexuality to language. Language both mediates the body and transcends it, for as the body loses ground, language becomes the sole guarantor that one is who one "does." Language weaves a web of deceit and half truths that at once seeks to contain and displace dangerous sexual impulses ("My son, Sebastian, was chaste. Not c-h-a-s-e-d!" [24]) and to harness those impulses to one's own advantage. That the subject's power resides in its sexuality is taken for granted; in fact, adapting Foucault's influential concept of power/knowledge, we might call the medium through which Williams's characters move *power/sexuality,* since the two are mutually constitutive aspects of the same discourse.[22] To enter the space of discourse is always to enter into the place of seduction, a power play that has as much to do with fantasy as with the body—as *Suddenly Last Summer*'s temptations in the garden attest.

Doctor Cuckrowicz, his English name signaling something edible and sweet, is the fly in Violet Venable's web. "Glacially brilliant" (10), Dr. Sugar is at once a stand-in for Sebastian and representative of the epicene young men to whom mother and son were both attracted. "You would have liked my son, he would have been charmed by you," Violet purrs (22). Violet's own appearance announces her as a brilliant construct, a grotesque triumph of artifice over nature. Violet's "withered bosom" is covered with a starfish of diamonds, and her hair is dyed "orange or pink" (9). Ice-cold daiquiris run in her veins instead of blood. Violet's silver-knobbed cane acts serially as crutch, magic wand, and weapon, for she is this drama's Prospero, its stage-manager, as well as leading lady. And like Prospero, Violet is supported by a bevy of "brave utensils," from the lift she has had installed to get her up and down stairs to the chair whose back her hapless maid cranks up and down, literally stiffening her employer's spine.[23] For Violet's body is in revolt. Dr. Sugar tells Catharine (without irony) that Violet is "a very sick woman" (62), but the bodily ground of her illness is uncertain. Violet herself admits to a "slight aneurism" (57), a convulsion in her brain that has paralyzed half her face. Her niece Catharine deems it a "stroke," which led to Sebastian's substituting Catharine herself as his traveling companion last summer, the summer whose events form the contested core of the play.

Violet has enticed Dr. Sugar to her lair in order to conduct a murder trial in which Catharine is the defendant and Violet herself the plaintiff, prosecutor, and judge. Dr. Sugar is to act both as jury and as potential executor of Violet's lethal will: he is a surgeon at Lion's View, a public hospital for which he performs experimental lobotomies. Violet has interred Catharine in an expensive private asylum, St. Mary's, in order to muzzle her account of Sebastian's death. The "Sebastian Venable Memorial Foundation" is prepared to make a generous donation to Lion's View should Dr. Sugar, ceding Catharine's insanity after hearing her story, agree to perform his operation.

Suddenly Last Summer, then, consists of a performance in which everyone is assigned his or her own role. They even appear as other than themselves: Dr. Sugar and George dress up as two versions of Sebastian, who himself dressed as a Renaissance prince, invoking Cesare Borgia rather than his namesake, St. Sebastian, yet another alter ego. But underneath Sebastian's clothes something essential is at stake: Catharine's brain, her very humanity and source of performativity—which in this world come very close to the same thing. Catharine's body is the site of final judgment, but not even those like Violet, who have power over others, can escape the body's sentence.

Yet the fate of Sebastian's body is played out in the discursive rather than biological arena. Dr. Sugar faces a dizzying exercise in hermeneutics: two conflicting spectral readings of Sebastian Venable's life and death. As dark matter Sebastian can only be known by his gravitational effects; the past being irretrievable, it is up to the Doctor (and the audience) to decide whether Violet or Catharine offers the more compelling version. If at one level the play is a courtroom drama, it is also a murder mystery without a body.[24] Put another way, Sebastian is an absent signifier under which slide conflicting signifieds. His Christian name suggests the Roman martyr of the third century, putative lover of Emperor Diocletian, destroyed in a hail of arrows; his surname conflates venality and cannibalism. Is Sebastian the celibate poet dedicated to the purity of his sacred art described by his mother or the sexual predator described by his cousin? Or both? Or neither?

Violet herself refuses to distinguish between Sebastian's life and art. "The work of a poet is the life of a poet and—vice versa, the life of a poet is the work of a poet, I mean you can't separate them" (12). To Violet her son's physical body and his corpus of work are coextensive. According to her, after nine months of labor Sebastian would produce his annual poem, one for each summer mother and son traveled together. But the pages of last summer's notebook are blank, and thus by Violet's logic Catharine is guilty of murder—criminalized for a sentence Sebastian never committed (to paper). In retrospect Violet reconstructs their travels together as a continuous artwork: "We would—carve out each day of our lives like a piece of sculpture . . . We were a famous couple. People didn't speak of Sebastian and his mother or Mrs. Venable and her son, they said, 'Sebastian and Violet . . . Violet and Sebastian'" (25). Violet echoes the identical twins of *Twelfth Night* with an incestuous flourish, implying that Violet and Sebastian shared more than their last name.

In Violet's memory-theater, only the mother could satisfy her son's appetites, and she is willing to destroy her niece to keep her central exhibit intact: "I'm devoting all that's left of my life, Doctor, to the defense of a dead man's reputation" (13). Violet brandishes Sebastian's poems "as if elevating the Host before the altar" (13). The Host is another human artifact consumed by the faithful, for Violet's temple is the book, and she herself the last defender of the faith.[25] But whereas Christ's sacrifice brought redemption, Sebastian's demise offers only sterility. Sebastian's writings are as unnourishing as the little white pills he ingested instead of food. His thin and costive poetry is not a poetry of the body but represents a denial of the body's propagative function. Sebastian's art, engendered through a poisonous combination of incest and narcissism, is stillborn. According to Violet, Sebastian himself saw his poetry's value as issuing from a dead voice and sought only posthumous fame. But Violet has it backward. Not Sebastian's life but his *death* was his "occupation"—perhaps his only successful poem of summer (11). Ironically, Sebastian's body had already rejected him as a child when rheumatic fever "affected a heart-valve" (13); once again an emotional lack finds its physical correlative. In Violet's Old Testament morality, her stroke and Sebastian's death must be answered with Catharine's lobotomy.

If the mother's temple is the book, the son's temple was the flesh. Sebastian went searching for a "clear image" of God (19) and found it in the grotesque spectacle of baby sea-turtles devoured alive by birds of prey on the beach of the Encantadas. "They were diving down on the hatched sea-turtles, turning them over to expose their soft undersides, tearing the undersides open and rending and eating their flesh" (16–17). This narrated scene both prefigures Sebastian's own demise and provides a mirror image of the play. Violet is the "half-dead" sea-turtle mother responsible for the "long and dreadful" birth (15); Catharine's brother George and her mother, Mrs. Holly, circle Catharine like vultures waiting for the kill; and Sebastian is shredded and devoured by a "flock of black plucked little birds" (91), the beggar-children he has sexually consumed and discarded on the beach at Cabeza de Lobo (a head both vulpine and already lobotomized).[26]

Catharine, too, is surrounded by raptors eager to cut out her brain. Her mother has already inscribed Catharine as an absence ("Not a soul even knows that you've come back from Europe" [44]), while her brother does not even feign interest in her health.[27] Catharine's family is there not to offer support but to coach her into a performance that will confirm Violet's truth and release their pickings: if Catharine capitulates, she and George inherit fifty thousand dollars each. There are further pressures on Catharine to change her story. Only her mother's signature holds Lion's View at bay, for Violet picks up the tab at the more expensive St. Mary's. If Catharine sticks to her story, she will literally lose her mind.

Perhaps only a lunatic would persevere in her version of the truth, but Catherine's subjectivity has been under siege for some time. "Suddenly last winter I began to write my journal in the third person," she tells Dr. Sugar, inviting him to fill in her blankness (64). For one thing, Catharine never gets to wear her own clothes. As the ingenue in a coming-out ball orchestrated by Violet—that curious performative ritual announcing sexual availability—Catharine wore Violet's mink stole, the remnant of another sacrificial victim too low on the food chain to survive and converted to a dead artifact. At Cabeza de Lobo, Sebastian put Catharine in a transparent white lisle bathing suit to lure his prey: "He'd grab my hand and drag me into the water, all the way in, and I'd come out looking naked!" (80). Sebastian understood that even nakedness is a performance, its illusion more titillating than the "real" thing. No less than Sebastian, Catharine performs herself in order to suit the discourse of others.

Designated mad, Catharine is locked up at St. Mary's, medicated, and subjected to insulin shock, electroshock, and the violent ward. As Violet concludes, with icy logic, "Nothing else is left for her" except lobotomy (31). The private economy of St. Mary's reproduces insanity while purporting to cure it, then the public economy of Lion's View disposes of the evidence under the guise of medical research, which brings in funds.

This consumer-driven economy is mirrored at Cabeza de Lobo, where predators like Sebastian feed off the public beach once the private beach is picked clean. Catharine's life at St. Mary's is a natural continuation of her theatrical career: she is under constant surveillance, and on visiting day "they send you to the beauty parlor" (41). Nevertheless, her life there is terminally restrictive. She has lost yard privileges for attempting to make contact with the outside world, and any loss of physical self-possession risks solitary confinement. Without an audience, Catharine will perish no less surely than if her brain is removed. Now, more than ever, her performance needs to *matter*.

The genius of Catharine's performance is to play sane rather than mad, or, as George puts it with grudging admiration, "crazy like a coyote" (47). Catharine warms up by stabbing out her cigarette on Sister's hand (the nurse is so bored with her own repetitive role that she barely bothers to express pain) but soon realizes this will not play to her new audience. Catharine instead appropriates the role Violet has written for Sebastian, that of "a sacrificial victim" (27). In her own testament, Catharine's only sin was to love in a world governed by exploitation. "He liked me and so I loved him," she says simply, casting herself as Desdemona to Sebastian's Othello.[28]

But Catharine's secret weapon is her sexuality. Although Violet flirts shamelessly with the Doctor, leaning on his shoulder and asking him to light her cigarettes, sex is a strategy best exploited by the young. In this arena Violet is no match for the drugged and pliant Catharine. Catharine parlays her injection with truth serum into an aphrodisiac, a welcome sexual intrusion. "Give me all your resistance . . . You are totally passive . . . you will do what I ask," commands Dr. Sugar, but his injection allows Catharine to seduce *him* (69). Violet's outraged tale of Catharine's sexual impropriety at the Mardi Gras ball hands Catharine the role of exploited ingenue, and she plays it to the hilt, retailing her spur-of-the-moment promiscuity in order to excite Dr. Sugar before throwing herself at him in a gesture that can be read as a spontaneous cri de coeur or a shrewd gambit: "Please hold me! I've been so lonely. It's lonelier than death" (71). Unfortunately, Dr. Sugar *is* death, or hers at any rate. The gambit fails, as Dr. Sugar's desires have been displaced into penetrating the brains of helpless young women.

If Violet holds the financial card, Catharine clearly holds its equivalent in the play's erotic economy. Violet's "disfiguring" stroke aside (a rhetori-

cal, as well as a physical, blemish), Sebastian must have already recognized
Catharine's ability to "do" sex better, just as Catharine's performance of the
"truth" of Cabeza de Lobo outstrips Violet's tale of the sea-turtles' sacrifice
by subsuming it. Discourse swallows discourse in a Darwinian competi-
tion as fierce as that enacted in the garden offstage. It is Catharine's supe-
rior histrionic ability, rather than her youthful appearance, that impressed
Sebastian and so galls Violet. No wonder Violet is haunted by Catharine's
teeming brain.

Catharine's drugged "vision" of what happened suddenly last summer is,
as it has to be, flawless. She begins by blaming herself for Sebastian's death:
"I failed him. I wasn't able to keep the web from breaking" (76). Catharine
concedes that only Violet could channel Sebastian's self-destructive appetites into poetry and save him from utter dissipation. Deprived of his "um-
bilical cord" last summer, Sebastian gave up his poem and began cruising
the public beach at Cabeza de Lobo for starving beggar-children. If Violet's
ideal is to perform life as if it were art, Sebastian's is to consume the body
as if it were food: "That's how he talked about people," Catharine says, "as
if they were items on a menu" (39). Fittingly, at a restaurant on the beach,
Sebastian is surrounded by hungry, naked children who torment him with
"gobbling noises" (84). Recognizing some of his former prey, Sebastian
flees but is overtaken. "When we got back to where my cousin Sebastian
had disappeared in the flock of featherless little black sparrows, he—was
lying naked as they had been naked . . . They had *devoured* parts of him"
(92). In the cannibalistic economy of Cabeza de Lobo, the children are by
turns disposable commodities and vengeful consumers.

Suggesting Saint Catherine of Ricci, Catharine's story is a religious vision of sorts, just as Sebastian's vision of the turtles had been, only with
Catharine playing iconoclastic "vandal" to Violet's priesthood of one (26).
Sebastian once planned to give himself over to a Buddhist mendicant order, and when the beggar-children cry for "*pan*," the bread of life, they are
fed their anti-Christ. Sebastian is a cruel God in a white suit who "thought
it unfitting to ever take any action about anything whatsoever!—except to
go on doing as something in him directed" (88–89). But Sebastian con-
trives his own death much as he designed every aspect of his life, and his
first attempt to control a human situation results in his own demise. In
Williams's theology, the sacred host consumed by the faithful is, in the last
instance, one's own body. Sebastian Venable is sacrificed to the pagan god
he reveres: the savage god of the turtles, his own divine image.

Providing the sinister verso to Violet's self-righteous recto, and usurping Violet's role as minister at Sebastian's crucifiction, Catharine has performed a transubstantiation in reverse. If Violet's Sebastian is the flesh made word, Catharine's Sebastian is the word made flesh. In the discourse of performance, where the word is always made flesh, Catharine has won. Her images are indelible, hence incontrovertible. Violet's raising her cane to strike Catharine is a histrionic gesture of defeat made by an upstaged actor, a Prospero-like abjuring of her magic and a final drowning of Sebastian's "g[u]ilt-edged volume" (13).

In the discourse of power, however, the jury is still out. The space left open by Sebastian's death is tentatively sketched in by Dr. Sugar, whose last words are ambiguous: "I think we ought at least to consider the possibility that the girl's story could be true. . . ." (93). The aporia with which *Suddenly Last Summer* ends is often finessed by the play's critics, who tend to make the Doctor over in their own image. According to Esther Merle Jackson, the Doctor is a moral figure who chooses justly and "reveals a sense of commitment to moral principle."[29] Benjamin Nelson, by contrast, argues, "His closing statement may be viewed as the one positive note, but if so how weak and timid it is. Sebastian's universe is much too overpowering."[30] After all, Dr. Sugar has everything to gain by choosing Violet's spectral reading over Catharine's: his job, his research, and the girl he cannot afford to marry. Finally, his use of Violet's dehumanizing phrase "the girl" does not bode well for Catharine, who has struggled so hard for recognition as a subject in her own right.

But how much are we, the audience, to credit the drugged Catharine's vision? The answer is that Catharine cannot be judged on any other than rhetorical grounds, since all physical evidence of Sebastian has vanished into dark matter. "One doesn't really believe *Suddenly Last Summer,* but neither does one quite disbelieve it—and the total effect is like that of a frightening nightmare that one can't fully shake off."[31] As in Robert Frost's disquieting poem "Design" (which might have been written by Sebastian), Williams draws the audience into a web in which each strand resonates "with an almost infernal beauty."[32] But, whereas Frost leaves open the yet more terrifying prospect that accident has directed the poem's scene of horror, Sebastian, the meticulous poet of death, leaves no part of his existence to chance.

We here come full circle to Fish's original notion of the homiletic *text* as self-consuming artifact. Fish infers that a "self-consuming" sermon faithful to the spirit of Augustine's *On Christian Doctrine* would open the reader's eyes rather than validate propositions, "persuading, if it did persuade, not to a point, but to a vision."[33] What more precise description of the sermon that is *Suddenly Last Summer?* Such a sermon, Fish continues, must continually point away from itself, proclaiming the insufficiency of the reader's frame of reference, together with its inability (which is also the reader's inability) "to contain, deal with, capture, say anything about, its putative subject, Christ . . . A sermon that is true to Augustine's *ars praedicandi* will in the end give itself over to God, just as it will give over to God the selves of its charges."[34] Shockingly remote from Donne or Herbert as it may seem, Williams's play is precisely the kind of work Milton's *Areopagitica* defends against the "excremental whiteness" produced by censorship.[35] It is as if the aesthetic of the bad physician (Dr. Sugar) has been replaced by that of the good physician (Tennessee Williams) after all.

In Williams's discourse, the only afterlife possible is the work itself. When Nonno dies in *The Night of the Iguana* at the age of ninety-seven, he leaves behind his most beautiful poem, even as his last word consumes his last breath. Sebastian Venable, the absent Christ-figure, is Williams's consummate self-consuming icon. He finally consummates his own marriage with death, the only union of which he is capable. Like Pynchon's V. or Nabokov's Sebastian Knight, the closer we approach to his mystery the further Sebastian recedes. Seeking to prove Sebastian's ability to transcend the body and its demands, Violet shows the Doctor two photographs of Sebastian taken twenty years apart at twin Venetian masked balls. The camera's is a vision of the body as frozen performance: "The [second] photograph looks older but not the subject" (23). Violet's fantasy is that a self-abnegatory care of the self (which the later Foucault would have called *askesis*) can subject time. "It takes character to refuse to grow old, Doctor . . . it calls for discipline, abstention" (23). Failing these, artifice will have to do. Sebastian's pageboy costume, his masked visage, the two-dimensional photograph, Violet's gloss, and Dr. Sugar's tentative response screen the truth of Sebastian's body from us with mediation upon mediation.

What remains when performance implodes, and the body takes its revenge, is power—which, as Boss Finley in *Sweet Bird of Youth* reminds us, is not an illusion.[36] In a sense, the body must accept its inscriptions from the beginning: Chance Wayne makes no attempt to escape castration, and Blanche is complicit in her own disintegration. Sebastian himself is always already inscribed, just as his punishment is written on the body. The fate of the body in Williams is to lose the ability to propagate itself except in discourse: Blanche escapes into a madness divorced from the body, while Sebastian, like Frost's spider, multiplies into ever-replicating images of himself. As in Frost's poem, each element of *Suddenly Last Summer* feeds off itself, until only the pattern remains. And in its own "design of darkness to appall," *Suddenly Last Summer* becomes the ultimate self-consuming artifact: an imploding performance engulfed, once the lights go out, by the ravenous black hole that is Sebastian Venable.[37] The cannibalistic performativity of Williams's artifacts is mirrored by the theatrical rhetoric itself. In a stunning *coup de théâtre,* Williams writes a play without a subject for hungry consumers utterly excluded from the frame of representation posited by realism.

Bugs in the Mind

The Archbishop's Ceiling
and Arthur Miller's Prismatic Drama

[T]he reality was what was happening in the dark.
—Arthur Miller

Written eight years since his last Broadway hit, and from a place of personal crisis in relation to his art, *The Archbishop's Ceiling* (1977) marks a significant departure in Arthur Miller's drama.[1] Ever since his first big success, *All My Sons* (1947), Miller had chronicled the American self under pressure, a pressure manifested as the past catching up with the present despite the self's attempt to deny that past. Yet in *The Archbishop's Ceiling,* set not in the United States but in Eastern Europe, the fugitive self pursued by the consequences of past acts of betrayal gives way to the self as a fiction: a maelstrom of conflicting forces that threaten to explode identity from within.

How, then, to express this internalized pressure within the framework of drama, in which conflict must somehow be externalized for an audience? Miller's revised notion of the self demanded a new dramaturgy, and one reason *The Archbishop's Ceiling* initially failed in performance is that its realistic production style obscured the fact that the play's true subject is not political repression, as most critics of the play suggest, but dramatic form itself.[2] Beneath a superficially conventional plot, which involves a dissident writer's choice between saving himself or his art, *The Archbishop's Ceiling* critiques the linear dramaturgy Miller inherited from Ibsen in order to embrace a prismatic, nonlinear dramatic structure. Miller's repudiation of a dramatic form he had earlier championed is signaled by the play's shift from staged technology to dark matter: in other words, from theatrical devices that drive the plot forward, as in Ibsen, to a single image, "the bugged ceiling of the mind," which transforms linear action into existential predicament.[3]

In drama, Miller writes, "It is necessary to employ the artificial in order to arrive at the real," and nowhere has this fact been more evident than in his skillful use of theater technology.[4] I refer not just to computerized or electronic devices and effects but to the concrete, theatrical means by which dramaturgical problems are solved onstage. In this sense, as Susan Bennett points out, "Technology has always been a part of theatre."[5] Every significant dramaturgy summons a technology adequate to it: the deus ex machina machinery of the Greeks, the trap door to Hell of the Elizabethan playhouse, the groove-and-shutter scenery of the Restoration, the nineteenth-century black box, and so on. But the traffic between theater and technology moves in both directions. New theatrical technologies in turn open up new dramatic opportunities for playwrights, as when the machinery concealed above the stage of the Blackfriars Theatre, which the King's Men acquired use of in 1608, inspired Shakespeare to grace his late romances with divine visitations. From the letter in *All My Sons* (1947) to the music in *Death of a Salesman* (1949) to the spotlight in *After the Fall* (1964) to the Brechtian projections in *Clara* (1986), Miller's increasingly sophisticated engagement with technology has far-reaching implications for his dramaturgy. For, if Miller's thematic quarry is what it means to be a morally accountable human being, electronic technology challenges the very existence of such a bedrock through its uncanny ability to double, fragment, and disperse the subject.[6]

Not coincidentally, at the very point in Miller's drama at which technology threatens to dissolve the self's coherence, it becomes dark matter. *The Archbishop's Ceiling* revolves around a listening device that may or may not be concealed in the ceiling of a former archbishop's residence, now frequented by local and foreign writers in an Eastern European police state.[7] The soot-covered ceiling features a baroque painting of cherubim and the four winds; in Miller's ironic vision, the bug has displaced God as omniscient, inscrutable observer and judge of human behavior. Miller has described *The Archbishop's Ceiling* as "a dramatic meditation on the impact of immense state power upon human identity and the common concept of what is real and illusory in a group of writers living in a small European capital today."[8] Given his emphasis on the precariousness of human identity, Miller's decision to remove the onstage figure of the listener, Martin, from his conception of the play raises the ontological stakes considerably.[9] Is the bug there or not there? More disturbingly, does it finally matter whether or not the authorities are listening? "Do you think God sees me?" asks Gogo in *Waiting for Godot,* voicing the same existential uneasiness that afflicts Miller's performers in *The Archbishop's Ceiling.*[10]

The play's *esse est percipi* conceit, "to be is to be perceived," borrowed from Bishop Berkeley by way of Beckett, has wider political ramifications.[11] Although *The Archbishop's Ceiling* is set in Eastern Europe, it embodies Miller's frustrated response to the "indefinition" and "exhaustion" of radicalism in the United States of the 1970s.[12] Miller's introduction to *The Archbishop's Ceiling,* a work of the 1970s, captures the sense of disillusionment within the American Left in the wake of the Kent State massacre: "Power everywhere seemed to have transformed itself from a forbidding line of troops into an ectoplasmic lump that simply swallowed up the righteous sword as it struck."[13] In the era of Watergate and Vietnam, the hidden listening device takes on an emblematic significance; the bug crystallizes Miller's conviction that "the visible motions of political life were too often merely distractions, while the reality was what was happening in the dark."[14] Still more disturbing, in Miller's view authoritarian power has so saturated the self that to some extent we are all speaking to the bugged ceiling of the mind.[15] Displaced from the United States onto an Eastern European stage, where power only *seems* to be more "sharply defined," *The Archbishop's Ceiling* is a political fable about how power undermines the "I" and turns resistance into performance (11). As (dis)embodied by the bug, power's massive force distorts not only the self but reality as well. Power's ungraspable tug cannot be resisted because it has been thoroughly internalized.

Yet in addition to its political freight, *The Archbishop's Ceiling* contains a metatheatrical dimension. It is a play about how drama *itself* confronts the challenge posed by the postmodern disintegration of the self to a traditional dramaturgy built on the link between psychological motivation and individual behavior. Miller has acknowledged inheriting this psychological dramaturgy from Ibsen, who himself adapted the structure of the nineteenth-century well-made play—along with its *raisonneurs,* reversals, and denouements—for morally forensic ends. "What is precious in the

Ibsen method is its insistence on valid causation, and this cannot be dismissed as a wooden notion," Miller insisted in the late 1950s.[16] In the psychological drama championed by Ibsen, what one does is what one is—and what one is is nothing less than the sum of one's actions up to the present moment. In this drama of "valid causation," motivation *is* character, and vice versa. Mrs. Alving, Hedda Gabler, John Gabriel Borkman, and the rest flee the consequences of their past failures of moral nerve, only to be squeezed in the vise of the well-made plot, which Richard Gilman defines as "the unfolding of a 'story' through the concatenation of incidents that build logically to a climax."[17] Miller's own image of Ibsen's achievement is more vivid: "the marvelous spectacle of life forcing one event out of the jaws of the preceding one."[18]

Such moral accountability traps Joe Keller in Miller's early play *All My Sons.* As Hersh Zeifman writes, "[T]he play's order stems from its relentless Ibsenite realism, a mimesis celebrating linearity, chronology, causality: the ghosts of the past—what Miller once termed 'the birds coming home to roost'—return to haunt the present and to shape its future."[19] With the implacability of an *Oedipus Rex,* the play brings Keller face to face with the fact that his shipment of faulty airplane parts during World War II, which resulted in the death of twenty-one pilots, is also responsible for the death of his pilot son Larry—who committed suicide on learning of his father's guilt. The very act Keller believed necessary to preserve the family business has destroyed his son, and this realization drives Keller to shoot himself.

Within the constraints of fourth-wall realism, Ibsen's challenge was to make the causal past tangible onstage without getting bogged down in interminable exposition. His solution was to borrow the fateful prop from the Scribean *pièce bien faite* in order to embody the past in "speaking" objects: Krogstad's letter in *A Doll's House,* Captain Alving's pipe in *Ghosts,* General Gabler's portrait and pistols in *Hedda Gabler.* In *All My Sons,* Miller makes similarly forensic use of the fateful prop. Causality crystallizes in the letter ex machina from Joe's dead son, Larry, which appears just in time to explain his suicide and precipitate Joe's own. Like Captain Alving's pipe or General Gabler's portrait, Larry's letter indicts from beyond the grave. It is not a symbol, like the stunted tree that metaphorically represents Larry on the set of *All My Sons,* but a *medium of communication.* Miller seizes on the device of the letter—one of theater's most primitive technologies—to solve an ancient dramatic problem (a Greek messenger would have accomplished the same job still less elegantly).

Miller's next play, *Death of a Salesman,* demonstrates a leap in Miller's mastery of theater technology, even as it marks his attempt to break out of "a method one might call linear or eventual in that one fact or incident creates the necessity for the next."[20] As Enoch Brater has shown, the play modulates between Willy Loman's inner dream-life and his present-day reality thanks to Miller's fluid use of a transparent, highly symbolic set, expressionistic lighting, and evocative flute music, as well as poetically expressive dialogue: "In *Salesman,* Miller's emblematic realism therefore holds the naturalistic and the symbolic in perfect equilibrium."[21]

Miller would push the expressionistic elements of his drama still further in *After the Fall* (1964), which Hersh Zeifman accurately calls an "expressionistic soulscape."[22] Entering middle-aged Quentin's tormented unconscious, we are plunged even further into "the inside of his head" (to borrow Miller's original title for *Death of a Salesman*). The set no longer pays lip-service to a realistic environment: "The action takes place in the mind, thought, and memory of Quentin," and Miller calls for "a lavalike, supple geography in which, like pits and hollows found in lava, the scenes take place."[23] Here Miller's key technological device for modulating between inner and outer experience is not music but the spotlight that, as in Beckett's *Play,* acts the role of inquisitor. A "sharp light" isolates Quentin on the stage and choreographs the action as figures from his haunted past move in and out of its focus.[24] The lighting repeatedly directs Quentin's attention to key moments of betrayal, moments underscored for the audience by the illumination of the concentration camp tower that looms at the rear of the set. Miller would not revisit such unabashed expressionism until his 1998 memory play, *Mr. Peters' Connections,* which also features a man seeking to draw the disconnected threads of his life together.

Miller is, above all, an anatomist of consciousness. He is fascinated by how individuals are seduced into ideologies that take the place of real, felt experience. Such anatomizing is at bottom reformist, since it ultimately envisions what William Demastes calls "a (re)construction of a world more fully predicated on a sense of moral responsibility involving truly disinterested actions benefiting our fellows via a fully rounded sense of social commitment."[25] But by the time of *After the Fall,* the unitary self that would undergird such a project was already beginning to splinter, and Miller began to seek more sophisticated theatrical means to stage his unraveling conception of character. As bigamist Lyman Felt puts it in *The Ride Down Mt. Morgan* (1991):

Look, we're all the same; a man is a fourteen-room house—in the bed-room he's asleep with his intelligent wife, in the living room he's rolling around with some bare-ass girl, in the library he's paying his taxes, in the yard he's raising tomatoes. And in the cellar he's making a bomb to blow it all up.[26]

In Miller's subsequent drama, the recurrent image of the split self represents an unintegrated identity that refuses to cohere into a morally accountable whole.

Miller stages this lack of coherence not through the video monitors beloved by theatrical postmodernists but through machines cunningly introduced into the action.[27] At the climax of *The Price* (1968), exhausted furniture dealer Gregory Solomon, overwhelmed by the weight of the past, cannot resist joining in with the "Laughing Record" on a wind-up Victrola that plunges him into nostalgia for his younger days as a vaudeville artist. In *Clara* (1986)—a short play that, uncharacteristically for Miller, makes use of Brechtian projections on a screen to indicate the contents of consciousness—a disoriented man whose daughter has just been murdered reacts to his voice as a young soloist on a phonographic record with a weak "Good Lord."[28] Yet these instances are just that—fleeting moments that underscore the capacity of the self to experience itself as Other, as uncannily outside one's own body. This divided or split self is not the same as the *illusory* self anatomized in *The Archbishop's Ceiling*.[29] In such later plays as *The Ride Down Mt. Morgan* and *Broken Glass* (1994), Miller would return to the divided protagonist whose task is to integrate past and present into a coherent self. But only in *The Archbishop's Ceiling* does the very self that underpins Miller's drama of moral accountability threaten to dissolve into an absurdist fiction. The existential threat posed by the bug unleashes a new dramaturgy based on a different principle than "valid causation": that of power.

Written thirty years after *All My Sons*, *The Archbishop's Ceiling* stages Miller's most insinuating technological device as dark matter—the invisible, possibly fictional bug—in order to pit the causal dramaturgy of motive against what one might call the *prismatic* dramaturgy of power. A prism, we recall, is a transparent solid (in this case a play) used to produce or analyze a continuous spectrum. Instead of a linear plot that dramatizes the protagonist's failed attempt to elude responsibility for his own actions—the pattern that tends to structure Miller's drama from *All My*

Sons onward—prismatic drama presents variations on a single theme. Within this "spatial" rather than linear dramaturgy, a play becomes a fugue of counterpointed melodies rather than an aria building to a crescendo.[30] There is little or no plot development to speak of; each character responds to a given situation in his or her own way, and that spectrum of responses *is* the action. No character is held responsible for his or her actions; there is no punishment or reward, as in melodrama, nor are we asked to judge who is behaving correctly or incorrectly, as in Ibsen's social drama. In prismatic drama, there is no protagonist, no plot, and no resolution—only variegated behavior in response to a common stimulus. Thus (to cite a few exemplary instances) *Troilus and Cressida* dramatizes the responses of a set of characters to war fatigue, *The Three Sisters* to unhappiness, *Waiting for Godot* to boredom, and *The Archbishop's Ceiling* to power.

The Archbishop's Ceiling hovers between the causal (in which X occurs) and the prismatic (in which X is refracted through mediums of different densities). Like an anamorphic painting, we can experience Miller's play from two competing perspectives. Depending on which perspective we take, the play's emphasis, and indeed its message, shifts. In the drama of causation, the play is a plea for personal responsibility in a world that has lost its moral bearings; in the drama of power, it is a wry acknowledgment of the impossibility of judging those whose actions no longer spring from coherent psychological motivation. Ingeniously, Miller dramatizes this clash not only through characterization but by juxtaposing outmoded and emergent technologies. Causal and prismatic principles are represented by two objects respectively: the pistol, that most Ibsenite of fateful props, which (in part) drives the linear action; and the bug, whose "not there, not not there" ambiguity pitches the characters into existential crisis. Crudely put, in the drama of the pistol, actions have discernible origins and clear consequences; in the drama of the bug, they have neither. It is no coincidence that the first object is material, the second phantasmal.[31]

At the start of *The Archbishop's Ceiling* we meet Adrian, a famous American writer who has arrived in a nameless Eastern European capital (presumably Prague) to visit old writer friends. Adrian is fleeing a pompous symposium on the contemporary novel at the Sorbonne, and in a conversation with Maya, a local playwright turned host of an innocuous radio show, it becomes apparent that Adrian is in crisis. He suffers from writer's block, a condition brought on by the fact that a pill has magically lifted the depression of his lover, Ruth. Overnight, the pill has transformed

Ruth into a happy and productive member of society: "It plugged her in to some . . . some power. And she lit up" (10). But if the self can be switched on and off like a light bulb by chemical means, then it cannot be held responsible for its own actions or even feelings. Adrian's psychologized brand of fiction has become pointless.

Adrian mistakenly believes that he can recover his moral bearings in a state whose repressive regime forces writers (as he thinks) either to take a firm stand against power or to connive with it: "You have no pills in this country, but power is very sharply defined here. The government makes it very clear that you must snuggle up to power or you will never be happy" (11). Adrian seeks to confirm a rumor spread by a fellow American: that Marcus and Maya, writers who enjoy a limited freedom denied their colleagues, invite fellow writers to orgies and tape the writers with young girls in order to compromise them with the government. Adrian's quest for moral certainties is ultimately in bad faith. He not only wishes to interview Maya in the interests of his research but to sleep with her as well—despite the fact that Maya is the lover of Adrian's absent host.

Miller depicts Adrian as a kind of vampire, a privileged outsider who seeks to revivify his voyeuristic art by exploiting the moral dilemmas of others. Adrian's situation mirrors Miller's own quandary in writing a play about his Czech colleagues. Adrian's crisis only intensifies in the course of the play, because his conception of the moral accountability of the "I" proves inadequate to the complexity of the situation. Under the archbishop's ceiling, the local writers must continually perform for an invisible god (the state), which may or may not be paying attention. The play tracks Adrian's bewilderment, suspicion, and anger at the fact that his friends seem largely unconcerned by their putative surveillance: "It's like some kind of continuous crime" (43). But performativity proves catching: the writers' condition soon infects Adrian, whose words sound increasingly hollow and self-serving.

Although Adrian is a novelist, he stands in for Miller the playwright, a man whose once firm faith in the moral accountability of the self has been shaken: "Here I'm laying out motives, characterizations, secret impulses—the whole psychological chess game—when the truth is I'm not sure anymore that I believe in psychology. That anything we think really determines what we're going to do. Or even what we feel" (9). What has shaken Adrian's faith is power, an intangible presence that compels action even as it disconnects acts and their consequences from individual agency.[32]

Adrian travels to Eastern Europe in search of a place where the struggle between the individual conscience and power has not collapsed into cheap melodrama on the one hand or amoral chaos on the other. His quest is precisely the one that impels the playwright: "Whether it matters anymore, what anyone feels . . . about anything. Whether we're not just some sort of . . . filament that only lights up when it's plugged into whatever power there is" (83).

Marcus, Adrian's urbane and cosmopolitan host, personifies Adrian's predicament. To Adrian, Marcus is a man without qualities, "a total blank" (14). Adrian's question—is Marcus a government agent?—is naive, almost what one might call a category mistake. By turns anthropologist, American soldier, literary editor, imprisoned dissident writer, and womanizing capitalist, the protean Marcus defies the principle and poetics of accountability. Marcus is a series of acts without a self, a man whose every remark is at once overdetermined and obscure. (Disconcertingly, he alone, besides Adrian, speaks perfect English.) Marcus embodies the principle of adaptation to power, symbolized by his apparent indifference to the bug that may or may not lurk in the ceiling of his residence: "How can I know what is in this room? How ludicrous can you get?" (66).

Marcus returns unexpectedly from a trip abroad, one of the perks mysteriously allowed him by the authorities. He arrives at the door accompanied by a beautiful Danish woman, Irina, and the country's greatest writer, Sigmund (whose name suggests Freud's double legacy of psychological motivation and overdetermined behavior). It turns out that Marcus's true motive is to convince his friend and rival Sigmund to emigrate. Marcus reports that in London he met a secret policeman who warned him that the flamboyantly dissident Sigmund faces arrest and imprisonment as retribution for publishing articles critical of the regime. Since exile to America would spell the end of his writing career—a kind of spiritual and artistic death—Sigmund must weigh the truth of Marcus's account, as well as Marcus's motivation, before making up his mind. Is Marcus driven by the urge to preserve political space for less openly confrontational writers, as he claims? Or is he spurred by jealousy over Sigmund's greater artistic powers and by Sigmund's affair with Maya to invent the tale of the policeman? A brief exchange with Adrian underscores the ambiguity.

ADRIAN: He's an agent.
SIGMUND: Is possible not.

ADRIAN: Then what is he?
SIGMUND: Marcus is Marcus. (50)

In short the inscrutable Marcus represents everything Adrian, the naive and insulated American, is unequipped to grasp.[33]

From the perspective of psychological causality, the play turns on the plot question: will Sigmund allow himself to be convinced to save himself by emigrating? As in *A Doll's House* and *Hedda Gabler,* objects propel the linear plot. First, there is the manuscript of Sigmund's novel, an apparent masterpiece that is snatched from his apartment at the beginning of the play and eventually (perhaps) returned as a demonstration of the regime's godlike mercy. Second, there is the pistol that Sigmund steals from Marcus's briefcase as insurance against arrest. If the offstage manuscript is a blatant McGuffin to get the plot rolling, the pistol is a tried-and-true way to ratchet up the dramatic tension in a very talky play: at various points Maya, Marcus, and Adrian each seek to retrieve the gun. But Miller's point here is metatheatrical. Sigmund steals the gun explicitly *as a prop.* If the authorities know he possesses it, they will be less likely to risk an international scandal by arresting him. Sigmund's recourse to the clunkiest of melodramatic devices is the logical response to his situation: "Is like some sort of theatre, no? Very bad theatre—our emotions have no connection with the event" (90). And, as if to protest the fact, Sigmund stages a defiant piece of performance art for the benefit of his unseen audience by placing the cocked gun on the strings of Marcus's piano—that most egregious symbol of bourgeois realism—and playing a crashing chord that sets it off. The gesture is, quite literally, melodramatic.

In keeping with its suspense plot, the ending of *The Archbishop's Ceiling* observes the classical structure of reversal, revelation, and resolution.[34] Sigmund's return of the pistol to Marcus marks a turning point in the action. By conceding that he no longer fears arrest, Sigmund tacitly accuses Marcus of lying to him. This in turn leads to the revelation that Marcus and Maya have cut a deal: in exchange for keeping their privileges (Maya's radio program, Marcus's passport), the couple must "deliver" Sigmund's emigration to the authorities. At the play's climax, Sigmund refuses to trade the ability to speak truth to power at home for cushy exile in an American university, and *The Archbishop's Ceiling* ends with Sigmund's invocation of the names of the great writers with whom he has corresponded. According to Miller's introduction, by bowing to the god of art, Sigmund transcends tyranny. But by portraying Sigmund as a martyr to the cause of art—albeit a flawed, narcissistic one—Miller buys a redemptive ending at the risk of replicating the very artifice he critiques. It is as if Sigmund has become a character in Adrian's failed novel: "Funny how life imitates art; the melodrama kept flattening out my characterizations" (20).

To Miller's credit, the play sustains another, more spectral reading, in which not Sigmund but Adrian is the protagonist. Seen from this perspective, the play is not an object lesson in moral authenticity but a study in the insidiousness of power, which is no longer a weapon (the pistol) but an environment ("the bugged ceiling of the mind"). In this much subtler drama, Adrian must absorb the Foucauldian lesson that power is a medium we move through rather than a tool wielded by the strong against the weak.[35] Every character, except the two foreigners (Adrian and Irina, who seems not to realize that her femininity is an elaborate masquerade), already grasps this. The presumed bug in the ceiling only magnifies the conviction that one is always talking or behaving for an audience, a conviction that is at root existential.

Here Miller exploits the phenomenology of theater itself. If Tennessee Williams's *Suddenly Last Summer* positions the spectator as a frustrated consumer of what is kept out of sight, Miller places his audience in the position of the bug. Dark matter ourselves, we are the invisible listeners (and observers) for whom the actors perform. The bug is at once a microphone and an amplifier that allows the characters to monitor their own inauthentic behavior. The truly disturbing thing about the bug—and the proof that in this play Miller transcends the drama's crudest devices, even as he trots them out—is that its actual presence is immaterial. Simply the belief that the bug *might* be there transforms life into "very bad theatre," and this is no less true in Washington than in Prague. "It would seem that the 'I' must be singular, not plural, but the art of bureaucracy is to change the 'I' of its subjects to 'we' at every moment of conscious life."[36]

In the prismatic drama, then, each character embodies a different accommodation with power, a set of strategies that has congealed into a way of life. Irina, Marcus's girlfriend, represents sheer ignorance, unless she, too, is a plant; significantly, Irina's husband is said to work for the BBC, another intangible yet all-pervasive technological presence. Maya, whose name means "illusion" in Hindi, inevitably comes to symbolize the country itself.[37] Not coincidentally, she sleeps with all the men (even the American!) in order to preserve what freedom of movement she has.[38]

Rather than use that freedom productively, Maya retreats into alcohol and the consumer-porn fantasies of *Vogue* magazine. Her redemptive feature is that she recognizes Sigmund as the conscience of her nation, and her motive throughout is to protect him (it is interesting to speculate what would have happened to the play's sexual politics had Maya been the writer with the greatest talent).

Marcus, as we have seen, epitomizes the fractured self that "ectoplasmic" power produces. It is impossible to determine whether or not Marcus is a government agent, hence guilty on Adrian's moral abacus, because his dance with power precludes a coherent subjectivity. Marcus's motivation is to survive, to maintain the freedom to continue performing. Since Sigmund's showy acts of rebellion threaten to force a crackdown by the authorities, Sigmund must be put safely out of the picture so that the dance can continue. As Marcus sourly notes, by playing power's game he has carved out the very political space that allows Sigmund the luxury to accuse him of selling out.[39]

Thus Sigmund, who in the drama of accountability embodies a principled stand of which the other writers are incapable, stands revealed in the drama of power as a performer addicted to an outmoded dramaturgy of moral calculus. Such is Marcus's accusation.

> You are a moral blackmailer. We have all humored you, Sigmund, out of some misplaced sense of responsibility to our literature. Or maybe it's only our terror of vanishing altogether . . . We have taken all the responsibility and left you all the freedom to call us morally bankrupt. But now you're free to go, so the responsibility moves to you. Now it's yours. All yours. We have done what is possible; now you will do what is necessary, or turn out our lights. (99)

No less addicted to performance than Marcus, Sigmund requires the persona of the dissident writer in order to sustain his oppositional art. His decision to stay (and, as it were, continue his performance) is as self-serving as Marcus's insistence that he leave. To Maya's plea for exculpation, "Is love not love because there is some profit in it? Who speaks only for his heart?," Sigmund responds, "I speak for Sigmund" (100–101). But Maya denies that "Sigmund" is any less a construct produced by power than the others: "They are your theme, your life, your partner in this dance that cannot stop or you will die of silence! They are in you, darling" (101). Beneath the hidden microphone, trapped onstage before a theater audience, Sigmund is less hero than poseur.

In the drama of accountability, Adrian is morally compromised beyond repair and merely provides a touchstone for Sigmund's principled stand. But in the drama of power, Adrian is a would-be *raisonneur* probing an alien dramaturgy. The first time we see him, he is lifting couch cushions and peering into the piano, trying to uncover the rumored bug. Adrian arrives in Eastern Europe on a mission to regenerate his art, only to find his worst suspicions confirmed. Saturated with the technology of power, the self is a "strategic zone" rather than an agent, and psychological causality a myth rather than an explanation (65). More chorus than protagonist by the end, Adrian is left echoing the question with which he began: "Whether it matters anymore, what anyone feels . . . about anything. Whether we're not just some sort of whatever power there is" (73). Under the archbishop's ceiling, the self is not a clockwork orange programmed by the state but Peer Gynt's onion: layers of performance without a core.

The Archbishop's Ceiling dramatizes not only the collision of American idealism with Eastern European realpolitik but the clash between two competing notions of the self and the dramaturgies they summon. In a sense the play's metatheatrical engagements are a response to its political ones, for *The Archbishop's Ceiling* reflects Miller's realization that the causal dramaturgy of *All My Sons* and *A View from the Bridge* is no longer adequate to the sociopolitical situation. Thus the play stages an outmoded dramaturgy that is critiqued theatrically by means of dark matter. Just as the presence of the audience turns the onstage action into a piece of theater, so the invisible bug turns the pistol into a prop and the characters into mouthpieces. If the drama of causation cannot resist lionizing Sigmund as a symbol of artistic integrity, in contrast to the American selfishly seeking artistic and sexual renewal, the drama of power reveals that we are all complicit with the bugged ceiling of the mind. In *The Archbishop's Ceiling*, Miller's subtlest piece of metatheater, theater itself becomes both master technology and master trope for exposing the incoherence of the subject, the performativity of behavior, and the chimera of psychological unity.

6

Invisible Wounds

Rehearsing Trauma on the Contemporary Stage

A black play is a white play when the lights go out.
—Suzan-Lori Parks

In the dark? how would you see that in the dark?
—Harper in *Far Away*

In Adam and Adrienne Kennedy's nightmarish memory play *Sleep Deprivation Chamber* (1996), the brutal beating of a young black man by a white policeman repeats itself over and over, both in narrative and before our eyes. These remorseless loops seem out of the conscious control of the narrating characters that conjure them into being. Interspersed with the horror, fragmented scenes of college students rehearsing a production of *Hamlet* unfold. Yorick's grave haunts *Sleep Deprivation Chamber* as a spectral presence both inside and outside the action; *Hamlet* is at once text and intertext, contents and envelope. What does it mean to *rehearse* within and beyond a scene of trauma that is itself an imitation of the real thing? What is the relationship between trauma and theatrical representation?

Contemporary anglophone playwrights frequently address collective traumas that transcend individual suffering: genocide, war, sexual abuse, terrorism, natural disasters, and other calamities.[1] Indeed, Christina Wald has posited "Trauma Drama" as a distinct genre that has evolved since the late 1980s.[2] Staging trauma poses a representational conundrum because trauma confounds chronology and eludes comprehension. According to Judith Herman, "Traumatic memories lack verbal narrative and context; rather, they are encoded in the new form of vivid sensations and images."[3] Trauma confuses cause and effect; in the words of Allen Meek, "[T]rauma's temporality constitutes an event that is always displaced in space and time. Trauma may not be consciously registered at the time of its occurrence but it returns in the form of intrusive memories, nightmares, compulsive acting-out and flash-backs."[4] A trauma-effect follows the trauma-event in time but precedes the trauma-event in terms of integration into the psyche, thereby raising the question of whether such "unclaimed experiences," as theorist Cathy Caruth calls them, can count as history or truth. Trauma is "experienced too soon, too unexpectedly, to be fully known and is therefore not available to consciousness until it imposes itself again, repeatedly, in the nightmares and repetitive actions of the survivor."[5] Further, "[W]hat returns to haunt the victim . . . is not only the reality of the violent event but also the reality of the way that its violence has not yet been fully known."[6] As a memory of something that has not (yet) happened to the subject, trauma disrupts both narrative and epistemology. That archetypal image of postmodern trauma, Mouth in Beckett's *Not I,* is an endless and recursive stream of words that emerges from and descends into babble.

If trauma's shattering force eludes comprehension by the speaking subject, the value and even the possibility of mimesis are called into question. Staging unclaimed experience carries the risk of reproducing its characteristic structures and affect without transforming, working through, or otherwise making it *usable* for an audience. Indeed, reproducing such experience would seem to resist catharsis or cure, inviting helplessness at best—*Not I*'s Auditor raises arms "in a gesture of helpless compassion"—and voyeurism at worst.[7] In perhaps the archetypal traumatic scene of postclassical Western drama, the sleepwalking scene from *Macbeth,* the doctor of physic (who in Ibsen would be the *raisonneur*) concedes that Lady Macbeth's disease is beyond his practice. The dream-logic of Lady Macbeth's hallucinatory rambling anticipates Mouth's logorrheic repetition-compulsion. With these challenges, psychic trauma haunts contemporary Anglo-American theater. It occupies the stage less as a bounded event, locatable within individual bodies and subjects, than as an invisible field that saturates bodies like malignant radiation.

Contemporary theater artists have departed from what might be called the standard (Freudian) model of theatrical trauma: the return of the repressed. Ibsen's *Ghosts* (1881) enacts this return as both neurotic symptom and hereditary disease: the sins of the father, Captain Alving, are visited on his syphilitic son Oswald while Mrs. Alving looks on in horrified and helpless witness. In this model trauma is a repressed, secret history that remorselessly comes to light until no secrets remain from the audience. Two tropes for this secret history recur over and over. The first is the dead or buried child familiar from Ibsen, O'Neill, and Shepard. The second is the revenant, the embodied apparition of the repressed past.[8] Howard Brenton's *The Churchill Play* (1974) opens with Winston Churchill bursting out of his coffin. Bill, a British soldier killed in Northern Ireland during the Troubles, disrupts an orgy in a London park with his unbearable sexual loneliness in Caryl Churchill's *Cloud 9* (1979). And at the end of Harold Pinter's *Party Time* (1991), which takes place in a police state, the ghost of one of the disappeared erupts into an elitist cocktail party to testify to his ordeal. Our witnessing of Jimmy's trauma brings the repressed to (blinding) light; as in a Passion Play, the ocular proof of trauma is located in the victim's visible, tortured body. This cathartic model remains an enduring presence in modern and contemporary theater. Thus Peter Shaffer's *Equus* (1973) traces a horrific trauma-effect (a young man's blinding of horses) back to sexual conflicts via psychiatry.[9] More recently, Edward Albee's queer tragedy *The Goat or Who Is Sylvia* (2002) presents a successful architect-hero who sacrifices his marriage on the altar of bestial love.[10]

By contrast, an emerging model of trauma as "a past that has never been present" has licensed playwrights to interrogate such received conventions as visible wounding, psychological unity of character, linear plot, reliable memory, and climactic catharsis.[11] Under the twin influences of psychoanalysis and deconstruction, trauma has been potently theorized as a hole or gap that makes direct memory, claimed subjective experience, and even self-presence impossible. On this understanding, theater's task is not so much bringing trauma to light—which would mean materializing something that isn't, properly speaking, there in the first place—as *rehearsing* or *reenacting* trauma's *Nachtraglichkeit* as gravitational effect.[12] If trauma is an inaccessible history that cannot be owned, rather than a repressed or distorted history that is disavowed, a major challenge for contemporary playwrights is *staging traumatic history as psychic absence*.[13] Elusive yet ubiquitous, trauma eats away at the representational structure of theater and the dramaturgical structure of realism alike. What was once a ghost that could be materialized, and hence exorcised, has become a black hole—an Elsewhere.

Catharsis and Traumatic Realism

Trauma comes from the Greek word for a physical wound, and ever since the Greeks theater has featured such wounding. Thus the very names Labdacos (lame), Laios (left sided), and Oedipus (swollen footed) present a family procession of walking wounded.[14] Yet Oedipus's self-blinding at the end of Sophocles' *Oedipus Rex* is literally obscene/offstage, *ob skene.* Reported by the Second Messenger, Oedipus's blinding takes place in our minds; the act itself is something we can only imagine. For Aristotle, Oedipus's wound purges the audience's pity and fear through vicarious identification. In the *Poetics,* Aristotle divorces trauma from mimesis; although pity and fear may successfully be aroused through "spectacular means," it is better when the trauma takes place "even without the aid of the eye," so that "he who hears the tale [of Oedipus] told will thrill with horror and melt to pity at what takes place."[15] Sophocles artfully blinds us to the act of blinding because, paradoxically, only through narrative can the event *happen* to us on a visceral level that transcends cheap spectacle. Staging trauma, then, entails a paradox. A fictional wound, represented onstage as a diegetic absence, wounds us vicariously in such as way as to heal us.[16] It is as if, through our identification with the tragic king-figure, our pity and fear can safely bleed out through the openings of Oedipus's eye sockets, which are themselves hidden by a mask when the Oedipus-actor returns onstage. At the founding of Western dramatic theory, *not* seeing facilitates traumatic knowledge and cathartic cure.

In common parlance, *trauma* puzzlingly refers both to the initial wounding (the trauma-event) and to its psychological aftereffects (the trauma-effect). This ambiguity ramifies within the interdisciplinary discourse that has come to be named trauma theory.[17] In Cathy Caruth's influential definition, trauma "describes an overwhelming experience of sudden, or catastrophic events, in which the response to the event occurs in the often delayed, and uncontrolled repetitive occurrence of hallucinations and other intrusive phenomena."[18] One paradigmatic instance is the post-traumatic nightmares experienced by World War I soldiers returning from combat, a repetition-compulsion that compelled Freud to revise his theory of dreams as unconscious wish-fulfillment in *Beyond the Pleasure Principle* (1920). The 1980 recognition of post-traumatic stress disorder by the American Psychiatric Association legitimated the evolution of the concept of trauma from physical to psychic wounding that took place in the latter half of the nineteenth century.[19]

According to Caruth, trauma overwhelms the psyche in such a way that the act does not *happen* to the victim except belatedly and symptomatically. Trauma manifests as a void or hole: "The historical power of the trauma is not just that the experience is repeated after its forgetting [as Freud noted], but that it is only in and through its inherent forgetting that it is first experienced at all."[20] Thus Caruth's privileged trope is not memory but possession: "The pathology consists . . . solely in the *structure of its experience* or reception: the event is not assimilated or experienced fully at the time, but only belatedly, in its repeated possession of the one who experiences it. To be traumatized is precisely to be possessed by an image or event."[21] Suddenly and without warning, a terrible event occurs that so threatens the self's integrity that the self dissociates in such a way so as not to experience it. After a period of effacement (latency), in which the sufferer may appear miraculously unharmed, various forms of unconscious repetition begin speaking through him or her symptomatically. The body becomes an involuntary rehearsal-machine, performing variations of a lost event that is not so much distorted as *unavailable*. It is not hard to draw the parallel between Caruth's model and Aristotelian tragedy, whose narrated trauma is at once the (invisible) event and its cure. But how can one narrate a history of trauma if trauma is something that never happened to the sufferer?[22] If history is a gap or void, how can it be communicated, represented, passed along?

Trauma's epistemology—or perhaps, its anti-epistemology, since by Caruth's definition trauma remains inaccessible to direct experience—troubles our conception of history itself. "For history to be a history of trauma means that it is referential precisely to the extent that it is not fully perceived as it occurs; or, to put it somewhat differently, that a history can be grasped only in the very inaccessibility of its occurrence."[23] Trauma revises our conception of history as necessarily referential, "based on simple models of experience and reference"—just saying what happened. Instead history becomes a displacement that arises "where *immediate understanding* may not."[24] History is inscribed as a kind of blind spot within the text (or self).[25] Although Caruth does not say this, history might even be a kind of theater: one that does not mimetically refer to a referential elsewhere but instead discloses a kind of gap or void *within* experience. We might call this a phenomenology without phenomena, since for Heidegger the phenomenal world is defined by its availability to consciousness (which is always intentional, that is, consciousness *of* something)—its thereness.[26] Such a ghostly theater would conceive of wounding as a kind of dark matter that hemorrhages beyond the fictive space.[27] We would not identify with traumatized characters as we identify with an Oedipus, for how could one identify with Beckett's Mouth, who is not even/no longer human, but a speaking cavity?[28]

In the wake of Beckett's exploded subject, contemporary playwrights have wrestled with how to represent trauma onstage. One solution to the representational conundrum with which I began is to press mimesis to its breaking point by staging violence as explicitly as possible. In a sense this strategy returns to the medieval tradition, but without its redemptive dimension.[29] What might be termed *traumatic realism* insists on staging the irreducible trauma-event, whose reality has arguably been obscured by theory's emphasis on the trauma-*effect* as an embodied forgetting. Traumatic realism seems particularly suited to the medium of film, since film techniques can mimic violence with absolute (one might say loving) fidelity without implicating the audience. Although the mimesis is hyperreal, we never worry about the actors getting hurt *in the process of our watching* (the making of the film is another matter). Conversely, no matter how well performed, mimesis onstage threatens to break down in the staging of extreme sexual and violent acts ("they can't *really* be doing that night after night"). We risk becoming distracted from the "what" by the "how" of the representation.

Theatrical immediacy produces mixed effects when it comes to graphic realism. A natural reaction to witnessing horror in the flesh is disgust; vomiting is, after all, a kind of catharsis, if perhaps not what Aristotle envisioned. Such visceral disgust has indeed been the reaction of many spectators to the graphic dramas of Sarah Kane, one of the most influential British playwrights of the 1990s. Kane was inspired by her fellow moralist Edward Bond, whose landmark play *Saved* (1965) arguably inaugurated traumatic realism on the contemporary English stage through its notorious depiction of the stoning to death of a baby in a pram.[30] Kane's first play, *Blasted* (1995), depicts the trauma of war by dramatizing such horrors as rape, the sucking out of a man's eyes, and the consumption of a (dead) baby. Kane's pulverizing drama takes the logic of trauma to the extreme:

it is not by "offending" but by traumatizing the audience that psychic and social change can be effected.[31]

The danger is that explicit brutality compounds trauma, assaulting (and alienating) the audience without transforming or purging it. As Shakespeare demonstrated some four hundred years before *Blasted* in *Titus Andronicus*, which also dramatizes cannibalism, the line between catharsis and voyeurism is thin. Horror takes place at the limits of mimesis. It is not that representation threatens to collapse altogether, as in Artaud's theater of cruelty, but that traumatic realism's simulations threaten to capsize theatrical illusion. An obscene event offstage can genuinely terrify; brought onstage, that event risks nausea or absurd laughter. This is precisely the risk Shakespeare courts by placing Gloucester's blinding onstage in *King Lear,* a tragedy that questions not only catharsis but meaning itself.[32]

Traumatic Irony: The America Play

Rejecting traumatic realism, the New Trauma playwrights stage trauma's gravitational effects with an emphasis on unseen terror rather than graphic horror. History and narrative become a series of effacements or gaps that the audience must fill in. By doing so, trauma is rehearsed rather than mapped, and the direct representation of trauma-events eschewed or mediated. Suzan-Lori Parks's *The America Play* (1994) considers African American history as a trauma that can never come into full visibility because American culture has disavowed it. Like Caruth, Parks conceives traumatic history in terms of possession. She writes:

> The history of Literature is in question. And the history of History is in question too. A play is a blueprint of an event: a way of creating and rewriting history through the medium of literature. Since history is a recorded or remembered event, theatre, for me, is the perfect place to "make" history—that is, because so much of African-American history has been unrecorded, dismembered, washed out, one of my tasks as playwright is to—through literature and the special strange relationship between theatre and real life—locate the ancestral burial ground, dig for bones, find bones, hear the bones sing, write it down.[33]

For a literary and theater artist, the act of writing history becomes an imaginative excavation in which the self simultaneously disappears and reveals itself. Theatrical performance is a place where trauma can unfold, but not in Kane's explicit sense; rather, "Theatre is an incubator for the creation of historical events."[34] These events are less empirical than phenomenological. The "something that through a production *actually happens*" is history itself—not the private response of an individual reader but the communal response of an audience that is invited, through the prism of trauma, to *remember* something that has never consciously happened to us, although we somehow know it in our bones.[35]

Despite its postmodern trappings, *The America Play* is—like *Death of a Salesman, Long Day's Journey Into Night,* or *Fences*—a classic family drama, whose son must come to terms with an absent father (*the* America play).[36] Accompanied by his mother, Lucy, Brazil searches for traces of the Foundling Father, who had gone west some thirty years before, abandoning his wife and young son, to seek his fortune.[37] The quest to recover the father represents the search for roots by a generation deracinated from Africa, the South, and cultural memory.[38] The Foundling Father is an African American gravedigger who subsequently impersonates Abraham Lincoln for a living. Both men are unnamed: the "Great Man" has passed into memory as an icon, and the "Lesser Known" appropriates Lincoln's identity through impersonation. He is, in short, a mimic man.[39] Dressed as Lincoln, who he is said to resemble, the Father sits in a fairground booth and allows paying customers to shoot him. American history is an amusement arcade whose initially nostalgic appeal has devolved into sadistic identification with a notorious assassin.[40]

As befits its notion of African American history as burial ground, *The America Play* takes place in "A great hole. In the middle of nowhere. The hole is an exact replica of the Great Hole of History."[41] The original hole was a theme-park attraction visited by the Father and Lucy on their honeymoon, and its "Reconstructed Historicities" fascinate the Father and parody (white) America's fondness for living museums and historical reenactments. At the Great Hole, "History" is reduced to a jumbled parade of impersonated icons from George Washington to Tarzan. The dehumanization and enslavement of displaced Africans, and the subsequent effacement of their traumatized bodies and psyches, form an unrepresentable hole in the American psyche.[42] Instead Parks offers us an "exact" replica—an ersatz parody of cultural amnesia, just as Lincoln is represented in act 1 by a pasteboard cutout, bust, and other "faux-historical knickknacks" (169). Parks satirizes our urge to memorialize an idealized past in sentimentalized, souvenir form as a gravitational effect of disavowed cultural trauma.[43]

The Foundling Father's identification with Lincoln feeds on a wish to be present in history, "to grow and have others think of him and remove their hats and touch their hearts and look up into the heavens and say something about the freeing of the slaves" (166). His imaginary identification is at once absurd, touching, and pathetic. The Father's emulation is driven by his desire to equal the Great Man in stature and leave something (having abandoned his wife and child) to posterity by following in his footsteps. Parks's anonymous gravedigger, whose profession is covering over human remains, seizes on the memes "Lincoln" and "the freeing of the slaves" as stand-ins for first-person experience and historical memory. Denied proper burial, the Father has died alone and unmourned—more Loman than Lincoln. His spirit remains locked in a repetition-compulsion of hollow reenactments: "The Lesser Known forgets who he is and just crumples. His bones cannot be found. The Greater man continues on" (173). Identity becomes self-forgetting, history repeats itself (the first time as parody, the second time as irony), and at the end of the act "*A gunshot echoes. Softly. And echoes*" (173).

The ever-repeating gunshot, an aftereffect that keeps on jangling the audience's nerves, is Parks's privileged figure for pain. The sourceless gunshot emanates not from a stage gun but from the great void of history itself. Like the Hole, another absent presence, it echoes an absence where memory should be. Phenomenological rather than mimetic, the gunshot imprints itself on the audience's nerves and memory.[44] Sound hemorrhages theatrical space-time and bleeds out into the auditorium (literally the place of hearing, as the *theatron* is the place of seeing). It does not represent a shot but *is* a shot, an act of auditory violence committed on our ears. Unlike an alienation effect, which would invite us to take up a critical perspective on the action—as, for example, *Hamlet*'s gravedigger invites us to view tragedy through the lens of irony—the gunshot is a trauma-effect. Its echoes carry unclaimed experience across the interval (stage time) and the fourth wall (stage space).[45]

Meanwhile, a more historically situated gunshot is debased by meretricious reenactment. Lincoln's mock assassination is repeatedly staged, as well as narrated, and the commerce between client and impersonator is rendered as pleasure in exchange for money. The thrill for the customer is equal parts sexual thrill and fetish for historical accuracy: "*Comes* once a week that one. Always chooses the derringer . . . He's one for History" (166, emphasis added). The Foundling Father muses, "A slight deafness in this ear other than that there are no side effects. Little ringing in the ears. Slight deafness. I cant complain" (169). The audience shares the impact: the bullets may be fake, but the sound is real. Here (unlike in traumatic realism) trauma bypasses mimesis.[46]

Act 2 begins with a replica gunshot that this time echoes "*Loudly*" instead of "*Softly*" (174). An effect without visible origin, the shot reverberates through the act as both assault and accusation. In Lucy's gloss of what the text calls Big Bang, "Once upon uh time somebody had uh little gunplay and now thuh gun goes on playing: KER-BANG! KERBANG-Kerbang-kerbang-(kerbang)-((kerbang))" (174). Lucy and Brazil have inherited the replica Hole, whose history lies in shards around them: "thuh bit from thuh mouth of thuh mount on which some great Someone rode tuh thuh rescue" (185). Mother and son spend the act excavating the Hole in search of the Foundling Father's bones (fragments they will shore against their ruins) so that his relics can be placed in a Hall of Wonders. Although the Father is dead and gone, traumatic echoes intensify. The shot that kills the surrogate "Lincoln" echoes the shot that killed the historical Lincoln. But that gunshot *itself* comes to stand in for the domestic and cultural histories (slavery, the civil war, emancipation, Jim Crow, the migration north) that are lost to the dispossessed Lucy and Brazil. Brazil has inherited the Foundling Father's knack for mimicry but not his identity. A professional mourner, he wails and gnashes, as appropriate, to provide gravitas to funerals. Brazil can memorialize his father only through rehearsing a pastiche of grief; he cannot experience his loss *as* loss but only as a void where the pain should be. Even his mourning—what Caruth might call unclaimed experience—is done for hire and belongs to someone else.

In its emphasis on inheritance, act 2 duplicates the coda to *Death of a Salesman*. Wife and son pronounce that the dead father had the wrong dreams, all, all, wrong: "His lonely death and lack of proper burial is our embarrassment . . . Diggin was his livelihood but fakin was his callin," intones Brazil (179). *The America Play* modulates Parks's anger at the way dominant narratives have effaced African American experience into caustic irony: "We're all citizens of one country afterall" (180). Among the "Greats" whom the Foundling Father enjoyed impersonating, alongside Washington and the Roosevelts, was Millard Fillmore. Parks expects us to remember that one of the thirteenth president's signal historic acts was signing the Fugitive Slave Act in 1850 (the "Bloodhound Law"), which declared that all runaway slaves be brought back to their masters, as part of the compromise between the free states of the North and the slave states of the South. Parks underscores the way that iconic signs ("Mister Millard Fillmore") become emptied of the content they once invoked. Can the Foundling Father's traces be turned into usable history?

As counterpoint to Lucy and Brazil's spectral quest, the Foundling Father's ghost appears and enacts scenes from *Our American Cousin,* the farce that Lincoln watched at Ford's Theatre on the day of his assassination.[47] Brazil digs up a number of objects culminating in a television on which the image of the Foundling Father's face appears, silently replaying the assassinations from act 1. Then the Foundling Father appears in the flesh, along with a waiting coffin. Parks makes the connection to Willy Loman explicit when Lucy invokes the "hundreds upon thousands" who wish to pay their respects at the funeral (195). The family reunion is played for bathos as the reunited trio stares at each other, and Lucy asks whether the Father is going to get into his coffin now or later. As a gift for his wife and son, the Father plays Lincoln once more, speechifying and then slumping in his chair as the shot fires. He freezes, sitting propped upright, becoming a waxwork-like exhibit in his own Great Hole. Brazil takes up his mantle as the master of ceremonies at the Hall of Wonders. The characters never escape their roles and never work through their trauma.

The target of Parks's acidulous satire is not only that slavery happened but that in cultural memory slavery has been reduced to the meme "Lincoln freed the slaves." A series of metonymic tropes (born in a log cabin, a nation mourned) now substitutes for African American experience. Lincoln's death—his assassination by John Wilkes Booth, who said something or other memorable at the time—stands in for "Lincoln," "Lincoln" stands in for "the freeing of the slaves," and "the freeing of the slaves" by a white president stands in for the traumatized psyches and bodies of enslaved Africans. *The America Play* wants to sing these bodies back into memory (where, as the Father reminds us in act 2, the nation mourned not slavery but the death of the sixteenth president). But because slavery is a trauma that *we* have not experienced, "History" can surface only as simulacra.

Rejecting linear narrative and catharsis, Parks recasts the rehearsal of trauma-effects as what she calls "Rep & Rev" (Repetition and Revision). Parks insists on the structural centrality of repetition not only within her work but within African and African American oral and literary traditions more broadly. Repetition takes place not only in the text but in the actor's body. Rep & Rev is "a literal incorporation of the past," a kind of staged history.[48] Parks simultaneously invokes her theatrical predecessors and kicks over their traces, anxious to avoid the didacticism and sentimentality of even the most accomplished American realist drama. Beneath the postmodern surface lies the anxiety that Parks is rewriting old plays, and she is. *Topdog/Underdog*'s thesis that young black men's symbolic emasculation is the central crisis of black culture recalls *A Raisin in the Sun,* for instance.[49] Parks is keenly aware that slice-of-life realism risks rehearsing tired tropes of racial oppression.[50] Her alternative conception of history as something created performatively in the "now" neutralizes the type of museum-theater that playwright George C. Wolfe affectionately if exasperatedly deems "The Mama-on-the-Couch Play."[51]

By burying the Father, *The America Play* literally re-hearses *Hamlet*'s "maimed" funeral rites and performs the culture's need for what performance theorist Joseph Roach calls "surrogation." According to Roach, surrogation is an omnipresent drive to fill historical voids, often traumatic to that culture, with substitutes that are often destroyed in turn once they prove unsatisfactory. Roach calls such scapegoat figures "effigies" and indicates the parentless and nameless Foundling Father as an example.[52] These haunted mediums are central to surrogation, which Roach defines as "the process of trying out various candidates in different situations— the doomed search for originals by continuously auditioning stand-ins."[53] Roach relates Parks's echoes to the "dead voices" overheard by Vladimir and Estragon in *Waiting For Godot,* where "the deferred memory of incalculable loss appears indirectly through the acoustical insinuation of ghostly voices into an austere soundscape eroded by silence."[54] The gravedigger can never be reintegrated into the family unit he abandoned, but his unsettled bones can be made to sing.

Traumatic Rehearsal: Sleep Deprivation Chamber

Whereas Richard Schechner has theorized performance as "restored" or "twice-behaved" behavior that migrates through time between bodies, trauma more closely resembles *rehearsed* or *deferred* behavior.[55] Trauma tilts toward the past or future; in the present it is foglike, ungraspable. We see it out of the corner of our eye, but whenever we try to set it directly in our sights, it vanishes. Trauma becomes visible only through its gravitational effects: the nightmarish repetition-compulsions of a Lady Macbeth, for example. Perhaps we might say that staged trauma is *twice-possessed behavior.*

The trauma-event possesses the subject as a repetition-compulsion rather than as integrated experience or memory, while the traumatized (fictional) character in turn possesses the actor, who bodies forth the trauma-effects. Witnesses to a double displacement, we are unmoored from clear coordinates in time, space, memory, and proprioception. What might it mean to rehearse trauma as that which can never be pinned down (as it is in *Party Time*) but asserts itself instead as compulsory spectral reading?

Behind its dead metaphor, rehearsal is a harrowing experience. The word *rehearse,* whose original English meaning is "to give an account of," comes from the Old French *rehercier,* "to go over again, repeat." Originally, however, the word meant "to rake over," from *re-* (again) and *hercier* (to rake). To rehearse something is to say it over again. But it is also to harrow, since a *hearse* was a large rake used for breaking up the soil. The word came to be applied to the harrowlike framework for holding candles over a coffin, and eventually, by association, to a vehicle for carrying a dead body. Rehearsal, then, is Janus-faced. To re-hearse means to repeat something that has already happened—to harrow it again, to bear the (dead) body once more on the bier of performance. But it also means to practice or prepare for an event that is yet to take place.[56] In this theatrical sense, which dates only from the 1570s, rehearsal is bracketed off as not quite, or not yet, the real thing. After all, if a theater-event is the *actual* performance then it isn't (quite) a rehearsal.

Acts performed in rehearsal occupy a peculiar status. According to J. L. Austin, any performative speech act spoken onstage, such as a marital vow, is "peculiarly hollow," an inefficacious performative unable to affect the status of the real.[57] A rehearsal of those stage vows would then be an imitation of an imitation. Both a telling-over and a dummy run, rehearsal collapses past and present, mimesis and diegesis, event and narrative.[58] Rehearsing joins a list of Janus-verbs associated with theater that blur *kinesis* and *mimesis:* acting, performing, playing. The tension between feigning and doing encapsulated in the phrase "performing an act" defines the ambiguous territory of theater itself. We might say that rehearsal is a model, in the sense that a model can mean both the template for subsequent duplication *and* the copies that are derived from that template. These two meanings erase the line between original and copy that the word supposedly demarcates. In its uncanny collapse of spatiotemporal categories, rehearsal models those psychic aftershocks of sudden, violent events that continually erupt into the *now*—repetitions that fall into the category of trauma.[59]

Yorick's grave haunts *Sleep Deprivation Chamber.* The play grew out of a 1991 incident in which Adam Kennedy, son of playwright Adrienne Kennedy, was brutally beaten by a policeman in the driveway of his father's house in suburban Virginia after being stopped for a broken taillight. Kennedy was then arrested and charged with assault and battery. Kennedy's fictional alter ego, Teddy Alexander, struggles to reconcile his nightmarish situation, in which a plea bargain may result in a suspended sentence but pressing the truth may lead to jail, with his other life as a privileged, middle-class college student at Antioch. The play also features Teddy's mother Suzanne, a chorus figure trying desperately to participate in her son's drama. A well-known writer, Suzanne sits at her writing desk and writes plaintive character references for her son, pleading with people of influence to intervene. Not only Suzanne's letters but her dreams figure prominently in the action. Eschewing linear narrative, the play stages trauma as a reverberating wound that cannot be integrated, only compulsively reenacted.[60]

The audience never forgets that it is in a theater. Key roles are taken by individual actors while the remaining roles are played by an ensemble. Theatrical space and time are fluid: short scenes bleed into each other, interrupting and repeating themselves with no clear dramatic arc, thereby exploding the "courtroom procedural" frame. The play refuses to cohere into the kind of family drama mocked by Parks in *The America Play.* Although both of Teddy's parents appear, this nuclear family has fractured. Teddy's parents are (by implication) separated, and his uncle suffers from depression and memory loss. Trauma hemorrhages outward to plunge the Alexander family into a legal and existential purgatory. The horror of physical assault triggers the terror of racial trauma, of historical persecution for crimes that one has not committed. The American "justice" system invokes the specter of the current mass incarceration of African American bodies—an invisible gulag previously beyond the ken of the "outstanding black American family" whose allegiance to middle-class values fails to insulate it from institutionalized racism (8).[61]

Sleep Deprivation Chamber treats cultural trauma as shrapnel that penetrates the subject yet cannot be integrated into a psychic whole. Suzanne struggles to hold together the coherent social self that in Kennedy's earlier plays had already fragmented into multiple personalities. Suzanne reads ubiquitous signs of social decay and communal breakdown (homeless men living under bridges, Uncle March's unsupervised dementia) as signs of the apocalypse. Uncle March, a retired Stanford professor once active in the civil rights movement, is increasingly treated as a relic by colleagues and students. Now given to wandering the hills around Palo Alto, the ghostly March embodies cultural amnesia (his very name invoking the 1963 march on Washington), as well as the collapse of communitarian vision into privatized individualism.

Without descending into traumatic realism, heavily mediated dream sequences recur in which Teddy is beaten or dismembered, often observed by Teddy himself. Teddy revisits himself in handcuffs, face swollen, interrogated by an unseen inquisitor. As a legal subject, Teddy is deemed responsible for his own abjection under the Kafkaesque law, even as his previous conception of himself as a free citizen disintegrates. Teddy's beating is captured on videotape; "*The brief film is very dark with violent sounds of Teddy's screams*" (20). But the video fails as court evidence, and the victim's inability to remember or articulate the forensic details demanded by the trial lawyers becomes an insistent theme. Meanwhile, Suzanne's nightmares are both narrated by her and acted out onstage by the ensemble. Narrative, memory, and dream converge in Suzanne's letter to the county manager.

> That morning in January [my daughter] Patrice called me crying, explaining how they had been sleeping when the sound of police sirens awakened them. The room appeared aflame with light and then a scream. It was Teddy. In the middle of that same night I dreamed about men living underneath the Westside Highway at 96th Street. (7)

Domestic tragedy cannot be separated from larger sociopolitical structures that abject American citizens, rendering them literally *unheimlich*.

Rehearsal in *Sleep Deprivation Chamber* does not so much represent the return of the repressed as the impossibility of owning one's own experience as a coherent individual subject.[62] As in much of Kennedy's earlier work, the "I" (agent-citizen-writer-witness) collapses under the pressures of internalized oppression. The first scene takes place in the Antioch College Theatre Department. We are backstage with a view of the rehearsal hall and stage, which are almost dark. The opening line is given to the student cast at the rehearsal table: "Ophelia, betrayal, disillusionment" (5). Later a student actor recites Old Hamlet's first lines, which retail not his murder but the crimes of which he himself is guilty. Old Hamlet's poisoning, "asleep at the moment of his murder," becomes a figure for trauma itself (16). Trauma possesses the characters, whose experience has slipped out of their control in both memory and narrative. Even one of the great family myths of Western literature, *Hamlet,* cannot save Teddy and instead haunts Suzanne as a kind of rebuke. Never dramatized, *Hamlet* appears only as ominous fragments. As director, Teddy controls rehearsals, but he cannot control his own fate. Denmark's revenant insists on the responsibility of the son to avenge the father's death; *Hamlet* underscores Suzanne's own fantasies of revenge, as well as her helplessness to intervene or even witness the beating and trial in person.

Like Parks's Great Hole of History, Yorick's unsettled grave is a dream-site occupied by phantoms. Shakespeare's grave is not only Yorick's but the hole where Ophelia is buried today and where Hamlet, Laertes, and the rest will presumably lie tomorrow. *Hamlet's* gravedigger began his work as sexton on the day of Hamlet's birth and will complete the cycle by burying him after the curtain falls. From the gravedigger's perspective, tragedy gives way to irony, since burial is all in a good day's work. As Beckett notes, the gravedigger is midwife, as well as sexton, and the grave a birth canal.[63] As Suzanne sleepwalks her way toward it, Yorick's grave re-hearses trauma as nightmarish repetition-compulsion and death wish. It is less the site of cultural amnesia than of traumatic dissociation itself. Alisa Solomon observes that Kennedy's four preceding "Alexander plays" dramatize "the process of turning memory into meaning."[64] The Kennedys now choose to short-circuit that Freudian trajectory.[65]

Sleep Deprivation Chamber dramatizes a crisis of retrodiction in which there is no longer "before" and "after." Teddy's assault and arrest are frozen in time, and there is no way to make sense of them within Suzanne and Teddy's previous frame of reference existentially, juridically, or artistically. Neither Suzanne nor the audience can read the fractured narrative backward in order to reconstruct the series of events within a cause-and-effect narrative that constructs citizen-subjects responsible for their fate. Like rehearsal itself, the action struggles to take place in the now, at the same time as it cannot help taking place in the now. *Sleep Deprivation Chamber* plunges the audience into the vertiginous depths of trauma, both as the sudden, unwilled incursion of the trauma-event into consciousness and as the uncanny sense that one's spirit has been possessed by nightmare and is marching, against one's will, toward the grave. The American family has become specters in its own lives: Suzanne and Teddy are doomed for a certain term to walk the night until the crimes committed against them are burnt and purged away.[66] A harrowing tragedy of repetition-compulsion, the play both dramatizes a sleep deprivation chamber and becomes one.

Traumatic Conscription: Far Away

If Parks and the Kennedys register racism's corrosive effects on individual identity and agency, for other contemporary playwrights, the conception of warfare as perpetual and indeterminate provides the most pressing challenge to theatrical representation. According to Mary Kaldor, a new type of organized violence developed during the last decades of the twentieth century. Such "new war" metastasizes within the context of globalization on the one hand and the erosion or disintegration of the autonomous state on the other. War is no longer the exclusive province of the state. Instead, "the new wars involve a blurring of the distinctions between war (usually defined as violence between states or organized political groups for political motives), organized crime (violence undertaken by privately organized groups for private purposes, usually financial gain), and large-scale violations of human rights (violence undertaken by states or politically organized groups against individuals)."[67] New war privatizes organized violence. The distinction between combatants and noncombatants breaks down as violence by both state and nonstate actors turns inward on citizens rather than being directed on an external enemy.

How can theater do justice to the experience of new war? One possible response has been to revive the documentary theater impulse, an impulse that Simon Shepherd aptly describes as "deferring to the real."[68] Such plays document war's effects on traumatized civilians based on interviews and other on-site research. Lynn Nottage follows this approach in her Pulitzer Prize–winning *Ruined* (2007), which dramatizes the plight of women targeted for sexual violence in the Democratic Republic of Congo. A documentary-based approach lends a sense of historical authenticity to such dramas of witness, which may feature otherwise fictionalized or composite scenes and characters. Moreover, placing trauma survivors within plots that follow recognizable dramatic arcs grants characters agency and offers a sense of hope. The question is whether such drama of witness can fully account for what is in essence a transformation in the *internal* and interpersonal landscape that threatens the boundaries of subjectivity itself.

Once warfare becomes a state of mind rather than a series of facts on the ground, as in the "war on terror" performatively declared by President George Bush on September 20, 2001, war becomes dark matter—in Julia Boll's suggestive phrase, the "unlisted character" of contemporary drama.[69]

While fearlessly experimental dramatist Caryl Churchill has never quite deferred to the real, her working methods often incorporate periods of intensive and collaborative research. Moving beyond the documentarian impulse that informs her (occasionally surreal) *Mad Forest: A Play from Romania* (1990), which was in part based on interviews conducted in Romania after the 1989 revolution, Churchill jettisons history in her grim fable *Far Away* (2000). *Far Away* dramatizes a state of war that is always elsewhere, unrepresentable, and absent, and yet at the same time present, internalized, and inescapable. Its three parts, while chronological, rehearse trauma from three different angles united by the theme of *conscription.* In part 1, whose dialogue between aunt and niece takes place in real time and uncannily mimics realism, the nature of the real is contested as a young girl, Joan, struggles to turn offstage trauma into narrative. In part 2, a now grown-up Joan pursues a flirtation with a fellow worker in a grotesque hat factory all the more sinister for its apparent normalcy. In part 3, which returns to the aunt's house, the characters face a global conflagration that has conscripted not only adults but children, animals, rivers, light, and sound. Environmental catastrophe and total war merge into a state of paranoia and defenselessness in which some social structures grotesquely remain (marriage and family) even as child-murder becomes normalized. By play's end trauma is less an individual psychological event than the very air the characters breathe.

Far Away's opening scene turns on what Joan has or has not seen in the dark. Visiting her aunt Harper for the first time, Joan has been awakened in the night by a shriek and has slipped out of doors to investigate, only to witness her uncle beating prisoners in a shed full of blood. Joan seeks comfort from her wary aunt and tries to construct a narrative that makes sense of a scene that defies rational explanation. Produced by the human voice but confounding language, the shriek is an apt figure for trauma; in Elaine Scarry's terms, it unmakes the world.[70] When Harper tries to convince Joan that the shriek was animal rather than human, Joan is dubious: "It was more like a person screaming."[71] She then revises her assertion in a speech act that teeters between the constative and the performative: "It was a person screaming" (6). Harper dismisses the child's testimony as the stuff of nightmares, but Joan refuses to take the bait: "Yes but I did see" (7). Hovering between the hypnopompic and the hypnagogic, the scene's competing narratives vie for factual purchase. Has the child awakened from or into nightmare?

Joan struggles to integrate the horrific scene into a plausible narrative—a bedtime story. She has not yet seen her aunt's house in daylight, making her *unheimlich* nighttime adventure doubly disorienting. At first tentatively, then with growing confidence, Joan relates an offstage sequence of events in which she witnesses her nameless uncle (whom the audience never sees) bundling a captive out of a lorry and into a shed and then beating him with a club. Clearly alarmed, Harper at first attempts to disavow Joan's testimony as the fruit of nightmare; after all, seeing in the dark is impossible. But when blood comes into play—Joan has slipped in it in her bare feet and tried to wipe it off—the wound contaminates the crime scene. Once Joan admits to seeing bloody children in the shed, Harper must switch tactics to protect her husband: "You've found out something secret" (11). Instead of denying the truth of Joan's witness, she conscripts Joan within a palatable melodrama. The heroic uncle was helping the prisoners escape, and Joan must remain silent so as not to endanger them. At this point Joan introduces a shocking new revelation.

> Why was uncle hitting them? . . . He was hitting a man with a stick. I think the stick was metal. He hit one of the children. (13)

The striking of the child represents a crisis in narrative confidence. Unconvincingly, Harper replies that Joan's uncle attacked a traitorous man and child in order to defend the other prisoners from betrayal. Joan repeats this as if testing a hypothesis, disguising a performative as a constative statement: "He only hit the traitors" (14). Joan offers to help what she now understands to be an underground railway movement, and Harper suggests that she help "clean up in the morning" (15).

Erasing the material traces of trauma symbolizes the child's complicity in adult violence, the necessary choosing of sides based on domestic or tribal loyalty. The trauma, suggests Churchill, is not merely the offstage violence in the shed but its normalization in the child's mind, its conversion into a mess that can simply be cleaned up. By rewriting her testimony and confusing her sense of right and wrong, Harper converts Joan into a child soldier, foreshadowing her future. But to villainize Harper is to fall into a melodrama the play subverts, for just conceivably Harper tells the truth. Right and wrong, truth and fiction, are undecidable. The uncle remains invisible, subject to spectral reading. Churchill offers us a troubling bedtime story, a meditation on the relationship among trauma, narrative, and complicity.

When Joan returns as a young woman in part 2, several years later, the childhood incident with the uncle is forgotten. But Joan is once again conscripted, this time by the institution of the state rather than the family. The play's middle scenes take place in a hat factory, where Joan and a young man named Todd (German for death) manufacture gaudy and ridiculous hats. The scenes drip with dramatic irony. "You'll find there's a lot wrong with this place," remarks Todd; "I'm the only person in this place who's got any principles" (16, 21). The play's central scene, unwitnessed by Joan and Todd, features a silent procession of ragged, beaten, chained prisoners, each wearing a fantastical hat, on their way to execution.[72] The morality of execution is never queried by the young couple—Todd watches the show trials on television, Joan ignores them—who grumble about their work conditions instead. Now under the influence of Todd rather than Harper, Joan is once again alienated from her own experience, but this time in the Marxist sense. A college-trained artisan who sells her labor professionally, Joan proudly turns artworks into disposable commodities. The hats' practical function has become purely decorative; the condemned have no need for hats. As "fascinators" (from Latin *fascinare*, "to bewitch"), they distract a public encouraged to see the march to execution as an amusing fashion show rather than a war of the state against its own citizens. Capitalist labor is itself a kind of trauma. From Todd and Joan's perspective, the "fantastic body of work" that they produce converts the condemned into disposable mannequins who give them a shot at the weekly design prizes (25). Todd and Joan lament the burning of the hats but not the burning of the human bodies, which evidently happens far away from the factory.

The play's final scene returns to Harper's house in daytime. Todd and Joan are married, and Todd is on leave from compulsory national service. The entire world is at war, including animals, children, flora, and inanimate objects: "The cats have come in on the side of the French" and have reportedly been killing Chinese babies (29). A deserter from the carnage, Joan has arrived at her aunt's house seeking refuge. But there is no place of safety in Churchill's mad dystopia, for war has become a way—the only way—of being-in-the-world. Harper, afraid that Joan has been traced to her house, descends into a state of paranoia posing as rationality: "Mallards are not a good waterbird. They commit rape, and they're on the side of the elephants and the Koreans. But crocodiles are always in the wrong" (33). Everything wars with everything else in a constantly shifting pattern of alliances that no one can keep straight. As the trio talk past each other, communication degrades and absurdism triumphs: "[T]he Latvian dentists have been doing good work in Cuba" (31).

As language unhooks itself from referentiality, war evacuates the "I" and substitutes a "we" on whose behalf "we" are fighting. "I think what we all think," Todd reassures Harper, although what Harper thinks changes from moment to moment. (Harper's name perhaps reflects her bardic function as a modern-day Homer.) The state has become evacuated of all recognizable landscape except shopping malls; consumer capitalism apparently thrives on a state of perpetual warfare. What distinguishes Churchill's protagonists from those of Parks and the Kennedys is that they are not victims but fully implicated in trauma's perpetuation. "I've shot cattle and children in Ethiopia," boasts Todd. "I've gassed mixed troops of Spanish, computer programmers, and dogs. I've torn starlings apart with my bare hands" (34). Todd chillingly describes working in abattoirs until "all you can see when you shut your eyes is people hanging upside down by their feet" (35). Todd's stunning of "pigs and musicians" recapitulates his dehumanizing work in the hat factory in the key of genocide. Joan retails her journey to the house past scenes of horror.

> It was tiring there because everything's been recruited, there were piles of bodies and if you stopped to find out there was one killed by coffee or one killed by pins, they were killed by heroin, petrol, chainsaws, hairspray, bleach, foxgloves, the smell of smoke was where we were burning the grass that wouldn't serve. (37)

The play ends abruptly and ambiguously with a tale of Joan deciding to ford a river without knowing whether or not it will help her swim or drown her.

In the inverse of traumatic realism, no violence occurs onstage; war remains dark matter. Churchill's parable denies the possibility of catharsis or narrative closure. Joan begins the play as an innocent witness to trauma and ends as an exhausted combatant in a war in which "everything's been recruited." Since the war exists both outside and within the characters, there is neither escape nor refuge nor respite. The earlier tactics of denial no longer serve in a weaponized universe. *Far Away* may be Churchill's bleakest play yet, but it is cautionary rather than cynical. Traumas that are disavowed as taking place "far away"—such as global warming, economic catastrophe, state terrorism, and the conscription of child soldiers—must be faced, warns Churchill, or else democracy and civilization will collapse into barbarism (unless they already have). To claim the status of righteous victim or loyal citizen is to perpetuate the horror. Aptly characterized by Aleks Sierz as a state-of-the-nation play, *Far Away* targets the psychological mechanism that tempts us to perceive a state of normalcy "here" and a state of exception "there."[73]

Traumatic Mediation: Attempts on Her Life

Among the most influential English plays of the 1990s, Martin Crimp's *Attempts on Her Life* (1997) is a satiric Passion Play whose protagonist's invisible, abused, and mediated body must be taken on faith. Described as "17 scenarios for the theatre," *Attempts* foregoes designated characters, plot, setting, and action. The script comprises dialogue without speech-headings and features an almost complete absence of stage directions or recognizable settings. There is no indication as to how many actors appear, nor how the play is to be realized onstage; only changes of speaker are indicated in the text. Ironically, given Crimp's critique of the society of the spectacle, the play's director is forced to fill the void by bringing the action into representation. To stage the attempts on "her" life requires an act of scopophilic violence against a protagonist who, voluntarily or not, has escaped the scene of representation entirely.

Crimp's experimental piece centers around a character variously named Anne, Annie, Anya, Annushka, and even (in her incarnation as a car) the Anny, who never speaks or appears in the script.[74] As a theatrical device she is by turns a murder victim, terrorist, porn star, tourist hostess, cult member, motor car, and artist documenting her own suicide attempts. Representation is an act of violence, as the pun in the title suggests. Like Sebastian Venable in *Suddenly Last Summer,* Anne is a self-consuming artifact devoured from within and without. Most critics have interpreted Anne as a figure for the unknowability of identity.[75] But Anne also signifies the mediatized conflation of trauma-event and trauma-effect. Having vanished without a trace, Anne becomes a conveniently empty cipher that allows for any and all projections onto her afterimages ("ALL THE THINGS THAT ANNE CAN BE" as Crimp's razzle-dazzle lyric "The Camera Loves You" puts it in scenario 4). The play's mediated projections, at once sadistic and objectifying, signify a traumatized global culture that reduces women to marketable commodities (25).[76]

Each scenario constructs Anne as a particular (dramatic) subject within a specific (theatrical) genre or tone. *Attempts on Her Life* begins with an overture, twelve answering machine messages left for the absent (dead?) protagonist. The messages introduce voices from Anne's life that will appear in subsequent scenarios, among them a cosmopolitan lover unsure if he is in Prague or Vienna; a terrorist leaving instructions; Anne's mother, cutting off funds; a car saleswoman; an enthused art critic or possibly agent; and a thug leaving death threats. Each voice demands something of Anne yet has failed her in some way; all are compromised, mediated, inauthentic. The machine automatically deletes the messages, which Anne will never hear.[77] The second scenario, titled "Tragedy of love and ideology," constructs not tragedy but a Merchant Ivory melodrama. What seem to be two writers work up a film scenario: "Summer. A river. Europe. These are the basic ingredients" (10). The notion of "basic ingredients" of course recalls Aristotle's *Poetics,* the original recipe book of tragedy. The voices are concerned to construct a "whole tragedy," a parody of Aristotle's definition of tragedy as the imitation of a complete action.[78] *This* Anne is constructed through her sexuality, as in a Hollywood filmscript—we first "see" her making love in a "luxury apartment, naturally, with a view over the entire city" (10). In this script Anne is an idealistic political activist who has (of course) fallen in love with a master of the universe. The writers are obsessed with rendering action visible, so that "tragedy unfolds before our eyes" (14). Crimp makes fun of the conventions of Hollywood lovemaking (such as the lack of condoms and the bathing in golden light). The "greatness" of the tragedy depends on depicting Anne as conventionally helpless to resist her passion for a masterful man whose values she despises.

The third scenario explicitly evokes the camera.[79] This time the unnamed characters seek to distill an image of trauma that will move the spectator. The image—a shorthand history of trauma—is a close-up of Anne (now Anya's) contorted face as she confronts a village scene in which "The women have been raped and then disemboweled. The men have hacked each other to pieces" (18). These atrocities soon reach absurd cinematic proportions: "The burning people running blazing between the fruit trees which bear their names, scorching the leaves, writhing on the blades of grass, while the soldiers stand by laughing" (19). The screen-writers (if this is what they are) then disagree on whether Anya should then scream "like something from an ancient tragedy" or advance toward the camera and let loose a string of bathetic expletives (20). The writers want to move the spectators from sympathy to empathy, for in the carnage of the valley "we strangely recognize ourselves. Our own world. Our own pain" (21). Witnessing Anya's suffering "strangely restores—I think it does—yes—our faith in ourselves" (22). The scenario debases Aristotelian recognition into narcissism. Anya's image flatters the audience with its own self-righteousness.

Anne is less a subject who eludes representation than a void where a subject should be. In the sixth scenario, "Mum and Dad," a picture emerges of a middle-class English childhood that degrades into depression and terrorism. "I feel like a screen," Annie is reported to have said: "She says she's not a real character, not a real character like you get in a book or on TV, but a *lack* of character, an *absence* she calls it, doesn't she, of character" (31). This particular Anne is complicit in her own commodification. She spends days on end pretending to be a television or a car. One moment Anne is caught in a snapshot "rubbing shoulders" with smiling slum-dwellers (29); the next she is a detached terrorist responsible for random acts of senseless violence (29). Here Anne looks on impassively as witnesses testify to the trauma-event.

> Is this really the same little Anne who now has witnesses breaking down in tears? Who now has long-serving officers of both sexes receiving counseling for the night-sweats, impotence, amenorrhea, trembling hands and flashbacks of human heads popping open as if in slow motion and the long long terrible wail of a buried unreachable child recurring as a kind of what's the word? (46)

The clichéd imagery reflects the mediated and packaged nature of global trauma. As a terrorist Anne "summed up the mood of a generation," appeared twice on the cover of *Vogue,* and sold the film rights to her story for 2.5 million dollars (46). Celebrity-terrorism grimly parodies the conflation of violence and entertainment that reflects our cultural moment.

In a scenario that seems to be set in an art gallery exhibit documenting Anne's suicide attempts, art critics glibly debate whether this is a landmark

conceptual work or narcissistic self-indulgence. Once more, language devolves into cliché: "It's entertaining. It's illuminating. It's dark. It's highly
personal and at the same time raises vital questions about the world we're
living in" (52). Crimp guys his own project.

> It's surely the point that a search for a point is pointless and that the
> whole point of the exercise—i.e. these attempts on her own life—*points*
> to that. It makes me think of the Chinese proverb: the darkest place is
> always under the lamp. (53)

Unsurprisingly, Crimp implies that any consumer of suffering dressed up
as highbrow art becomes a complicit voyeur: "Isn't she saying the only
way to avoid being a victim of the patriarchal structures of late twentieth-
century capitalism is to *become her own victim?*" (55). In a debased culture
where art is judged on its shock value, the salvific Passion Play—Anne's
"broken and abused" body is said to be "almost Christ-like"—has mutated
into a fetishized iconography of death (57).

Crimp's target is wider than an English art-scene dominated by "Cool
Britannia" artists like Damien Hirst or Tracey Emin, however. The conver-
gence of globalization, new war, terror, and consumer capitalism has led
to a surreal or hyperreal society in which the simulacra of civilization—
"art galleries, halogen lamps, charming cafes and attractively displayed
shoes"—numb us to widespread carnage and social breakdown (63). Yet
fear and trauma keep bursting through the membrane of civilization. In
the play's most disturbing scenario, "Pornó," a very young girl testifies before what seems to be an international tribunal; her words are dispassion-
ately translated into an African, South American, or Eastern European
language. The girl mechanically testifies that participating in pornography
is a financial investment that does not prevent her from leading a normal
life with "all the normal interests of a girl of her age" (73). Her recitation
is interrupted by what seem to be lapses in a memorized script; a voice
prompts her with increasing impatience, as if anxious that the girl make
a convincing impression. The girl performs dissociation, as if testifying to
something that happened to someone else's body. Eventually she breaks
down, and the text moves from third to first person: "I can't" (75). Another
speaker takes over. In one of the play's rare stage directions, Crimp is careful to note, "*She seems to have forgotten what to say: but this should imply a
distress which is never allowed to surface. She looks for a prompt*" (74). The

girl (Anne?) speaks in platitudes that mask a traumatic personal history unavailable to direct experience. Eventually the scene transmutes into a bizarre ensemble musical number, accompanied by passionate gypsy violin, in which individual suffering dissolves into a parodic chorus of faith in a utopian future.

Throughout *Attempts on Her Life,* trauma refuses to provide a coherent story or a subject. A horrible anecdote about a man who stabs a woman thirty-seven times in the presence of her sleeping child, witnessed by his own son, becomes an article mentioned in a letter to Anne that is never read and never replied to. Adopting prismatic rather than linear dramaturgy, with Anne herself as the prism, Crimp interrogates what it means to *be* a body in an age of relentless media saturation. Every scenario presents a different attitude toward testimony or witness: police procedural, melodramatic fiction, public hearing, advertisement, interview, art criticism. Post-identity and post-representation, Anne is simultaneously the object and subject of violence. As dark matter she can be Christ-figure, contested narrative, ordeal artist, It-Girl, or hallucination, according to our needs. Detectable only by her gravitational after-effects, Anne figures trauma as at once disembodied, ungraspable, and irresistible.

Traumatic Empathy: Anna Deavere Smith

Rehearsed rather than exorcised, trauma hemorrhages the contemporary stage space through its gravitational effects: nightmare, somnambulism, the breakdown of language, the fragmentation of the subject, and compulsive repetition. If the cathartic model traffics in revenants, the New Trauma features unfillable holes and gaps. The ghost of Old Hamlet becomes Yorick's (empty) grave. As dark matter trauma defies direct representation and shatters realism; mimesis is suspect, as is the Aristotelian goal of catharsis through identification with fictional beings. Staging psychic absence through techniques that extend or reject psychological verisimilitude, contemporary playwrights rewrite Aristotle in order to forge new connections between trauma and theatricality. Ironically, Suzanne Alexander, whose life has collapsed into nightmare, lectures on "The Construction of a Play with Aristotelian Elements." Such a construction would of course nullify the very trauma the Kennedys wish to stage. As Philip C. Kolin remarks, "Characters in Kennedy's plays never reach a catharsis; their psychic wounds just bleed, and bleed."[80] What unites the New Trauma playwrights, and distinguishes them from traumatic realists like Bond and Kane, is skepticism toward theater as cathartic or curative.

Yet the New Traumatists do not dominate the scene of contemporary drama and performance art. African-American performance artist and playwright Anna Deavere Smith takes a more sociological approach, for instance. Smith's long-term project, *On the Road: A Search for American Character*, documents traumatized communities in their own words. The communities she selects tend to have been silenced by the dominant culture, media coverage, and American mythography. Recovering living history, Smith interviews and then embodies her subjects by duplicating their speech and gestures. Closer to Erving Goffman than Judith Butler, Smith's quarry is less compulsory performativity than social performance: "[P]art of me is becoming them through repetition—by doing the performance of themselves that they do. I become the 'them' that they present to the world."[81] Smith takes pains to duplicate verbal breakdowns and slips as exactly as possible, recognizing that it is precisely in the moments when public language breaks down that trauma speaks through the body. Through what might justly be called spectral *listening*, unclaimed experience can be reclaimed for the polis.

Smith begins from the standpoint that America, as Rabbi Isidor Chemelwitz ruefully puts it in Tony Kushner's *Angels in America*, is "the melting pot where nothing melted."[82] Our challenge as a nation is to *become* Americans—to negotiate our cultural differences without essentializing, collapsing, or sentimentalizing them. Although she does not say so explicitly, in performance Smith's body—marked by gender, class, and race, yet, through theatrical alchemy, able to inhabit differently marked bodies—wants to *become* America: a container for others' experience, living museum rather than Great Hole. By mirroring others' experience faithfully, and without effacing racial, gender, or sexual difference, Smith allows America's trauma to speak through her. The performer becomes at once verbatim documentarian and speaking ghost, bringing history into the now.

At the wrenching conclusion of *Fires in the Mirror: Crown Heights, Brooklyn, and Other Identities* (1992), which documents the 1991 Crown Heights riots that occurred in the wake of the accidental killing of a black child named Gavin Cato by a Lubavitch rebbe's motorcade, Smith incarnates Carmel Cato, Gavin's father. Although we have heard dozens of voices from both sides of the conflict, Gavin himself is absent from the play, as is Yankel Rosenbaum, the Jewish scholar killed in retaliation on the same day. The two victims are rendered invisible by the aftermath of grievance, accusation, self-justification, paranoia, and publicity mongering that still possess both communities. Having given all the interviewees the opportunity to express themselves in their own words, in Smith's extraordinary performance as Cato, we witness embodied grief mixed with wounded pride.

Smith's riveting portrayal of Cato embodies spectral reading. The trauma-event of Gavin's death remains invisible, but beneath Cato's proudly spoken words, a hidden landscape of grief ripples to the surface. Trauma emerges in the gaps within and between articulation. Smith notes:

> What I'm ultimately interested in is the struggle. The struggle that the speaker has when he or she speaks to me, the struggle that he or she has to sift through language to come through. Somewhere I'm probably also leaving myself room as a performer to struggle and come through.[83]

The struggle between Goffmanian self-presentation and inexpressible grief opens up a space for empathy without voyeurism. "[Y]ou can repeat every word I say," Cato concludes.[84]

Comparing Smith to a shaman, Richard Schechner labels her method "incorporation" rather than conventional acting: "To incorporate means to be possessed by, to open oneself up thoroughly and deeply to another human being."[85] Putting her faith in living testimony, Smith returns us to a curative model of trauma. Yet Smith's aim is neither exorcism nor catharsis but witness, and her dramaturgy is palimpsestic rather than Aristotelian. In *Fires in the Mirror,* the mirrored characters echo each other across a gulf of black-Jewish misunderstanding, generating irony and pathos in equal measure.[86] Performing barefoot in white shirt and black pants, Smith subtends the performances as a ghostly presence behind her uncanny mimicry. Her own difference from her subjects is both visible and invisible, creating an uncanny effect of presence/absence. In her ability to act as a container whose subjects' trauma is simultaneously not there and not not there, Smith exemplifies the enduring power of the invisible to shape drama, theater, and performance. Her embodiment of Carmel Cato's anguish exemplifies what Caruth calls "the enigma of the otherness of a human voice that cries out from the wound."[87]

Smith's haunting performances remind us that, scripted or not, performance is *always* spectral. The paradox of dark matter is that something hidden is disclosed even as it eludes our sight. Whether hallucinated demons, offstage sex, masked women, self-consuming protagonists, invisible surveillance, or contemporary trauma, theater conjures the unseen in the service of its imaginative poetics. Aristotle recognizes the power of dark matter in his remarkable claim that effective tragedy can dispense with theatrical representation altogether.[88] Aristotle threatens to make theater itself into a specter, a ghost haunting the feast of tragic poetry. While we would not go so far as to bring down the curtain on theater once and for all, the ghost behind the curtain remains crucial. "I became an actor because the curtain's there in the auditorium, and I wanted to be behind the curtain," explains master actor Michael Gambon. "I wanted to be in the secret world of the curtain and the stage door and the backstage and the other world—and with the audience out there . . . I like to retain the mystery."[89]

Notes

Introduction

1. "The Visit to the Sepulchre (Visitatio Sepulchri) from *The Regularis Concordia* of St. Ethelwold," in *Medieval Drama,* ed. David Bevington (Boston: Houghton Mifflin, 1975), 27–28.

2. "The Resurrection of The Lord (from Wakefield)," in *Medieval Drama,* ed. David Bevington (Boston: Houghton Mifflin, 1975), 620.

3. The Wakefield audience has just seen Christ incarnated by an actor who arose from the sepulchre and delivered a 107-line complaint.

4. Frank Wilczek, *The Lightness of Being: Mass, Ether, and the Unification of Forces* (New York: Basic Books, 2008), 225–26.

5. Gravitational pull is a Newtonian concept; such instantaneous action-at-a-distance is inconsistent with the principle of relativity. Thus, in Einstein's general theory of relativity, gravity is not a force acting between distant bodies but the curvature of space-time itself.

6. In the late 1990s astronomers postulated a previously unknown and all-pervasive dark energy to explain why the expansion rate of the universe is speeding up rather than slowing down. Einstein left room in his equations for such a "cosmological constant."

7. "We have been handed a Universe that is overwhelmingly dark to our eyes and our telescopes—one that is roughly three parts dark energy to one part dark matter, with only a pinch of the familiar sprinkled throughout the cosmos like a handful of glitter on a vast sea of dark felt." Evalyn Gates, *Einstein's Telescope: The Hunt for Dark Matter and Dark Energy in the Universe* (New York and London: W. W. Norton, 2009), 4.

8. See Hanna Scolnicov, "Theatre Space, Theatrical Space, and the Theatrical Space Without," in *Themes in Drama IX: The Theatrical Space,* ed. James Redmond (Cambridge: Cambridge University Press, 1987), 11–26; Michael Issacharoff,

Discourse as Performance (Stanford, CA: Stanford University Press, 1989); Anne Ubersfeld, *L'école du spectateur: Lire le théâtre 2* (Paris: Éditions Sociales, 1991); Karel Brušák, "Imaginary Action Space in Drama," in *Drama und Theater: Theorie-Methode-Gesschichte,* ed. Herta Král Schmid and Hedwig Král Schmid (Munich: Otto Sagner, 1991), 144–62; Gay McAuley, *Space in Performance: Making Meaning in the Theatre* (Ann Arbor: University of Michigan Press, 1999), especially 17–23; and William Gruber, *Offstage Space, Narrative, and the Theatre of the Imagination* (New York: Palgrave Macmillan, 2010).

9. Marvin Carlson, "Indexical Space in the Theatre," *Assaph* 10 (1994): 4. I am grateful to the author for this reference. See also Keir Elam, *The Semiotics of Theatre and Drama* (London and New York: Routledge, 1980), 21–27.

10. Issacharoff, in *Discourse as Performance,* claims, "Mimetic space does not require mediation; in contrast, diegetic space is mediated by verbal signs (the dialogue) communicated verbally and not visually" (56). Critiquing such a distinction between perceived (onstage) and conceived (offstage) space, McAuley remarks, "Fictional place is 'conceived' whether it is on or off (Nora's drawing room is not, in fact, a drawing room)" (*Space in Performance,* 29–30). The distinction between enacted (mimetic) and narrated (diegetic) modes of representation goes back to Aristotle's *Poetics;* useful discussions of offstage space in ancient Greek theater can be found in Lowell Edmunds, *Theatrical Space and Historical Place in Sophocles'* Oedipus at Colonus (Lanham, MD: Rowman & Littlefield, 1996); and Rush Rehm, *The Play of Space: Spatial Transformation in Greek Tragedy* (Princeton, NJ: Princeton University Press, 2002).

11. See, for example, Peggy Phelan, *Unmarked: The Politics of Performance* (New York: Routledge, 1993), 146–66; and Elinor Fuchs, "Presence and the Revenge of Writing: Re-thinking Theatre after Derrida," *Performing Arts Journal* 9 (1985): 163–73. Janelle Reinelt, "Staging the Invisible: The Crisis of Visibility in Theatrical Representation," *Text and Performance Quarterly* 14 (1994): 97–107, critiques Phelan's "utopian" insistence on rupturing the representational economy, writing that "resistance [to the hegemonic] does not lie in denying the power of the visible, but rather in co-opting it" (105). Like Elin Diamond, who in *Unmaking Mimesis: Essays on Feminism and Theater* (London: Routledge, 1997) appropriates Irigarayan mimicry and Brechtian *gestus* to dismantle patriarchal mimesis, Reinelt reclaims representation as a viable political practice.

12. See especially Jacques Derrida, "The Theater of Cruelty and the Closure of Representation," trans. Alan Bass, in *Mimesis, Masochism, and Mime: The Politics of Theatricality in Contemporary French Thought,* ed. Timothy Murray (Ann Arbor: University of Michigan Press, 1997), 40–62. Conversely, for Jane Goodall, in *Stage Presence* (Abingdon, UK: Routledge, 2008), "The real challenge may be not to demystify presence, but to discover just how this mysterious attribute has been articulated and what kinds of imagery surround it" (7). Suzanne M. Jaeger, "Embodiment and Presence: The Ontology of Presence Reconsidered," in *Staging Philosophy: Intersections of Theater, Performance, and Philosophy,* ed. David Krasner and David Z.

Saltz (Ann Arbor: University of Michigan Press, 2006), 122–41, likewise challenges Derrida's critique of presence from a phenomenological perspective.

13. Performed at the border of ontology and phenomenology, theatrical "acts" have little to do with facts on the ground but can infect people nonetheless— sometimes with fatal consequences. Thus Elizabethan antitheatricalists remained both puzzled and phobic about what the professional theater actually was and did, and also liable to confuse it with (black) magic—a parallel the theater itself invited. See Andrew Sofer, "Felt Absences: The Stage Properties of *Othello*'s Handkerchief," *Comparative Drama* 31 (1997): 367–93; and Jody Enders, *Death by Drama and Other Medieval Urban Legends* (Chicago: University of Chicago Press, 2002).

14. My formulation pays homage to Richard Schechner's famous "not me . . . not not me" model of the performer; see Richard Schechner, "Restoration of Behavior," in *Between Theater and Anthropology* (Philadelphia: University of Pennsylvania Press, 1985), 35–116. Since beginning this project, I have come across three passing (and poetic) references to narrative and theatrical "dark matter": Alice Rayner, "Rude Mechanicals and the *Specters of Marx*," *Theatre Journal* 54 (2002): 539; Elinor Fuchs, "EF's Visit to a Small Planet: Some Questions to Ask a Play," *Theater* 34 (2004): 5; and H. Porter Abbott, "Narrative," in *Palgrave Advances in Samuel Beckett Studies,* ed. Lois Oppenheim (London: Palgrave Macmillan, 2004), 11. While fleetingly suggestive, none develops the analogy or relates it to recent scientific developments.

15. While my area of study is scripted, postclassical Western theater, the dark matter in global performance modes like commedia dell'arte, Noh, Butoh, Kabuki, and Kathakali fascinates in its own right. For instance, are the Bunraku puppeteers— like our own black-clad stagehands—there, not there, or not not there? Such walking blackouts present a riddle that is as much phenomenological as ontological. According to Alice Rayner, *Ghosts: Death's Double and the Phenomena of Theatre* (Minneapolis: University of Minnesota Press, 2006), "When a stage crew comes on during an intermission to change scenery or props in full view of an audience, it announces in effect, 'we are here and not here, doing real things that you see, but do not see as representational because they are actual. We are here working, but we are not signifying'" (140).

16. The pivotal yet unrepresented sexual encounter between Alec and Tess in Thomas Hardy's *Tess of the d'Urbervilles* (1891), which may or may not be a rape, exemplifies narrative dark matter. John Fowles's spectral reading of Hardy's novel, *The French Lieutenant's Woman* (1969), renders visible the dark matter of *Tess* by dramatizing the sexual act.

17. A striking instance of terror is W. H. Auden's poem "O What Is That Sound," which is really a verse play in dialogue. Theatricalized terror, in the sense I use it here, is not to be confused with the blind panic produced by violent acts of terrorism.

18. See Andrew Sofer, "Spectral Readings," *Theatre Journal* 64 (2012): 323–36. To combat kinamnesia, theater practitioners often fetishize material talismans like the "gypsy coat" passed down by Broadway ensemble members from production to pro-

duction. Diana Taylor adumbrates the performance repertoire of embodied memory in *The Archive and the Repertoire: Performing Cultural Memory in the Americas* (Durham, NC: Duke University Press, 2003). Joseph Roach, "Performance: The Blunders of Orpheus," *PMLA* 125 (2010): 1078–86, argues that performance studies' bias toward the living repertoire leaves performances "adrift in the present, unmoored from prior iterations of them that might be imagined, if not known, like the actions and events reconstructed partially but with forensic conclusiveness at an archaeological site or crime scene" (1079).

19. An ingenious spectral reading in its own right, Peter Shaffer's 1965 farce *Black Comedy* reverses its lighting scheme so that blackouts are played in the light and illuminated scenes in the dark—thereby producing what can only be called light matter.

20. Colin McGinn, *Mindsight: Image, Dream, Meaning* (Cambridge, MA: Harvard University Press, 2004). McGinn's mindsight is not to be confused with the neurological phenomenon known as blindsight, in which people who are perceptually blind in a particular area of their visual field nonetheless demonstrate some response to visual stimuli.

21. See Andrew Sofer, *The Stage Life of Props* (Ann Arbor: University of Michigan Press, 2003), 1–29. The existence of five dimensions is not, relativistically speaking, accurate. Einstein's relativity refutes Newton's view of space as a transcendent stage, against whose backdrop matter and energy play their parts, and of time as a neutral observer outside the action (as it were). Instead, time becomes a fourth dimension or axis (albeit one that cannot be visualized by our three-dimensional brains), while—according to general relativity—space, time, matter, and energy become mutually constitutive.

22. Cosmic dark matter's makeup remains unknown because its elementary particles do not interact with the electromagnetic force. Nevertheless, scientists have begun to map dark matter's large-scale distribution by observing how it bends light from distant galaxies through gravitational lensing (discussed in chapter 3). Dark matter acts as a lattice around which luminous galaxies and galaxy clusters assemble; see Richard Massey *et al.*, "Dark Matter Maps Reveal Cosmic Scaffolding," *Nature* 445 (18 January 2007): 286–90. The hunt for dark matter continues: in July 2012 scientists reportedly detected a thin thread of dark matter, some 2.7 billion light-years away, whose mass is about 60 trillion times that of the sun. Having found the Higgs boson, the European Organization for Nuclear Research (CERN) laboratory in Geneva now plans to make individual particles of dark matter.

23. The young Samuel Beckett neatly summarized this perspective when he praised Proust's "non-logical statement of phenomena in the order and exactitude of their perception, before they have been distorted into intelligibility in order to be forced into a chain of cause and effect." Samuel Beckett and George Duthuit, *Proust and Three Dialogues* (London: John Calder, 1965), 86.

24. Bert O. States, *Great Reckonings in Little Rooms: On the Phenomenology of Theater* (Berkeley, Los Angeles, and London: University of California Press, 1987), 7.

25. Jeffrey Andrew Weinstock, *Spectral America: Phantoms and the National Imagination* (Madison: University of Wisconsin Press, 2004), 3.

26. Wolfgang Iser, "The Reading Process: A Phenomenological Approach," *New Literary History* 3 (1972): 279–99. See also Greta Olsen, ed., *Current Trends in Narratology* (Berlin and New York: De Gruyter, 2011).

27. Jacques Derrida, *Specters of Marx*, trans. Peggy Kamuf (New York: Routledge, 2006), 10. Derrida's invocation of Marx has been not uncontroversial in materialist circles; see Michael Sprinkler, ed., *Ghostly Demarcations: A Symposium on Jacques Derrida's* Specters of Marx (New York: Verso, 1999). Colin Davis, "*État Présent:* Hauntology, Spectres, and Phantoms," *French Studies* 59 (2005): 373–79, provides a useful genealogy of hauntology.

28. Marvin Carlson, *The Haunted Stage: The Theatre as Memory Machine* (Ann Arbor: University of Michigan Press, 2001), 7.

29. Joseph Roach, *Cities of the Dead: Circum-Atlantic Performance* (New York: Columbia University Press, 1996), 80.

30. Peggy Phelan, *Mourning Sex: Performing Public Memories* (London and New York: Routledge, 1997), 2.

31. "The materiality of the performance is ghostly if for no other reason than that performance event is not an object but an event of consciousness generated by repetition." Rayner, *Ghosts,* xvii.

32. McAuley, *Space in Performance,* labels the backstage area "practitioner space" and notes, "Apart from the stage and its machinery, the practitioner space is significantly the least documented, least analyzed, least theorized area of theatre space" (26).

33. Hence the enduring playhouse tradition of the ghost light, which appeases any resident ghosts (and allows them to perform onstage) once actors and audiences have left the building. See Spencer Jay Golub, *Infinity (Stage)* (Ann Arbor: University of Michigan Press, 2001), 143–69.

34. If a ghost appears onstage, that ghost is not dark matter but part of the visible fabric of the play. David Savran reads the prevalence of ghosts in late-twentieth-century American drama as "the materialization of new anxieties" in "The Haunted Stage," the introduction to his *The Playwright's Voice: American Dramatists on Memory, Writing, and the Politics of Culture* (New York: Theatre Communications Group, 1999), xiii–xxi. For Elaine Scarry, in "On Vivacity: The Difference between Daydreaming and Imagining-under-Authorial-Instruction," *Representations* 52 (1995): 1–26, listening to a ghost story in the dark exemplifies how verbal fictions instruct us to create an image whose own diaphanous properties are "second nature" to the human imagination: "It is not hard to successfully imagine a ghost. What is hard is successfully imagining an object, any object, that does *not* look like a ghost" (13).

35. For the tendency of semiotic, phenomenological, and materialist approaches to dematerialize theater's physical matter, see Sofer, *The Stage Life of Props;* and "Spectral Readings." W. B. Worthen, *Drama: Between Poetry and Performance* (Mal-

den, MA: Wiley-Blackwell, 2010), 35–93, discusses "the repressing of the material" from New Criticism through performance studies.

36. I cite *The Riverside Shakespeare,* 2nd ed., ed. G. Blakemore Evans *et al.* (Boston: Houghton Mifflin, 1997).

37. McGinn, *Mindsight:* "[B]*ecause* images [unlike percepts] are attention-dependent, [we feel] they are subject to [our] will[s]" (28). All percepts imply presence. As McGinn sums up Sartre's argument, "[T]he percept 'posits' its object as existing and present (even when it is a hallucination), but the image 'posits' its object as absent or not existing" (29). Macbeth cannot *not* see the dagger as long as his eyes are open.

38. It is, however, a figure *for* language. "The mystery of meaning is that it doesn't seem to be located anywhere—not in the word, not in the mind, not in a separate concept or idea hovering between the word, the mind, and the things we are talking about." Thomas Nagel, *What Does It All Mean? A Very Short Introduction to Philosophy* (Oxford: Oxford University Press, 1987), 43.

39. Huston Diehl, in "Horrid Image, Sorry Sight, Fatal Vision: The Visual Rhetoric of *Macbeth,*" *Shakespeare Studies* 16 (1983): 191–203, reads *Macbeth* as centrally concerned with "the problematic of vision" and the dagger as an emblem of sin to which Macbeth is blind.

40. The emollient nostrum "It was only a dream" makes little sense to a card-carrying phenomenologist. Like a surgery, just because a dream is *over,* and happened to *no one else,* does not mean that it never happened.

41. Mime is a special instance of dark matter beyond the scope of this study.

42. Ralph Richardson, interview with Derek Hart, in *Great Acting*, ed. Hal Burton (London: BBC, 1967), 69. I am grateful to Cary Mazer for this reference. Directed by John Gielgud, Richardson played Macbeth for the Stratford-upon-Avon Festival in 1952.

43. This is not to say that performances that take place in the dark abjure indexical signs. Odyssey Theatre Ensemble's *Theatre in the Dark* (2012), a ninety-minute performance that plunges both actors and audiences in darkness for the duration of the show, makes extensive use of indexical sound effects, including sound-making props.

44. W. B. Worthen, "'The written troubles of the brain': *Sleep No More* and the Space of Character," *Theatre Journal* 64 (2012): 79–97.

45. My brief discussion of *Sleep No More* raises the question of whether, as mute witnesses, *all* audiences constitute dark matter; I am grateful to Ric Knowles for this question. To my mind metatheatrical moments of (say) aside, soliloquy, and fourth-wall breaking—as when Clov turns his telescope on the audience in *Endgame*—deliberately invoke an invisible audience precisely so as to disturb the gravitational field. Such distortions in the representational fabric would be negated, or at least diluted, by the claim that an audience functions as dark matter throughout any given performance. McAuley, in *Space in Performance,* similarly notes, "The power

of the metatheatrical and ideological impact of such spatial use justifies a separate subcategory" of offstage space, which she names "the *audience off*" (31–32).

46. See Richard Panek, *The 4 Percent Universe: Dark Matter, Dark Energy, and the Race to Discover the Rest of Reality* (New York: Mariner, 2011).

47. Eric V. Linder, "The Universe's Skeleton Sketched," *Nature* 445 (18 January 2007): 273.

48. As for the tree itself, it refuses to resolve into a symbol of anything except the passing of time, nor does it permit the clowns to hang themselves. Suicide, suggests Beckett, is no solution to the problem of being *in* time. The tree thus recapitulates the lesson of *Uncle Vanya*'s morphine pill, which Vanya steals from Astrov.

49. Linder, "The Universe's Skeleton Sketched."

50. Susan Glaspell, *Trifles*, in *The Harcourt Anthology of Drama, Brief Edition*, ed. W. B. Worthen (Boston: Thomson Heinle, 2002), 631–36. The quotation is from page 633.

51. Massey *et al.*, "Dark Matter Maps Reveal Cosmic Scaffolding." In 1936 Einstein predicted the gravitational lensing of one star by another. He dismissed it as a curiosity of no practical use and (mistakenly) added, "Of course, there is no hope of observing this phenomenon directly" (cited in Gates, *Einstein's Telescope*, 71).

52. "The deflection of light by massive objects is, in a very real sense, a lens through which we can scan the heavens and search for dark matter and dark energy. Gravitational lensing has the potential to launch a new scientific revolution by making it possible to map out the invisible sector of the universe. It is a new and powerful telescope—*Einstein's telescope*." Gates, *Einstein's Telescope*, 77.

53. Theater historians must correct for such distortions through the necessary scrim of imaginative reconstruction in the present. For the challenges facing contemporary theater historiography, see, for example, Judith Milhous and Robert D. Hume, *Producible Interpretation: Eight English Plays, 1675–1707* (Carbondale: Southern Illinois University Press, 1985); Thomas Postlewait and Bruce McConachie, eds., *Interpreting the Theatrical Past: Essays in the Historiography of Performance* (Iowa City: University of Iowa Press, 1989); Thomas Postlewait, *The Cambridge Introduction to Theatre Historiography* (Cambridge: Cambridge University Press, 2009); Charlotte M. Canning and Thomas Postlewait, eds., *Representing the Past: Essays in Performance Historiography* (Iowa City: University of Iowa Press, 2010); and Henry Bial and Scott Magelssen, eds., *Theater Historiography: Critical Interventions* (Ann Arbor: University of Michigan Press, 2010).

54. It is hard to overestimate the effects of Eucharistic controversy on the development of Western drama and theater. See, for example, Miri Rubin, *Corpus Christi: The Eucharist in Late Medieval Culture* (Cambridge: Cambridge University Press, 1992); Michal Kobialka, *This Is My Body: Representational Practices in the Early Middle Ages* (Ann Arbor: University of Michigan Press, 1999); Sofer, *The Stage Life of Props*, 31–60; and Sarah Beckwith, *Signifying God: Social Relation and Symbolic Act in the York Corpus Christi Plays* (Chicago: University of Chicago Press, 2003).

55. The logical positivists, who extolled the principle of verificationism, declared that only empirically verifiable (or tautological) propositions are meaningful. This claim's logic was famously demolished by Willard Van Ormond Quine.

56. For the productive engagement of theater and performance studies with cognitive neuroscience, see, for example, Mary Thomas Crane, *Shakespeare's Brain: Reading with Cognitive Theory* (Princeton, NJ, and Oxford: Princeton University Press, 2001); Bruce McConachie and F. Elizabeth Hart, eds., *Performance and Cognition: Theatre Studies and the Cognitive Turn* (London and New York: Routledge, 2006); Bruce McConachie, *Engaging Audiences: A Cognitive Approach to Spectating in the Theatre* (New York: Palgrave Macmillan, 2008); Rhonda Blair, *The Actor, Image, and Action: Acting and Cognitive Neuroscience* (New York: Routledge, 2008); and Tobin Nellhaus, *Theatre, Communication, Critical Realism* (New York: Palgrave Macmillan, 2010).

57. Karl Popper, *The Logic of Scientific Discovery* (London: Hutchinson, 1959).

58. Einstein's 1905 *Annalen der Physik* essay, "On an Heuristic Viewpoint concerning the Production and Transformation of Light," *Annalen der Physik* 17 (1905): 132–48, suggested the quantization of all light radiation and eventuated in his 1921 Nobel Prize.

59. Radio drama exemplifies dark matter but is not the subject of this book, having been well served by several previous studies. See, for example, Elissa S. Guralnick, *Sight Unseen: Beckett, Pinter, Stoppard, and Other Contemporary Dramatists on Radio* (Columbus: Ohio University Press, 1995). By presenting a blind protagonist onstage, plays like Frederick Knott's *Wait until Dark* (1966) convert fictional dark matter into bright matter for the nonce. The sighted actor must then imaginatively convert percept (bright matter) into image (dark matter)—thereby *reversing* the process of spectral reading.

60. This popular device, otherwise known as the "Godot Effect," transcends theater. Thus Gloriana in Spenser's *The Faerie Queene,* the first English epic, never appears directly but holds the poem's structure in place.

61. Arthur Miller, *Timebends: A Life* (New York: Grove Press, 1987), 573.

62. Cathy Caruth, *Unclaimed Experience: Trauma, Narrative, and History* (Baltimore and London: Johns Hopkins University Press, 1996).

63. Gruber (*Offstage Space,* 129–34) reads Godot diegetically, and the Boy's description of Godot as a "messenger speech" in the Greek tradition: "Mimesis and diegesis run side by side, as it were, functioning as two interdependent modes of theatrical representation" (131).

64. Herbert Blau, *Take Up the Bodies: Theater at the Vanishing Point* (Urbana: University of Illinois Press, 1982), reminds us that theater and theory share a common Greek root (*theasthai,* "to watch"). "Theater is theory, or a shadow of it . . . In the act of seeing, there is already theory" (1). See also Maaike Bleeker, *Visuality in the Theatre: The Locus of Looking* (Houndmills: Palgrave Macmillan, 2008); and Alan Ackerman, *Seeing Things: From Shakespeare to Pixar* (Toronto: University of Toronto Press, 2011).

Chapter 1

1. For Alleyn's costume as Faustus, see Samuel Rowlands's satirical tract *The Knave of Clubbes* (London: 1609): "The Gull gets on a surplis, / With a crosse upon his breast, / Like *Allen* playing *Faustus*, / In that manner he was drest." According to Michael Hattaway, "The Theology of Marlowe's *Doctor Faustus*," *Renaissance Drama*, n.s., 3 (1970): 64, "Alleyn wore a surplice and cross and used Psalters and New Testaments." Hattaway cites Rowlands as his source, but Rowlands makes no mention of Psalters and New Testaments in connection with Alleyn. Presumably Hattaway relies on Valdes's lines "Then haste thee to some solitary grove, / And bear wise Bacon and Albanus' works, / The Hebrew Psalter, and New Testament" (1.1.155–57). Alleyn must have carried some kind of magical book in the conjuring scene, as indicated by the title page illustration of the 1616 B-text quarto. But it is hard to imagine the actor weighed down by several tomes in performance, as this would have made the stage business of conjuring too awkward. The relevant lines from *The Knave of Clubbes* are in Samuel Rowlands, *The Complete Works of Samuel Rowlands* (New York: Johnson Reprint Co., 1966), vol. 2, n.p. My citations to both A- and B-texts of *Doctor Faustus* are from Christopher Marlowe, *Doctor Faustus and Other Plays*, ed. David Bevington and Eric Rasmussen (Oxford and New York: Oxford University Press, 1995). Unless otherwise noted, citations are to the A-text.

2. John Melton, *Astrologaster, or, The Figure-Caster* (London, 1620), cited (without attribution) in Park Honan, *Christopher Marlowe: Poet and Spy* (Oxford: Oxford University Press, 2005), 219.

3. "Certaine Players at Exeter, acting upon the stage the tragical storie of Dr. Faustus the Conjurer; as a certaine number of Devels kept everie one his circle there, and as Faustus was busie in his magicall invocations, on a sudden they were all dasht, every one harkning other in the eare, for they were all perswaded, there was one devell too many amongst them; and so after a little pause desired the people to pardon them, they could go no further with this matter; the people also understanding the thing as it was, every man hastened to be first out of dores." This and other accounts of the *Faustus* players unwittingly conjuring an actual devil are collected in E. K. Chambers, *The Elizabethan Stage* (Oxford: Clarendon Press, 1923), 3:423–24.

4. William Prynne, *Histrio-Mastix* (London, 1633), cited in *Marlowe: The Critical Heritage 1588–1896*, ed. Millar Maclure (London: Routledge and Kegan Paul, 1979), 48.

5. David Bevington, "Introduction to *Doctor Faustus*," in *English Renaissance Drama: A Norton Anthology*, ed. David Bevington, Lars Engle, Katharine Eisaman Maus, and Eric Rasmussen (New York: W. W. Norton, 2002), 249.

6. In her survey of reputed devil sightings in medieval theater, Jody Enders, in *Death by Drama and Other Medieval Urban Legends* (Chicago and London: University of Chicago Press, 2002), 100, wonderfully asks, "Just who was it that was seeing things that were not there—early spectators? ecclesiastical and municipal officials? theater historians? some strange combination of them all?" I concur with Kristen

Poole ("The Devil's in the Archive: *Doctor Faustus* and Ovidian Physics," *Renaissance Drama*, n.s., 35 [2006]: 191–219) that reports of real devils appearing at performances of *Faustus* invite us to suspend new historicist skepticism in favor of historical phenomenology. When it comes to early modern experiences of what we now dismiss as supernatural, "the distinction between the psychological and the physical, or between the physical and the spiritual, or between the metaphorical and the literal ceases to hold" (210).

7. I use the expression "Elizabethan audiences" as well as "Elizabethan spectators" because theatergoers in the period spoke of going to "hear" a play. This is not to underestimate the powerful resources and impact of Elizabethan stage spectacle, which are particularly notable in the B-text of *Doctor Faustus*.

8. David Z. Saltz, "How to Do Things on Stage," *Journal of Aesthetics and Art Criticism* 49 (1991): 31–45, challenges Searle's claim that theatrical performance drains speech acts of illocutionary power. Saltz posits what he calls "a game model of dramatic action, wherein actors do not merely imitate actions as they would be performed off stage, but really do commit illocutionary acts within the theatrical context" (41).

9. The literature on necromancy in the period is too extensive to list here. Useful works include Keith Thomas, *Religion and the Decline of Magic: Studies in Popular Beliefs in Sixteenth and Seventeenth Century England* (New York: Oxford University Press, 1997); Stuart Clark, *Thinking with Demons: The Idea of Witchcraft in Early Modern Europe* (Oxford: Oxford University Press, 1997); Frances Yates, *The Occult Philosophy in the Elizabethan Age* (London: Routledge, 2001); and Lorraine J. Daston and Katharine Park, *Wonders and the Order of Nature, 1150–1750* (New York: Zone Books, 1998). For devils on the English stage, see John D. Cox, *The Devil and the Sacred in English Drama, 1350–1642* (Cambridge: Cambridge University Press, 2000).

10. In 1604 Dee unsuccessfully appealed to James I for exoneration of the charge of conjuring demons. See Peter J. French, *John Dee: The World of the Elizabethan Magus* (London: Routledge and Kegan Paul, 1984).

11. David Riggs, *The World of Christopher Marlowe* (New York: Henry Holt, 2004), 176–77.

12. Ibid., 177.

13. Enders, *Death by Drama*, notes, "Superstition had it that there could be no 'playing around' when it came to speaking his name, lest the Devil manifest himself in person with deadly consequences. His pointy ears were always listening, always ready to parse someone's words or to give a binding contractual meaning to any smug or careless utterance. With its own propensities toward performativity, drama had always been well placed to review precisely such utterances" (94).

14. J. L. Austin, *How to Do Things with Words* (Cambridge, MA: Harvard University Press, 1962), 5.

15. Ibid., 6. John R. Searle, in "How Performatives Work," in *Essays in Speech Act Theory*, ed. Daniel Vanderveken and Susumu Kubo (Amsterdam and Philadelphia:

John Benjamins, 2002). 85–107, points out that Austin's distinction between performative actions and constative sayings "didn't work, because stating and describing are just as much actions as promising and ordering, and some performatives, such as warnings, can be true or false. Furthermore statements can be made with explicit performative verbs, as in 'I hereby state that it is raining'" (86). While acknowledging Searle's critique, I retain Austin's distinction between describing and *producing* a state of affairs through speech because it cuts to the heart of the Renaissance ambiguity over conjuring.

16. Austin, *How to Do Things with Words,* 14. Precisely this risk of inefficacy tempts us to disguise our most arrant performatives ("I give this paper a B+") as constatives ("This is a B+ paper"), hoping the magic will stick.

17. Ibid., 22.

18. For interesting discussions of what is at stake in the "marriage scene" between Orlando and "Ganymede" in *As You Like It,* see Susanne L. Wofford, "'To You I Give Myself, for I Am Yours': Erotic Performance and Theatrical Performatives in *As You Like It,*" in *Shakespeare Reread: The Texts in New Contexts,* ed. Russ McDonald (Ithaca, NY, and London: Cornell University Press, 1994), 147–69; and James Shapiro, *1599: A Year in the Life of William Shakespeare* (London: Faber and Faber, 2005), 238–39. See also Saltz, "How to Do Things on Stage," 33.

19. "For, ultimately, isn't it true that what Austin excludes as anomaly, exception, 'non-serious,' *citation* (on stage, in a poem, or a soliloquy) is the determined modification of a general citationality—or rather, a general iterability—without which there would not even be a 'successful' performative? So that—a paradoxical but unavoidable conclusion—a successful performative is necessarily an 'impure' performative, to adopt the word advanced later on by Austin when he acknowledges that there is no 'pure' performative." Jacques Derrida, "Signature Event Context," *Glyph* 1 (1977): 191.

20. Judith Butler, "Performative Acts and Gender Constitution: An Essay in Phenomenology and Feminist Theory," *Theatre Journal* 40 (1988): 527. This position is fleshed out in Butler's *Gender Trouble: Feminism and the Subversion of Identity* (New York and London: Routledge, 1990).

21. Judith Butler, *Bodies That Matter: On the Discursive Limits of "Sex"* (New York and London: Routledge, 1993), 234. Rehearsing the point in a 1996 interview, Butler explains, "[Performance] presumes a subject, but [performativity] contests the very notion of a subject." Judith Butler, "Gender as Performance" (interview), in *A Critical Sense: Interviews with Intellectuals,* ed. Peter Osborne (London and New York: Routledge), 112. It is unfortunate that the adjectival form of *performative* has come to mean both "performatized" and "performance-y."

22. Thus Elin Diamond presses theatrical performance into service as a kind of Butlerian laboratory for exposing the ruse of gender: "Performance . . . is the site in which performativity materializes in concentrated form." Elin Diamond, *Unmaking Mimesis* (London and New York: Routledge, 1997), 47. Compare W. B. Worthen, "Drama, Performativity, and Performance," *PMLA* 113 (1998): 1093–1107: "As a cita-

tional practice, dramatic performance—like all other performance—is engaged not so much in citing texts as in reiterating its own regimes; these regimes can be understood to cite—or, perhaps subversively, to resignify—social and behavioral practices that operate outside the theater and that constitute contemporary social life" (1098).

23. As Mona Lloyd observes, "[I]t is hard to see what precisely renders a performance discrete from the performative context of gender since both rely upon recitation of the same norms and conventions . . . Since the performative produces that which it names, and since gender is understood in performative terms as the effect of the intersection of discourses and practices of gender, and since these discourses and practices also underpin performances, it suggests that performance is itself performative. The distinction seems to be of little help. Indeed it raises more questions than it answers." Mona Lloyd, "Performativity, Parody, Politics," *Theory, Culture & Society* 16 (1999): 209.

24. This despite the fact that the 1995 volume *Performativity and Performance,* ed. Andrew Parker and Eve Kosofsky Sedgwick (New York and London: Routledge, 1995), was expressly devoted to the task. For a Marxist critique of Butler's position as late capitalism's nostalgia for individual agency, see Julia A. Walker, "Why Performance? Why Now? Textuality and the Rearticulation of Human Presence," *Yale Journal of Criticism* 16 (2003): 149–75.

25. Mary Thomas Crane, "What Was Performance?," *Criticism* 43 (2001): 174.

26. "An excellent Actor." *New Characters (drawne to the life) of severall Persons, in severall qualities,* in *The Works of John Webster,* ed. David Gunby, David Carnegie, and MacDonald P. Jackson (Cambridge: Cambridge University Press, 2007), 3:483–84.

27. Crane, "What Was Performance?," 172.

28. Ibid.

29. Ibid.

30. Ibid. Compare the antitheatricalist conviction that the Elizabethan transvestite theater sexually inflamed its (male) audiences through contagion: "Then these goodly Pageants being ended, euery mate sortes to his mate, euery one brings another homeward of their way very friendly, and in their secret conclaues (couertly) they play the Sodomits, or worse." Philip Stubbes, *The Anatomie of Abuses,* 7th ser., ed. Margaret Jane Kidnie (1583; rpt., Tempe, AZ: Renaissance English Text Society, 2002), 204.

31. Ibid., 173.

32. Philip Butterworth, *Magic on the Early English Stage* (Cambridge: Cambridge University Press, 2005), 3.

33. Ibid., 2. *Pace* Butterworth, in the context of Marlowe's own notoriety, *juggler* and *conjurer* seem to have been used interchangeably. Richard Baines's infamous 1593 letter to the Privy Council attributes to Marlowe the opinion that "Moyses was but a juggler" (cited in David Scott Kastan, ed., *Doctor Faustus: A Norton Critical Edition* [New York: W. W. Norton, 2005], 127). Puritan Thomas Beard (relying on testimony by Kyd and Baines) claims in 1597 that Marlowe averred "Moses to be but

a conjurer and seducer of the people" (*Theatre of God's Judgments*, cited in Bevington and Rasmussen, *Doctor Faustus and Other Plays*, viii). Butterworth does not note that Tyndale and other Protestant Reformers of the sixteenth century denigrated the Roman Catholic consecration as "conjuring" (*Oxford English Dictionary* [Oxford: Oxford University Press, 1971] 3.7.a; earliest citation, 1535), although *juggling* seems to have been a preferred term. The Eucharistic formula uttered by the priest ("Hoc est corpus meum") was no doubt the most contested performative of the period; see Judith H. Anderson, *Translating Investments: Metaphor and the Dynamic of Cultural Change in Tudor-Stuart England* (New York: Fordham University Press, 2005). For a subtle reading of *Faustus'* anti-Eucharistic parody, see Marjorie Garber, "'Here's Nothing Writ': Scribe, Script, and Circumscription in Marlowe's Plays," *Theatre Journal* 36 (1984): 301–20. Shifting the focus from speech acts to acts of onstage writing, Garber argues that "the act of writing or signing conveys, not just a struggle between contending characters, but a struggle for mastery of stage and text between the playwright and his inscribed characters" (301).

34. C. T. Onions, *A Shakespeare Glossary*, enlarged and revised by Robert D. Eagleson (Oxford: Clarendon Press, 1986), 56.

35. Citations to *Othello* are from *The Riverside Shakespeare*, 2nd ed., ed. G. Blakemore Evans *et al.* (Boston and New York: Houghton Mifflin, 1997).

36. For the knotty textual history of the play, see Eric Rasmussen, *A Textual Companion to Doctor Faustus* (Manchester and New York: Manchester University Press, 1993).

37. See David Bevington, "Staging the A- and B-Texts of *Doctor Faustus*," in *Marlowe's Empery: Expanding His Critical Contexts*, ed. Sara Munson Deats and Robert A. Logan (Newark: University of Delaware Press, 2002), 43–60. Recent editor David Scott Kastan summarizes, "The B-text, then, represents the play more or less as it came to be performed later in its stage history . . . [T]he two texts do not reflect only the distinction between a largely 'authorial' text and a 'theatrical' one—that is, between the play as its author [*sic*] may have imagined it and the work as it survived and inevitably mutated in the theater . . . But, even more, the two versions of the play in fact trace significantly different tragic trajectories, the B-text externalizing and theatricalizing what the A-text makes a matter of private conscience and conviction." See Kastan, *Doctor Faustus*, x.

38. Just as parody can make an original seem campier in retrospect—call it the Austin Powers effect—*Faustus* may have played quite differently with audiences in the wake of, say, Greene's *Friar Bacon and Friar Bungay* (published 1594) or Jonson's *The Devil Is an Ass* (1616), both of which make fun of conjuring, as does Rowland's satirical tract *The Knave of Clubbes*. The B-text indicates that increasing garishness marked the play's theatrical evolution (as when Faustus's scattered limbs are displayed to the audience in act 5, scene 3). Note Thomas and Tydeman: "The likelihood that *Doctor Faustus* was written in late 1588 or 1589 suggests that it is Marlowe, rather than Robert Greene, who should be credited with pioneering the vogue for plays about magicians in the early 1590s"; see Vivien Thomas and William Tydeman,

eds., *Christopher Marlowe: The Plays and Their Sources* (London and New York: Routledge, 1994), 172.

39. "The evidence Marlowe supplies in the play for an evaluation of Faustus' magic is inconclusive, and our judgment must depend on our widest conception of the play's meaning." Hattaway, "The Theology of *Doctor Faustus*," 61. Nevertheless, this truism has not stopped critics from arguing that *Faustus* is first and foremost polemical, even if the A- and B-texts' divergences create headaches for interpreters. The critical debate between orthodoxy and heterodoxy is usefully summarized in the editors' introduction to David Bevington and Eric Rasmussen, eds., *Christopher Marlowe, Doctor Faustus A- and B-texts (1604, 1616)* (Manchester and New York: Manchester University Press, 1993), 15–31.

40. Gareth Roberts, "Marlowe and the Metaphysics of Magicians," in *Constructing Christopher Marlowe*, ed. J. A. Downie and J. T. Parnell (Cambridge: Cambridge University Press, 2000), 59.

41. Ibid. These putative spectators respectively represent popular belief (faith in charms, spells, cunning women, etc.); the condemnation of *all* magic as bound up with witchcraft, together with a dismissal of the popular belief that magicians could control spirits, as articulated by the orthodox demonologists of the time (call it the King James version); and "high non-Satanic occult magic," Roberts's umbrella term for neoplatonism, Kabbalah, the Hermetic Arts, and so forth. Renaissance conjuring books, as well as figures such as Prospero, belong to this latter tradition of white magic. Necromancers claimed to command spirits without needing to enter into a pact with the devil (i.e., become witches). Orthodox demonologists tended to dismiss the distinction, which quickly collapses in *Doctor Faustus* (Faustus and his friends speak of raising "spirits" in act 1, scene 1, but "devils" in act 1, scene 3). Roberts doubts that a "Marlowe" exists behind the text(s) who sides with one of these three positions. Kristen Poole, in *"Dr. Faustus* and Reformation Theology," in *Early Modern English Drama: A Critical Companion,* ed. Garrett J. Sullivan Jr., Patrick Cheney, and Andrew Hatfield (New York and Oxford: Oxford University Press, 2006), concurs: "Like the culture that produced it, the theology of *Dr. Faustus* is messy, ambiguous, and often contradictory" (102).

42. Roberts, "Marlowe," 73. For instance, in their 1993 Revels Plays edition (*Christopher Marlowe*), Bevington and Rasmussen offer an ingenious explanation of the contradiction whereby Mephistopheles comes of his own accord when Faustus conjures in act 1, scene 3, but is then summoned against his will by the clowns in act 3, scene 2 (170n).

43. Daniel Gates, "Unpardonable Sins: The Hazards of Performative Language in the Tragic Cases of Francesco Spiera and Doctor Faustus," *Comparative Drama* 38 (2004): 59–82.

44. Ibid., 70.

45. Ibid., 60. Gates conflates the A- and B-texts as "Marlowe's play." Critics such as Michael H. Keefer and Bevington understand the two texts as presenting diver-

gent views on magic. Like Roberts, I view each text as presenting various contradictory early modern understandings of magic, rather than as representing a single ideology that can confidently be attributed to Marlowe.

46. On the London theater's appropriation of church vestments and properties, see Stephen Greenblatt, "Shakespeare and the Exorcists," in *Shakespearean Negotiations: The Circulation of Social Energy in Renaissance England* (Berkeley and Los Angeles: University of California Press, 1988), 112–13.

47. Andrew Sofer, *The Stage Life of Props* (Ann Arbor: University of Michigan Press, 2003), 61–88. For the argument that the London playhouses compensated for the Elizabethan regime's suppression (by about 1580) of most of the ritual practices and popular celebrations of late medieval Catholic culture, see Louis Montrose, *The Purpose of Playing: Shakespeare and the Cultural Politics of the Elizabethan Theatre* (Chicago and London: University of Chicago Press, 1996).

48. Gates, "Unpardonable Sins," 62. Gates deconstructs his own argument when he concedes, "The juxtaposition of . . . two contrasting views of language [in Spiera's story] shows how easily magical language can slide into the theatrical, and vice versa, how theatrical language can develop a force that verges on magic" (69). What fascinates Marlowe and his collaborator is not that religion is cardboard but that religion is a kind of performative production that is or can be magical in its perlocutionary effects. Intriguingly, Baines's (unreliable) letter claims that Marlowe, L. Ron Hubbard–like, considered inventing his own religion: "That if he were to write a new Religion, he would undertake both a more Exellent [*sic*] and Admirable methode and that all the new testament is filthily written" (cited in Kastan, *Doctor Faustus*, 128).

49. Gates, "Unpardonable Sins," 63.

50. See Andrew Sofer, "Felt Absences: The Stage Properties of *Othello*'s Handkerchief," *Comparative Drama* 31 (1997): 367–93.

51. One might compare the parallel instance of "coming out" as a performative utterance whose unpredictable effects exceed the will of the speaker but one that is often misread as a constative utterance that notes a preexistent state of affairs. I am grateful to Kevin Ohi for this insight.

52. For the emergent early modern notion of personation as something beyond merely "playing a role," see Frank Kermode, *The Age of Shakespeare* (New York: Modern Library, 2003), 64. For the view that Elizabethan dramatic personation transcended semiosis and became "participation," see Anthony B. Dawson, "Performance and Participation: Desdemona, Foucault, and the Actor's Body," in *Shakespeare, Theory, and Performance,* ed. James C. Bulman (London: Routledge, 1996), 29–45.

53. "Early modern actors did not yet 'perform' plays, and early modern audiences did not attend 'performances'"; see Crane, "What Was Performance?," 172.

54. William Blackburn, "'Heavenly Words': Marlowe's Faustus as a Renaissance Magician," *English Studies in Canada* 4 (1978): 13n12, notes that Mephistopheles's

claim that he was not compelled to appear by Faustus's conjuring does not appear in the *Faust-book* source and so was "presumably invented by Marlowe for a specific purpose of his own."

55. In the B-text, intriguingly, Lucifer and four devils enter before Faustus at the top of the scene. It is not clear whether this confirms the "orthodox" reading of the inefficacy of Faustus's magical speech. In the A-text, Faustus asks Mephistopheles, "Did not my conjuring speeches raise thee? Speak" (1.3.42); in B he asks, "Did not my conjuring raise thee? Speak" (1.3.42).

56. Michael H. Keefer, "Verbal Magic and the Problem of the A and B Texts of *Doctor Faustus*," *Journal of English and Germanic Philology* 82 (1983): 324–46, argues that the A-text systematically inverts magical faith in the transitive power of magical words by showing them to bind only Faustus himself: "The blasphemous rhetoric which [Faustus] uses is not a net to catch the world, but a web in which he himself becomes entangled" (339). Yet Keefer concedes that Faustus's act 5 speeches "are permeated by a verbal magic which is transitive . . . on the audience . . . The effect is paradoxical, for Marlowe's magic works on us through the utter failure of his protagonist's" (345–46). Here Keefer's sense of magic slides from the illocutionary to the perlocutionary. The fact that the A-text's clowns conjure Mephistopheles against his will presents a problem for Keefer's thesis and must be explained away as belonging to the 1602 additions by Birde and Rowley recorded by Henslowe (343). For Keefer the B-text's treatment of verbal magic is incoherent and contradictory (344).

57. "Though not themselves performatives, they are *about* performatives and, more properly, they cluster *around* performatives . . . Periperformative utterances aren't just about performative utterances in a referential sense: they cluster around them, they are near them or next to them or crowding against them; they are in the neighborhood of the performative"; see Eve Kosfosky Sedgwick, *Touching Feeling: Affect, Pedagogy, Performativity* (Durham, NC, and London: Duke University Press, 2003), 68.

58. Faustus's line seems to fulfill the Austinian requirements for a "first person singular present indicative active" performative. Austin labels such utterances, in which "hereby" can be credibly inserted following the first-person pronoun, "explicit" performatives (*How to Do Things with Words*, 61). Compare the B-Text's more evasive "Ay, Mephistopheles, I'll give it him" (2.1.48). On the repetition of the bond-signing, see Poole, "Devil's in the Archive."

59. "What means this show?" asks Faustus following the dumb show of act 2, scene 1. "Nothing, Faustus, but to delight thy mind withal, / And to show thee what magic can perform," replies Mephistopheles, cementing the theatrical parallel (2.1.83–85). *Pace* the *Oxford English Dictionary*, to "perform" here clearly means to stage acts of theater.

60. Gates, "Unpardonable Sins," 59.

61. The A-text mistakenly prints this scene following what is commonly accepted as the Chorus to act 4 and the brief clown scene that Bevington and Rasmussen move to become act 2, scene 2. On the obvious misplacement of the clown

scenes by the A-text printer, see Bevington and Rasmussen, *Christopher Marlowe*, 287–88. While I am persuaded by Bevington and Rasmussen's reordering of the comic scenes, the "correct" order of the scenes bears no relation to my argument.

62. Possibly animal heads, similar to the ass's head placed on Bottom in *A Midsummer Night's Dream,* were attached to the actors as patently theatrical magic. The idea that witchcraft can transform men into animals was a popular view, but it was rejected by orthodox demonologists. "The comic scenes are the stuff of popular stories about magic: garbled demonic names, comic familiarity with devils, accidents with a magician's books" (Roberts, "Marlowe," 67). Nevertheless we must beware an overly symmetrical alignment of the comic scenes with popular belief and the supposed "Marlowe scenes" with orthodoxy.

63. Sedgwick, *Touching Feeling,* 67.

64. Elizabeth Cary's *The Tragedy of Mariam* likewise celebrates the imperative stage cue as performative magic. "Had I not nam'd him, longer had he stay'd," marvels Cary's Salome at her ability to conjure Silleus simply by naming him (1.4.324). Elizabeth Cary, *The Tragedy of Mariam, the Fair Queen of Jewry,* ed. Barry Weller and Margaret W. Ferguson (Berkeley and Los Angeles: University of California Press, 1994).

65. Judith Butler, *Excitable Speech: A Politics of the Performative* (New York and London: Routledge, 1997), 5. Butler goes on to caution against reifying the magical power of injurious speech (as she claims Catharine MacKinnon and others have done). Instead, Butler recommends exploiting the inevitable "time-lag" between illocution and perlocution so as to neutralize hate-speech by resignifying it.

66. See, for example, Pauline Honderich, "John Calvin and Doctor Faustus," *Modern Language Review* 68 (1973): 1–13; and William M. Hamlin, "Casting Doubt in Marlowe's *Doctor Faustus," Studies in English Literature* 41 (2001): 257–75.

67. Cited in James Knowlson, *Damned to Fame: The Life of Samuel Beckett* (New York: Simon and Schuster, 1996), 342. No Beckett scholar to my knowledge has sourced the quotation in Augustine's works; Beckett probably found it elsewhere.

68. For the ways in which the actor's struggle with the text mirrors Faustus's struggle against damnation, see Johannes H. Birringer, "Between Body and Language: 'Writing' the Damnation of Faustus," *Theatre Journal* 36 (1984): 335–56.

69. Plagiarizing from Reginald Scot's 1584 exposé of witchcraft as mere jugglery, *Discouerie of Witchcraft,* Samuel Rid offers this counsel to aspiring jugglers in *The Art of Iugling or Legerdemaine:* "You must also have your words of Arte, certaine strange words, that it may not onely breed the more admiration to the people, but to leade away the eie from espying the manner of your conuayance, while you may induce the minde, to conceiue, and suppose that you deale with Spirits: and such kinde of sentences, and od speeches, are vsed in diuers mannuers, fitting and correspondent to the action and feate that you goe about. As *Hey Fortuna, furia, numquam, Credo,* passe passe, when come you sirrah: or this way: hey Jack come aloft for thy masters aduantage, passe and be gone, or otherwise: as *Ailif Cafil, zaze,* Hit, metmeltat, Saturnus, Iupiter, Mars, Sol, Venus, Mercurie, Luna? Or thus: *Drocti, Micocti, et*

senarocti, velu barocti, Asmarocti, Ronnsee, Faronnsee, hey passé passe: many such obseruations to this arte, are necessary, without which all the rest, are little to the purpose," cited in Butterworth, *Magic on the Early English Stage,* 84.

70. Gates, "Unpardonable Sins," 62.

71. Wofford, "To You I Give Myself," 167.

72. Onions, *A Shakespeare Glossary,* defines *mere* in this sense as "Absolute, sheer, downright" (169). We recall that in Hamlet's imagination, things rank and gross in nature possess the world "merely." Celia R. Daileader, *Eroticism on the Renaissance Stage: Transcendence, Desire, and the Limits of the Visible* (Cambridge: Cambridge University Press, 1998) reminds us that "the theater trope . . . tends to carry magic with it; with an almost mathematical regularity, depictions of the circular stage bring forth associations with necromancy, and sex" (133).

73. Blackburn ("Heavenly Words") argues that the problem is not that magical spells do not work, but that "Faustus never really gives it a try" because of his incompetence as a conjuror (5). His is not a failure of magical language *per se,* but of his mastery of language. Blackburn usefully points out that Faustus initially intends to be a magus rather than a witch in league with the devil.

74. Riggs, *World of Christopher Marlowe,* 237. The anxiety over theater's potentially performative language further manifests itself in the B-text's censorship of the play's oaths, presumably in the wake of 1606 act forbidding the use onstage of "the holy name of God or of Christ Jesus, or of the Holy Ghost or of the Trinity." Cited by Bevington and Rasmussen in their introduction to the Revels Plays edition (*Christopher Marlowe,* 76).

Chapter 2

1. The word *misprision* and its variants pepper the play. As critics from Leonard Barkan to Jonathan Bate attest, Shakespeare also entertains critic Harold Bloom's more idiosyncratic sense of misprision as the deliberate misreading of a literary forerunner (here, Ovid) so as to carve out one's own territory.

2. "*Changeling* was a rather elastic term in early modern England and could refer to any substitute for another person or to general fickleness in addition to the literal fairy brat substituted for a healthy human infant." Regina Buccola, *Fairies, Fractious Women, and the Old Faith: Fairy Lore in Early Modern British Drama and Culture* (Selinsgrove, PA: Susquehanna University Press, 2006), 73–74.

3. The play was probably performed at court on January 1, 1604, but its early performance history is unknown. The title page of Q1 (1600) notes "*as it hath beene sundry times publickely acted, by the Right honourable, the Lord Chamberlaine his servants.*" For an illuminating stage history, see Gary Jay Williams, *Our Moonlight Revels: A Midsummer Night's Dream in the Theatre* (Iowa City: University of Iowa Press, 2002).

4. Dennis Kay, *Shakespeare: His Life, Work, and Era* (New York: Quill William Morrow, 1992), 194–95.

5. C. L. Barber, *Shakespeare's Festive Comedy: A Study of Dramatic Form and Its*

Relation to Social Custom (Princeton, NJ: Princeton University Press, 1959), 154–57. Annabel Patterson, "Bottom's Up: Festive Theory in *A Midsummer Night's Dream*," in *A Midsummer Night's Dream: Critical Essays,* ed. Dorothea Kehler (New York and London: Garland, 1998), 165–78, complicates Barber's reading by adducing less socially conservative theories of festival.

6. Jan Kott, *Shakespeare Our Contemporary,* trans. Boleslaw Taborski (New York: W. W. Norton, 1964), 228. Kott's reading informed Peter Brook's landmark 1970 production of *A Midsummer Night's Dream* at the Royal Shakespeare Theatre, which emphasized Bottom's phallic potency and the fairies' sexual threat. For a measured reassessment of Kott's well-endowed Bottom, see David Bevington, "'But We Are Spirits of Another Sort': The Dark Side of Love and Magic in *A Midsummer Night's Dream*," in *A Midsummer Night's Dream,* ed. Richard Dutton (New York: St. Martin's Press, 1996), 24–37.

7. Louis Adrian Montrose, "'Shaping Fantasies': Figurations of Gender and Power in Elizabethan Culture," in *Representing the English Renaissance,* ed. Stephen Greenblatt (Berkeley: University of California Press, 1988), 35.

8. Dympna Callaghan, *Shakespeare without Women: Representing Gender and Race on the Renaissance Stage* (London and New York: Routledge, 2000), 150–51.

9. Gail Kern Paster, *The Body Embarrassed: Drama and the Disciplines of Shame in Early Modern England* (Ithaca, NY: Cornell University Press, 1993), 141.

10. John J. Joughlin, "Bottom's Secret . . . ," in *Spiritual Shakespeares,* ed. Ewan Fernie (London and New York: Routledge, 2005), 130–56.

11. The best-known contemporary instance of quantum dramaturgy is Michael Frayn's successful 1998 play *Copenhagen,* which dramatizes a meeting between Niels Bohr and Werner Heisenberg in 1941. Simon McBurney's *A Disappearing Number* (2007) explores infinity and string theory through a double plot featuring peripatetic mathematicians. Nick Payne's *Constellations* (2011) ingeniously ramifies an ordinary love affair through the quantum multiverse hypothesis; for scientists' somewhat bemused responses, see Sarah Hemming, "Exit, Pursued by a Quark," *Financial Times,* November 4, 2012, 15. "Whodunit" plays in which the audience's vote retroactively determines the murderer also exploit quantum uncertainty; I am grateful to Bonnie Tenneriello for this observation.

12. Natalie Angier, *The Canon: A Whirligig Tour of the Beautiful Basics of Science* (Boston and New York: Houghton Mifflin, 2007) 91. As if glossing Angier, Demetrius marvels, "These things [the events of the night] seem small and undistinguishable, / Like far-off mountains turned into clouds." Hermia replies, "Methinks I see these things with parted eye, / When everything seems double" (4.1.187–90). Clearly Shakespeare wishes us to retain some of Hermia's fuzziness of vision even as the spell wears off. Tony Tanner points out in his *Prefaces to Shakespeare* (Cambridge, MA: Belknap Press, 2010) that the word *undistinguishable,* like the word *glimmering,* occurs more than once in *A Midsummer Night's Dream* and in no other play by Shakespeare (114).

13. See Andrew Sofer, *The Stage Life of Props* (Ann Arbor: University of Michigan Press, 2003), 173–83.

14. Conversely the offstage Indian boy, the *Dream*'s other locus of dark matter,

is pure wave, an immaterial disturbance in a medium. We do not know how old he is, what he looks like, or who his father is. Like Bottom, he is at once eroticized and infantilized. Indian-boy criticism is something of a growth industry in *Dream* studies; see, for example, Thomas R. Frosch, "The Missing Child in *A Midsummer Night's Dream*," *American Imago* 64 (2008): 485–511; Kate Chedzgoy, *Shakespeare's Queer Children: Sexual Politics and Contemporary Culture* (Manchester: Manchester University Press, 1995); and Ania Loomba, "The Great Indian Vanishing Trick: Colonialism, Property, and the Family in *A Midsummer Night's Dream*," in *A Feminist Companion to Shakespeare*, ed. Dympna Callaghan (Malden, MA: Blackwell, 2000), 163–87. "The changeling boy is mysteriously absent in *A Midsummer Night's Dream*, but in a sense he is everywhere," notes David Marshall in "Exchanging Visions: Reading *A Midsummer Night's Dream*," *Journal of English Literary History* 49 (1982): 9. Stubbornly quantized, the boy frustrates attempts to pin him down.

15. Louis Montrose, *The Purpose of Playing: Shakespeare and the Cultural Politics of the Elizabethan Theatre* (Chicago and London: University of Chicago Press, 1996), 180.

16. Ibid., 191.

17. Citations from the *Dream*, as for all Shakespeare's plays quoted in this chapter, are from *The Riverside Shakespeare*, 2nd ed., ed. G. Blakemore Evans *et al.* (Boston and New York: Houghton Mifflin, 1997). The Riverside takes Q1 (1600), which was evidently prepared from a manuscript in Shakespeare's hand, as its copy-text. The First Folio text of the play (F) published in 1616 takes Q2 (1619) as its basis, together with a theatrical manuscript (probably the King's Men's prompt-book). Because the *Dream* is a doubled text, I have relied on facsimiles of both editions. F's fuller stage directions likely reflect the stage practice of Shakespeare's company.

18. "The name of the weaver Bottom in particular links him directly to this translated sense of weaving, since the bottoms of thread long acknowledged to be behind his name also served in the period as the familiar material figure for precisely such an extending or spinning out of discourse." Patricia Parker, *Shakespeare from the Margins: Language, Culture, Context* (Chicago and London: University of Chicago Press, 1996), 95–96. Parker notes the phallic shape of the bottom, or core, on which a weaver's yarn is wound. On whether Bottom's name can be associated with the buttocks *a posteriori*, as it were, see Cedric Watts, "The Name 'Bottom' in *A Midsummer Night's Dream*," in *Borrowers and Lenders: The Journal of Shakespeare and Appropriation* 5 (2010): n.p.

19. John Keats, letter to George and Tom Keats, December 21, 27 (?),1817, in *Complete Poems and Selected Letters of John Keats* (New York: Modern Library, 2001), 492.

20. Louis Montrose, in *The Purpose of Playing*, 191, observes, "The contrast between amateur and professional modes of playing is incarnated in the *performance* of Bottom—by which I mean the professional player's performance of Bottom's performance of Pyramus . . . The fully professional collaboration between the imaginative playwright and the protean player of the Lord Chamberlain's Men—between Will

Shakespeare and the celebrated comedian and dancer Will Kemp—creates the illusion of Bottom precisely by creating the illusion of his incapacity to translate himself into other parts."

21. Marvin Carlson, *The Haunted Stage: The Theatre as Memory Machine* (Ann Arbor: University of Michigan Press, 2001). For a discussion of how Kemp's outsized personality bent Shakespeare's semiotics into shape, see David Wiles, *Shakespeare's Clown: Actor and Text in the Elizabethan Playhouse* (Cambridge: Cambridge University Press, 1987).

22. Bruce R. Smith, "Studies in Sexuality," in *Shakespeare: An Oxford Guide,* ed. Stanley Wells and Lena Cowen Orlin (Oxford: Oxford University Press, 2003), 436. Wiles, *Shakespeare's Clown,* characterizes the postlude jig as "a form of soft commercial pornography" (46). It is difficult to hazard to what extent Kemp's notorious earthiness bled into his characterization of Bottom the clown. Wiles avers that Kemp "never submerged his own personality in the role that he played" (55) and speculates that Shakespeare and his contemporaries deliberately left their scripts open-ended with regard to the clown's sexuality and marital status because of the knowledge that their romantic comedies would be rounded off by a jig (53). Mainly associated with The Curtain and The Fortune, jigs were suppressed north of the river in 1612.

23. Wiles, *Shakespeare's Clown,* 55. Once again it is hard to place Bottom/Kemp inside or outside the play. Was Kemp's customary jig replaced by the scripted Bergomask dance (perhaps featuring Bottom) that apparently takes place before the court *prior* to Puck, Titania, and Oberon's final reappearance—thereby containing Kemp/Bottom within the fictive envelope? Or did Kemp's jig/ballet burst the bounds of Shakespeare's script and trump the fairies' bride-bed blessing? The theater historian is at a loss.

24. William C. Carroll, "Romantic Comedies," in *Shakespeare: An Oxford Guide,* ed. Stanley Wells and Lena Cowen Orlin (Oxford: Oxford University Press, 2003), 177. On the *Dream* specifically, Henry S. Turner, in *Shakespeare's Double Helix* (London: Continuum, 2007), writes, "As in all myths, desire is the life-blood of its action, the underlying motivation of every character and a force that becomes by turns romantic, giddy, obsessive, violent, and supernatural in its power" (22).

25. Susan Zimmerman, "Introduction," in *Erotic Politics: Desire on the Renaissance Stage,* ed. Susan Zimmerman (New York and London: Routledge, 1992), 6.

26. Smith, "Studies in Sexuality," 438. Smith locates dark matter within an unrepresentable orifice on the early modern stage: "[I]n ontological terms, in terms of its state of being, the anus presents a void, a dark vortex. As such, the anus exposes the limits of language in marking and controlling the human body" (439). I am less certain that the early moderns equated anuses with aporia.

27. Valerie Traub, *Desire and Anxiety: Circulations of Sexuality in Shakespearean Drama* (London and New York: Routledge, 1992), 2, 16.

28. Celia R. Daileader, *Eroticism on the Renaissance Stage: Transcendence, Desire, and the Limits of the Visible* (Cambridge: Cambridge University Press, 1998). In her survey of erotic activity in the 216 surviving dramatic works performed in London's

commercial theaters between 1595 and 1621, Daileader discovers that "some 95 percent feature at least one scene foregrounding what we would now call 'heterosexual' erotic activity, despite the obvious complication posed by the absence of female performers" (2). See her appendix 1, 143–44.

29. Some of the discussions I have found useful are in John Elsom, *Erotic Theatre* (London: Secker and Warburg, 1975); Karen Newman, *Fashioning Femininity and English Renaissance Drama* (Chicago and London: University of Chicago Press, 1991); Valerie Wayne, ed., *The Matter of Difference: Materialist Feminist Criticism of Shakespeare* (Ithaca, NY: Cornell University Press, 1991); Stephen Orgel, *Impersonations: The Performance of Gender in Shakespeare's England* (Cambridge: Cambridge University Press, 1996); Mario Di Gangi, *The Homoerotics of Early Modern Drama* (Cambridge: Cambridge University Press, 1997); Laurence Senelick, *The Changing Room: Sex, Drag, and Theatre* (London and New York: Routledge, 2000); Stanley Wells, *Looking for Sex in Shakespeare* (Cambridge: Cambridge University Press, 2004); and Will Fisher, *Materializing Gender in Early Modern Literature and Culture* (Cambridge: Cambridge University Press, 2010). Richard Rambuss, "*A Midsummer Night's Dream*: Shakespeare's Ass Play," in *Shakesqueer: A Queer Companion to the Complete Works of Shakespeare,* ed. Madhavi Menon (Durham, NC: Duke University Press, 2011), 234–44, explores Bottom as an example of interspecies queerness over and above the transgressive homoeroticism limned by other critics.

30. "[T]he prohibition against female actors, working in tandem with social decorum, encouraged the offstage placement of heterosexual intercourse; paradoxically, to make it remotely convincing, it would have to remain unseen." Daileader, *Eroticism on the Renaissance Stage,* 48.

31. Thomas Middleton and Thomas Dekker, *The Roaring Girl*, in *English Renaissance Drama: A Norton Anthology,* ed. David Bevington, Lars Engle, Katharine Eisaman Maus, and Eric Rasmussen (New York and London: W. W. Norton, 2002), 1371–1451.

32. Lisa Jardine, *Still Harping on Daughters: Women and Drama in the Age of Shakespeare* (Brighton: Harvester Press, 1983); Callaghan, *Shakespeare without Women.* But see also Valerie Traub, *The Renaissance of Lesbianism in Early Modern England* (Cambridge: Cambridge University Press, 2002).

33. It may be that the codpiece makes visible not so much desire itself as (more generically) potency. I am grateful to Tracy Davis for this observation.

34. Christopher Marlowe, *Edward II*, in *English Renaissance Drama: A Norton Anthology,* ed. David Bevington et al. (New York and London: W. W. Norton, 2002), 351–420.

35. "The apparel of women . . . is a great provocation of men to lust and lechery because a woman's garment being put on a man doeth vehemently touch and move him with the remembrance and imagination of a woman: and the imagination of a thing desirable doth stir up the desire." John Rainolds, *Th'Overthrow of Stage-Plays* (London, 1599).

36. For a useful discussion of invisible characters, see Barbara D. Palmer, "Staging Invisibility in English Early Modern Drama," *Early Theatre* 11 (2008): 113–28.

37. The First Folio (F) has a somewhat confusing second entrance for Bottom after the stage has cleared at line 3.1.111.

38. See chapter 1. Theseus later makes fun of the "madman" for hallucinating "more devils than vast hell can hold," a possible reference to *Faustus*' hell-mouth property and, more broadly, to affect-contagion among lunatic, lover, and poet in the Elizabethan playhouse (5.1.9).

39. R. A. Foakes's New Cambridge edition of the *Dream* includes a useful illustration by C. Walter Hodges on possible ways of staging Titania's bower in 2.2 and 3.1. *A Midsummer Night's Dream*, ed. R. A. Foakes (Cambridge: Cambridge University Press, 2003), 34. Foakes points out that Titania need not be visible from the time when Oberon drugs her to the time when Bottom awakens her, and that Oberon could easily have drawn a curtain around her bower on the line "Wake when some vile thing is near" (2.2.34). Foakes and Hodges equate Titania's canopied bank in act 2 with her seductive bower in 4.1, suggesting that the same (discovery) space was employed.

40. Madeleine Forey, "'Bless thee, Bottom, bless thee! Thou Art Translated!': Ovid, Golding, and *A Midsummer Night's Dream*," *Modern Language Review* 93 (1998): 321–29, reads the ass-head as Shakespeare's comment on Golding's anxiety regarding Ovid. Taking up Shakespeare's debt to Golding, David Lucking, in "Translation and Metamorphosis in *A Midsummer Night's Dream*," *Essays in Criticism* 61 (2011): 137–54, observes that "the concomitant to [Bottom's translation] is that he has experienced a kind of theophany, a revelation of the sacred. If he has crossed the boundary dividing the human from the bestial, he has also traversed another threshold, and found himself consorting on equal terms with the denizens of a magical world" (148).

41. Kott, *Shakespeare Our Contemporary*, 111.

42. Ibid., 116.

43. Notes Kott, "All these animals represent abundant sexual potency, and some of them play an important part in sexual demonology. Bottom is eventually transformed into an ass. But in this nightmarish summer night, the ass does not symbolize stupidity. From antiquity up to the Renaissance the ass was credited with the strongest sexual potency and among all the quadrupeds was supposed to have the longest and hardest phallus." Ibid., 115.

44. "[B]estiality arguably encompasses a large part of the play's overt eroticism; the spectacle of Titania and Bottom embracing and sleeping together comes as close to enacted sexual intercourse as any scene in Shakespearean comedy . . . In overall effect, *A Midsummer Night's Dream* is a bit like a Protestant marriage-manual constructed out of animal pornography." Bruce Thomas Boehrer, "Bestial Buggery in *A Midsummer Night's Dream*," in *The Production of English Renaissance Culture*, ed. David Lee Miller, Sharon O'Dair, and Harold Weber (Ithaca, NY, and London: Cornell University Press, 1994), 132.

45. Gail Kern Paster and Skiles Howard, eds., *A Midsummer Night's Dream: Texts and Contexts* (Boston and New York: Bedford and St. Martin's, 1999), 295–96.

46. Bottom's bawdy quibble on "serving his own turn" figures onanism as a trope for self-love. In another part of the forest, Helena unwittingly invokes sexual self-gratification as a potential solution to her frustration at Demetrius's erotic antipathy, using the common Elizabethan pun on *die:* "I'll follow thee and make a heaven of hell, / To die upon the hand I love so well" (2.1.243–44).

47. Matters are complicated by occasional discrepancies between Q1 and F. Act divisions all derive from F; none exist in Q1. In F, at the end of act 3, the direction "*They sleepe all the Act*" indicates that the four lovers must remain in their positions (possibly through an interval) and that the action is understood to be continuous between acts 3 and 4. Norton Shakespeare editor Stephen Greenblatt conjectures that since the stage is apparently cleared at 3.2.412, when Puck draws away Lysander and Demetrius to fight, a new scene begins. If so, Shakespeare introduces yet another gap in stage time.

48. See the useful essays by Rosemarie Bank, Michal Kobialka, Sarah Bryant-Bertail, and Karl Topefer in "Physics and the New Historiography," ed. Rosemarie Bank, *Journal of Dramatic Theory and Criticism, special issue,* 5 (1991): 63–136. Bank's preface to "Physics and the New Theatre Historiography" claims, "For a theatre researcher, the displacement of the traditions of Newton, Hegel, and Darwin and the perception of a new spatio-temporal landscape are unavoidable and inescapable features of the quantum relative universe" (64). See also Carol Anne Fischer, "Quantum Theatre: A Language for the Voices of Contemporary Theatre" (MA thesis, San Jose State University, 2004); and Paul Johnston, "Quantum Performance: Scientific Discourse in the Analysis of the Work of Contemporary British Practitioners" (PhD thesis, University of Wolverhampton, 2006).

49. Manjit Kumar, *Quantum: Einstein, Bohr, and the Great Debate about the Nature of Reality* (New York and London: W. W. Norton, 2010), xiii.

50. Werner Heisenberg, *Physics and Philosophy: The Revolution in Modern Science* (New York: Harper Perennial, 2007), 81.

51. Rivka Galchen, "Dream Machine: The Mind-Expanding Universe of Quantum Computing," *New Yorker,* May 2, 2011, 35.

52. John Polkinghorne, *Quantum Theory: A Very Short Introduction* (Oxford: Oxford University Press 2002), 33. Polkinghorne offers an ingenious musical analogy. To know the pitch of a note, we need to analyze its frequency of sound; but to know its frequency, we need to listen to a note through several oscillations (treating it like a wave), which means that we cannot know the precise instant *when* that note was sounded (treating it as a punctum) at the same time as we measure its pitch. We cannot unwave the nature of sound in order to fix the discrete, pitched note in time.

53. Niels Bohr, *Atomic Physics and Human Knowledge* (New York: John Wiley, 1958).

54. This might help to explain how in John Archibald Wheeler's logic-defying "delayed choice" experiments, a photon that is made to split at point A into two

sub-beams can somehow hedge its bets by following both right-hand and left-hand paths, *and* following only *one* path.

55. Freeman Dyson, in "The 'Dramatic Picture' of Richard Feynman," *New York Review of Books,* July 14, 2011, 40, notes, "The fashionable theorists reject [Feynman's] dualistic picture of nature, with the classical world and the quantum world existing side by side. They believe that only the quantum world is real, and the classical world must be explained as some kind of illusion arising out of quantum processes." Such a view reverses the very classical Theseus's odd conviction that he is real, whereas the miniscule fairies are fictional.

56. Marjorie Garber, *Shakespeare After All* (New York: Anchor Books, 2004), 224.

57. Katharine M. Briggs, *The Anatomy of Puck: An Examination of Fairy Beliefs among Shakespeare's Contemporaries and Successors* (London: Routledge, 1959), refuted the claim that Shakespeare invented tiny fairies, which was first made in Minor White Latham, *The Elizabethan Fairies: The Fairies of Folklore and the Fairies of Shakespeare* (New York: Columbia University Press, 1930). Harold F. Brooks, "Introduction," in *A Midsummer Night's Dream* (London and New York: Methuen, 1979), catalogs pre-Shakespearean diminutive fairies, lxx–lxxv, although Diane Purkiss, *At the Bottom of the Garden: A Dark History of Fairies, Hobgoblins, and Other Troublesome Things* (New York: New York University Press, 2000), 85–93, asserts that the vogue for miniaturizing fairies began in the late sixteenth century. Lewis Spence, in *British Fairy Origins* (London: Watts, 1946), 10–12, notes that sixteenth-century fairy lore suggests that fairies can assume different degrees of stature at will. I am grateful to Tracy Davis for her help with English fairy lore.

58. Peter Holland, "Introduction," in *The Oxford Shakespeare: A Midsummer Night's Dream,* ed. Peter Holland (Oxford: Clarendon Press, 1994), 23 (Holland's line numbers omitted).

59. For Turner, Titania's fairy attendants "are emblematic of the insubstantial, the minute, the atomic, and even the nanotechnological (which we could describe as the goal-directed modification of natural objects at a small scale)" *(Shakespeare's Double Helix,* 90).

60. Although we know Kemp played Bottom and assume a boy actor took the role of Titania, we do not know if men or boys played Puck and Titania's retinue. It may be that Puck was played by an adult, as in the Lord Admiral's play *Grim the Collier of Croydon* (1600). It is charming to assume that Titania's diminutive train was played by boys, as Brooks assumes, but I concur with Holland (following William A. Ringler Jr.) that Titania's retinue was likely doubled by the adult actors who also played the mechanicals. This would shrink the overall cast size down to sixteen, the usual number for the Lord Chamberlain's Men. Neither Q1 nor F offers cast lists for *Dream,* but the Riverside lists twenty-one speaking parts. Even if the play premiered at an aristocratic affair that provided extra boys for the nonce, it would not have been cost effective for Shakespeare to script a play beyond the capacities of his professional company.

61. Matthew Woodcock, "Spirits of Another Sort: Constructing Shakespeare's Fairies in *A Midsummer Night's Dream*," in *A Midsummer Night's Dream: A Critical Guide*, ed. Regina Buccola (London: Continuum, 2010), 127. "Fairies are thus 'playful' in a Derridean sense: they raise the possibility that we might apprehend a centre with which to understand them—be it an allegorical interpretation, a belief system or a textual tradition—but this always transpires to be a stimulus for further interpretation" (116). Not unlike subatomic particles, or even atoms themselves, "fairies may be little more than airy nothings that might indeed easily dissolve should we try and examine them too intently" (117).

62. Polkinghorne, *Quantum Theory*, 21–22.

63. Erwin Schrödinger, *Science and Humanism* (Cambridge: Cambridge University Press, 1951), 47.

64. Werner Heisenberg, *Physics and Beyond: Encounters and Conversations* (New York: Harper & Row, 1971).

65. Heisenberg, *Physics and Philosophy*, 160. Einstein famously retorted that God does not play dice with the universe. But the notorious Einstein-Podolsky-Rosen (EPR) experiment, designed to refute a probabilistic interpretation of reality, backfired on Einstein by proving the seemingly absurd: instantaneous "telepathy" between two photons separated in space. This defeated Einstein's belief that a particle's speed and position are localized on the particle independent of observation. On the quantum level, at least, "here" is in some sense identical to "there," and reality is nonseparable rather than carved into bits.

66. Niels Bohr, *Atomic Theory and the Description of Nature* (Woodbridge, CT: Ox Bow Press, 1987), 18.

67. William Gruber, in *Offstage Space, Narrative, and the Theatre of the Imagination* (New York: Palgrave Macmillan, 2010), discusses *Miss Julie* and other scenes of offstage sex (57–75). Gruber points out that whereas offstage violence is often narrated by an onstage character, "the theatre has tended historically to frame actions involving sexual activity not as retrospective narratives but as gaps or omissions" (58).

68. Kumar, *Quantum*, 213.

69. Galchen, "Dream Machine," 35.

70. J. B. Priestley explores this interpretation in his unjustly overlooked play *Dangerous Corner* (1932), a fascinating example of quantum dramaturgy. Inspired by theorist J. W. Dunne, Priestley's better-known *Time and the Conways* (1937) explores the notion that past, present, and future exist simultaneously.

71. Matthieu Ricard and Trinh Xuan Thuan, *The Quantum and the Lotus: A Journey to the Frontiers Where Science and Buddhism Meet* (New York: Three Rivers Press, 2001), 43.

72. Ann Thompson and Neil Taylor's 2006 Arden edition prints the texts of 1603 and 1623 and the text of the 1604–5 second quarto in two separate volumes. Ann Thompson and Neil Taylor, eds., *Hamlet*. The Arden Shakespeare. 3rd series (London: Thomson Learning, 2006). Ann Thompson and Neil Taylor, eds., *Hamlet*,

The Texts of 1603 and 1623. The Arden Shakespeare. 3rd series (London: Thomson Learning, 2006). Paul Benjamin Bertram and Bernice W. Klimans's *The Three-Text Hamlet* (New York: AMS Press: 1991), a parallel text version, allows us to follow Shakespeare's three Danish princes simultaneously. An enjoyable account of recent Shakespearean editorial controversies can be found in Ron Rosenbaum, *The Shakespeare Wars: Clashing Scholars, Public Fiascoes, Palace Coups* (New York: Random House, 2006).

73. See W. B. Worthen, *Shakespeare and the Authority of Performance* (Cambridge: Cambridge University Press, 2007).

74. "Quantum physics . . . revealed that an electron in an atom can be in one place, and then, as if by magic, reappear in another without ever being anywhere in between, by emitting or absorbing a quantum of energy. This was a phenomenon beyond the ken of classical, non-quantum physics. It was as bizarre as an object mysteriously disappearing in London and an instant later suddenly reappearing in Paris, New York, or Moscow." Kumar, *Quantum*, xiii.

75. "Act 4" is perhaps more textual than phenomenological marking; the 1600 Q1 text has no act break.

76. To match Jack with Jill, Oberon must cheat nature by leaving Demetrius permanently in the thrall of the love-juice, an irony overlooked by critics like Tanner.

77. Or, rather, there seem to be *two* Oberons in superposition. Q1's Oberon enters at the top of the act with Titania and her train; F's Oberon enters with Puck only once Titania and Bottom fall asleep. This particular quantum wave-packet collapses in performance, since the actor playing Oberon cannot be onstage and offstage at the same time. Such quantum uncertainty runs throughout the *Dream*. Defying classical logic, the text itself allows woodbine to be both honeysuckle (2.1.251) and not honeysuckle (4.1.42), and Cobweb to be at once fetching honey offstage and scratching Bottom's head at 4.1.23 in both Q1 and F. Whether Bottom's or Shakespeare's, this slip is indeed a head-scratcher (to avoid quantum superposition, some editors amend "Cobweb" to "Peaseblossom").

78. Emma Katherine Atwood, "A Defense of Bottom: Translation and the Liminal Body" (forthcoming), nicely refers to "the polite antisociality" of Bottom's sleep in this scene and points out that Bottom's drowsiness comically punctures Titania's phallic wish "To have my love to bed and to arise" (3.1.171).

79. On the other hand, we can also interpret Bottom's lassitude in this scene, Kott-like, as the consequence of Titania's earlier sexual demands offstage.

80. Oberon's shift here from anger to pity anticipates Prospero's more weighty choice (at Ariel's prompting) to move *The Tempest*'s genre from revenge tragedy to tragicomedy. Jealous Oberon, the most complex character in the *Dream,* is the only figure capable of growth through experience and of surprising himself.

81. Gruber, *Offstage Space*, 9.

82. Oberon's blessing of "fortunate issue" to the mortal pairs (5.1.405–08) is ironic on Shakespeare's part, but how lightly or heavily is hard to determine. Educated spectators would know that Theseus and Hippolyta's offspring will be the

ill-starred Hippolytus, destroyed by his father's curse once his besotted stepmother, Phaedra, accuses him of attempted rape. But this is dotage in another key.

83. Tanner, *Prefaces to Shakespeare,* 135. Tanner divides the did-they-or-didn't-they critical opinions into English, American, and Eastern European schools of thought before impishly concluding, "I suppose it depends where you are born" (135).

84. "The love juice is the distilled essence of erotic mobility itself, and it is appropriately in the power of the fairies. For the fairies seem to embody the principle of what we might call polytropic desire—that is, desire that can easily alight on any object, including an ass-headed man, and that can with equal instantaneousness swerve away from that object and on to another." Stephen Greenblatt, "Introduction" to *A Midsummer Night's Dream,* in *The Norton Shakespeare,* 2nd ed., ed. Stephen Greenblatt, Walter Cohen, Jean E. Howard, and Katharine Eisaman Maus (New York and London: W. W. Norton, 2008), 845. In its dizzying speed, mobility, and randomness, desire itself partakes of quantum uncertainty.

85. Michael Hoffman's 1999 film adaptation of the *Dream* gives Kevin Kline's Bottom a wife, for example.

86. Having perhaps too neatly proposed narcissism as the solution to erotic suffering, Shakespeare writes a comedy in which narcissism is the problem. *Twelfth Night*'s Orsino and Olivia must be led out of the mirror-world of self-love toward compulsory heterosexuality. Interestingly, the play rejects same-sex love (which may or may not transcend the erotic) as a solution to the problem of desire: devoted Antonio, emblem of un-Illyrian constancy, is excluded from the denouement's happy pairings. But then Antonio is the anti-Bottom. A spectacularly bad pirate, whose job is after all to take what does not belong to him, Antonio devotes himself utterly to Sebastian and has no self to fall back on.

87. Conversely, for Turner, Theseus "evacuates desire into the airless, absolute space of a non-human legal principle" (*Shakespeare's Double Helix,* 28).

88. A parallel invisible scene occurs when Oberon has the Indian boy led to his "bower," signaling his official transfer from the female to male sphere (4.1.60–61). Whether Oberon has sexual designs on his Ganymede remains unclear. The onstage/offstage pairing of bowers recalls the onstage/offstage pairing of Gertrude's closet (which we see) and Ophelia's closet (which is narrated but never represented). Hamlet's desire for Ophelia, if it *is* desire rather than just a silly pantomime intended to throw Claudius off the scent, is literally left in the closet.

89. Traub, *Desire and Anxiety,* 2.

90. Brooks, "Introduction," xc.

91. Cited in Kumar, *Quantum,* 320.

92. Ludwig Wittgenstein, *Culture and Value,* ed. G. H. von Wright, trans. Peter Winch (Chicago: University of Chicago Press), 83e.

93. "Changing speech prefixes suggest that Bottom's famous affability is not the result of a firm allegiance to a single, imperturbable identity but of a willingness to accept, and finally transform, numerous identities offered by his theatrical and social

circumstances." Lina Perkins Wilder, "Changeling Bottom: Speech Prefixes, Acting, and Character in *A Midsummer Night's Dream*," *Shakespeare* 4 (2008): 58. By speculating that Bottom *assumes* "numerous identities offered by his theatrical and social circumstances," however, Wilder reifies the very character she wishes to deconstruct.

94. Random Cloud, "'The very names of the Persons': Editing and the Invention of Dramatick Character," in *Staging the Renaissance: Reinterpretations of Elizabethan and Jacobean Drama*, ed. David Scott Kastan and Peter Stallybrass (New York and London: Routledge, 1991), 88–96. Wiles, in *Shakespeare's Clown*, similarly states, "Shakespeare constructs character as a set of functions, a set of relationships. The dynamics of the stage situation are more important to him than the internal consistency of a single character" (74).

95. See, for example, Angus Fletcher, *Time, Space, and Motion in the Age of Shakespeare* (Cambridge, MA: Harvard University Press, 2007); Peter D. Usher, *Shakespeare and the Dawn of Modern Science* (Amherst, MA: Cambria Press, 2010); and Howard Marchitello, *The Machine in the Text: Science and Literature in the Age of Shakespeare and Galileo* (Oxford: Oxford University Press, 2011).

96. Norman Rabkin, *Shakespeare and the Common Understanding* (New York: Free Press, 1967). Rabkin extends Bohr's notion of complementarity so broadly that it becomes something more akin to negative capability: the very stuff of art itself.

97. Christopher Pye, *The Vanishing: Shakespeare, the Subject, and Early Modern Culture* (Durham, NC, and London: Duke University Press, 2000); Jonathan Gil Harris, *Untimely Matter in the Time of Shakespeare* (Philadelphia: University of Pennsylvania Press, 2009), 3.

98. Cited in Rosemarie Bank, "The Theatre Historian in the Mirror: Transformation in the Space of Representation," *Journal of Dramatic Theory and Criticism 3* (1989): 219–28. According to Bank, Carlson delivered this remark in his address for a Status of Theater Research panel at the 1985 annual meeting of the American Society for Theatre Research in New York (228).

99. Elizabeth Spiller, *Science, Reading, and Renaissance Literature: The Art of Making Knowledge, 1580–1670* (Cambridge: Cambridge University Press, 2004), 1. Spiller argues that "early modern science is practiced as an art and, at the same time, that imaginative literature provides a form for producing knowledge. Within this context . . . literary texts gain substance and intelligibility by being considered as instances of early modern knowledge production" rather than just topical commentaries on new scientific discoveries (2).

100. Einstein's "On an Heuristic Viewpoint concerning the Nature of Light'" appeared in *Annalen Der Physik* in 1905.

101. Brian Greene, *The Elegant Universe: Superstrings, Hidden Dimensions, and the Quest for the Ultimate Theory* (New York: Vintage, 2000). Greene's book inspired Nick Payne's multiverse play *Constellations* (2012).

102. Joseph Roach, "It," *Theatre Journal* 56 (2004): 559.

103. I am thinking here, for example, of logical positivism, A. J. Ayer's verificationism, and Karl Popper's principle of falsification.

104. Cited in Galchen, "Dream Machine," 40.

105. Mercutio's zany Queen Mab speech is a kind of antisonnet: a compulsive burst of language that spins off into entropic chaos. It is as if the wish to imaginatively penetrate the infinitesimal and inconstant fairy world drives Mercutio to distraction. The idea of atoms (from the Greek *atomos,* something indivisible), introduced by Leucippus and Democritus in the sixth century BCE, was eclipsed by Aristotle's quartet of elements (earth, air, fire, and water). Atoms then resurfaced as a concept in the late sixteenth century. See Bernard Pullman, *The Atom in the History of Human Thought* (Oxford: Oxford University Press, 1998).

Chapter 3

1. Most critics of the play acknowledge the importance of its Carnival setting (Behn transposed her source-play, Thomas Killigrew's *Thomaso, or The Wanderer,* from Madrid to Naples). For the cultural valence of eighteenth-century masquerade, see Terry Castle, *Masquerade and Civilization: The Carnivalesque in Eighteenth-Century English Culture and Fiction* (Stanford, CA: Stanford University Press, 1986). For Mikhail Bakhtin, writing in *Rabelais and His World,* trans. Helen Iswolsky (Cambridge, MA: MIT Press, 1965), Carnival is "the place for working out, in a concretely sensuous, half-real and half-play-acted form, a *new mode of interrelationship between individuals,* counterposed to the all-powerful socio-hierarchical relationships of noncarnival life" (122–23).

2. *The Rover*'s first recorded production was on March 24, 1677. It was presented at court in 1680, 1685, 1687, and 1690 and was performed almost every year from 1703 until 1750 and remained (albeit in bowdlerized versions) in the repertory until 1757, an extraordinary run. The play was staged in 1790 in a sanitized version by John Philip Kemble, *Love in Many Masks,* which managed only nine performances. It then disappeared from the stage until the late 1970s.

3. Katharine Eisaman Maus, "'Playhouse Flesh and Blood': Sexual Ideology and the Restoration Actress," *English Literary History* 46 (1979): 609. Maus notes, "[Playwright] George Farquhar became enamored of a woman who used her mask to pique his interest; only after writing her several declarations of love, and perhaps going to bed with her, would she allow him to see her face . . . The mask was seductive because it obscured the reality beneath, because it confused the lowest part with the highest, and eventually annihilated distinctions of rank" (608–9). Nor was masking confined to women of the period: "Charles II . . . his royal person concealed behind a mask, loved to party anonymously with aristocrats and rich Londoners" (610).

4. J. L. Styan, *Restoration Comedy in Performance* (Cambridge: Cambridge University Press, 1986), 114. On February 18, 1668, Samuel Pepys's diary records his being distracted—and entertained—by Sir Charles Sedley's interrogation of an anonymous masked lady during a performance of *The Maid's Tragedy.* Harold Pinter's *The Homecoming* (1965) turns on the same question: Lenny (who, as a pimp, has a professional interest) tries to place his brother Teddy's wife Ruth as either a "woman of

quality" or a whore, only to be outsmarted. Pinter's neo-Restoration comedy even ends with a mock "proviso scene" in which Ruth negotiates her terms as house prostitute.

5. See, for example, Laura Mulvey, "Visual Pleasure and Narrative Cinema," *Screen* 16 (1975): 6–18; Teresa de Lauretis, "Sexual Indifference and Lesbian Representation," in *Performing Feminisms: Feminist Critical Theory and Theatre,* ed. Sue-Ellen Case (Baltimore and London: Johns Hopkins University Press, 1990), 17–39; Peggy Phelan, *Unmarked: The Politics of Performance* (London: Routledge, 1993); and Elin Diamond, *Unmaking Mimesis: Essays on Feminism and Theater* (London and New York: Routledge, 1997). According to the logic of patriarchal signification, a woman onstage (or onscreen) stands for the sign "Woman"; Griselda Gambaro dramatizes this conundrum in her powerful 1974 play *Stripped.*

6. Aphra Behn, *The Rover,* 2nd ed., ed. Anne Russell (Toronto: Broadview Editions, 2004). All subsequent citations are to this edition.

7. P. A. Skantze, *Stillness in Motion in the Seventeenth-Century Theatre* (London and New York: Routledge, 2003), argues, "While accounting for bodies performing and receiving might seem an effort disconcertingly speculative to all of us who have been trained to rely on text, and to believe that that reliance provides 'firm' evidence, without this effort to re-animate kinesthetic exchange in time and space, our understanding of the relation of readers to playtext, audience to performed work, remains static" (5–6).

8. Such a masculinist reading of *The Rover* seems initially supported by Behn's 1681 sequel, *The Second Part of the Rover,* which brings back Willmore and Blunt (but not Hellena, whose place is supplied by La Nuche, a courtesan more receptive to Willmore's values) for further libertine adventures. However, the sequel did not prove a living play; apparently audiences preferred the more ambiguous (and balanced) sexual politics of *The Rover,* which held the stage for decades.

9. Laurence Senelick, in *The Changing Room: Sex, Drag, and Theatre* (London and New York: Routledge, 2000), 142, notes, "By 1608 playgoers had already seen more than twenty comedies predicated on gender disguise, and in the following three decades nearly fifty plays utilized the female page disguise." Influential discussions of the transvestite stage include Lisa Jardine, *Still Harping on Daughters: Women and Drama in the Age of Shakespeare* (Brighton: Harvester Press, 1983); Laura Levine, "Men in Women's Clothing: Anti-theatricality and Effemination from 1589 to 1642," *Criticism* 28 (1986): 121–43; Jean E. Howard, "Crossdressing, the Theatre, and Gender Struggle in Early Modern England," *Shakespeare Quarterly* 39 (1988): 418–40; Valerie Traub, *Desire and Anxiety: Circulations of Sexuality in Shakespearean Drama* (London and New York: Routledge, 1992); Susan Zimmerman, ed., *Erotic Politics: Desire on the Renaissance Stage* (New York and London: Routledge, 1992); and Stephen Orgel, *Impersonations: The Performance of Gender in Shakespeare's England* (Cambridge: Cambridge University Press, 1996). Several of their arguments exist in variant published versions as the writers' ideas developed.

10. Dympna Callaghan, *Shakespeare without Women: Representing Gender and*

Race on the Renaissance Stage (London and New York: Routledge, 2000), denies the very possibility of female mimesis under such material conditions of performance, writing that "early modern women were absent from Shakespeare's stage" (8).

11. For the ghostly history of female-female eroticism, see Valerie Traub, *The Renaissance of Lesbianism in Early Modern England* (Cambridge: Cambridge University Press, 2002).

12. Thomas Middleton and Thomas Dekker, *The Roaring Girl*, in *English Renaissance Drama: A Norton Anthology,* ed. David Bevington, Lars Engle, Katharine Eisaman Maus, and Eric Rasmussen (New York and London: W. W. Norton, 2002), 1371–1451.

13. *The Roaring Girl* is ghosted by the real Mary Frith, who was frequently in trouble with the law. The play's epilogue promises those displeased by the play a cameo appearance by the roaring girl herself "some few days hence" (Epilogus, line 35).

14. See Andrew Gurr, *Playgoing in Shakespeare's London,* 2nd ed. (Cambridge: Cambridge University Press, 1996), 50–80.

15. Kynaston's rocky transition from female to male roles is fancifully dramatized in the film *Stage Beauty* (2004), starring Billy Crudup.

16. "[B]y the middle of 1661 actresses were an established feature of the English stage," as they had been in France, Italy, and Spain by the latter part of the sixteenth century. Elizabeth Howe, *The First English Actresses: Women and Drama, 1660–1700* (Cambridge: Cambridge University Press, 1992), 24.

17. Maus, "Playhouse Flesh and Blood," 602.

18. Epilogue to *The Libertine,* cited in Maus, "Playhouse Flesh and Blood," 602. Spectators were allowed to visit the actresses in the tiring house in various stages of undress; on January 23, 1667, Pepys recorded that he and his wife both kissed Nell Gwyn on one such backstage visit, "and a mighty pretty soul she is." *The Diary of Samuel Pepys,* ed. Robert Latham and William Matthews (London: G. Bell and Sons, 1974), 8:27.

19. Howe, *The First English Actresses,* xi. See also John Harold Wilson, *All the King's Ladies: Actresses of the Restoration* (Chicago: University of Chicago Press, 1958); Sandra Richards, *The Rise of the English Actress* (New York: Palgrave Macmillan, 1993); and Beate Braun, *Restoration Actresses during the Reign of Charles II with Special Regard to the Diary of Samuel Pepys* (Trier: Wissenschaftlicher Verlag Trier, 1995). For further discussion, see Andrew Sofer, "The Fan of Mode: Sexual Semaphore on the Restoration and Early-Eighteenth-Century Stage," in *The Stage Life of Props* (Ann Arbor: University of Michigan Press, 2003), 117–65.

20. This relationship is fictionalized in Stephen Jeffrey's 1994 play *The Libertine,* later filmed with Johnny Depp as Rochester, Samantha Morton as Barry, and John Malkovich as King Charles (ghosted by his own mesmerizing performance as Rochester in Steppenwolf Theatre's American premier, which featured Martha Plimpton as Barry). Aphra Behn's entanglements with Charles II, Nell Gwyn, and Lady Davenant are fancifully treated in Liz Duffy Adams's amusing 2009 comedy *Or, [sic]*.

21. "Elizabeth Barry," in *A Biographical Dictionary of Actors, Actresses, Musicians, Dancers, Managers, and Other Stage Personnel in London, 1660–1800,* ed. Philip H. Highfill Jr., Kalman A. Burnim, and Edward A. Langhans (Carbondale: Southern Illinois University Press, 1973–93), 1:313–25.

22. Janet Todd, "Introduction," in Aphra Behn, *Oroonoko, The Rover, and Other Works,* ed. Janet Todd (London: Penguin Books, 2003), 1.

23. Einstein predicted such space-time dimples in 1911; Arthur Eddington famously confirmed gravitational lensing while observing a solar eclipse in 1919.

24. The first gravitationally lensed object, known as the Twin Quasar (Twin QSO) or "Old Faithful," was discovered in 1979. The "twins" are in fact doubled images of the same quasar.

25. Richard Ellis, "Gravitational Lensing: A Unique Probe of Dark Matter and Dark Energy," *Philosophical Transactions of the Royal Society A* 368 (2010): 975.

26. "In a manner akin to the Polynesian seafarers who sense islands out of their sight through the deflected direction of ocean waves, cosmologists can map a concentration of the Universe's unseen mass through the gravitational deflection of light coming from sources behind it." Eric V. Linder, "The Universe's Skeleton Sketched," *Nature* 445 (January 18, 2007): 273.

27. Richard Ellis, interview with Wendy Barnaby (video podcast), *Philosophical Transactions of the Royal Society* website, http://rsta.royalsocietypublishing.org/content/suppl/2010/01/26/368.1914.967.DC1.html%20.

28. One measure of the mask's ability to warp its wearer's signal is the voice. Although the audience always recognizes the speaker by her voice, and hence can keep track of who is who behind the vizard, by convention the onstage characters do not. It is as if masked womanhood produces a generic *feminine* voice instead of a singular *female* one.

29. Russell, "Introduction," 25.

30. Jessica Munns, "'I by a Double Right Thy Bounties Claim': Aphra Behn and Sexual Space," in *Curtain Calls: British and American Women and the Theater, 1660–1820,* ed. Mary Anne Schofield and Cecilia Macheski (Athens: Ohio University Press, 1991), 193–210.

31. Catherine Gallagher, "Who Was That Masked Woman? The Prostitute and the Playwright in the Comedies of Aphra Behn," in *Rereading Aphra Behn: History, Theory, and Criticism,* ed. Heidi Hutner (Charlottesville and London: University Press of Virginia), 74.

32. Susan Green, "Semiotic Modalities of the Female Body in Aphra Behn's *The Dutch Lover,*" in *Rereading Aphra Behn: History, Theory, and Criticism,* ed. Heidi Hutner (Charlottesville and London: University Press of Virginia), 141.

33. Lesley Ferris, *Acting Women: Images of Women in Theatre* (New York: New York University Press, 1989), 74. Ferris extends Callaghan's woman-as-sign argument from the Renaissance to the Restoration: "Just as women were physically absent from their initial aesthetic representation on the Greek stage, so too they are 'absent' from their roles on the Restoration stage" (73).

34. Mark S. Lussier, "'Marrying That Hated Object': The Carnival of Desire in Behn's *The Rover*," in *Privileging Gender in Early Modern England*, ed. Jean Brink (Kirksville, MO: Sixteenth Century Journal Publishers, 1993), 232.

35. Richard Bevis, *English Drama: Restoration and Eighteenth Century* (London and New York: Longman, 1988), 71. Bevis notes "the sheer number of masks, veils, fans, screens, aliases, impersonations, ironic colloquies, and feigned appearances on the Restoration stage" (30).

36. Tomography comprises any kind of cross-sectional imaging technique that uses penetrating waves such as x-rays, magnetic fields, photons, seismic waves, or radar. The resulting two-dimensional "slices" can then be integrated into a three-dimensional image (tomogram). Thus, although the surface of Venus is hidden to the naked eye by a thick cloud cover, its surface can be accurately mapped by bouncing radio waves off the surface. The *Titanic*'s whereabouts were divined tomographically.

37. *Redshift* refers to the way the light shed by distant objects that are moving away from us noticeably shifts toward the red end of the spectrum. Cosmologists measure redshift via a series of spectra of the same star taken at different times; they then integrate those spectra statistically in order to map how rapidly the star is traveling. This technique is called *astrotomography*. Such observations confirm that the expansion of the universe is accelerating—presumably under the influence of some mysterious dark energy—defying dark matter's gravitational pull.

38. The gaze is an important concept in much feminist, psychoanalytic, and postcolonial criticism; see Jeremy Hawthorn, "Theories of the Gaze," in *Literary Theory and Criticism: An Oxford Guide,* ed. Patricia Waugh (Oxford: Oxford University Press, 2006), 508–18.

39. Marvin Carlson, "The Haunted Body," in *The Haunted Stage: The Theatre as Memory Machine* (Ann Arbor: University of Michigan Press, 2001), 52–95.

40. Once can extend the astronomical analogy. In the type of gravitational lensing known as "microlensing," an observed star appears temporarily brighter, without changing its shape, due to the magnification induced by a foreground object that crosses the line of sight of the observer. For Joseph Roach, in "Nell Gwyn and Covent Garden Goddesses," in *The First Actresses: Nell Gwyn to Sarah Siddons* (Ann Arbor: University of Michigan Press, 2011), 72, the Restoration's celebrity actresses lensed "the sacred monarch's ancient charisma." But in *The Rover* it is Willmore, "a rover of fortune, yet a prince aboard his little wooden world" (5.1.492–93), whose occasional microlensing—an additional glow from behind, as it were—ghosts Charles II.

41. Behn's offstage nunnery also codes lesbian desire: "I should have stayed in the nunnery still, if I had liked my lady Abbess as well as she liked me" (3.1.38–39). Homoerotic currents run through *The Rover*. Pedro and Antonio's attraction plays out through violent rivalry for Angellica's and Florinda's bodies, while Blunt shares a kiss with Frederick, ostensibly so that he can taste Lucetta's mouth—a badge of homosocial traffic between men (2.1.31–32).

42. Ophelia's death—in Gertrude's description, not so much a suicide as a *letting herself drown*—demands to be read as a rebuke to Elsinore's silencing of women, even as her madness critiques the sexual double standard and speaks truth to uncomprehending power. Jealous of the exegetical attention paid to Hamlet's transformation, especially in act 2, Ophelia apparently goes mad out of hermeneutic envy.

43. Heidi Hutner writes, in "Revisioning the Female Body: Aphra Behn's *The Rover,* Parts I and II," in *Rereading Aphra Behn: History, Theory, and Criticism,* ed. Heidi Hutner (Charlottesville and London: University Press of Virginia), 106–7, "Hellena's donning of the mask is a form of resistance to the repression of feminine desire. Masked, she believes she will rule herself . . . The female disguise . . . promises freedom, but that freedom only functions within the context of the seventeenth-century marriage market and its class-based assumptions about feminine value."

44. The women are shadowed by a chaperone, Callis, who extends male surveillance in the absence of Don Pedro and the sisters' father, who never appears. Like the empty seat at Gateshead Hall in *Jane Eyre,* the father's absence in *The Rover* underscores the point that women suffer not at the hands of individual men but from a patriarchal system that operates independent of particular fathers who may or may not be well disposed toward women.

45. On a split stage Willmore flirts with Hellena, Florinda reads Belvile's palm, and Valeria flirts with Frederick in dumb show. Absent from act 1, scene 1, and silenced by her mask, Valeria does not audibly speak until act 3, scene 1.

46. "[T]he commodification of women in the marriage market is Aphra Behn's first and most persistent theme." Elin Diamond, "*Gestus* and Signature in Aphra Behn's *The Rover,*" *English Literary History* 56 (1989): 534. Because the women's masquerade "defers but does not alter the structure of patriarchal exchange," for Diamond *The Rover* demands a Brechtian reading that critiques the ideology encoded by the "apparatus of representation" itself (534).

47. An outspoken critic of the double standard, Angellica has received the lion's share of critical attention, which has tended to see the courtesan as the playwright's stand-in; see, for example, Gallagher, "Who Was That Masked Woman?"; and Hutner, "Revisioning the Female Body." But Angellica is "outspoken" in more than one sense—Willmore's philippic against the cozening sex (one part Hamlet, one part *The Honest Whore, Part 1*) reduces her to speechlessness. "Thou hast a pow'r too strong to be resisted," she marvels before being led off to bed (2.2.150).

48. This claim is retrospectively ironized once Willmore, having conquered Angellica, learns (from her) that his nameless gypsy is worth several hundred thousand crowns.

49. Anne Quin, who created Angellica, was one of the first actresses to appear on the English public stage. She may conceivably have been the very first, playing Desdemona on December 8, 1660, for the King's Company. Quin (then Anne Marshall) may also have played "Angelica Bianca" in Behn's source-play, Killigrew's *Thomaso,* during the 1664–65 season. See the entry for Mrs. Anne Quin in *A Biographical Dictionary,* 242–44. Quin's appearance as Behn's Angellica in March 1677

seems to mark her return to the stage after an almost ten-year absence (possibly to raise a family)—a piece of living theatrical history for the Dorset Garden audience (one can imagine her singing "I'm Still Here"), unlike Elizabeth Barry, whose stage career likely began just a year and a half before *The Rover*'s premier.

50. Adding insult to injury, the gold that Angellica supplies Willmore as a gift comes from the deceased uncle who previously kept Angellica; it is therefore Pedro, Hellena, and Florinda's family money. Willmore tosses Florinda one of Angellica's pistoles before assaulting her (3.5.58).

51. Skantze, in *Stillness in Motion,* notes, "Behn's frequent description of her main characters as 'inconstant' renders them a kind of moving emblem of the world in motion" (113).

52. It is not only Willmore who flattens out Hellena's signification. For Angellica, looking on unseen, the masked gypsy is "the other woman": an emblem of sexual threat that can be occupied by *any* individual.

53. Some portion of the female audience at Dorset Garden watched the stage action through the eyeholes of their *own* vizards. At various points in the play, Behn genders her imagined spectatorship: "'Tis pretty to see with how much love the men regard her," observes Frederick of Angellica, "and how much envy the women" (1.2.310–11). Possibly this is a metatheatrical comment on Anne Quin, who created Angellica. The once-accepted claim that the notorious Nell Gwyn created Angellica is erroneous; see Russell, "Introduction," 32.

54. Behn emphasizes throughout *The Rover* that romantic idealism and sexual sadism are complementary aspects of patriarchy. Lucetta's successful gulling of Blunt—he is robbed and must exit her house through the sewer—leads him to swear sexual vengeance on all women and to attack Florinda in act 4.

55. Howe, in *The First English Actresses,* estimates that nearly a quarter of all plays produced on the public stage in London from 1660 to 1700 contain one or more breeches roles and observes, "Almost every actress appeared at some time or other in a breeches role" (57).

56. Frances M. Kavenik, in "Aphra Behn: The Playwright as 'Breeches Part,'" in *Curtain Calls: British and American Women and the Theater, 1660–1820,* ed. Mary Anne Schofield and Cecilia Macheski (Athens: Ohio University Press, 1991), 177–92, sees Behn's breeches roles as liberatory for the heroines who play them. However, Howe, in *The First English Actresses,* concludes that "breeches roles became little more than yet another means of displaying the actress as a sexual object" (59). Hutner, in "Revisioning the Female Body," claims that Willmore turns Hellena's "phallic disguise" against her as "another means to disrupt the female character's act of self-assertion" (59). Perhaps the answer to why Behn has Hellena disguised as a boy in *The Rover* is because there was no reason not to.

57. Howe, *The First English Actresses,* 56.

58. Kavenik, in "Aphra Behn," misreads Hellena's male role-play as an embrace of Willmore's promiscuous values: "Behn fully extends [*sic*] the capabilities of the

breeches part beyond the assumption of more ordinary masculine prerogatives to include sexuality" (184). But far from being "firmly committed to his ethos through-out," as Kavenik claims, Hellena *rejects* free love.

59. Petr Bogatryev, "Semiotics in the Folk Theater," trans. Bruce Kochis, in *Semiotics of Art: Prague School Contributions,* ed. Ladislav Matejka and Irwin R. Titunik (Cambridge: MIT Press, 1976), 35–50. For Willmore women are fungible; after parting from Angellica, he follows the masked Valeria offstage (4.3.35).

60. Deborah C. Payne, "Reified Object or Emergent Professional? Retheorizing the Restoration Actress," in *Cultural Readings of Restoration and Eighteenth-Century English Theater,* ed. J. Douglas Canfield and Deborah C. Payne (Athens: University of Georgia Press, 1995), quotes one contemporary (Robert Gould) lampooning Barry in 1709 as "a Dowd / So very basely born so very Proud" and "Covetous" that "she'll prostitute with any, / rather than wave the Getting of a Penny" (19).

61. Barry's 1680 performance of La Nuche in *The Second Part of The Rover* opposite William Smith, reprising Willmore, must have ironically echoed her earlier performance of Hellena; the audience watched the "same" woman first reject (in part 1) and then embrace (in part 2) Willmore/Smith's free love proposal.

62. For gratuitous rape scenes as sexual exploitation of the Restoration actress, see Howe, *The First English Actresses,* 43–49.

63. In comedy any "father" can play the correct role. As dark matter the offstage priest, like the heroines' and Pedro's father (whose imminent return shadows the play), affirms the patriarchal frame within which Behn's comedy operates. Another name for the gravitational field produced by offstage fathers is romantic comedy itself. Such comedy typically contains subversion by allowing for (some) free choice of marital partners without shaking the superflux of class, gender, and money. According to what might be called the Egeus principle, the patriarchal institution of marriage can comfortably accommodate the occasional thwarting of a *particular* father's will. See chapter 2.

64. Belvile hints that Frederick might be better suited to a life of gay bachelorhood (5.1.159–62).

65. Or perhaps this is not so surprising. Cave Underhill's Blunt was apparently one of the play's most popular characters along with Willmore. William Smith and Underhill reprised their roles in *The Second Part of The Rover* in 1681 (the Bettertons did not take part), and Blunt seems to have been played increasingly for laughs. In part 1, Blunt carries his fantasy of ripping off "false faces" to play's end (5.1.544).

66. Here Behn departs from her source, Killigrew's *Thomaso,* whose Angellica leaves the country together with a plea for forgiveness. Hutner, in "Revisioning the Female Body," reads Angellica as cross-dressed in the pistol scene (108); I find no textual support for this assertion.

67. "Hellena, the virgin heiress, attempts to turn her world upside down—to transgress class and gender boundaries—but she is eventually and willingly brought back into the patriarchal fold" (ibid., 103).

68. In what might be a slip of Behn's pen, Hellena's fortune suddenly becomes a hundred thousand crowns dearer. Because Hellena inherits from her uncle, she cannot be disinherited.

69. Hellena remains in male guise until play's end, to Willmore's evident delight; the success of Hellena and Willmore's marriage depends on keeping the play of gazes mutually exciting but not deceptive. Whether or not Hellena forsakes the mask once and for all, she leaves the space of *The Rover* unmasked and never appears onstage again (she dies before part 2 begins, even as Barry retakes the stage as the prostitute La Nuche).

70. Taking on Rochester's former role as acting coach, Behn herself carefully supervised Barry's performance. According to actor John Bowman, who played Frederick at Drury Lane in 1710, "Mrs. Behn, upon her writing of *The Rover, or Banisht Cavalier,* took the utmost pains to instruct that Actress, who was to play the part of Helena [*sic*] in that Comedy; and that the beauty of Mrs. Barry's action on this Occasion, proved the foundation of the great fame she afterwards gained." Anne Russell, "Appendix B: From Early Accounts of Behn's Life," in Aphra Behn, *The Rover,* 2nd ed., ed. Anne Russell (Toronto: Broadview Editions, 2004), 213.

71. I count four discovery scenes in *The Rover:* Lucetta's chamber in 3.3, Blunt's creeping out of the sewer in 3.4, imprisoned Belvile in Antonio's lodging in 4.1, and Blunt reading in his chamber in 4.5.

72. "In her plays, Behn builds framed theatrical moments and in turn breaks the frame in order to provide the audience with a set-up of fixity and the correcting (sometimes simply inevitable) influence of motion . . . The give and take of Behn's particular work in the theatre can only be interpreted through an understanding of staging, of motion, of moments carefully choreographed and collected together to be dispersed again." Skantze, *Stillness in Motion,* 106, 113.

73. Jane Spencer, "Introduction," in *The Rover and Other Plays,* ed. Jane Spencer (Oxford: Oxford University Press, 1995), xii. See also Jocelyn Powell, *Restoration Theatre Production* (London: Routledge and Kegan Paul, 1984).

74. Previous works that ridiculed the telescope include Tomkis's *Albumazar* (1615), Jonson's *The Staple of News* (1625), Shadwell's *The Virtuoso* (1676), and Butler's *The Elephant in the Moon* (1676). See Hugh G. Dick, "The Telescope and the Comic Imagination," *Modern Language Notes* 58 (1943): 544–48. I am grateful to Mary Crane for this reference.

75. Aphra Behn, *The Emperor of the Moon,* in *The Rover and Other Plays,* ed. Jane Spencer (Oxford: Oxford University Press, 1995). Spencer's introduction emphasizes Behn's interest in astronomy; she also speculates that Baliardo's telescope was turned on the audience.

76. Behn clearly addressed a female *reading* public. Her prologues are defensive about criticism from women readers, and her preface to *The Lucky Chance* states, "All I ask, is the Priviledge [*sic*] for my Masculine Part the Poet in Me" (cited in Russell, "Introduction," 15).

77. *London Chronicle,* February 22–24, 1757, cited in Russell, "Introduction," 34.

78. This is not counting Kemble's *Love in Many Masks* (1790).

79. Howe, in *The First English Actresses,* notes, "After playing Hellena Barry remained the [Duke's] company's leading comic actress for ten years, the number of prologues and epilogues she spoke at this time conveying how popular she had become" (81). She then specialized in tragic roles until her retirement.

Chapter 4

1. Leonard Casper, "Triangles of Transaction in Tennessee Williams," in *Tennessee Williams: 13 Essays,* ed. Jac Tharpe (Jackson: University Press of Mississippi, 1980), 196.

2. *Suddenly, Last Summer,* the lurid 1959 film adaptation—directed by Joseph L. Mankiewicz, written by Gore Vidal, and starring Elizabeth Taylor's chest—solves the problem of (not) representing Sebastian by keeping his face out of frame. Gilles Deleuze theorizes the out-of-frame film technique in *Cinema 1: The Movement-Image* (Minneapolis: University of Minnesota Press, 1986). I am grateful to Frances Restuccia for this reference.

3. See Brian Parker, "A Tentative Stemma for Drafts and Revisions of Tennessee Williams's *Suddenly Last Summer* (1958)," *Modern Drama* 41 (1998): 303–26.

4. Tennessee Williams, *Suddenly Last Summer* (New York: New American Library, 1958), 9. Subsequent references to this edition are cited parenthetically in my text.

5. W. B. Worthen, *Modern Drama and the Rhetoric of Theater* (Berkeley: University of California Press, 1992), 17.

6. Ibid., 18.

7. Ibid., 149.

8. Ibid., 69.

9. Ibid., 18.

10. Judith Butler, *Gender Trouble: Feminism and the Subversion of Identity* (New York and London: Routledge, 1990), 25.

11. Ibid., 140.

12. Judith Butler, *Bodies That Matter: On the Discursive Limits of "Sex"* (New York: Routledge, 1993), 9.

13. Such an attempt at subversive resignification backfires on the masked heroines in Aphra Behn's *The Rover;* see chapter 3.

14. C. W. E. Bigsby, *Modern American Drama, 1945–1990* (Cambridge: Cambridge University Press, 1992), 34.

15. If we read *Sweet Bird of Youth* as a kind of supernova event, it is as if the gravitational collapse of a massive star has magically produced a brand new (neutron) star ready for her close-up instead of a black hole like Sebastian.

16. "Power must be understood . . . as the multiplicity of force relations immanent in the sphere in which they operate and which constitute their own organization . . . Power is everywhere; not because it embraces everything, but because it

comes from everywhere . . . [P]ower is not an institution, and not a structure; neither is it a certain strength we are endowed with; it is the name that one attributes to a complex strategical situation in a particular society." Michel Foucault, *The History of Sexuality*, vol. 1: *An Introduction*, trans. Robert Hurley (New York: Vintage Books, 1990), 92–93.

17. Tennessee Williams, *A Streetcar Named Desire* (New York: New American Library, 1947), 99.

18. Stanley Fish, *Self-Consuming Artifacts: The Experience of Seventeenth-Century Literature* (Berkeley: University of California Press, 1972), 3.

19. Ibid., 43.

20. Ibid., 1.

21. Tennessee Williams, *Cat on a Hot Tin Roof* (New York: New American Library, 1955), 113.

22. See Michel Foucault, *Power/Knowledge: Selected Interviews and Other Writings, 1972–1977*, ed. Colin Gordon (New York: Pantheon Books, 1980). Foucault begins his exposition of power/knowledge in *Discipline and Punish: The Birth of the Prison* (1975), trans. Alan Sheridan (London: Penguin, 1997), and develops the concept in subsequent works.

23. *The Tempest*, 3.2.100. I cite *The Riverside Shakespeare*, 2nd ed., ed. G. Blakemore Evans et al. (Boston: Houghton Mifflin, 1997).

24. Susan Glaspell's *Trifles* (1916) is a murder mystery without a murderer: neither Minnie Wright nor her deceased husband (and presumed victim) appears onstage. Like *Suddenly Last Summer*, *Trifles* depicts spectral reading as forensic act.

25. For Williams's Eucharistic imagery, see John S. Bak, "Suddenly Last Supper: Religious Acts and Race Relations in Tennessee Williams's 'Desire'," *Journal of Religion and Theatre* 4 (2005): 122–45.

26. *Suddenly Last Summer* criticism overwhelmingly links the trope of cannibalism to the play's homosexual themes, often but not always reading it biographically and psychoanalytically in light of Williams's own conflicted sexuality. See John M. Clum, "'Something Cloudy, Something Clear': Homophobic Discourse in Tennessee Williams," *South Atlantic Quarterly* 88 (1989): 161–79; Robert F. Gross, "Consuming Hart: Sublimity and Gay Poetics in *Suddenly Last Summer*," *Theatre Journal* 47 (1995): 229–51; Steven Bruhm, "Blond Ambition: Tennessee Williams's Homographesis," *Essays in Theatre/Etudes Théâtrales* 14 (1996): 97–105; Annette J. Saddik, "The (Un)Represented Fragmentation of the Body in Tennessee Williams's 'Desire and the Black Masseur' and *Suddenly Last Summer*," *Modern Drama* 41 (1998): 347–54; and Kevin Ohi, "Devouring Creation: Cannibalism, Sodomy, and the Scene of Analysis in *Suddenly, Last Summer*," *Cinema Journal* 38 (1999): 27–49.

27. The vacuous George, appearing in Sebastian's wardrobe, is literally cut from Sebastian's cloth.

28. "She loved me for the dangers I had passed, / And I loved her that she did pity them" (*Othello*, 1.3.166–67). *Othello* is another drama in which a human sacrifice invokes pagan gods, in this case the ancient rites of Venus. Desdemona is offered

up as a propitiatory sacrifice to the Aphrodite she so remarkably resembles in act 2, scene 1, while Othello performs his own execution as both judge and judged. For Williams's sources in classical myth, see Pau Gilabert Barberà, "Literature and Mythology in Tennessee Williams's *Suddenly Last Summer:* Fighting against Venus and Oedipus," *Barcelona English Language and Literature Studies* 15 (2006): 1–11.

29. Esther Merle Jackson, *The Broken World of Tennessee Williams* (Madison: University of Wisconsin Press, 1965), 147.

30. Benjamin Nelson, *Tennessee Williams: The Man and His Work* (New York: Obolensky, 1961), 253.

31. Philip T. Hartung, "The Voice of the Turtles" (review of *Suddenly Last Summer*), *The Commonweal* 71 (January 1, 1960), 396, cited in Nelson, *Tennessee Williams,* 259.

32. Nelson, *Tennessee Williams,* 259.

33. Fish, *Self-Consuming Artifacts,* 41.

34. Ibid., 42.

35. John Milton, *Areopagitica,* in *John Milton: A Critical Edition of the Major Works,* ed. Stephen Orgel and Jonathan Goldberg (Oxford and New York: Oxford University Press, 1991), 248.

36. Tennessee Williams, *Sweet Bird of Youth* (New York: New American Library, 1959), 73.

37. Describing the implosion of any given performance field, Richard Schechner, "Restoration of Behavior," in *Between Theater and Anthropology* (Philadelphia: University of Pennsylvania Press, 1985), captures the sense of gravitational collapse at *Suddenly Last Summer*'s curtain: "Catharsis comes when something happens to the performers and/or characters but not to the performance itself. But when doubt overcomes confidence, the field collapses like popped bubble gum. The result is a mess: stage fright, aloneness, emptiness, and a feeling of terrible inadequacy when facing the bottomless unappeasable appetite of the audience" (113).

Chapter 5

1. The play opened at Washington's Kennedy Center on April 30, 1977, and ran for just thirty performances. Unfortunately, the production (directed by Arvin Brown) underestimated the audience and transformed the play into political melodrama. Miller's subtler, original version was first published in 1984; it was subsequently staged at the Cleveland Playhouse in 1984, followed by productions at the Bristol Old Vic in 1985 and the Royal Shakespeare Company in 1986. Christopher Bigsby, *Arthur Miller, 1962–2005* (London: Weidenfeld & Nicolson, 2011), 258–71, outlines *The Archbishop's Ceiling*'s production and publication history. For George Coates's 1999 avant-garde San Francisco production, see Ruby Cohn, "Manipulating Miller," in *Arthur Miller's America: Theater and Culture in a Time of Change,* ed. Enoch Brater (Ann Arbor: University of Michigan Press, 2005), 191–201.

2. See, for example, Dennis Welland, *Miller: The Playwright* (London and New

York: Methuen, 1985), 156–68; June Schlueter, "Power Play: Arthur Miller's *The Archbishop's Ceiling*," *CEA Critic* 49 (Winter 1986–Summer 1987): 134–38; and William W. Demastes, "Miller's 1970s 'Power' Plays," in *The Cambridge Companion to Arthur Miller*, ed. Christopher Bigsby (Cambridge: Cambridge University Press, 1997), 139–51. Bigsby, in *A Critical Introduction to Twentieth-Century American Drama*, vol. 2 (Cambridge: Cambridge University Press, 1984), views *The Archbishop's Ceiling* as a play about the nature of the real, in which "the social and the psychological defer in some degree to the ontological" (236).

3. Arthur Miller, *Timebends: A Life* (New York: Grove Press, 1987), 573; here Miller refers to *The Archbishop's Ceiling* as "a play of shaded meanings and splintered implications."

4. Arthur Miller, "On Broadway: Notes on the Past and Future of American Theater," *Harpers*, March 1999, 47.

5. Susan Bennett, "Comment," *Theatre Journal* 51 (1999): 358.

6. See Johannes Birringer, "Contemporary Performance/Technology," *Theatre Journal* 51 (1999): 361–81.

7. One can compare the sophistication of the bug as an emblem of amorphous power to Harold Pinter's eponymous dumbwaiter, a much cruder symbol of political coercion. In *The Dumb Waiter* (1960), Pinter uses the device of the speaking tube to ventriloquize an oppressive offstage character—a nod to Strindberg's *Miss Julie* (1888). Alice Griffin, in *Understanding Arthur Miller* (Columbia, SC: University of South Carolina Press, 1996), mistakenly refers to the bug as "a mechanical device" (159) and calls the play "[m]ore conventional in its form" than Miller's earlier drama of the 1980s (168).

8. *New York Times*, May 3, 1977, cited in Welland, *Miller*, 139.

9. One might compare this to Samuel Beckett's decision to allow the Auditor to be omitted from the television production of *Not I*, which similarly raises the stakes. For an account of Miller's revisions to *The Archbishop's Ceiling*, see Welland, *Miller*, 156–62.

10. Samuel Beckett, *Waiting for Godot*, in *The Collected Plays of Samuel Beckett* (London and Boston: Faber and Faber, 1986), 71.

11. Beckett's short play *Catastrophe*, written for Václav Havel, represents Beckett's own response to the predicament of Eastern European writers and bears comparison to *The Archbishop's Ceiling*, as does Tom Stoppard's *Professional Foul*, which is likewise dedicated to Havel. Miller's Sigmund is clearly based on Havel (with shades of Joseph Brodsky).

12. Miller, "Conditions of Freedom: Two Plays of the Seventies," in *The Archbishop's Ceiling* and *The American Clock* (New York: Grove Press, 1989), vii. Subsequent citations from *The Archbishop's Ceiling* are to this edition and are cited parenthetically in the text.

13. Ibid.

14. Ibid., viii.

15. "We're all impersonators in a way. We are all impersonating something, in-

cluding ourselves . . . We have all become actors." Cited in Christopher Bigsby, *Arthur Miller and Company* (London: Methuen, 1990), 163.

16. Arthur Miller, introduction to *Collected Plays*, vol. 1 (New York: Viking Press, 1957), 21.

17. Richard Gilman, *The Making of Modern Drama* (New York: Farrar, Straus and Giroux, 1974), 203.

18. Miller, introduction to *Collected Plays*, 22.

19. Hersh Zeifman, "All My Sons after the Fall: Arthur Miller and the Rage for Order," in *The Theatrical Gamut: Notes for a Post-Beckettian Stage*, ed. Enoch Brater (Ann Arbor: University of Michigan Press, 1995), 107–8. The Miller quotation is from Bigsby, *Arthur Miller and Company*, 49.

20. Miller, introduction to *Collected Plays*, 23.

21. Enoch Brater, "Miller's Realism and *Death of a Salesman*," in *Arthur Miller: New Perspectives*, ed. Robert A. Martin (Englewood Cliffs, NJ: Prentice Hall, 1982), 114. Brenda Murphy provides a useful account of *Salesman*'s "subjective realism," and Miller's subsequent rejection of this technique, in "Arthur Miller: Revisioning Realism," in *Realism and the American Dramatic Tradition*, ed. William W. Demastes (Tuscaloosa: University of Alabama Press, 1996), 189–202.

22. Zeifman, "All My Sons," 113.

23. Arthur Miller, *After the Fall*, in *Collected Plays*, vol. 2 (New York: Viking Press, 1981), 127.

24. Ibid., 128.

25. Demastes, "Miller's 1970s 'Power' Plays," 149.

26. Arthur Miller, *The Ride Down Mt. Morgan* (London: Penguin, 1991), 81.

27. An early use of such a device occurs in *Death of a Salesman*, when Howard's tape recorder uncannily jumps to life and terrifies Willy. However, the "self" on the tape is not Willy but Howard's small son. For Miller's careful use of objects as "pivots of human action and revelation," see Marianne Boruch, "Miller and Things," *Literary Review* 24 (1981): 548–61. For the postmodern use of technology to represent the fragmentation of the self, see Matthew Causey, "The Screen Test of the Double: The Uncanny Performer in the Space of Technology," *Theatre Journal* 51 (1999): 383–94; and Matthew Causey, *Theatre and Performance in Digital Culture: From Simulation to Embeddedness* (New York: Routledge, 2009).

28. Arthur Miller, *Clara*, in *Danger: Memory!* (New York: Grove Press, 1986), 65.

29. *The Ride Down Mt. Morgan* (1991) restages the divided self, but here the technology is much cruder. At various points in the play the actor playing Lyman (a paralyzed character confined to a hospital bed) steps out from behind his plaster cast, dressed in a hospital gown, and addresses the audience while a dummy "Lyman" remains in bed.

30. It should be noted that Miller, in *Collected Plays*, vol. 1, 24, saw himself as jettisoning linear dramaturgy as early as *Death of a Salesman*: "What was wanted now was not a mounting line of tension, nor a gradually narrowing cone of intensifying suspense, but a bloc, a single chord presented as such at the outset, within which all

the strains and melodies would already be contained." Yet *Salesman* retains a tragic line of action that reveals the betrayal at the heart of Biff and Willy's alienation (the woman in the hotel) and climaxes in Willy's realization of his son's love and Biff's rejection of the values that have destroyed his father. It is in *The Archbishop's Ceiling* that Miller's musical analogy is fulfilled, and "a single chord" quite literally sounded.

31. For a discussion of the anamorphic use of stage objects in early modern drama, see Andrew Sofer, *The Stage Life of Props* (Ann Arbor: University of Michigan Press, 2003), 89–115.

32. Stephen A. Marino considers power relations in *The Archbishop's Ceiling* through the prism of Rollo May, rather than Foucault, in *A Language Study of Arthur Miller's Plays: The Poetic in the Colloquial* (Lewiston, NY: Edwin Mellen Press, 2002), 120–34.

33. Constructed around stochastic probabilities rather than locatable essence, Marcus exemplifies quantum characterization, which I discuss in chapter 2.

34. "The sitting room setting, the copious bar, the curious intruder, an unsolved crime, all these might suggest an Agatha Christie mystery." Neil Carson, *Arthur Miller,* 2nd ed. (Houndmills: Palgrave Macmillan, 2008), 102.

35. Michel Foucault defines *power* as "the multiplicity of force relations" that produce subjects in *The History of Sexuality,* vol. 1: *An Introduction,* trans. Robert Hurley (New York: Vintage Books, 1990), 92. Foucault's analysis helps explain *The Archbishop's Ceiling*'s ambivalence toward Sigmund's final, heroic gesture: "These points of resistance [within power relationships] are present everywhere in the power network. Hence there is no single locus of great Refusal, no soul of revolt, source of all rebellions, or pure law of the revolutionary. Instead there is a plurality of resistances, each of them a special case . . . [B]y definition, they can only exist in the strategic field of power relations" (95).

36. Miller, "Conditions of Freedom," x.

37. See Steven R. Centola, "The Search for an Unalienated Existence: Lifting the Veil of Maya in Arthur Miller's *The Archbishop's Ceiling,*" *Journal of Evolutionary Psychology* 21 (2000): 230–37.

38. Although sex is one arena of power in Miller's work, he does not tend to posit power/sexuality as a single, mutually constitutive discourse, as does Tennessee Williams (see my discussion in chapter 4).

39. If Miller takes Marcus's point, he betrays his greater sympathy for the rebellious Sigmund by artistically castrating his rival. As Marcus's ex-lover Maya confesses, "[H]e can't write anymore; it left him . . . (*In anguish:*) It left him!" (85).

Chapter 6

1. The challenge of staging trauma is not limited to the modern era. See *Staging Pain, 1580–1800: Violence and Trauma in British Theater,* ed. James Robert Allard and Mathew R. Martin (Burlington, VT: Ashgate, 2009); and Catherine Silverstone, *Shakespeare, Trauma, and Contemporary Performance* (New York: Routledge, 2011).

2. Christina Wald, *Hysteria, Trauma, and Melancholia: Performative Maladies in Contemporary Anglophone Drama* (New York: Palgrave Macmillan, 2007). For Wald contemporary theater stages trauma as a "malady" that tropes performative gender identity. Wald distinguishes Trauma Drama from the drama of witness: "Rather than depicting abuse, Trauma Drama puts on view the post-traumatic, psychic repetition-compulsions and traces the protagonists' attempt to come to terms with their traumatisation" (156). See also Timothy Murray, *Drama Trauma: Specters of Race in Performance, Video, and Art* (London: Routledge, 2007), which analyzes trauma across a variety of art forms in terms of Laplanche's enigmatic signifier. For trauma in postdramatic theater, see Karen Jürs-Munby, "'Did You Mean Post-Traumatic Theatre?': The Vicissitudes of Traumatic Memory in Contemporary Postdramatic Performances," *Performance Paradigm* 5 (2009): 1–33.

3. Judith Herman, *Trauma and Recovery* (New York: Basic Books, 1997). 38.

4. Allen Meek, *Trauma and Media: Theories, Histories, and Images* (New York and London: Routledge, 2010), 5. Inspired by Giorgio Agamben's notion of biopolitics, Meek offers a politicized genealogy of trauma theory that stretches beyond Freud to include Barthes, Benjamin, and Adorno.

5. Cathy Caruth, *Unclaimed Experience: Trauma, Narrative, and History* (Baltimore and London: Johns Hopkins University Press, 1996), 4. Caruth continues, "[T]rauma is not locatable in the simple violent or original event in an individual's past, but rather in the way that its very unassimilated nature—the way it was precisely not known in the first instance—returns to haunt the survivor later on."

6. Ibid., 6.

7. Samuel Beckett, *Not I*, in *The Complete Dramatic Works* (London: Faber and Faber, 1986), 375.

8. "From Ibsen on, modern drama has been troubled by ghosts. Their ubiquity stems in part from the fact that they conveniently represent the past that is dead but that refuses final interment." Joseph Roach, "The Great Hole of History: Liturgical Silence in Beckett, Osofisan, and Parks," *South Atlantic Quarterly* 100 (2001): 312. The critical literature on haunting as a figure for trauma is extensive; see, for example, Kathleen Brogan, *Cultural Haunting: Ghosts and Ethnicity in Recent American Literature* (Charlottesville: University Press of Virginia, 1998); Marvin Carlson, *The Haunted Stage: The Theatre as Memory Machine* (Ann Arbor: University of Michigan Press, 2001); and Alice Rayner, *Ghosts: Death's Double and the Phenomena of Theatre* (Minneapolis: University of Minnesota Press, 2006). Rayner's poetics transforms material presence into double vision: "The greatest mystery of theatrical ghosting is not that the ghosts are disembodied spirits from some ineffable realm, heaven or hell, and hence imaginary. The mystery, rather, is that they are fully embodied and material but are unrecognized without a certain mode of attention, a certain line of sight that can perceive the mysterious thing that is distinct from, yet embodied by, the theatrical object" (xvii). Rayner shifts Carlson's ghosting (X reappears as X1) to the phenomenological level: ghosts are uncanny disturbances in the fabric of the knowable rather than recycled matter.

9. Shaffer attempts, not very convincingly, to distance *Equus* from Freudian psychodrama by stirring in some R. D. Laing. The psychiatrist, Dysart, suffers a midlife crisis in which he questions the efficacy of treatment that aims to "adjust" passionate visionaries like his young patient to ordinary English unhappiness.

10. Both *Equus* and *The Goat* were commercially successful despite their content, perhaps indicating the audience's comfort with trauma's more shocking manifestations as long as they remain subsumed within recognizable (Aristotelian, Freudian) dramatic structures. Albee subtitles *The Goat* "Notes toward a Definition of Tragedy."

11. The quotation is from Jane Kilby, "The Writing of Trauma: Trauma Theory and the Liberty of Reading," *New Formations* 47 (2002): 217.

12. "[A] play might have restorative efficacy either by rehearsing the trauma-event or by figuring such a need—perhaps to prepare us for trauma. Major elements of the play remain available as a rehearsal of and for traumatic loss." Patrick Duggan and Mick Wallis, "Trauma and Performance: Maps, Narratives, and Folds," *Performance Research* 16 (2011): 6. Although Duggan and Wallis use *rehearse* in the sense of *repeat,* in their model rehearsal seems at once belated and apotropaic.

13. "It's a fabricated absence . . . It's the story that you're told that goes, 'once upon a time you weren't here.'" Suzan-Lori Parks, interviewed by Steven Drukman, cited in Steven Drukman, "Suzan-Lori Parks and Liz Diamond: Doo-a-diddly-dit-dit," *Drama Review* 39 (1995): 67.

14. Richard Kearney, "Writing Trauma: Catharsis in Joyce, Shakespeare, and Homer," *ABC Religion and Ethics,* July 19, 2012. http://www.abc.net.au/religion/articles/2012/07/19/3549000.htm. Kearney attributes this observation to Claude Lévi-Strauss and adds, "[M]yths are machines for the purging of wounds: strategies for resolving at a *symbolic* level what remains irresolvable at the level of lived *empirical* experience." Kearney's model of narrative catharsis translates incurable wounds, which can never be properly registered or recorded in the first place, into ghostly "scars" that can be "worked through" over time.

15. *Aristotle's Poetics,* trans. S. H. Butcher (New York: Hill and Wang, 1961), 78.

16. Aristotle seems less interested in expunging our pity and fear once and for all than in temporarily rebalancing those emotions (which, after all, serve a valuable function) so as to bring us to a state of better health. The cure is never conclusive; not unlike chiropractic patients, we must return to the theater for constant tune-ups with no end in sight.

17. Foundational treatments include Shoshana Felman and Dori Laub, *Testimony: Crises of Witnessing in Literature, Psychoanalysis, and History* (New York: Routledge, 1992); Cathy Caruth, ed., *Trauma: Explorations in Memory* (Baltimore and London: Johns Hopkins University Press, 1995); Caruth, *Unclaimed Experience;* Ruth Leys, *Trauma: A Genealogy* (Chicago: University of Chicago Press, 2000); and Dominick LaCapra, *Writing History, Writing Trauma* (Baltimore and London: Johns Hopkins University Press, 2001).

18. Caruth, *Unclaimed Experience*, 11.

19. See Roger Luckhurst, "Mixing Memory and Desire: Psychoanalysis, Psychology, and Trauma Theory," in *Literary Theory and Criticism: An Oxford Guide*, ed. Patricia Waugh (Oxford: Oxford University Press, 2006), 497–507.

20. Caruth, *Unclaimed Experience*, 17.

21. Cathy Caruth, "Introduction," *American Imago* 48 (1991): 3.

22. "The experience of trauma, the fact of latency, would thus seem to consist, not in the forgetting of a reality that can hence never be fully known; but in an inherent latency within the experience itself." Caruth, *Unclaimed Experience*, 17.

23. Ibid, 18. In its strongest form, trauma theory risks disempowering survivors by insisting on a split subject who is unable to psychically process, integrate, and witness the trauma-event. Thus according to Holocaust survivor Dori Laub, in "Truth and Testimony: The Process and the Struggle," in *Trauma: Explorations in Memory*, ed. Cathy Caruth (Baltimore and London: Johns Hopkins University Press, 1995), *"the event produced no witnesses. . . .* The Holocaust created in this way a world in which one *could not bear witness to oneself"* (65–66). Vivian M. Patraka, in *Spectacular Suffering: Theatre, Fascism, and the Holocaust* (Bloomington: Indiana University Press, 1999), argues that "Theatre reiterates the Holocaust . . . by announcing itself as performative" (6). Magda Romanska describes the Holocaust-inspired work of Grotowski and Kantor as "post-traumatic" in *The Post-Traumatic Theatre of Grotowski and Kantor* (London: Anthem Press, 2012).

24. Caruth, *Unclaimed Experience*, 11. Caruth's paradigm for the kind of history she champions is Freud's. Caruth offers a *midrash* on *Moses and Monotheism*, just as Freud's book is itself a *midrash* on Exodus. By making Jewish history unconscious, Freud deprives it of what Caruth calls "referential literality" (16).

25. I think of the dead silence in Austen's *Mansfield Park* that follows Fanny Price's query about her uncle Sir Thomas Bertram's Antigua plantation, which (as Edward Said pointed out) invisibly supports the genteel household, as just such a displacement. It is as if slavery momentarily stops the novel dead in its tracks before the wheels of narrative grind on.

26. "'Phenomenology' means to let that which shows itself be seen from itself in the very way in which it shows itself from itself." Martin Heidegger, *Being and Time*, trans. John Macquarrie and Edward Robinson (San Francisco: Harper & Row, 1962), 58.

27. In film, sound becomes a key vehicle for transforming the frame in this way: "At any moment the frame can haemorrhage [*sic*] toward an unseen area simply by including a sound whose source is not seen." Tom Gunning, *The Films of Fritz Lang: Allegories of Vision and Modernity* (London: BFI Publishing, 2000), 165. I am grateful to Donna Kornhaber for this reference.

28. Mouth's vociferous denial of an "I" behind traumatic experience recalls Blanchot's notion of disaster as that which cannot be experienced by a linear being-in-time. "It is the disaster defined—hinted at—not as an event of the past, but as the

immemorial past which returns, dispersing by its return the present, where, ghostly, it would be experienced as a return." Maurice Blanchot, *The Writing of the Disaster*, trans. Ann Smock (Lincoln: University of Nebraska Press, 1995), 17.

29. See Jody Enders, *The Medieval Theater of Cruelty: Rhetoric, Memory, Violence* (Ithaca, NY: Cornell University Press, 1999).

30. The Lord Chamberlain prosecuted those involved in the production of *Saved* in a historic case that influenced the 1968 abolition of government censorship of licensed English theater, thereby opening the door to Kane and other traumatic realists. Ironically, *Saved* was a highly moralistic protest against social disenfranchisement. Aleks Sierz emphasizes the moralism underpinning the so-called New Brutalist playwrights of the 1990s in *In-Yer-Face Theatre: British Drama Today* (London: Faber and Faber, 2001).

31. By labeling Sarah Kane and Edward Bond "traumatic realists," I do not mean to imply any allegiance to naturalistic drama on their part. Since traumatic realists freely depart from realism as a style, traumatic literalists might be a preferable term.

32. For an enlightening discussion of Gloucester's blinding, see Erika T. Lin, *Shakespeare and the Materiality of Performance* (New York: Palgrave Macmillan, 2012), 3–22.

33. Suzan-Lori Parks, "Possession," in *The America Play and Other Works* (New York: TCG, 1995), 4.

34. Ibid., 5.

35. Ibid., 4.

36. Christine Woodworth discusses Parks's children as "performative genealogies of their family histories or larger histories" in "Parks and the Traumas of Childhood," in *Suzan-Lori Parks: Essays on the Plays and Other Works,* ed. Philip C. Kolin (Jefferson, NC: McFarland, 2010), 140–55. The quotation is from page 141.

37. Parks's debunking of rugged individualism, westward expansion, and Manifest Destiny recalls similar demythologizings of the west by Arthur Miller (*The Misfits*) and Sam Shepard (*True West*). It will not have escaped Parks, a careful student of dramatic history, that *Hamlet*'s gravedigger has been a sexton for exactly thirty years.

38. Parks shares with her forerunners August Wilson and Lorraine Hansberry a consciousness of African Americans' double deracination. The migration north is seen as a traumatic rupture from agrarian to urban culture, a turning one's back on one's ancestry. But, whereas Wilson and Hansberry cast the dramatic project as returning to, or at least coming to terms with, the previous generation's values, Parks resists a solution she fears is sentimental (embodied by Cory's decision to attend his father's funeral in *Fences*—joining Miller's Biff Loman, as it were, at the graveside— and by Walter Younger's embrace of Big Papa's values in *A Raisin in the Sun*: the essential dignity of free labor despite the daily humiliations of racism). For a discussion of trauma in Wilson's drama, see Sinikka Grant, "'Their Baggage a Long Line of Separation and Dispersement': Haunting and Trans-generational Trauma in *Joe Turner's Come and Gone," College Literature* 36 (2009): 96–116.

39. "Mimicry conceals no presence or identity behind its mask." Homi K.

Bhabha, "Of Mimicry and Man: The Ambivalence of Colonial Discourse," in *The Location of Culture* (London: Routledge, 1994), 88. Peggy Phelan, in *Mourning Sex: Performing Public Memories* (London and New York: Routledge, 1997), defends mimicry as "the fundamental performance of this cultural moment." Phelan's hope is that by enacting losses through her own strategy of performative writing, "loss itself helps transform the repetitive force of trauma and might bring about a way to overcome it" (12).

40. Parks's satiric debasement of history recalls Stephen Sondheim and John Weidman's sour musical *Assassins* (1990), which also features a murderous funfair.

41. Suzan-Lori Parks, *The America Play*, in *The America Play and Other Works* (New York: TCG, 1995), 159. All parenthetical citations in my text are to this edition.

42. Lucy describes the original Great Hole as a paraded history in which African Americans cannot see their own images reflected: "*Like* you, but *not* you. You know: *Known*" (196).

43. For New York's Ground Zero as a pilgrim site for those seeking a material connection to the mediated trauma of 9/11, see Laura E. Tanner, "Holding On to 9/11: The Shifting Grounds of Materiality," *PMLA* 127 (2012): 58–76.

44. Jeanette R. Malkin, in *Memory-Theater and Postmodern Drama* (Ann Arbor: University of Michigan Press, 1999), observes, "Nonsemiotic noises are often written onto [Parks's] pages as musical moans that evoke an uninscribed—perhaps uninscribable—preliterate world." Although not preliterate, the gunshots also produce noise: a situation in which there is *too much* information for a spectator/auditor to distinguish a discrete signal equivalent to a musical tone.

45. Harvey Young, "Touching History: Staging Black Experience," in *Embodying Black Experience: Stillness, Critical Memory, and the Black Body* (Ann Arbor: University of Michigan Press, 2010), 119–66, discusses how Parks "challenge[s] the muting effect of historical erasure or historical misrepresentation by centering not the voice but the [speaking] body" in her play *Venus*. See also Jennifer L. Griffiths, *Traumatic Possessions: The Body and Memory in African American Women's Writing and Performance* (Charlottesville: University of Virginia Press, 2009).

46. I am grateful to the participants in Bernadette Myler's Theater and Democracy seminar at Harvard's Mellon School of Theater and Performance Research for an illuminating discussion of *The America Play* and its gunshots in particular (June 14, 2012).

47. The Foundling Father thus parodies both master tropes of the standard dramaturgical model of trauma I identified earlier: the buried child and the revenant. Parks might well have titled the play *(Un)buried Father.*

48. Suzan-Lori Parks, "from Elements of Style," in *The America Play and Other Works* (New York: TCG, 1995), 10.

49. The same thesis, translated to a Chicano/a context, can be found in Cherríe Moraga's *Shadow of a Man* (1990).

50. Parks insists that "Black presence on stage is more than a sign or messenger of some political point," but it seems impossible for her to use the category "black

drama" without feeling herself in a representational bind. Suzan-Lori Parks, "An Equation for Black People Onstage," in *The America Play and Other Works* (New York: TCG, 1995), 21. Bruce Norris's *Clybourne Park* (2010) dramatizes the white neighborhood to which the Younger family moves in *A Raisin in the Sun,* thereby rendering visible the dark (or in this case white) matter of Hansberry's play. This "antimatter" tradition goes back at least as far as Stoppard's *Rosencrantz and Guildenstern Are Dead* (1966) and more recently includes David Roby's *Unseen Character* (2011), eighteen monologues by unseen characters in *The Glass Menagerie.*

51. George C. Wolfe, *The Colored Museum* (New York: Dramatists Play Service, 2010).

52. Roach, "The Great Hole of History," 309.

53. Joseph Roach, *Cities of the Dead: Circum-Atlantic Performance* (New York: Columbia University Press, 1996), 3.

54. Roach, "The Great Hole of History," 312. Although Roach does not mention them specifically, Parks's gunshots indeed echo Beckett's dead voices (which for Roach convey the dark matter of the Great Hunger). To my ear the shots also echo the voices of the serfs that Trofimov hears coming from every haunted tree in *The Cherry Orchard.* Martin Crimp picks up Chekhov's motif in scenario 3 of *Attempts on Her Life.*

55. "Performance means: never for the first time. It means: for the second to the nth time. Performance is 'twice-behaved behavior.'" Richard Schechner, "Restoration of Behavior," in *Between Theater and Anthropology* (Philadelphia: University of Pennsylvania Press, 1985), 36.

56. For Schechner "rehearsals make it necessary to think of the future in such a way as to create a past" (ibid., 39).

57. J. L. Austin, *How to Do Things with Words* (Cambridge, MA: Harvard University Press, 1962), 22. See chapter 1.

58. For the intimate connection between reenactment and failure in contemporary performance, see Rebecca Schneider, *Performing Remains: Art and War in Times of Theatrical Reenactment* (London and New York: Routledge, 2011). Schneider's sly grammar (is the "Performing" of her title noun, gerund, or modifier?) enacts the collapse of temporalities I associate with rehearsal.

59. "Repetition compulsion . . . has a peculiar time scheme: *after* the event there is an attempt to act as if in preparation *before* it. This is also the case with sexual trauma: the event takes place in childhood, but it is only understood as traumatic later, after reaching sexual maturity." Luckhurst, "Mixing Memory and Desire," 500–501.

60. If Arthur Miller was led in the direction of prismatic drama by a loss of faith in the morally accountable self in the Watergate era, the Kennedys' rejection of linear drama is driven by a loss of faith in a morally accountable legal system in the Rodney King era. For further discussion of prismatic dramaturgy, see chapter 5.

61. See Michelle Alexander, *The New Jim Crow: Mass Incarceration in the Age of Colorblindness* (New York: New Press, 2012).

62. Karl Abraham and Maria Took, in *The Shell and the Kernel: Renewals in Psychoanalysis,* trans. Nicholas Rand (Chicago: University of Chicago Press, 1994), point out that the return of the repressed is not the correct formulation for an eruption of traumatic material (the Holocaust, slavery, etc.) outside the personal experience of the subject. What returns is not the repressed, then, but a secret history that may be transgenerational.

63. "Down in the hole, lingeringly, the gravedigger puts on the forceps." Samuel Beckett, *Waiting for Godot,* in *The Complete Dramatic Works* (London: Faber and Faber, 1986), 84.

64. Alisa Solomon, "Foreword," in Adrienne Kennedy, *The Alexander Plays* (Minneapolis: University of Minnesota Press, 1992), xvi.

65. In Kennedy's *Letter to My Students on My Sixty-first Birthday by Suzanne Alexander,* a narrative retelling of *Sleep Deprivation Chamber,* it is not Teddy's Uncle March but his father David who has gone missing. In this version of the story, which otherwise parallels the play, Teddy plays Hamlet rather than directing the production, rendering his confrontations with his father's ghost unbearably poignant for Suzanne. Both *Letter to My Students* and the related play *Motherhood 2000* appear in Adrienne Kennedy, *The Adrienne Kennedy Reader* (Minneapolis: University of Minnesota Press, 2001). For Lesley Ferris and Johanna Frank, in "A Discourse on Staging a Writer's Worlds," *Modern Drama* 55 (2012): 70–89, "*Sleep Deprivation Chamber* is the final product of a progression of plays that, ultimately, reveals that both language and image can never fully signify or make visible embodied experience" (73).

66. Written before *Sleep Deprivation Chamber,* *Motherhood 2000* dramatizes the very vengeance against Teddy's assailant, and hence dramatic closure to the tragedy, that its sequel suggests is impossible.

67. Mary Kaldor, *New and Old Wars: Organized Violence in a Global Era* (Cambridge: Polity Press, 1999), 2. I am grateful to Julia Boll for this reference.

68. Simon Shepherd, *The Cambridge Introduction to Modern British Theatre* (Cambridge: Cambridge University Press, 2009), 158–64. Shepherd spotlights Theatre Workshop's *Oh What a Lovely War* (1963). Notable recent examples of documentary theater, each of which addresses trauma (though not necessarily war), are London's Tricycle Theatre's series of verbatim tribunal plays, Moisés Kaufman and Tectonic Theater Project's *The Laramie Project* (2000), Jessica Blank and Eric Jensen's *The Exonerated* (2002), Alan Rickman and Katharine Viner's *My Name is Rachel Corrie* (2005), Robin Soans's *Talking to Terrorists* (2005), and Gregory Burke's Scottish drama *Black Watch* (2006).

69. Julia Boll, "The Unlisted Character: Representing War on Stage," in *The New Order of War,* ed. Robert Brecher (New York: Rodolpi, 2010), 167–80. Boll reads *Far Away* allegorically: in a state of "total war," there is neither recognizable conflict nor a graspable objective reality, and so characters in new war drama become reactive survivors rather than actors.

70. Elaine Scarry, *The Body in Pain: The Making and Unmaking of the World* (Oxford: Oxford University Press, 1987). Kennedy alludes to Scarry's influential work

in *A Letter to My Students.* The body in pain becomes a site of interrogation in such plays as Pinter's *One for the Road* (1984), Martin McDonagh's *The Pillowman* (2003), and Mark Ravenhill's *The Cut* (2006), as well as in the work of ordeal artists such as Stelarc, Orlan, Bob Flanagan, and Angelika Festa. For the avant-garde body as a site of trauma, see Kristine Stiles, "Never Enough Is *Something Else:* Feminist Performance Art, Avant-Gardes, and Probity," in *Contours of the Theatrical Avant-Garde: Performance and Textuality,* ed. James M. Harding (Ann Arbor: University of Michigan Press, 2000), 239–90.

71. Caryl Churchill, *Far Away* (London: Nick Hern Books, 2003). All parenthetical citations in my text are to this edition.

72. In the original production, the Royal Court enlisted scores of volunteers to emphasize the magnitude of the slaughter.

73. Aleks Sierz, *Rewriting the Nation: British Theatre Today* (London: Methuen, 2011), 75. Sierz usefully surveys British dramatists' treatment of war in the decade between 2000 and 2010, when "Fear was the new world order" (71).

74. Martin Crimp, *Attempts on Her Life* (London: Faber and Faber, 1997). All parenthetical citations are to this edition. In scenario 7, "The new Anny" is described in terms of the slick images of a car commercial. Crimp's sleek, inviolate automobile symbolizes escape from and immunity to the violence of a collapsing global system: "No one is ever dragged from the *Anny* by an enraged mob" (40). Both Crimp and Churchill stress the symbiosis of consumer capitalism and social breakdown.

75. This is evident in many reviews of *Attempts on Her Life.* David Edgar, in *State of Play: Playwrights on Playwriting* (London: Faber and Faber, 1999), comments, "Crimp's purpose is not only to question whether we can truly know another human being, but whether we can regard other people as existing at all independent of the models we construct of them" (31). Mary Luckhurst, "Political Point-Scoring: Martin Crimp's *Attempts on Her Life,*" *Contemporary Theatre Review* 13 (2003): 47–60, emphasizes themes of sexual objectification and violence on and by women.

76. That Crimp's target is globalization is signaled by his textual note that the company of actors "should reflect the composition of the world beyond the theatre" (unpaginated). Anne recalls Karen in David Hare's teleplay *Wetherby* (1985), a university student without affect or purpose whose vacancy drives others to madness, rage, and despair. Karen, whose favorite occupation is watching television, is a symptom of contemporary culture. Director Katie Mitchell, who directed *Attempts on Her Life* at Milan's Piccolo Theatre in 1999 and the 2007 National Theatre revival, remarks that "on one level, the play is a vision of global capitalism and how it menaces children"; cited in Aleks Sierz, *The Theatre of Martin Crimp* (London: Methuen Drama, 2006), 198. In addition to Mitchell, Sierz's book includes insightful interviews with Tim Albery, who directed the Royal Court premiere, and Gerhard Willert, who directed the German premier in Munich at the Bayerisches Staatsschauspiel in 1998.

77. Crimp indicates in the script that scenario 1 may be cut—presumably to avoid creating the impression that Anne is an actual individual.

78. Crimp's characterless play may be seen as an ironic gloss on Aristotle's claim that "without action there cannot be a tragedy; there may be without character." Aristotle continues, "Character [in tragedy] is that which reveals moral purpose, showing what kind of things a man chooses or avoids." *Aristotle's Poetics*, 63, 64.

79. These references inspired director Katie Mitchell to use live video-feed as the fundamental staging strategy in her 2007 revival at the Lyttelton. The play became a send-up of media manipulation.

80. Philip C. Kolin, *Understanding Adrienne Kennedy* (Columbia: University of South Carolina Press, 2005), 20. More optimistically, Jenny Spencer, in "Emancipated Spectatorship in Adrienne Kennedy's Plays," *Modern Drama* 55 (2012): 19–39, views *Sleep Deprivation Chamber* and *Motherhood 2000* as emancipating rather than traumatizing the reader [*sic*], who is challenged "to rewrite the script for her own pleasure and use" (37).

81. Carol Martin, "Anna Deavere Smith: The Word Becomes You," *The Drama Review* 37 (1993): 51.

82. Tony Kushner, *Angels in America: A Gay Fantasia on National Themes* (New York: Theatre Communications Group, 1995), 16.

83. Martin, "Anna Deavere Smith," 52.

84. Anna Deavere Smith, *Fires in the Mirror: Crown Heights, Brooklyn, and Other Identities* (New York: Anchor, 1993), 139.

85. Richard Schechner, "Anna Deavere Smith: Acting as Incorporation," *The Drama Review* 37 (1993): 63.

86. This is not to say that Smith and her directors do not carefully sequence her work. While the script is verbatim, chunks of it are edited and rearranged for dramatic effect.

87. Caruth, *Unclaimed Experience*, 3.

88. "The Spectacle has, indeed, an emotional attraction of its own, but, of all the parts, it is the least artistic, and connected least with the art of poetry. For the power of Tragedy, we may be sure, is felt even apart from representation and actors." *Aristotle's Poetics*, 62.

89. Michael Gambon, cited in Mel Gussow, *Michael Gambon: An Acting Life* (New York: Applause, 2005), 214.

Glossary

Antimatter play. A play that appropriates dark matter from previous drama and renders it visible to the audience; examples include *Rosencrantz and Guildenstern Are Dead* (1966) and *Clybourne Park* (2010).

Classical dramaturgy. Everyday laws (e.g., cause and effect) apply to the world of the play; compare *quantum dramaturgy.*

Complementarity principle. The particle and wave aspects of a quantized phenomenon cannot be disassociated. Instead, because of the experimental interaction between that phenomenon and the apparatus used to measure it, they complement each other.

Conjuration, conjure. Early modern term for performative magic: the calling into being of that which it names, such as a demon or a doctorate.

Copenhagen interpretation. Atoms and other subatomic phenomena form a world of potentials and possibilities rather than of things and facts. Contrasts with Einsteinian realism, in which the world is what it is independent of observation and such things as atoms "really" exist. By extension the notion that no autonomous, fictional world subtends a given theatrical performance.

Dark matter. Matter of an unknown nature that emits no radiation. Its existence is deduced from its gravitational effects on the motions of stars and galaxies.

Egeus principle. Within romantic comedy, a kind of ideological homeopathy in which occasional instances of free marital choice immunize patriarchal marriage against structural subversion.

Godot effect. The deliberate withholding of a central character from direct representation in a play.

Gravitational lensing. The bending of distant objects' light by matter (whether dark or luminous) that intervenes between light source and observer. Such a lens magnifies and distorts the object's image, allowing cosmologists to look back in cosmic time, measure the rate of the universe's acceleration, and map the distribution of intervening dark matter.

Kinamnesia. The tendency of a culture's unscripted performances to slip out of collective memory over time.

Microlensing. A form of gravitational lensing in which a foreground star passes in front of a background star, causing the background starlight to brighten and bend through a ring-shaped region. By extension a theatrical effect in which distant or absent personages temporarily "shine through" current performers.

New Traumatists. A group of contemporary playwrights suspicious of the adequacy of linear plot, traditional psychology, graphic realism, and Aristotelian catharsis for the representation of collective trauma; compare *traumatic realism.*

Noise. A situation in which too much semiotic or phenomenological information prevents a spectator from distinguishing a discrete "signal" equivalent to a musical tone.

Ophelia strategy. The decision to protest patriarchal signification and/or sexual commodification by withdrawing from representation altogether.

Particle. A discrete, bulletlike entity, such as a photon, that can be measured in time and space.

Power/sexuality. Sexuality conceived as a transpersonal medium rather than an internal attribute of individual subjects. Viewed this way, sexuality and power relations are mutually constitutive.

Prismatic dramaturgy. Spatializes variations on a chosen theme rather than tracing causes and effects through linear plot.

Quantum characterization. Character defined as a "probability wave" spread out in time and space until observed by an audience.

Quantum dramaturgy. Indeterminacy of plot and character governs the dramatic world; compare *classical dramaturgy.*

Self-consuming artifact. A performative character that uses him- or herself up in performance and disappears without a trace. The dramatic equivalent of a black hole.

Semiotic redshift. A measure of the difficulty of reconstructing theatrical history proportional to its distance from the observer in space and time.

Spectral criticism, spectral reading. A critical approach that measures dark matter's gravitational effects on visible bodies and incidentally illuminates theater's full spectrum.

Superposition principle. An unobserved fictional character can be in different states of being simultaneously, not unlike a quantized particle. Thus Philostrate is (Q1) and is not (F1) Master of the Revels in act 5 of *A Midsummer Night's Dream.*

Tomographic criticism. A form of spectral reading in which a composite, three-dimensional image of an object (tomogram) can be reconstructed by integrating a series of planar projections (cross sections).

Trauma. In recent theory both the trauma-event itself and the belated acts of repetition-compulsion that mark the sufferer's inability to internalize or process the event at the time of its occurrence.

Traumatic realism. The graphic and explicit representation of shocking violence onstage, presented with as much verisimilitude as possible however "unrealistic" the given fictional circumstances.

Uncertainty principle. The impossibility of determining a subatomic particle's position and speed at the same time, because the act of shedding light on the particle to determine position disturbs its movement, whereas the use of low-energy light to avoid such disturbance increases the uncertainty of its position. The principle implies that no observer-free objective reality can be perceived.

Wave. The flappy, spread-out aspect of an entity, as opposed to its particulate aspect; a disturbance in a particular medium.

Index

Italicized page numbers followed by the letter *f* designate figures; those followed by the letter *g* designate Glossary listings.

Caruth, Cathy. *See also* trauma
　Freud as model for, 193n24
　on possession by traumatic history, 121,
　　123
　trauma model of, 14, 118, 120–22, 126,
　　191n5, 193n22
　the wound as dark matter for, 144
Catastrophe (Beckett, 1982), 188n11
catharsis. *See also* drama, Aristotelian; re-
　demption; transformation, theatrical
　as climactic, 119
　as dramatic closure, 14, 114, 197n66
　as gravitational collapse, 187n37
　as healing, 120, 121, 192n12, 192n14
　King Lear's questioning of, 123
　as performative cure via *not* seeing, 120
　resistance to by staged trauma, 14, 118,
　　142
　via trauma as return of the repressed, 119
　via vicarious wounding as paradoxical,
　　120
　from visceral disgust, 122–23
　and voyeurism, 123
Cat on a Hot Tin Roof (Williams, 1955),
　93, 94
causation, valid. *See also* drama, linear
　in classical dramaturgy, 5, 39–40
　confusing of in new models of trauma,
　　118, 132
　indexical signs as expression of, 3–4
　vs. performative magic, 12, 17, 23
　psychological tracing of in linear dramas
　　of motive, 91–92, 106–10, 113–14
　vs. self-fragmentation in dramas of
　　power, 108–10, 114–16
Changeling, The (Middleton and Rowley,
　1653), 44, 69
character, dramatic. *See also Poetics*; self;
　warfare
　vs. *absence* of, 139–140
　contradictory possibilities of, 54–55,
　　63–64
　and critical impulse to reify, 62
　endowing of with past history, 63, 107
　as incoherent mouthpiece, 105, 115, 116
　as lens, 76, 81

　as morally accountable and coherent
　　subject, 105, 106–7, 115
　as performative, 22
　personation of, 28
　as relational and interactive illusion, 63,
　　92, 175n94
　unraveling of unity of, 92, 108, 110, 116,
　　119
character, offstage, 13, 15, 39–40, 135, 136,
　169n39. *See also Waiting for Godot*
character, quantized. *See also* quantum
　characterization
　fuzziness of in space and time, 40, 49–
　　51, 52, 56, 58, 165n12
　partially veiled reality of, 53
　as probabilities vs. locatable essence,
　　49–51, 54, 190n33
　spectral reality of, 65
Charles II, 68, 70–71, 176n3
Chekhov, Anton, 10, 110, 153n48
Cherry Orchard, The (Chekhov, 1904),
　196n54
Christ. *See also* Eucharistic imagery; God
　absent body of as dark matter, 1–3, 11
　actor incarnation of, 147n3
　Doctor Faustus in relation to, 30,
　　34–35
　ghostly presence of, 2, 5
　Passion Play of, 2
　redemption through sacrifice of, 97
Churchill, Caryl, 14, 117, 119, 134, 135–38,
　198n74. *See also Far Away*
Churchill Play, The (Brenton, 1974), 119
Clara (Miller, 1986), 105, 109
"Cloud, Random" (pseud.), 63
Cloud 9 (Churchill, 1979), 119
Clybourne Park (Norris, 2010), 196n50,
　201g
the codpiece, 44, 69–70, 72, 168n33
comedy, 13, 61–62, 83. *See also* romantic
　comedy; tragicomedy
complementarity principle, 50, 175n96,
　201g
conjure, 24–25, 201
conjuring. *See also* black magic; *Doctor
　Faustus*; performativity